Linn's
Complete
Stamp Collecting
Basics

Michael Baadke

Published by *Linn's Stamp News*, the largest and most informative stamp news-paper in the world. *Linn's* is owned by Amos Press Inc., 911 Vandemark Road, Sidney, Ohio 45365. Amos Press also publishes *Scott Stamp Monthly* and the Scott line of catalogs.

Library of Congress Cataloging-in-Publication Data

Baadke, Michael.
  Linn's complete stamp collecting basics / Michael Baadke.
      p. cm.
Includes index.
      ISBN 1-932180-05-2
  1. Stamp collecting. I. Title: Complete stamp collecting basics. II.
Title.
HE6213.B3 2004
769.56--dc22

                                                            2003024765

For
Herman and Valeska Baadke
who introduced me to the pleasures of writing and stamp collecting

and
Patti and Katie
who keep me smiling long after the stamps are put away

Contents

Introduction

There have been many books written about stamps and the stamp hobby, but nearly all of them tell about one specific area or collecting specialty. Our intent in producing this new book was to provide an overview that would help the beginner collector understand all the basics of the hobby, but we also intend for it to serve as a useful reference tool as the collector gains experience.

Anyone who has an interest in stamps and is thinking about starting a collection will begin by asking some important fundamental questions. Do I collect new stamps or used stamps? Do I collect stamps of the United States or other countries? Where do I keep my stamps? How do I learn more about them?

These are the kinds of questions we wanted to help answer. Many of those answers depend, in part, upon your own personal interests, but this book provides the information that will help you find the answers that work best for you.

This book is created primarily from a series of weekly Refresher Course columns that I wrote for *Linn's Stamp News* from December 1995 until I was named editor of *Scott Stamp Monthly* in March 2001. Encouraged by *Linn's* book editor Donna Houseman and Amos Press editorial director Michael Laurence, I've re-edited and revised many of those columns, selected new and updated images, and considered how best to present it all in book form. We've used about one-third of the 270 or so columns I wrote, and arranged them to cover the primary subject areas that stamp collectors encounter.

The first section will get you started with basic information about stamps and covers, plus ideas for building your collection, tips on how to handle and store your collection, and where to look to learn more about the stamps you collect.

After that, you'll find more details about the wide variety of stamps that are out there, various collecting specialties you may enjoy, the tools and supplies that stamp collectors use, and much more.

There aren't many hobbies that seem to have the staying power of stamp collecting. I've been a stamp collector for nearly 40 years, and I've met many people who have enjoyed the hobby for 50 years, 60 years and longer.

Many collectors know that the first adhesive postage stamp issued by any nation was the Penny Black, a British 1-penny stamp from 1840 picturing Queen Victoria. But the stamp hobby extends even farther back in history, for there are many collectors who study how mail was delivered long before the postage stamp was ever dreamed of.

It's a vast hobby that encompasses many centuries of history and literally every single country in the world. And yet, it's possible to pick any aspect of it that you happen to enjoy, large or small, and create a collection that can educate you, entertain you and delight you for a lifetime.

Michael Baadke, March 2004

Acknowledgments

Eleven years ago I was hired as a staff writer for *Linn's Stamp News* by publisher Michael Laurence and managing editor Elaine Boughner. They provided me with some wonderful opportunities, for which I am very grateful, and taught me what I needed to know to make a career out of writing about stamps.

While writing the *Linn's* Refresher Course column, I frequently relied upon friends and colleagues at *Linn's* and Scott Publishing for answers, advice, ideas and even material to borrow for illustrations. Those individuals include Michael Schreiber, Denise McCarty, Rob Haeseler, Chad Snee, Jim Kloetzel, Bill Jones, Martin Frankevicz, David Akin and many others. Credit for many of the images in this book goes to our talented photographer, Verlon Walden, who was always ready with some new way to create the perfect shot. Garry Leapley and the production staff at Amos Press digitally processed those finished prints and scanned new images with care and precision. Designers Johanna Peters and Cinda McAlexander put it all together to create a layout that is both effective and appealing.

Linn's book editor Donna Houseman has supported this project with patience and worked hard to see it through. I'm grateful for her encouragement and great help.

Thanks are also due to a number of writers and philatelists I consulted and worked with while at *Linn's*, including Ken Lawrence, Steven J. Rod, John Hotchner, Toke Nørby, Calvet Hahn, George Amick, Stan Showalter, Bob Dumaine and Varro Tyler. By its nature this book also owes much to the investigations and discoveries of many philatelic researchers and historians, past and present, who have shared their findings with others.

The staff of the American Philatelic Society, including executive director Robert E. Lamb, former education director Kathleen Wunderly, Ellen Stuter, Ken Martin, Gini Horn and Mercer Bristow, has always provided help when asked. Representatives of the United States Postal Service in Washington, particularly Don Smeraldi, Cathy Yarosky and Terrence McCaffrey, have answered my questions more often than anyone could count. A vast number of collectors, stamp dealers, experts and friends, far too many to name, were kind enough to help when asked, and I appreciate them all.

Chapter 1
Hobby Basics

How do we collect? Let us count the ways

It's a big hobby.

People who are not involved in the stamp hobby may think stamp collectors just put stamps into albums. Ho-hum.

The fact is, most stamp collectors study the stamps they collect, learn a lot about the subjects shown on the stamps, and learn even more about the countries and colonies all over the world that have issued stamps.

Noncollectors aren't aware of the incredible variety that is found in the stamp hobby. There are even plenty of collectors who don't know that this hobby offers a spectrum of collecting possibilities that is nearly endless.

Although the term "stamp collecting" is quite common, the term "stamp hobby" is often used to describe the many different collecting areas that exist. Others use the term "philately" (pronounced, "fih-LAT-l-ee") to describe stamp collecting and related collecting areas.

Some of these areas can be placed into various categories, like "stamps," "covers," "markings" and so on, but some collections just can't be pigeonholed. And almost all of these areas intermingle with one another, creating a great stamp-hobby stew that everyone can enjoy. Most covers, for instance, contain both stamps and markings. But let's begin with the hobby's most familiar collectible items.

Stamps: A careful look at stamp collecting alone turns up hundreds of different paths the collector may follow. Some start out by simply buying the latest new issues from the post office. A collector in the United States, for example, may make regular trips to the local post office to buy new U.S. stamp issues as soon as they are released.

Some collectors buy single stamps. Some buy blocks of four stamps or plate blocks (special blocks with margin paper attached that includes a plate number). Some buy full panes of stamps.

Figure 1. Most people know about the United States and Italy, (above, left and right). Fewer may know of the Faeroe Islands (left), but its stamps are just as collectible.

It is even possible to buy full press sheets of selected U.S. commemorative issues directly from the U.S. Postal Service. These uncut sheets are made up of multiples of the stamp panes that are sold at post office windows.

Buying collectible stamps from the post office is done not only in the United

Figure 2. Examples of back-of-the-book issues include semipostal stamps (top), airmails (center) and special delivery stamps (bottom).

States, but in countries all over the world. The stamp collector in Australia may buy each new Australian stamp issue as it arrives at his post office. These new, undamaged and unused stamps are called "mint" stamps.

Collectors also may buy mint stamps from other countries, either from stamp dealers (at a stamp shop, a stamp show, or by making a mail-order purchase) or by mail directly from the country of their choice. Some of these countries are well-known. Some are not.

Three mint stamps are shown in Figure 1. At top left is a stamp from the United States, and at top right is a stamp from Italy. Most people know at least a little about these two countries. At bottom left is a stamp from Faeroe Islands. Fewer people may know anything about Faeroe Islands, located in the northeast Atlantic Ocean, but many stamp collectors have bought, collected and studied Faeroese postage stamps and learned a great deal from them.

Collectors can even collect stamps from countries or areas that no longer exist and no longer issue stamps. Such stamps can be bought from stamp dealers.

Stamps like those shown in Figure 1 have all been used as postage for mail sent from the issuing countries.

Some stamps are designated for special purposes, such as those shown in Figure 2. At the top is a semipostal stamp from Belgium. Part of the sale price of this stamp goes toward a specially designated charity. At the center is an airmail stamp from Greece. This stamp is intended to pay a special airmail rate for letters sent from Greece to other countries. At the bottom is a special delivery stamp from the United States. This stamp was issued more than 100 years ago to provide a more immediate delivery of the mail.

These types of stamps and many others like them usually are listed in stamp catalogs after the regular postage stamp issues, and are therefore often referred to as "back-of-the-book" issues.

A stamp collector may develop a special interest in these particular issues. Other similar back-of-the-book items are postage due stamps, Official stamps, parcel post stamps and more. Learning about the special purposes these stamps serve is part of the stamp hobby.

Postally used stamps also are extremely collectible and often serve as the basis for a beginner's stamp collection. Many great collectors never even look for mint stamps, because they prefer an issue that has served its intended purpose: the delivery of the mail. Most stamps are struck with a postmark when they carry the mail and the postmark is usually visible on the face of the postally used stamp, as shown in Figure 3.

Again, the collector may choose to look for the stamps of a single country or geographic area. It may be his own country or that of some faraway land. And it may be that the collector looks for regular postage stamps or a special back-of-the-book issue.

To collect older issues, the collector can make purchases from stamp dealers or at stamp shows. This is true for mint or used stamps. Sometimes collectors trade with each other to help build collections.

Some collectors try to specialize their stamp-collecting interests, choosing to collect only commemorative stamps (usually colorful larger issues that are on sale for a limited time) or definitive stamps (usually smaller stamps that are on sale for a much longer period) or some back-of-the-book area.

In some ways, specializing or defining a stamp collection can help reduce the cost spent on stamps. A collector of German definitive stamps, for instance, does not spend money trying to collect all the German commemorative stamps.

Figure 3. A postally used stamp usually has markings on it from the strike of a postmark.

Other collectors may choose to collect only booklet stamps or coil stamps. Some collectors choose not to collect self-adhesive issues, while others choose to collect only self-adhesive issues.

Many collectors look for stamps not because of the country that issued them, but because of the subject or topic that appears on the stamp. Topical or thematic collectors may look for any special topic that interests them, from animals to occupations, specific individuals, sports or literally anything at all. For many topical collectors, it does not matter if the stamp is mint or postally used, definitive or commemorative, or back-of-the-book.

Collectors of errors, freaks and oddities search for printing mistakes made on stamps. These collectors may look for only specific kinds of errors, or errors from only one country, and may look for either unused or used versions.

For many of these collectors, collecting stamps alone often is not enough. They may seek other philatelic items to add to their collections.

Covers: When a stamp is used to mail an item, that mailed item is referred to as a "cover." Other covers might be unmailed but bear special postal markings.

Most often a cover is an envelope with a stamp that has been sent through the mail. Some covers might not even have a stamp on them. For example, covers mailed before 1840, when the first postage stamp was issued in Great Britain, often had the cost of postage marked on them with pen. Some modern covers sent by certain military personnel or government officials are accepted and delivered without stamps.

Figure 4 shows a cover mailed Aug. 10, 2001, from Dayton, Ohio, to Sapporo, Japan. Although the cover is fairly simple, it serves as an example of how the 80¢ Mount McKinley stamp paid the 1-ounce airmail postage rate in effect at the time.

Covers provide a great deal of information about the mailing systems of the world. When a cover is complete, and the stamp has not been removed, it is called

Figure 4. When a cover is saved "intact," the collector can see how the stamp was used to pay postage to a specific destination. In this case, the 80¢ stamp paid postage in 2001 to carry a letter from the United States to Japan.

Goetz Heermann
The Cover Exchange
Toyohira P.O. Box 2
Sapporo 062-8691
JAPAN

AIRMAIL

"intact." An intact cover is part of "postal history," often telling where, when and how an item was mailed.

Other types of covers can include parcel wrappings, picture postcards and postal cards, oversized envelopes and much more.

A collector who specializes in a certain type of stamp also may collect that stamp "on cover." For instance, someone with an interest in the U.S. special delivery stamp shown at the bottom of Figure 2 most likely would enjoy owning a cover that was mailed using that stamp.

A collector may choose to specialize by collecting only one kind of stamp, covering all of its postal usages, including mint stamps, used stamps, stamps on covers, errors and varieties.

First-day covers are another popular collecting area, and the first-day cover collector is again faced with many different choices. First-day covers are covers that are postmarked on the first day a stamp was issued. The classic cover at the top of Figure 5 is an Oct. 1, 1883, first-day cover for the 2¢ red-brown George Washington issue. This early use is an ordinary-looking addressed envelope with a handcancel. This classic cover illustrates a great reason why collectors must be careful about removing stamps from covers.

The 1883 2¢ Washington is a fairly common stamp, and a postally used single stamp is listed in the Scott *Specialized Catalogue of United States Stamps & Covers* with a value of less than $1. Relatively few first-day covers are known of this issue, however, and although the cover at the top of Figure 5 has only one stamp on it, its value is in the thousands of dollars.

Removing the stamp from this cover would be a disaster.

The cover at the bottom of Figure 5 was issued March 3, 1997, by the country of Luxembourg for its Tourism series stamps. Like most modern first-day covers, the envelope is unaddressed, it bears a colorful cachet (a design on the left side of the envelope) and has a specially designed handcancel that marks the cover as first day of issue (in this case, "Jour d'emission"). It is nowhere near as valuable as the 1883 cover, but it is still a very attractive collectible.

Cover collectors have at least as many different collecting choices as stamp collectors. The two collecting areas certainly overlap frequently.

But wait, there's more: Is that everything there is to the stamp hobby? It's not even close.

There are revenue stamps, Christmas seals, souvenir cards, first-day programs, philatelic literature, Pony Express covers, meter stamps, essays and proofs, year sets, postal stationery and countless other collecting possibilities.

A beginning stamp collector quickly finds that there are many different collecting areas to choose from, and often may start out by collecting a little bit of everything. That's a fine way to get one's feet wet in the hobby, but it is a good idea to look for ways to refine your collecting habits.

Defining what you want to create with your stamp collection requires some discipline, but it will better serve you in the end. If you spend a lot of money on items unrelated to your collection, you may have less money to obtain items that actually would benefit your collection.

As you become an advanced collector, you may work to maintain two, three or more collections, perhaps in very different areas. Keep in mind, however, that focusing on the development of your collection gives you a better opportunity to create something that you will enjoy for many years.

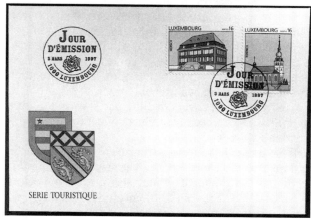

Figure 5. Early first-day covers show the first day of use for an issued postage stamp (top). Modern first-day covers (bottom) often are created specially for collectors.

This is the place to start looking for stamps

What's the one thing that every stamp collector wants?

If you guessed stamps, you're probably right. While some stamp collectors only look for covers, most of the people who call themselves stamp collectors are on the lookout for stamps.

Some stamp collectors find stamps for free nearly every day, while others pay thousands of dollars for just one stamp.

Can you really find stamps for free? The answer is yes. One appeal of the stamp hobby is that you can begin your collection by saving the postally used stamps that come on your daily mail.

You can harvest stamps from greeting cards and letters that you receive from friends and relatives. Let them know that you're a stamp collector, and you'll find that many will be willing to save the stamps from their daily mail — including the mail they get from you.

Figure 6. Many stamp collectors regularly gather boxes full of postally used stamped envelopes from local businesses, agencies or schools that would otherwise throw them away.

Ask your friends to save entire envelopes for you. That way, you can watch for unusual postal markings or interesting mailing uses, such as registered mail, that you may want to save on an intact cover. You may be surprised by the number of people who remember that they have a stash of old stamps or old envelopes, or even a stamp collection that's been abandoned for decades. They may be happy to give them to you because they know you will appreciate them.

Your own daily mail may not yield a stamp landslide, but there are many businesses that get lots of mail every day from bill-paying customers or other correspondents who use stamps. If you can approach someone at such a business and ask them to save their empty envelopes for you, you may find a rich source for all kinds of interesting stamps.

Think of the possibilities: a business running a write-in contest, your insurance or utility company, your doctor's office, your child's school office, your church or synagogue, even your city's tax office. You can probably think of other potential sources that will yield boxes of stamped covers like the one shown in Figure 6. For this type of collection program to succeed, you must collect the envelopes promptly so they aren't in anyone's way.

Some stamp collectors look for discarded envelopes in office dumpsters or in the trash containers in post office lobbies. There's even an amusing name for this activity: It's called dumpster diving. As strange as it may seem, some collectors have found great prizes this way, such as Express Mail envelopes bearing high-value stamps or registered mail envelopes from overseas.

It's always a good idea to obtain permission from someone in charge before you do your dumpster diving, whether it's at the post office or any other public place.

Hunting free stamps can be fun, but at one time or another most collectors wind up buying stamps to add to their collections.

You might begin with stamp mixtures and packets sold by stamp dealers or advertised for sale in *Linn's Stamp News*. A modern worldwide on-paper mixture may yield a great selection of stamps like those shown in Figure 7. While mixtures often contain duplicate stamps, packets of stamps are usually off-paper and all different. Carefully read the stamp dealer's description before you place your order.

Other mail-order stamp dealers offer stamp approvals, which are stamp selections sent to your home for examination. If you wish to purchase some or all of the stamps, you send payment to the dealer, along with the remaining stamps that you did not purchase. Read over the approval terms carefully so you know the kinds of stamps the dealer will send you, how long you may examine the stamps, whether postage costs are paid by you or the dealer, and so on.

Figure 7. A worldwide stamp mixture may yield on-paper stamps like these. Some dealers offer packets of mint or used stamps, or approval selections sent through the mail.

If you are lucky enough to have a retail stamp dealer doing business in your town, he may be an important source for the stamps and supplies you need for your collection. Look for stamp shops in the yellow pages of your telephone book under the headings "Stamps for Collectors," "Coins and Stamps" or "Hobbies."

The local stamp dealer may stock different packets and mixtures that you can examine before buying. Most also carry sets and individual stamps for purchase. If you talk with the local stamp dealer and let him know your interests, he may be able to help you track down the kinds of stamps you are looking for.

Figure 8. Stamp collectors find plenty to look for at stamp shows, where dealers gather to sell stamps and supplies.

You'll find many stamp dealers attending stamp shows and exhibitions that are held each weekend all over the country. The stamp show gives you a great opportunity to look over the selections of several dealers and make new contacts for future purchases.

Figure 8 shows a number of collectors at a stamp show examining the offerings at a stamp dealer's table. If you've never been to a stamp show before, you're sure to be amazed at the great selection of stamps you'll find. Watch for news of upcoming shows in *Linn's*, or check with your local stamp club or post office.

Many stamp dealers now trade on the Internet, and stamp collectors are finding a number of different online stamp shopping options. These include fixed-price sales and exchange offers, as well as popular online auctions. Of course, anyone purchasing items over the Internet should be cautious when dealing with individuals they do not know.

A collector is shown viewing one online stamp site in Figure 9.

Traditional stamp auctions have been a popular method of purchase among collectors for many years. Some of the world's greatest stamp rarities have been sold through established auction houses, but there are many auctions that offer more affordable stamps as well.

Auction houses provide catalogs that tell the date, time and location of the auction and describe the items in the sale. Buyers may request copies of the catalog by mail from auction houses advertising in *Linn's*. Some catalogs are free, while others may cost a few dollars.

Figure 9. The Internet provides a number of different ways to buy stamps. Collectors who use the Internet for their stamp purchases should pay attention to security concerns.

You can place your auction bid by mail in most cases. Anyone new to auctions can learn more about participating by carefully reading the details provided in the auction catalog.

Collectors looking for brand new stamp issues will also find many different options. New-issue stamp dealers frequently advertise in *Linn's Stamp News* and *Scott Stamp Monthly*, as do agents of postal authorities worldwide. Some postal agencies regularly produce illustrated mail-order catalogs showing their latest stamp releases. Catalogs from the postal services of Denmark, the United States and the United Nations are shown in Figure 10.

Figure 10. Postal authorities around the world create and distribute illustrated mail-order stamp catalogs like these colorful examples from Denmark, the United States and the United Nations.

The stamp sources described here will get you started. As you read more about the stamp hobby and talk with other stamp collectors, you'll find that looking for stamps can be almost as much fun as adding them to your collection.

Handle and store your collection with care

One thing every car owner hates to see is that first ding or scratch in a new car's body. The car may have been perfect in every respect when it was driven off the dealer's lot, but the first mishap to mar the new car, no matter how tiny, somehow alters it forever.

Stamp collectors go through similar suffering when they realize a choice stamp obtained for their collection has been damaged in one way or another.

In 1989 one of the famous U.S. Jenny Invert airmail stamp errors of 1918, of which only 100 are known, suffered an inadvertent trip through a vacuum cleaner. Although the stamp was retrieved from the appliance and dusted off, the journey left it creased, soiled and torn.

The owner, a well-off East Coast collector, reportedly responded to the mishap by saying, "Thank goodness it's something I can replace."

Since they often sell for more than $150,000 each, most of us will never own a Jenny Invert. If we did, our reactions probably would be more dismal if the stamp were vacuumed into damaged condition.

There are really two important reasons why collectors go to great lengths to keep their stamps and covers in the best condition possible. The condition of a stamp or cover can greatly affect the item's value. Damaged items trade or sell for considerably less than the same items in undamaged condition.

Probably just as important, though, is the way that the collector feels about having damaged items sprinkled throughout a collection. Not every collector can afford the finest example of each stamp, but most collectors take care in selecting their stamps. It's much more satisfying to know each stamp in the collection has maintained its condition because of proper handling and storage than it is to look through a collection and spot damage to stamps that could have been avoided.

Individual stamps are among the most fragile items in the stamp hobby. Even a new mint stamp can be torn, creased or stained with just a moment's inattention.

Many collectors handle stamps with their hands or fingers. Sometimes this can hardly be avoided, such as when a collector separates a single stamp from a pane. To help prevent damage to stamps, particularly mint (unused) stamps, collectors often use stamp tongs whenever possible. The tips of stamp tongs are specially designed for picking up and holding postage stamps. The tips are rounded and highly polished, making them safe for this delicate task.

Standard tweezers, which resemble stamp tongs to some degree, should not be used with stamps because the ridged tips can crease or cut fragile stamp paper.

Human skin is always coated with some oily residue. Even a good solid hand-washing reduces that skin oil for only a very brief time. When skin oil is transferred to a stamp, even in minute quantities, it can act over time to discolor or dull the stamp.

Certainly every collector should wash and dry his hands carefully before touching stamps, but using stamp tongs practically eliminates the chance of soiling stamps with skin oil or other residue.

Figure 11 shows a collector attempting to pick up a stamp with his fingers. Notice that the stamp is bending as the collector struggles to pluck it off the tabletop. At the right of Figure 11, the same collector finds it easier to lift the stamp using a pair of stamp tongs. The stamp is held firmly, and the danger of bending or creasing the stamp is eliminated.

Collectors often keep their stamps and covers safe in albums or stock books.

The fragile edges of stamps can be damaged with careless handling. On perforated stamps, the pointed tips, known as "teeth," can be bent, creased or torn easily.

In an album or stock book, stamps and covers are stored flat in a fixed position, so the opportunity for damage is greatly reduced.

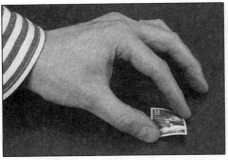
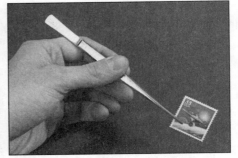

Figure 11. Using fingers to handle stamps easily can result in damage (left). Specially manufactured stamp tongs (right) are inexpensive and much safer for stamps.

Stamps, covers, albums and stock books always should be stored in an area where humidity and temperature are kept at reasonable and fairly constant levels. The combination of heat and humidity can activate the adhesive on the back of many stamps, causing them to stick to album or stock book pages.

The added element of pressure on album pages or stock book pages can further aggravate the situation. When pages are packed tight with stamps, the adhesive has an even greater chance of sticking to the page.

Albums and stock books should never be overstuffed with stamps or pages. This can be tough on the pages and on the stamps, making either or both susceptible to damage.

Another way to avoid pressure on stamps is to make sure albums and stock books are stored upright, as shown in Figure 12. When an album lies flat on its side, the weight of the pages on top puts a lot of pressure onto the bottom pages. Storing the album upright distributes that weight evenly and reduces the pressure on the stamps and the album binder.

When an album is not in use for extended periods, it is recommended that the collector periodically open it and carefully turn each page to ensure that all stamps are still affixed properly and that pages separate easily.

Figure 12. Store stamp albums and stock books upright on shelves in a room with safe temperature and humidity levels.

Special album slipcases are available from some album manufacturers to further protect the stamps inside.

Stamps and albums always should be kept out of direct sunlight and away from dust. Storing stamps in a cabinet with a door is one way to accomplish both of these goals. Sunlight can fade the colors of stamps and album binders. Heat from sunlight or other sources can cause binders to crack and album pages to yellow.

Even repeated moderate exposure to room light can affect the colors of many postage stamps, either by fading them or by changing their appearance. Stamps displayed in frames for any length of time are likely to show evidence of damage from light.

Collectors should never place food or beverages near stamps, covers or albums.

Figure 13 shows a disaster waiting to happen, with coffee and snacks right next to an open stamp album. Spills or drips can cause immediate and irreparable damage to stamps or an album. Even the crumb of a cookie dropping unnoticed onto an album page can create a permanent stain on the page or on a stamp.

Covers — including first-day covers, postcards, mailed envelopes and wrappers — all need to be handled and stored with the same care and common sense that is applied to stamps. Jamming covers together into tightly stuffed boxes easily can result in creases or damaged corners.

Storage boxes for covers should always have enough room for covers to be removed easily. But if there is too much room inside the storage box, covers may slide around loosely and suffer bent corners when other covers stack up on top of them. Cover boxes should be made of archival material that will not oxidize and stain covers.

Figure 13. Don't ever bring food or drink this close to your collection. Just one small mishap could result in disaster.

For added protection, individual covers can be kept in transparent cover sleeves. There are several varieties of sleeves available, offering varying degrees of protection.

The example shown in Figure 14 is made from a sturdy transparent plastic that is chemically neutral so it will not damage the paper of the cover or stamp. The firm plastic resists bending or folding. Also available are inexpensive polybag sleeves, which are best used as temporary storage for large quantities of less valuable

Figure 14. Transparent sleeves protect covers from dirt and fingerprints but still allow viewing from both sides.

covers. The clear plastic provides protection from dirt and fingerprints, but the thinner, flexible material does not protect against bending.

Some collectors use glassine envelopes to store covers or stamps. These are also best used only temporarily. Because the paperlike glassine material is easily bent or creased, the collector must ensure that the envelopes are stored in a manner that protects the contents from harm.

Cover albums are available with transparent pages that hold covers securely and allow easy viewing. Cover albums provide the best protection for covers, but they are also considerably more expensive than sleeves or glassine envelopes.

All the collector tools and supplies mentioned here are available from stamp dealers and stamp-hobby suppliers. These products serve to protect your favorite collectibles, so you can enjoy them for years to come — long after that new car has been consigned to the junkyard.

There's a stamp catalog that's right for you

It may be hard to comprehend, but stamp catalogs exist that identify nearly every postage stamp ever created in the entire world.

There have been so many stamps issued throughout history that to list them all and show images of representative stamps, the Scott *Standard Postage Stamp Catalogue*, shown in Figure 15, is published in six large volumes.

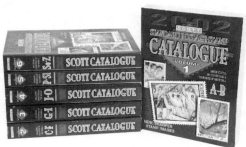

Scott catalogs are carefully researched and compiled by Scott Publishing Co., a division of Amos Press of Sidney, Ohio.

Each volume of the Scott catalog contains comprehensive stamp listings for countries arranged in alphabetical order by country name.

Scott Publishing Company, publisher of the Scott catalog line, does not sell the stamps in the catalog. It illustrates, describes and values stamps so that collectors can identify the stamps in their collections.

Figure 15. The Scott *Standard Postage Stamp Catalogue* is a six-volume set that lists and values the postage stamps that have been issued throughout the world. The entire catalog is updated each year.

The stamps of the United States are listed first in Vol. 1, followed by all the countries of the world beginning with the letters A and B. Vol. 6 ends with the 24 stamps issued by Zululand between 1888 and 1896. The entire 6-volume set is revised each year. More than half-a-million different stamps are listed in the complete set.

Each stamp in the Scott standard catalog is listed with useful information, such as the issue date, the process used to print the stamp, the perforation gauge (a measurement of how close together the perforation holes are) and an individual Scott catalog number.

Many collectors and dealers use the Scott catalog number to precisely identify a specific stamp.

For example, a collector who refers to Mexico Scott 1062 is describing the 40-centavo Dancing Dogs stamp in Figure 16, issued by Mexico on April 10, 1974, to commemorate an exhibition of pre-Columbian art held that year in Mexico City. If you look in the Mexico section of the Scott standard catalog for Mexico Scott 1062, you will find an illustration of the Dancing Dogs stamp and additional information about the issue.

The standard postage stamp catalog provides values for most of the stamps that are listed, both in unused condition and postally used. These values approximate what a retail stamp dealer would charge a customer who wanted to purchase any specific single stamp or set.

Figure 16. When a collector refers to a stamp by its country and Scott catalog number, it precisely identifies a specific stamp. The 1974 Dancing Dogs stamp shown here, for example, is Mexico Scott 1062.

For each individual stamp or stamp set listing, at least one stamp is shown in black and white to illustrate the basic design. Often the catalog also provides a brief bit of information about the stamp subject, telling why the stamp was issued.

There are different worldwide catalogs published in other countries. Many of these catalogs use their own numbering systems.

A collector with an interest in just one country or region may prefer a stamp catalog that describes only the stamps in the specific collecting area.

For beginner collectors, a pocket catalog that simply identifies each stamp and lists them in chronological order may be all that is needed.

Figure 17. Pocket catalogs provide the stamp collector with a handy reference guide, but they normally do not include detailed information.

Two such catalogs for United States stamps are shown in Figure 17. At left is *The Postal Service Guide to U.S. Stamps*, published by the United States Postal Service. At right is the Scott *U.S. Pocket Stamp Catalogue*. Both of these catalogs use Scott catalog numbers to identify the listed stamps.

Pocket catalogs generally provide limited information. The illustrations and listings simply help the collector determine which stamps are needed to fill out the collection. When the collector wants to learn more about his stamps, he can turn to a specialized stamp catalog.

The Scott *Specialized Catalogue of United States Stamps & Covers* is shown in Figure 18.

Collectors of U.S. stamps find substantially more information in the specialized catalog than is available in any pocket or standard catalog. For instance, the Scott U.S. specialized catalog includes information about plate numbers on coil and booklet stamps that is lacking in other catalogs. More varieties and errors are listed in the specialized catalog, as well as other details about stamp issues such as plate block descriptions and information about stamp printers and designers.

The descriptions shown in Figure 19 may help to explain how the listings differ in the pocket, standard and specialized catalogs.

All three listings in the example are for the 15¢ Organized Labor stamp (Scott

1831) issued by the United States in 1980. The listings are shown near actual size.

All three catalogs include an illustration of the stamp design.

The pocket catalog listing, shown at top in Figure 19, identifies the stamp by Scott catalog number, denomination and issue name, and it gives values for a single stamp in unused and postally used condition.

Also listed is an error variety, Scott 1831a, which is an imperforate pair of the Organized Labor stamp. "Imperforate" means the stamps have no perforations separating them from each other or adjacent margin paper.

The description in the center of Figure 19, from Vol. 1 of the Scott standard catalog, has all of the pocket catalog information, as well as the exact date of issue, printing method ("Photo.," short for "photogravure" or "gravure") and perforation gauge ("Perf. 11").

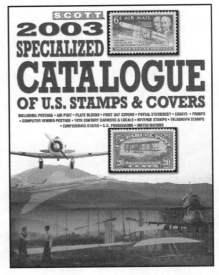

Figure 18. The Scott *Specialized Catalogue of United States Stamps & Covers* provides in-depth information about United States stamps and their many varieties.

At the bottom of Figure 19 is the listing for the Organized Labor stamp from the Scott U.S. specialized catalog.

Still more information is included: the name of the designer, listings and values for plate number blocks of 12 stamps and ZIP blocks of four stamps, and the format in which the stamp was printed, "Plates of 200 subjects in four panes of 50." The U.S. specialized catalog illustration is also larger.

The specialized catalog also contains many listings that aren't found in standard catalogs. Among these are descriptions of U.S. proofs and essays (test printings and artwork created before the stamps are printed); expanded revenue stamp listings; first-day-cover listings, including information about official first-day cities; detailed specialized listings for booklet stamps; and much more.

1831 15c Organized Labor .... .30 .20
a. Imperf., pair.......... *375.00*

Organized Labor
1980, Sept. 1 Photo. *Perf. 11*
1831 A1218 15c multicolored .30 .20
a. Imperf., pair *375.00*

ORGANIZED LABOR ISSUE
Designed by Peter Cocci.
PHOTOGRAVURE
Plates of 200 subjects in four panes of 50.
1980, Sept. 1 Tagged *Perf. 11*
1831 A1218 15c **multi** .30 .20
P# block of 12, 6# 3.50 —
Zip block of 4 1.25 —
a. Imperf., pair *375.00*

Figure 19. Listings for the 1980 Organized Labor stamp issued by the United States, from the Scott *United States Pocket Stamp Catalogue*, the Scott standard catalog, and the Scott U.S. specialized catalog. Each provides a certain depth of detail for the collector.

Stamp collectors can even find stamp catalogs on compact discs (CD-ROM) that are read by computer. Scott Publishing Co. offers many of its catalogs on CD, as shown in Figure 20.

Just as Scott, a U.S. company, creates a specialized catalog for

Figure 20. Scott stamp catalogs on CD-ROM provide the computer user with the same information found in conventional print catalogs.

U.S. stamps, many companies in other countries create specialized catalogs for their own stamps. Figure 21 shows four such catalogs. Clockwise from top left are the Michel specialized Germany catalog, the Zumstein catalog of Switzerland and Liechtenstein, the Prangko catalog for Indonesia and the AFA catalog for Denmark. Each catalog presents more information than the collector is likely to find in the general worldwide catalog, but most foreign catalogs also are written in the language of the country of origin.

Stamp catalogs are sold by dealers in philatelic literature, many of whom advertise in *Linn's Stamp News*, *Scott Stamp Monthly* and other stamp-hobby publications. They are also available from stamp dealers or directly from the publisher.

Figure 21. A number of catalog publishers worldwide have created specialized catalogs for the stamps issued by their own countries. Many such catalogs are published in the language of the country where the catalog was created.

Chapter 2
Stamp Terminology

Come to terms with the language of stamps

An important way that you can develop your skills as a stamp collector is to learn about the hobby by reading books and journals, along with the wealth of information that is presented weekly in *Linn's Stamp News*.

In *Linn's* and other publications you will come across words and phrases that are used by stamp collectors to describe important aspects of the stamp hobby. In some of these publications, there may not be an explanation of the term that is used, and that can be frustrating if you are trying to learn more about stamp collecting.

When you read about stamp collecting and you encounter an unfamiliar abbreviation, check through the earlier part of the material you are reading to see if those initials relate to something that was already mentioned.

For instance, in a *Linn's* article about plate number coils, the phrase "plate number coils" will be written out one time; thereafter, the writer will refer to the coils as "PNCs." By looking back through the article, you can see that "PNC" stands for "plate number coil."

Here are a few common words and phrases that stamp collectors frequently use.

Covers are envelopes, postal cards or parcel wrappers that have had stamps applied to them. Usually, when an item is called a cover, it has been sent through the mail and received postmarks and cancels on the stamps.

Actually, any mailed envelope that you receive at your home or business could be considered a cover. Some are worth saving, some perhaps not.

Figure 22. This first-day cover for the 20¢ Preserving Wetlands commemorative has a decorative cachet at the left side of the envelope that complements the stamp.

A **first-day cover** is a specially prepared envelope that has a cancel dated for the first day of issue for a particular stamp or item of postal stationery.

Some first-day covers are plain, addressed covers that have been sent through the mail. Others may be unaddressed or have a special design that is called a **cachet**. In Figure 22 is shown a first-day cover for the 20¢ Preserving Wetlands commemorative stamp with a cachet (pronounced "ka-SHAY"). The cachet decorates the first-day cover.

If you go to the post office, you may hear someone ask to buy a sheet of stamps. The clerk will certainly sell that customer 20, 50 or 100 stamps as they wish, but stamp collectors have two specific terms they use to describe that type of item. A **pane** of stamps is what the customer is buying at the post office. Why is it called that and not a sheet? It's called a pane because the word **sheet** is used to describe the full printing press sheet of stamps that will include a specific number of panes.

For instance, the 32¢ Utah Statehood stamp that was issued Jan. 4, 1996, was sold at the post office in a full pane of 50 stamps. However, when the stamps were printed by Sterling Sommer Inc. in Tonawanda, N.Y., they came off the printing press in full sheets of 200 stamps, which means four panes on one uncut sheet. The sheet was cut into individual panes, and only then were the panes packaged and sent to post offices for sale.

A **plate block** or **plate number block** is a special part of the stamp pane that many collectors enjoy saving. Many plate blocks consist of four stamps from a corner of the pane and include the margin of the pane that has the number of the printing plate that was used to print the entire press sheet.

Collectors who save plate blocks do not remove any of the margin paper from around the block of stamps. One example of a U.S. plate block is illustrated in Figure 23: the 13¢ John F. Kennedy stamp issued May 29, 1967. On the Kennedy plate block in Figure 23, you can see the plate number 29114 in the margin paper along the left side of the block.

On some stamp issues from panes, it may take more than four stamps to create a plate block, particularly if the stamp issue has multiple designs. In those cases, it is a good idea to check the Scott *Specialized Catalogue of United States Stamps & Covers* or *Scott Stamp Monthly* magazine to see in what form the plate block should be saved.

The marginal paper around the edge of a stamp pane is often called the **sel-vage**. On the Kennedy block in Figure 23, the selvage extends around the left side and top of the block.

If a stamp issue has multiple designs, it is said that the stamp designs are **se-tenant**. The United States Postal Service issues many se-tenant designs, often in panes of commemorative

Figure 23. A plate block of the 13¢ John F. Kennedy stamp consists of four stamps from the corner of a pane, along with the surrounding selvage, including the plate numbers from the printing sheet (seen at left).

Figure 24. Stamps that are attached to one another but have different designs, such as this strip of American Indian Dances stamps, are called se-tenant.

stamps, or in booklets of stamps.

On June 7, 1996, the USPS issued a pane of 20 32¢ American Indian Dances stamps. There are five different designs of stamps, and each design is repeated four times on the pane. The five designs are shown in Figure 24. Because they are different designs on stamps that are attached to one another, they are called se-tenant.

A plate block of the American Indian Dances stamps, according to the Scott U.S. specialized catalog, consists of 10 stamps with all marginal selvage attached.

Another popular way to collect stamps is to save **coil** stamps. At the post office, you may hear customers ask for a "roll" of stamps. What they want to buy is a coil of 100 stamps. Such coils are easy to keep in small dispensers, and mailers can detach stamps from the coil one at a time to place on letters. These rolled-up strips of stamps are also available in much larger sizes than just 100 stamps, for use in machines or commercial mailers.

A stamp that is placed on a letter is called the **frank** or **franking**. A cover that is franked has postage applied for mailing. Even after the cover has been through the mail and delivered, the stamp may still be called the franking.

A **meter stamp** also may be considered a franking. Meter stamps are often used by businesses and governments to easily apply postage to mail that is being sent out. The meter stamp is created by a **postage meter**, a special machine that is regulated by the Postal Service but is kept on the premises of a business.

Shown in Figure 25 is a cover that has been franked with a meter stamp. The **denomination** of the meter stamp is 34¢, the first-class letter rate in effect when the envelope was mailed in August 2001.

The denomination is the number that is printed on any kind of stamp to show the value of it. Almost all U.S. stamps have a denomination printed on them, although a few have been issued without denominations when rates have recently changed.

A **nondenominated** U.S. stamp is shown in Figure 26. Instead of numbers, the stamp has a large letter G printed on the front. Postal Service employees can look up the value of this stamp and find that it is worth 32¢ in postage. Earlier nondenominated stamps, marked by the letters A-F, have lesser values. Some other nondenominated stamps do not have letter codes. Nondenominated stamps from other countries use other methods to indicate the stamp's value.

Figure 25. Shown is a common cover franked with a meter stamp that has a denomination of 34¢. The terms "cover," "franking," "meter stamp" and "denomination" are explained in this chapter.

The large letter G, and all the other lettering on the stamp in Figure 26, is called the stamp's **inscription**. It is the part of the design with lettering or numbers. The remainder of the design, in this case the American flag, is called the **vignette**.

The term vignette has been used most commonly to describe a pictorial stamp design element that is surrounded by a border. However, the 10th edition of the *Merriam-Webster's Collegiate Dictionary* also describes vignette as "the pictorial part of a postage stamp design as distinguished from the frame and lettering."

If you don't understand a term or phrase, sometimes a standard desk dictionary will give you most or all of the information that you need. Even "cover," the first term described here, is listed in the dictionary as "an envelope or wrapper for mail."

The more you read and learn about the stamp hobby, the more you will enjoy it.

Stamp collecting terms with foreign origins

There are many different hobbies that are known around the world, but stamp collecting is probably one of the most universally recognized. Postal services worldwide recognize that there are collectors almost everywhere, and they try to create and distribute stamp designs that will appeal to collectors of one sort or another.

The international aspect of stamp collecting has influenced the language of the hobby. Many of the terms and phrases that are used to describe different aspects of stamps and collecting have origins in languages other than English.

One of the more familiar terms is the formal word **philately**, which is used to specify the hobby of stamp collecting. Many collectors have heard the term "philately." It is even

Figure 26. The G stamp is nondenominated — it does not have a number showing the value. The G stamp with a white background has a face value of 32¢.

part of the name of the largest collector organization in the United States: the American Philatelic Society. A person who enjoys and studies stamp collecting is called a **philatelist**.

The roots of these words come from two Greek words. "Philo" means a love of something. "Ateleia" means something that is untaxed.

A French stamp collector named Georges Herpin created the word in the 1860s. It describes a stamp collector as one who loves something that is untaxed: the postage stamp. The term probably was intended to describe the recipient of a mailed stamp, who did not have to pay a tax because the postage was prepaid.

Greek words were used by a French stamp collector to describe a hobby enjoyed around the world. How do collectors in the United States pronounce these words?

Though the definitions are fairly consistent, even major dictionaries don't fully agree on the pronunciation. Philately is most often pronounced "fih-LAT-l-ee," which is hard to put into print, but not too difficult to say. The pronunciation for philately in the 10th edition of the *Merrian Webster's Collegiate Dictionary* combines the "t" and the second "l" with no vowel sound in the third syllable: "fih-Latl-ee." Remember that the "a" in "philately" sounds like the "a" in "bat," and that the stress is on the second syllable. The word almost sounds like the word "flatly."

Philatelic, the adjective that describes something related to stamp collecting, is pronounced "fil-lah-TE-lik." It's almost like four words combined, "fill-a-tell-lick," with the emphasis on "tell." Philatelist, meaning stamp collector, is pronounced, "fih-LAT-l-ist."

It's ironic that the most difficult words in the stamp collector's vocabulary are those describing the hobby and practice of stamp collecting.

Many other words in the stamp hobby may be puzzling to the collector who is unfamiliar with them.

Bourse is pronounced "boorce." It describes a gathering where philatelic items are bought and sold. Most frequently you'll see the word "bourse" used to describe the dealers' tables at a stamp show or exhibition. The word "bourse" distinguishes the selling area from the exhibit area of a stamp show.

Burelage is pronounced "byu-REL-idge." Burelage is a fine network pattern of lines or dots used on the paper that stamps are printed upon. In some cases burelage is used to make forgery of the stamp difficult. This type of pattern can be seen on the back of some 19th-century stamps from Queensland. The Scott *Standard Postage Stamp Catalogue* describes the pattern as a **moiré** (pronounced "mwa-RAY").

Burelage can be seen in the designs of several issues from Mexico's Exporta postage stamps, first issued in 1975. Figure 27 shows Scott 1505, issued in 1988. The fine line of a burelage is a "burele" (pronounced "byu-REL").

Figure 27. The designs of some stamps from Mexico's Exporta series feature a burelage, a network of fine lines printed over the stamp. Shown is Mexico Scott 1505.

Figure 28. The special design on a cover is called a cachet. The image of Duke Ellington at left is the cachet.

To show how unusual some of these words are, I looked in 11 dictionaries before I located the pronunciation of "burelage" in the 1947 unabridged second edition of Webster's *New International Dictionary of the English Language*.

A much more common philatelic term is **cachet**, which describes a special design on a cover (a prepared envelope). For example, shown in Figure 28 is a first-day cover of the 22¢ Duke Ellington stamp issued April 29, 1986. The cachet on this cover is the artwork at left showing Ellington and a piano keyboard. The word "cachet" is pronounced "ka-SHAY." The first letter "a" is once again pronounced like the "a" in the word "bat."

Facsimile is pronounced "fak-SIH-muh-lee." An exact replica of an issued stamp is called a facsimile. Usually, these reproductions are not intended to defraud a stamp collector and can be distinguished by marks that identify them as facsimiles. A facsimile that is intended to deceive collectors and pass as the genuine object is called a forgery.

There are two words used to describe common printing methods that some collectors may be unfamiliar with. **Gravure** printing is accomplished by the chemical etching of a printing plate or cylinder with an image of finely screened dots. The word "gravure" is pronounced "grah-VYUR." **Intaglio** printing is accomplished by the impression of an engraved image that has been reproduced in recess onto a printing plate or cylinder. The word "intaglio" is pronounced "in-TAHL-yo."

Machin is the last name of the artist who designed one of the most familiar definitive stamp series in the world. Arnold Machin created a plaster cast profile of Great Britain's Queen Elizabeth II. His design has been used on stamps from that country since 1967, and new varieties continue to be issued in the 21st century. One example from the extensive Machin series of definitives, Great Britain Scott MH66, is shown in Figure 29.

The name "Machin" is most commonly pronounced, "MAY-chin," although

Figure 29. The design of this British definitive stamp shows a plaster cast portrait of Queen Elizabeth II. The artist who created the design is Arnold Machin.

other pronunciations have been heard.

The next four terms are all derived from French words. Each describes some characteristic of a postage stamp.

Roulette is a method of stamp separation that is used instead of perforation. It has been used in the United States on stamps such as Scott 2892, the G-rate 32¢ Flag coil stamp issued in 1994. Rouletting consists of a straight-line series of slits through the stamp paper that incompletely separates the stamps. The stamps can be separated by gently pulling them apart, causing the connecting points of paper to tear neatly. "Roulette" is pronounced "roo-LETT."

Se-tenant means two stamps that are attached to one another but have different designs. Many U.S. stamps are se-tenant. For instance, the 1995 Civil War stamps were issued in a single pane with 20 different stamp designs. These stamps are all considered se-tenant, since all the designs are different. "Se-tenant" is pronounced "say-ten-AWH," but many collectors put an American twist to the pronunciation, and say, "say-TEN-ent."

Tête-bêche describes attached stamps that are inverted with relation to one another. That is, if you look at one stamp right side up, the attached stamp is printed upside down.

"Tête-bêche" is pronounced "tet-BESH." It's a combination of two French words meaning "head against foot."

The two stamps shown in Figure 30 illustrate both the terms "se-tenant" and "tête-bêche." These stamps from Denmark are se-tenant because there are two different stamps attached to one another, and they are tête-bêche because each stamp is upside down in relation to the other.

Finally, the term **vignette** is used to describe that part of a postage stamp design that consists of a picture, as opposed to a frame or lettering. "Vignette" is pronounced "vin-YET."

The stamp shown in Figure 31 is the $1 Surrender at Saratoga definitive issued by the United States in 1994. The vignette is the central design area that is surrounded by a ring of small round circles, almost like a pearl necklace. The vignette on this stamp shows British Gen. John Burgoyne as he surrenders to American Gen. Horatio Gates.

There are certainly many other stamp terms that may be difficult to understand or pronounce. In many cases, such terms can be found in a good dictionary, often with the philatelic meaning described.

In some cases the words described here have pronunciation variations that are used in different parts of the world. If you're talking about stamps with another collector, though, you're likely to do just fine with the descriptions provided here.

Figure 30. These two stamps from Denmark are se-tenant and tête-bêche.

Stamp-hobby abbreviations can be decoded

The stamp hobby has a language all its own. Collectors and stamp dealers regularly discuss their interests using terms that are quite unfamiliar to noncollectors. That language becomes even harder to comprehend when the terminology is abbreviated in print. Yet there are dozens of symbols and abbreviations commonly used throughout the stamp hobby that can mystify newer collectors and puzzle even more advanced collectors who are unfamiliar with them.

The chart shown here is *Linn's Stamp News* guide to philatelic symbols and abbreviations that are commonly used in print. It contains more than 80 symbols and abbreviations that you might find in dealer price lists, in classified or display advertising, or even in editorial text in stamp-hobby specialty publications.

Following are explanations of symbols and abbreviations you may spot as you become more involved in the stamp hobby.

The first two symbols on the chart are a star or

Figure 31. The vignette on this $1 stamp is the pictorial design in the center.

Linn's guide to philatelic symbols and abbreviations

To help the philatelic newcomer, *Linn's* presents this list of most frequently used symbols and abbreviations:

★ or * — Mint
◉ — Used
⊞ — Block
☐ — Piece
⊠ — Cover
ABNC — American Bank Note Co.
APO — Army Post Office, Air Force Post Office
APS — American Philatelic Society
ASDA — American Stamp Dealers Association
Av. or Avg. — Average
BEP — Bureau of Engraving and Printing
Bklt. — Booklet
BNA — British North America
BOB — Back-of-the-book
BPO — British Post Office
Canc. or Ccl. — Canceled or Cancellation
CDS — Circular Datestamp
CMS — Complete Matched Set
Comm. — Commemorative
Cpl. — Complete
CTO — Canceled to Order
CV — Catalog Value
Def. — Definitive
DPO — Discontinued Post Office
EFOs — Errors, Freaks and Oddities

Est. — Estimated
F — Fine
FDC — First-Day Cover
FFC — First-Flight Cover
FPO — Fleet Post Office
G — Good
GD — Gum Disturbance
GPO — General Post Office
HH — Heavily Hinged
HPO — Highway Post Office
IC — Iron Curtain
Imperf. — Imperforate
IRC — International Reply Coupon
LH — Lightly Hinged
LP — Line Pair
MB — Minimum Bid
MC — Maltese Cross
MD — Minor Defect(s)
ME — Mail Early
Mi. — Michel catalog
MI — Marginal Inscription
MNH — Mint, Never Hinged
MPO — Mobile Post Office
MPP — Mailer's Precancel Postmark
M/S — Miniature Sheet
MS — Matched Set
NG — No Gum
NH — Never Hinged
OG — Original Gum
Opt. or Ovpt. — Overprint

P — Poor
PB — Plate Block
PCL — Precancel
Perf. — Perforated or Perforation
PM — Postmaster or Postmark
Pmk. — Postmark
PNC — Plate Number Coil
PS3 — Plate Strip of 3
PS5 — Plate Strip of 5
RG — Regummed
RPO — Railway Post Office
S or Sup. — Superb
S/A — Self-adhesive
SASE — (Self)-addressed, Stamped Envelope
Sc. — Scott catalog
SE — Straight Edge
Seten. — Se-tenant
SG — Stanley Gibbons catalog
S/S or SS — Souvenir Sheet
UNPA — U.N. Postal Admin.
USPS — U.S. Postal Service
UPU — Universal Postal Union
VF — Very Fine
VG — Very Good
VLH — Very Lightly Hinged
w/o — Without
Wmk. — Watermark
W/W or WW — Worldwide
XF — Extremely Fine
Yv. — Yvert et Tellier catalog

asterisk to represent the word "mint," and a large dot within a circle to represent the word "used." These terms refer to the condition of a stamp or group of stamps. A mint stamp is unused and undamaged, with full gum on the back (if

that's how it was issued), in the same condition it should be when it leaves the stamp printer. The word "used" describes a stamp that was placed on an envelope, postcard or parcel to show that postage was paid. The used stamp is commonly struck with a postmark.

Figure 32. Stamp dealers sometimes use special symbols to indicate if a stamp is in mint condition (the 1996 German stamp shown at left) or postally used (the example at right).

Figure 32 shows two examples of Germany Scott 1934, a 100-pfennig stamp issued in 1996. The stamp at left is in mint condition. It is unmarked on the front and has full undisturbed gum on the back. The stamp at right was used to mail a letter. After it traveled through the mail, a stamp collector soaked it from the envelope paper, so it no longer has gum on the back. The front of the stamp shows a postmark from the northern German city of Flensburg.

A stamp dealer's price list or advertisement may offer both stamps shown in Figure 32, using the symbols representing "mint" and "used" to differentiate the two.

APS refers to the American Philatelic Society, a national organization of stamp collectors in the United States. The APS participates in national stamp shows and exhibitions, operates a stamp sales division, publishes the monthly magazine *American Philatelist*, provides access to insurance for collections and has the most extensive public-access philatelic library in the United States.

ASDA is the American Stamp Dealers Association, a large nationwide organization of individuals and businesses involved in the stamp trade. Along with the APS and the United States Postal Service, the ASDA also serves as a major stamp show sponsor. Because the ASDA requires that its dealer members follow specific ethical guidelines, many stamp collectors prefer buying and selling from dealers who are ASDA members.

FDC stands for first-day cover. It refers to any cover (most often an envelope or postcard) that is postmarked on the first day of issue for the stamp affixed to it.

A modern FDC from the United States is shown in Figure 33. In the upper-right corner is the 22¢ John J. Audubon stamp of 1985. The postmark across the stamp includes the words "FIRST DAY OF ISSUE." Older FDCs may not have this type of souvenir postmark. Instead, the postmark simply bears the date of issue for the stamp on the cover.

CDS is an abbreviation for circular datestamp. It refers to a round, dated portion of a postmark used to cancel stamps. The stamp shown on the cover in Figure 33 has been canceled by a postmark that has two parts. The CDS is the circular part at left that reads "NEW YORK, NY" and is dated "APR 23 1985." The straight lines at right that cancel the stamp are known as killer bars.

In the case of this special souvenir cover, the CDS gives the date and location

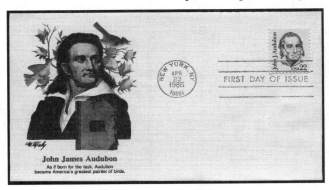

Figure 33. A first-day cover (FDC) is postmarked on the day of issue for the stamp franking the cover. The 22¢ John J. Audubon stamp was issued April 23, 1985, in New York City.

where the 22¢ Audubon stamp was issued. On regular mail, the CDS gives the date and location where the item was first postmarked or mailed.

The CDS exists in many different styles. Post office window clerks in the United States often use a round dated handcancel without killer bars.

PB refers to plate block, a collecting format popular with some collectors in the United States for many years. Plate blocks are groups of four or more stamps with attached margin paper that includes the plate numbers or cylinder numbers used for that issue. Figure 34 shows a plate block of the 33¢ Los Angeles-class Submarine stamps issued March 27, 2000.

Plate blocks for stamp issues with multiple designs may consist of more than four stamps. The exact configuration of the plate block for each U.S. issue, when applicable, is described in the Scott *Specialized Catalogue of United States Stamps & Covers*.

Opt. or **Ovpt.** is an abbreviation for overprint. An overprint is a message imprint applied to unused stamps by the postal authority that issues the stamps.

Stamps are officially overprinted for many reasons. Some overprints announce a new name for the issuing country. Other overprints, called surcharges, change the value of the stamp.

Figure 35 shows an overprinted stamp from the United States, part of the 1929 Kansas-Nebraska issue. The 6¢ James Garfield stamp of 1927, Scott 638, was overprinted "Kans." as part of a program created to thwart stamp theft from post offices. "Kans." or "Nebr." overprints were applied to 22 different issues.

Overprinted stamps often receive their own catalog listings. The 6¢ Garfield with

Figure 34. The abbreviation "PB" is sometimes used to refer to a plate block of United States stamps. Shown is a plate block of the 33¢ Submarines issue released March 27, 2000 (Scott 3372).

"Kans." overprint in the illustration is Scott 664.

The definitions provided here are general, and exceptions may exist for some of them. As you become more familiar with the stamp hobby, you will learn to recognize many of the symbols and abbreviations that are commonly used.

Figure 35. Overprints are added to unused stamps by the issuing postal authority. Regular stamps overprinted "Kans." or "Nebr." were issued by the United States in 1929 as part of a program to reduce post office burglaries.

Chapter 3
Building a Collection

Soak stamps to help build your collection

Stamp collecting is one of the few hobbies that you can enter without any cost. All you need is a pair of scissors, a cup of water and yesterday's mail.

Many collectors remove postally used stamps from envelopes by soaking them in water. Once free from the envelope paper, the stamps can be dried, flattened and added to a collection.

Stamp soaking is an activity practiced by stamp collectors everywhere. The steps for successful stamp soaking are fairly simple, and the end result is often a terrific collection of postally used stamps.

Collectors soak stamps in water because almost any other method of removing the stamp from paper is likely to damage the stamp. If a collector pulls up on a stamp corner to peel it off an envelope, for instance, it is almost certain that a layer of paper from the stamp will tear free and remain stuck to the envelope. The resulting stamp is damaged with what collectors call a "thin": any area where a layer of stamp paper is missing. The stamp will probably be creased or even torn as well.

The condition of your postage stamps is always very important. Some collectors do not save damaged stamps at all, while others may use them to fill empty spaces on album pages until undamaged examples can be found.

Many collectors soak stamps from the daily mail, while others buy on-paper mixtures of postally used stamps to sort through and soak.

Collectors can find offers of stamp mixtures for sale among the many classified ads in the back pages of *Linn's Stamp News*.

Here are some step-by-step instructions for stamp soaking that should help you build your collection in no time.

1. Inspect your covers. Covers are the envelopes, postcards and parcel wrappings that make up the mail. Collectors get many of their stamps from covers, but there are times when cutting off the stamp is a bad idea.

Covers that indicate that special mail services have been used, such as registered mail or certified mail, should be saved intact. Chances are that such a cover will be more valuable to a collector or stamp dealer than the stamps alone.

Similar markings, such as return-to-sender, postage due and so on, are also likely to be of interest to a specialist collector.

If you're not sure if a cover should be cut, set it aside until you can find out more information, or check with a knowledgeable collector or a stamp dealer.

2. Cut the stamps off the envelopes. Once you've decided the covers you have don't need to be saved intact, you can begin to cut the stamps off, as shown in Figure 36. Always be very careful not to cut any part of the actual stamp. Trim around the stamp, leaving at least one-quarter inch of paper on all sides for safety's sake.

If a stamp is cut, it's considered damaged. If the damaged stamp is common, choose another example of the same issue for your collection.

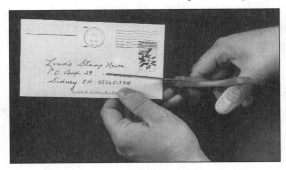

Figure 36. Careful trimming with scissors removes the stamp from the envelope, leaving it on a backing of envelope paper.

Don't cut printed stamps from stamped envelopes or postal cards. These are the stamps that are printed directly on the stationery, not the stamps applied by the mailer. Such stamps don't soak off. Postal stationery items should be saved intact, though some collectors save the printed stamps from envelopes as cut corners, often cut to 2 inches by 4 inches in size.

Instead of cutting or discarding such items, consider starting your own postal stationery collection or trade the items with a friend.

3. Sort your clipped stamps. If you have a large number of stamps, it may help to sort them before soaking and soak only as many as you can handle to start. Stamps can be sorted by country or geographic region, by issue dates (older vs. newer stamps), by topic or by some other designation you choose. Sorting before soaking saves time sorting the stamps afterward.

Also look out for colored envelope paper at this point. The dye used to color envelope paper often is not colorfast, which means it may begin to seep out into water and stain your stamps. Even manila envelope paper can be a hazard. Red or green paper used for holiday greeting-card envelopes, such as the example shown in Figure 37, is particularly dangerous.

Stamps on manila paper can be soaked together, but immediately after they float free of the paper, remove them from the bath and place them into clean water.

Stamps on darker colored paper should be soaked separately, perhaps in running water, or not at all. It's usually better to find another example of the same stamp on white paper.

Some collectors suggest that adding a little salt to a cold-water soak reduces the dangers of colored paper. Try this method first with stamps that you won't mind risking, and see if it works for you.

Figure 37. Dye from colored paper envelopes may run in water when soaked, staining the stamps. Soak such stamps separately or look for another example of the same stamp on white paper.

4. Soak your stamps. Find two sturdy, clean containers: one to soak your stamps and one to rinse your stamps.

You can soak stamps in something as small as a cereal bowl or you can go for a larger container. The on-paper stamps will float near the surface of the water, so you want enough area at surface level to enable you to keep an eye on your stamps as you tend to them.

Fill both containers using water that is room temperature or a little warmer. Place the stamps you want to soak face up in one container, as shown in Figure 38.

Dunk the stamps under water using your fingers or stamp tongs to get them wet on the face. Some collectors soak stamps face down, but soaking the stamps face up makes it easy to see when the stamp has floated free of the envelope paper.

Some stamps will come free within just a few moments. Others may require a soak of a half-hour or more before they float away from the paper.

Figure 38. After a few minutes of soaking in a pan of clean water, most of the stamps will float free of the envelope paper.

Wet stamps are even more fragile than dry stamps, so patience is an important virtue at this stage of the game. Pulling a stubborn wet stamp away from the envelope paper will probably damage the stamp. Let the tough stamps soak a little longer, and they should eventually fall away from the paper.

5. Rinse. When a stamp comes free of the paper, use tongs to pick up the stamp and place it into the clean-water rinse container. Discard the leftover envelope paper.

Some collectors prefer to use broad-tipped stamp tongs to handle wet stamps, as shown in Figure 39. Tongs with pointed tips may pierce the wet stamp paper.

Other collectors prefer to use their fingers to handle wet stamps. In either case, take care not to bend perforation tips or stamp corners, or otherwise damage the stamp.

A 10-minute soak in the clean-water rinse will help remove any remaining adhesive residue from the stamps.

6. Dry. After they are rinsed, the stamps can be transferred to a towel or clean absorbent paper to air-dry for 10 to 15 minutes, as shown in Figure 40. This reduces some of the moisture on the surface of the stamp, but the stamp should still be damp.

7. Flatten. Collectors prefer nice flat stamps to add to their collections. There are several different ways that collectors choose to flatten their soaked stamps.

Figure 39. Stamp tongs with broad tips make it easier to handle wet stamps safely.

One of the easiest methods involves using a stamp-drying book, as shown in Figure 41. These books have alternating glossy and absorbent pages.

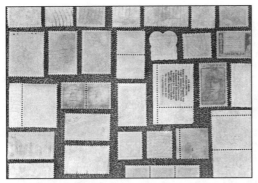

Figure 40. After the soaked stamps are rinsed in clean water, they can be air-dried on a towel or clean absorbent paper.

Figure 41. Stamps can be flattened using a drying book, as shown here, or between pieces of clean cardboard. Collectors use many different methods to flatten soaked stamps.

Beginning at the back of the book, stamps are placed face up on the clean glossy page. That way, the stamps can be removed from the page later even if a little adhesive remains on the back of the stamps.

When the glossy page is covered with stamps, the absorbent page ahead of it is turned to cover the stamps. The next glossy page is then turned so more stamps can be placed on it and the process is repeated.

Once all the stamps are in the drying book, a heavy weight (such as a thick book) is placed upon the closed drying book for several hours.

Collectors also may press stamps flat by sandwiching them between thin cardboard and wax paper, and then weighting them with a heavy object.

Some collectors place stamps within the pages of a telephone book.

You may try one of these methods or even find your own way to get nice flat stamps to show off in your collection.

Stamp shows are a treat for every collector

I love going to a stamp show.

For a stamp collector, a trip to the stamp show is like a kid visiting the candy store. There's so much to see and do, and while you can't take it all home with you, it's a lot of fun to look and dream.

The stamp show gives you a chance to see outstanding collections and exhibits, look for stamps and covers that you can add to your own collection, learn more about your hobby by attending open seminars and meetings, and spend some time with people who share your interests.

To help you enjoy it all, most stamp shows create a free program that lists all the events and participants so it's easy to see what's going on.

I picked up the program shown in Figure 42 when I visited the Chicagopex 98 show in Rosemont, Ill., just outside of Chicago.

Why is it called Chicagopex? Many U.S. stamp shows have "pex" at the end of their names: The letters are an abbreviation for "philatelic exhibition."

CHICAGOPEX '98

112ᵗʰ ANNUAL EXHIBITION
NOVEMBER 6, 7 & 8, 1998

ROSEMONT O'HARE EXPO CENTER
ROSEMONT, ILLINOIS

HONORING

200 Years of Expansion Beyond the Mississippi

150ᵗʰ Anniversary of the Treaty of Guadalupe-Hidalgo

100ᵗʰ Anniversary of the Trans-Mississippi Issue

Figure 42. Stamp shows usually provide a program that collectors can use to plan how they will spend their time.

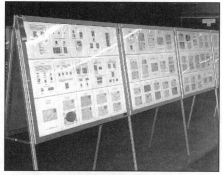

Figure 43. Stamp exhibits are an important part of major stamp shows. Exhibits are judged, and exhibitors receive awards. The show program provides a list of the exhibits on display.

Don't let the fancy phrase fool you. Although you may see stamps on display worth thousands of dollars, the stamp show isn't a dress-up affair. Collectors come to shows in jeans and sneakers more than they do in suits and ties. Dress comfortably and plan to enjoy yourself.

When I visit a show I like to start by taking a few minutes to get familiar with the show program. Sometimes I have all day to spend at the show, but other times I may only have a few hours. When time is tight, I use the program to plan out exactly what I want to see.

Let's start with the stamp exhibits. Not all shows have exhibits: Those that don't are usually called a bourse (I rhyme it with "course," and no one's corrected me yet). Even when there are exhibits, the collection of dealers at a show is sometimes referred to as "the bourse."

When there are exhibits at the show, they're usually all listed in the program and identified by frame numbers. The framed exhibits look like the photograph shown at the top of Figure 43. Below the photograph is an exhibit listing from the Chicagopex 98 program.

Each exhibit has a title that gives some idea of what's being exhibited.

The exhibits usually are specialized collections that someone has spent years putting together and wants to show off to others. That kind of sharing is really great because it helps other collectors get ideas about how to shape their own collections.

At most shows a panel of judges looks over each exhibit and awards one a grand prize and another a reserve grand (which basically means second place, but it's still a very prestigious award).

Every exhibit is given an award, a ribbon or a certificate of participation. The awards typically include a gold, vermeil (pronounced "ver-MAY"), silver or bronze award. Vermeil means "gilded silver," so it falls between gold and silver.

Many shows hold a judge's critique. This is an open forum where exhibitors

33

Figure 44. Stamp dealers at the show bourse offer a wide range of items for sale and help answer collector questions.

meet with judges to learn what they can do to improve their exhibits (and maybe win a higher award the next time out). The critique is open to everyone, and it is another good place to learn more about exhibiting and putting together a collection.

Many large stamp shows like Chicagopex are participants in the American Philatelic Society's World Series of Philately exhibition circuit. The grand-award winner at each WSP show is invited to exhibit at the annual APS Stampshow, which takes place in a different city each year. Of all the grand-award winners for the year, one is selected Champion of Champions, a remarkable achievement for any collector.

Make sure you visit the exhibits, but don't lose track of time. You'll want to look over the incredible offerings of the many dealers taking part in the show.

Have you ever spent time in a retail stamp store? It's always a pleasure for me to spend some time looking over the treats in a retail shop. Now imagine 10 or 20 or even 50 or 75 little stamp shops all in one place.

At the stamp show, you can find just about anything you may be looking for, including stamps, covers, books and catalogs, pages from stamp collections and lots of different supplies.

Specialist dealers may offer only stamps from one country or region, while others may have a worldwide selection from which to choose.

Often you'll find a dealer selling postally used stamps for a nickel apiece, while other dealers may offer rarities that sell for thousands of dollars.

When the dealer asks you "What do you collect?" let him know your interests. He'll tell you if he has what you're looking for, or he may suggest a dealer at the show who will be able to help you out.

Figure 44 shows stamp dealer Bob Dumaine as he assists a customer at a show.

Once again the show program helps you by listing the dealers at the show and their locations in the bourse. The program also may describe the particular kind of items they handle.

At larger shows you can sit in on open seminars to learn more about many different

Figure 45. Stamp expert Ken Lawrence talks to a collectors about the United States Liberty series at a stamp show.

aspects of collecting. These meetings are also listed in the program.

Experts and other collectors discuss their favorite topics, sometimes showing slides or selections from their own collections. Stamp expert and philatelic writer Ken Lawrence is shown at a stamp show in Figure 45 giving a talk on the U.S. Liberty stamp series of 1954.

Some United States national-level shows host first-day ceremonies for new stamps. Collectors who attend the ceremony usually get a free program souvenir with the new stamps affixed and specially canceled.

Figure 46. Some larger shows host first-day ceremonies for new stamps. Stamp artist Jimmy Wang autographed souvenir folders at the 1999 ASDA Spring Mega-Event in New York City.

Figure 46 shows a souvenir folder from the first-day ceremony for the United Nations Endangered Species stamps issued April 22, 1999, at the ASDA Postage Stamp Mega-Event show in New York City. Stamp designer Jimmy Wang was at the event and autographed my folder for me (and happily did so for dozens of other collectors who asked).

Even if there isn't a first-day ceremony, many shows sell souvenir covers with special pictorial cancels that mark the day of the show. These covers are fun collectibles, and they help the sponsoring club raise money to pay for the cost of running the show.

Lots of clubs also sponsor youth tables for beginning collectors, offering free or inexpensive stamps for kids and plenty of advice for novices.

Dozens of stamp shows take place every month in cities and towns all over the country (and all around the world, for that matter). For information on upcoming shows near you, check the Stamp Events calendar each week in *Linn's Stamp News*. Many shows charge no admission fee. Those that do usually set a very reasonable cost.

If you enjoy the hobby of stamp collecting, you're bound to enjoy your visit to the stamp show. Maybe I'll see you there!

Stamp mixtures and packets offer variety

Stamp packets and mixtures are popular ways for collectors to obtain stamps.

Many stamp collectors begin building their collections with stamps and covers they receive at home on envelopes in the mail. Others obtain discarded envelopes from their workplace, nearby schools, places of worship and businesses they patronize.

As you become interested in a particular collecting area and look for specific stamps, you can visit retail stamp stores and contact mail-order stamp dealers to buy the stamps you need.

When you look through advertisements for packets or mixtures, there are many different considerations that you should keep in mind as you read the descriptions of the stamp offers. Packets are collections of stamps that are selected by a dealer and are specifically assembled for sale. In some bookstores and hobby shops, you may see packets that contain "200 U.S. stamps" or "100 animal stamps from around the world." In most cases, the stamps in packets are off-paper, meaning they were clipped from envelopes, soaked, dried and flattened, then assembled into packets.

A packet also may consist of stamps that have never been used and are uncanceled. These are called mint stamps.

Mixtures are more difficult to define. Many stamp mixtures contain stamps that are still on the paper corners of envelopes. They may be sorted by country or worldwide region, or by stamp size.

Smaller stamps are usually definitives, like the U.S. stamps featuring flags or famous Americans, and are often very common. Larger stamps are usually commemoratives. They may have colorful pictures to honor specific events, people, locations or attractions.

The smaller stamp at left in Figure 47 is a German definitive stamp. The larger stamp from Guernsey at right is a commemorative pictorial. These are two types of stamps that you might find in a mixture.

Whether you are interested in buying a packet or a mixture, to avoid disappointment you need to know what the advertisement is describing.

Figure 47. Definitive stamps, like the example from Germany at left, are usually small and often only one color. The commemorative stamp from Guernsey at right is larger and has a more colorful pictorial design.

Many stamp dealers offer packets and mixtures for direct sale through ads in stamp publications like *Linn's Stamp News* and *Scott Stamp Monthly*.

Each week, at the beginning of *Linn's* classified ads, you can find an index of the classifications that exist. Mixtures and packets are listed under separate headings. Other classified sections also carry mixture and packet offers. Almost all of the categories under "Foreign stamps for sale" include such offers.

As you read through these various classifications, you will find descriptions that tell you what you will receive for your money. What you don't read may be just as important.

Dealers are charged by the number of words in an ad, so the descriptions often will be brief. An ad offering a packet of 200 different worldwide topical pictorials may result in a selection like that shown in Figure 48. Most of the stamps are large and colorful, and many include topics such as space, chess, horses, flowers and others. Of the 200 stamps received, however, 160 were canceled-to-order (CTO). Most of the CTOs were stamps issued in communist bloc countries from 1970-90.

CTOs are created by postal authorities specifically for sale in stamp packets to

Figure 48. A packet of 200 different worldwide pictorials offers a wide variety of colorful stamps, but does it include the kind of stamps you're looking for?

collectors. They can be identified by crisp cancels and full gum on the back of the stamps. Such stamps were never used and were canceled so they never can be used. Because of the nature of CTOs, they are not found in on-paper mixtures.

Many collectors prefer postage stamps that have actually been used on mail. For that reason, some ads for packets will state, "No CTOs." This means the packet you buy will not contain any CTOs.

The packet in Figure 48 was purchased for $3.15. Almost all of the stamps in it were valued by the Scott *Standard Postage Stamp Catalogue* at the minimum value. None is valued higher than 40¢.

The advertisement for the mixture shown in Figure 49 described it as an ounce of Scandinavian commemoratives. The cost was $5.50. The mixture provided stamps from seven countries, with many high-value stamps from Iceland in particular. There were remarkably few duplicates in this mixture. Often a mixture will include duplicate stamps, unless the ad specifically states "all different" or "no duplicates."

At the other extreme is the mixture shown in Figure 50. The small mountain of stamps shown is only part of what was described as a "mission mixture." Almost all of the stamps included are British definitive stamps known as "Machins" that depict a portrait of Queen Elizabeth II. The name comes from Arnold Machin, who designed the queen's portrait on these stamps.

There are literally hundreds of stamps in this mixture, and many are alike. Why would anyone want such a mixture?

A collector who specializes in Machin stamps might search through this batch looking for unusual varieties or hard-to-find values. For instance, from the pile in Figure 50, a collector can find the many 19-penny orange stamps in Figure 51, and look through them for the two different less-common lithographed varieties. The original 19p orange issue was printed by the photogravure method. There are similar varieties for a number of different

Figure 49. A more expensive mixture of on-paper stamps may provide some higher-value, harder-to-find stamps.

Figure 50. This mountain of stamps consists almost entirely of common British definitives. Many of the stamps look almost identical. Are there stamp collectors who would actually enjoy sorting through a huge pile like this?

Machin definitives.

Several terms and phrases appear regularly in advertisements for mixtures and packets to give some idea of what's included (or what's not included).

All different tells you that all the stamps you receive will be different from one another. You also may see the phrase "no duplication." Therefore, if the ad says, "some duplication," you can expect that you will receive more than one copy of some stamps. And, if the ad doesn't mention duplication in any way, it's quite likely that you will receive duplicates.

Large pictorials can include larger size commemorative stamps, usually more colorful than the smaller definitives. Remember the two stamps in Figure 47? The stamp at right in that illustration would be considered a large pictorial. However, the description "pictorial" refers to any stamp with a picture and can include more common larger definitive stamps or Christmas issues.

If an advertisement doesn't describe whether the stamps are pictorial, commemorative or definitive, it's quite possible that the mixture you receive will be

Figure 51. A stamp collector might sift through the mound in Figure 50 to find specific collectible varieties. All the stamps in this picture are 19-penny orange definitives.

made up of fairly common definitive stamps. Unless the ad specifies the type of stamp, it's really up to the dealer what to include.

No dunes is a phrase used to tell the collector that the mixture will not contain stamps from a specific group of Arab sheikdoms known as the Trucial States: Ajman, Dubai, Fujeira, Manama, Qatar, Ras al Khaima, Sharjah and Umm al Qiwain. The Mutawakelite Kingdom of Yemen is often included in this group.

From the mid-1960s to early 1970s, these entities issued huge numbers of pictorial stamps, usually as CTOs, for sales to collectors. Most of these stamps have not been found used as postage.

Because many experts do not consider the dunes issues to be actual postage stamps, the Scott catalog does not list them. However, some collectors enjoy the colorful designs on the issues. Dunes issues are commonly found in inexpensive packets and approvals. If an advertisement offers large pictorials, you may see many of these dunes issues included, unless the phrase "no dunes" is used in the description.

SCV stands for Scott catalog value. The phrase SCV $60, for instance, tells you that the stamps being offered are listed with a value totaling $60 in the current Scott *Standard Postage Stamp Catalogue*.

Other details to consider as you look over advertisements for mixtures and packets are the quantity of stamps that you would like to buy and the areas of the world that the stamps come from.

One ounce of on-paper mixture of postally used stamps will yield an average of 100 stamps. To get quality higher-valued stamps, you probably have to spend a little more on your purchase and seek out ads that offer better material.

Many stamp dealers will include additional offers with their mixtures in the hope that you will order again and become a regular customer.

Take a close look at what else the dealer can provide. If you were satisfied with your first mixture or packet, you may find that you have discovered a reliable dealer who will be happy to help you with your stamp-collecting needs.

How to enjoy buying stamps 'on approval'

As you review advertisements in stamp-hobby publications, you may come across items that are offered "on approval." The selling of stamps "on approval" is a marketing strategy that has been used by dealers for decades.

It's also a sales method that is often misunderstood by newer collectors.

The concept of purchasing items on approval has been used in many areas outside the stamp hobby as well. Buying on approval provides the seller an opportunity to show the merchandise he has available for purchase, and it allows the customer to take a closer look at the items at home and decide if they are worth buying.

Because the customer has agreed to this relationship, he has a responsibility to make sure the merchandise he does not buy is properly returned to the seller.

Stamps on approval follow this simple concept: Stamp dealers send stamps through the mail to the home of a collector. The collector examines those stamps to determine if he would like to purchase them. He returns the stamps he doesn't want to buy. Of course, the buyer also includes payment for the stamps he decides to keep.

Collector and dealer usually meet when the collector reads an approval ad in a stamp-hobby newspaper like *Linn's*. The advertisement describes the type of stamps that the collector may be able to purchase from the dealer. Often the collector can choose to buy mint stamps or postally used stamps, singles or sets, worldwide issues or stamps from specific geographic locations. Sometimes the approvals dealer will indicate whether the stamps are expensive or less costly issues.

Sometimes collectors will come across an ad that offers a nice set of stamps for a good price, and the ad states that the collector will receive "other stamp offers on approval," or wording to that effect. That means if you take advantage of the special offer, you also are agreeing to receive stamps on approval by mail.

The stamp dealer will send you selections of stamps that you look over. If you want to buy some of the stamps, you return the stamps you don't purchase, along with payment for the stamps you do purchase. Usually the collector must pay the return postage for the approvals. Sometimes the dealer pays for the return of the stamps.

The dealer sets a time period, like two weeks, by which the stamps are to be returned. Usually the dealer will let you know how often he will send stamps.

The ways that the stamps will arrive can vary. Some dealers send their stamps in a book with pages, as shown in Figure 52. Each stamp has been affixed to the page with a stamp hinge, and all the stamps shown in the illustration have cancels. Such stamps are either postally used or canceled-to-order (CTO). Remember, stamps that are CTOs are usually unused stamps that have had cancels marked on them so they cannot be used for postage, but they can be added to collections.

Approval stamps in booklets are sometimes individually priced with a note written near the stamp, or the dealer may simply mark the cover of the book with one price — like 5¢ — to indicate that each stamp in the book costs the same. The collector can select the stamps he likes and carefully remove from the page each hinged stamp he wants to buy.

Another way that dealers send stamps on approval is in packets — usually glassine envelopes, as shown in Figure 53. Each packet contains many different stamps, and there is a price per stamp marked on the packet. In the Figure 53 illustration, for instance, there are stamps from Germany available for 15¢ each.

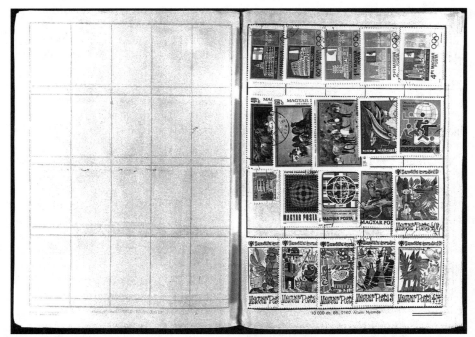

Figure 52. Approval dealers may send books with canceled stamps hinged on the pages. The stamps may be individually priced, or all the stamps may be priced the same.

Figure 53. Approvals in packets let the collector select the stamps he wants to buy at a set price. Unwanted stamps are returned along with payment for stamps that were bought.

The collector may choose as many as he likes, paying only for the stamps he keeps.

Other dealers put individual sets in separate glassine envelopes, as shown in Figure 54. The envelope may have only one stamp or one set, and each stamp or set is individually priced on the outside of the glassine envelope.

Approval dealers stay in business by selling stamps. If you ask for approval stamps and then do not buy any, or do not buy enough for the dealer to make a profit, he will probably discontinue the service. That doesn't mean you have to buy stamps every time, but the dealer will expect you to make regular purchases from the selection.

The collector also can choose to end the relationship whenever he pleases, provided all accounts are settled and all of the dealer's stamps have been properly returned. All it takes is a note requesting that the dealer no longer send any stamps on approval.

Stamp dealers advertise many different kinds of approvals, often based on geographic areas ("Canada," "U.S.," "Asia," and so on).

"Penny" or "Nickel" approvals are stamps of lesser value that are offered for low prices. There aren't many penny stamp offers anymore, but stamps for 4¢-10¢ are commonly found.

Figure 54. Some stamp dealers package each stamp or set individually, marking the price clearly on the packaging.

"Personalized Approvals" are approval offerings that are prepared specifically to match the collector's interests. Though the dealer may offer stamps from all over the world, he will send you only the specific kinds of stamps that you request.

"Topical Approvals" means the stamps being offered have strong topical appeal in the designs.

"Worldwide" means the stamps you receive could come from anywhere in the world.

"New Issues" are normally mint (unused) stamps that have just been released.

Approval ads under the heading "Covers" often offer first-day covers for sale, though other types of covers may be offered under this heading.

If you're interested in buying stamps using the approval method, you have a lot to choose from. Read the advertising carefully and select a dealer who can provide the kind of stamps that you will want to add to your collection. That stamp dealer may help you create the collection you've been hoping for.

At the auction, you get to name your price

Stamp auctions provide collectors (and dealers) with an opportunity to set their own prices when they purchase stamps or covers. However, the price a bidder chooses has to be high enough to beat out the bids of other potential buyers.

There are usually three principal players in every auction sale: the seller (or consignor), the auctioneer and the bidder.

The seller's material being sold at the stamp auction is divided into lots by the auctioneer who conducts the sale. A lot may consist of a single stamp or cover, or it may be a group of items.

Lots are offered for sale to potential buyers who make offers to purchase by bidding. There may be only one bidder who has an interest in a certain lot, but often there are several bidders competing at the same time. The bidder who offers the most for the lot is the winning bidder, and he agrees to purchase the lot for the price of that bid.

Most auctions do not require that a bidder attend in person. Bidders can send their offers in the mail, by fax, by phone, or by hiring an auction agent as a bidding representative.

There are a number of different types of auctions, ranging from stamp club auctions, where the bidding is friendly and the average lot price is low, to the most prestigious public auctions, where high-priced rarities can sell for as much as a million dollars after a passionate bidding battle.

Some collectors believe the auction process is complicated or they do not understand how auctions work, so they are reluctant to participate.

Any collector who regularly purchases stamps and covers should consider learning more about auctions, for often these sales give the collector an opportunity to obtain stamps and covers at prices well below normal retail values. In fact, many of the most active bidders at auctions are stamp dealers, obtaining material that they will later sell to collectors at higher prices. The auction often gives the collector the chance to obtain items at the wholesale prices the dealers themselves pay.

Two well-known types of auctions are the public auction and the mail-bid auction. In some ways the two are very similar, but there are important differences.

2066

2066	★★	11c **Dark Green (434)**, a gorgeous mint single, with virtually perfect centering within uncharacteristically wide margins for a perf. 10 issue, especially intense color and impression on bright fresh paper, pristine o.g., Never Hinged, Extremely Fine, a large margined gem, 1999 P.F. Certificate. Cat. $35 **(photo)**

Figure 55. Shown here are catalogs for public auctions and mail-bid auctions (top). Listings in the catalog (bottom) describe each lot and provide additional information for the prospective bidders.

For each type of sale, auction catalogs are printed and made available to prospective buyers. The catalog contains a list of the lots that will be sold at auction, often with photographs of the more interesting items.

A number of different stamp auction catalogs are shown at the top of Figure 55. A typical auction listing for one lot, a single stamp, is shown at the bottom of Figure 55.

Collectors can obtain catalogs by writing or calling the auction house. Unless you are an established customer, there may be a charge of a few dollars to recover some of the expense of printing and mailing. Larger, more elaborate catalogs cost more.

Auction houses regularly advertise in stamp-hobby publications. The ads tell how to obtain their catalogs.

The auction catalog also contains very important information about bidding and payment. This information is often titled "terms of sale." An example of terms of sale from one auction house is shown in Figure 56.

Almost all auction houses add a buyer's premium, often 10 percent of the winning bid, so a collector who is bidding must keep in mind that this additional fee will be added to his bill. In some cases sales tax is also charged. This is just some of the information contained in the terms of sale. Other details may include how to place bids, payment methods, collecting your lots, and more.

It is essential that bidders read and understand the terms of sale before participating in an auction. Auction house employees are usually happy to clear up any confusion you may have in the days before the sale, but they probably cannot take time to explain the entire process over the telephone or in person.

The terms of sale vary from one auction house to the next, so all bidders must check the terms for each sale in which they plan to participate.

Terms of Sale

1. Lots will be sold to the highest bidder at a slight advance over the second highest bid. Should there be a dispute between bidders, the decision as to the successful bidder and the re-offering or resale of the lot under dispute shall rest entirely on the discretion of the auctioneer. The auctioneer shall regulate the bidding and reserves the right to refuse any bid believed by him not to be made in good faith — **no buy bids will be accepted.** Bid as high as you are willing to pay; the lot will be purchased for you as much below your limit as bidding allows.

2. A buyer's commission of 10% of total purchases will be added to all invoices.

3. Terms of sale are cash upon receipt of invoice (we gladly accept VISA & MasterCard).

4. Purchasers who have established adequate credit may, at the auctioneer's discretion, have lots shipped along with the invoice. Payment is due upon receipt of invoice. Any amount still due after 30 days will have a service charge of 1⅛% per month added to the invoice.

5. All lots sold can be expected to be genuine and as described. In the event of a discrepancy, the lot may be returned intact within 7 days of receipt of shipment. The following lots may not be returned:
   a. Lots containing 10 or more stamps.
   b. Lots which were photographed may not be returned for centering, perforation faults or other details visible from the photo.
   c. Lots described as faulty.
   d. Lots viewed in our offices or through postal viewing.
   e. Lots described "as is."

6. **If expertization is requested,** the following provisions apply:
   a. The buyer will pay for the item to be expertized upon receipt of invoice.
   b. Requests for expertization of stamps with certificates dated within the last five years will not be granted (other than at auctioneer's discretion).
   c. Mail bidders must notify auctioneer in writing, of requests for expertization when the bids are placed. Floor bidders will notify the auctioneer of extension requests at conclusion of sale.
   d. All items will be submitted by Matthew Bennett, Inc., unless prior arrangements are made.
   e. All items will be submitted to a mutually agreeable committee (for U.S. stamps, this will usually be The Philatelic Foundation).
   f. An expert committee's failure to render an opinion is not grounds for return of a stamp.
   g. In the unlikely event of a negative opinion, Matthew Bennett, Inc., will refund the cost of the lot **plus** expertization fees **and** the interest calculated as per the prime rate at the time of payment.
   h. No items may be returned if they are altered in any way, i.e., an indelible backstamp.

Figure 56. Bidders must understand the terms of sale before participating in any stamp auction.

Each catalog also includes a bid sheet to use with mail or fax bids. Bidders write down one bid for each lot they hope to purchase; the amount should be the most they are willing to spend to obtain the lot.

Bids must be placed in specific increments, depending on the value of the bid. A sample chart is shown in Figure 57. Actual increment levels vary from sale to sale. This chart shows that bids up to $300 must be given in $10 increments. Therefore, a bid of $240 is acceptable, but a bid of $238 is not. Depending on the terms of sale, the $238 bid would likely be reduced automatically to $230.

Often the auction catalog will list an estimated sale price or a recent stamp catalog value for each lot. Bidders may bid less or more than that estimate.

However, most auction houses will disregard bids they believe are unrealistically low. If you bid $5 for an unused 1847 5¢ Benjamin Franklin stamp of the United States (catalog value $5,250) with the hope that your bid will be the only one received, you might as well not bother. An auctioneer who accepts such a bid would be out of business very quickly because no seller would trust him to auction his material.

Bid increments			
Up to	Increase	Up to	Increase
$10	$.50	$500	$20
$24	$1.00	$1,000	$25
$50	$2.00	$2,500	$50
$75	$2.50	$5,000	$100
$100	$5.00	$7,500	$250
$300	$10.00	$10,000	$500
More than $10,000 at approximately 5% increments			

Figure 57. Auction bids must follow increment levels set by the auction house. These levels vary from auction to auction.

If you bid high, you may obtain the item you want without having to pay the full amount of your bid. Most auction houses award successful bids at one increment above the second highest bid. Therefore, if your bid on one lot is $120, and the next highest bid is $80, you will win the lot for $85, using the increment chart shown in Figure 57.

It is important to understand that in close bidding the full amount of your bid will be accepted if you are the winning bidder, and you will be responsible for paying the full amount of your bid plus the buyer's premium. Obviously it's important to consider your budget when placing bids. If you win every bid at your maximum level, you have to pay all the money you bid, plus the buyer's premium.

Public auctions are held at a location open to the public. Anyone interested may attend, and anyone attending who registers may bid during the auction. Figure 58 shows a well-attended public auction in Chicago. Sometimes there will be only a few bidders in attendance because most bids come in by mail or fax.

Mail-bid auctions do not have this type of public forum. Instead, the auction is conducted on the basis of mail bids only.

Another difference between the public auction and the mail-bid auction is that prospective bidders may examine the items offered at public auction during specified viewing times at the auctioneer's offices. This is generally not possible for most

Figure 58. Floor bidders and observers may attend public auctions, but mail bids are also accepted. With mail-bid auctions, there is no event where floor bidders participate.

mail-bid auctions.

Both types of auctions usually offer return policies if an item has been misdescribed by the auction house. In some cases, however, an auction house may have a "no return" policy on some or all lots that are sold "as is" or that include a certain number of items. Once again, the terms of sale should spell out return policies.

In any case, it is wise to look for dealers who are members of established stamp organizations such as the American Stamp Dealers Association or the American Philatelic Society. These groups have rules of ethics by which their members must abide.

The auctioneer represents the sellers of the items at auction. Instead of submitting mail or fax bids to the seller's representative (the auctioneer), many bidders prefer having someone representing them at the public auction.

Auction agents work for prospective buyers, submitting bids in person during the sale. They charge a fee, generally a small percentage of the price of each lot purchased.

One important benefit of using an agent is having someone familiar with auction bidding to obtain items for you at the lowest possible cost. Agents also can examine public auction lots on behalf of clients and answer questions the client may have about the lot or the auction in general.

Auction agents advertise in stamp-hobby periodicals. Some auction houses provide the names and phone numbers of agents who are regularly present at their sales.

Even among public auctions the type of sale may vary considerably. Some auctions deal primarily in stamps of one country or region, such as the United States, Scandinavia or Asia. Other auctions may feature stamp errors or some other specialty.

Look for auction houses that cater to your specific interests and request a catalog to review. Once you find a sale that offers the type of material you're looking for, get familiar with the terms of sale. With a little study and some careful consideration, you have a good chance of becoming a successful auction bidder.

For many, it started at the local stamp store

The story of how I became interested in stamp collecting is similar to many such stories told by collectors around the world.

My father had been a stamp collector most of his life, gathering items from correspondents around the world, including a great number of stamps and covers from his brother in East Germany. He also began a collection of mint plate blocks from the United States in the early 1960s. Some of the stamps in his worldwide collection had been gathered by his father.

His foreign collection was housed in great black binders on heavyweight quadrille pages, and his plate blocks were protected by stamp mounts and affixed to preprinted album pages.

I watched him work on his stamps from time to time, and when I was 10 years old, I went with him to a stamp store called the Bookery in Grand Rapids, Mich., (where we lived) to pick up collecting supplies. That trip to the dealer convinced me that stamp collecting was for me. There were amazing things in that shop, not all of them related to the stamp hobby.

The front window displayed a number of glass globes with four small black flags inside arranged on a wire like a weather vane, spinning endlessly, powered solely by the rays of the sun. These solar-powered gizmos shared the front window with a flock of colorful glass cartoon birds that dipped their beaks into small shot glasses of water and then righted themselves over and over again like some remarkable out-of-sync bowing ballet. I still don't know the physics behind those whimsical knickknacks, but to a 10-year-old boy it was nothing short of magic.

There weren't many stamps in that front window, probably owing to the fact that exposure to sunlight quickly fades the colors of stamps. Inside the shop were the wonders of the stamp-collecting world that most of us now take for granted. Long glass cases displayed full sheets of stamps from the United States and the rest of the world. Colorful sets of stamps from virtually everywhere on the planet were arranged on sturdy displays.

There were stamp tongs, catalogs, albums, stock pages, mounts, hinges and everything else that my father used to put his collection together, but in varieties and quantities that I had never imagined.

Each Saturday morning my father would work for a few hours in his downtown office, and I would go with him. After I'd torn all the stamps and postage meter impressions off his incoming mail — I wish now that I had saved the complete covers — I'd go to the Grand Rapids Public Library and to a bookstore that I liked to visit.

The stamp dealer's store became another Saturday morning stop, and it was there that I made my first-ever stamp purchase. My interest in soccer drew me to a set of canceled Polish stamps commemorating the 1966 World Cup Soccer Championship, which I seem to recall paying 35¢ for. The Scott catalog value is now $2.80 for the set, so my first stamp investment has held up well over the years. The high value of that set, Scott 1405-12, is shown in Figure 59.

When I went into the stamp store I was always comfortable, because the people who worked there let me spend as long as I wanted to look at all the remarkable items they had for sale. There were coins and coin-collecting supplies there too, and sometimes I'd look for some of the wheat-back pennies that were missing out of my blue Whitman penny collecting book.

Figure 59. A set of soccer stamps from 1966 made a great first purchase for a budding stamp collector.

But the stamps and supplies held most of my interest. For all the time I spent there I probably didn't buy enough to turn much profit for the store owner, but my questions always were answered with patience and a smile. Sometimes I would be shown some wonderful stamp item that I could never afford, but I got a great deal of pleasure just seeing such things.

By the time I got into high school I was neglecting my collection, and my visits to the stamp store came to an end. I moved away from Grand Rapids when I was 19.

Over the years I've been in many different stamp stores, and I've always enjoyed myself, whether I was just looking around or I had a specific purchase in mind.

One day I thought back to that first stamp shop and how the encouragement I received there helped the stamp hobby become the important part of my life that it is today. The Bookery is still going strong in Grand Rapids (a picture of the shop is shown in Figure 60), though it's now at a different location than when I first visited it in the mid-1960s. I placed a call to store owner Ken Engen and spoke with him about how stamp dealers and stores like his play an important role in keeping the stamp hobby strong.

"Service is probably the most important thing," Ken told me. When a customer enters his shop, Ken or one of his part-time employees is there to answer questions and provide suggestions. Ken and a regular customer are shown looking through some of the store's stock in Figure 61.

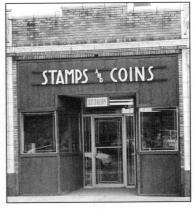

Figure 60. The local stamp store provides collectors with a convenient way to purchase supplies and look for stamp finds. Shown is the Bookery in Grand Rapids, Mich.

Helping young collectors or those just starting out in the hobby is an important part of what the stamp dealer has to offer. It can be hard for a beginner to get specific answers to questions about the stamp hobby, but the stamp dealer can be a great source of information.

"I'm willing to spend a few minutes to talk to them about how to start and what to do," Ken said. Stamp supplies continue to be a big part of his inventory, including hundreds of file drawers filled with album pages and supplements. Many of them are hard-to-find items that are no longer in print. Ken keeps albums for beginners in stock as well and makes up starter stamp packets for young collectors.

One question he gets regularly is "How do I collect?" "You collect any way you want to," Ken replies. "You do want to talk to somebody who will mention some different things and give you some ideas, but yeah, you collect any way you want to."

Once the collector knows what he wants to collect, the stamp dealer can help him build that collection. Even if the dealer doesn't carry a specific item the collector is looking for, he may be able to suggest other sources for particular stamps. Some dealers can watch for material that appeals to the interests of their regular customers.

Figure 61. Stamp store owner Ken Engen (right) discusses a selection of stamps with customer Al Roberts.

The Bookery first opened in 1930. Ken's been the man in charge since

1978, though he began working there the same year as my first visit in 1966.

Like most general stamp stores, the inventory at the Bookery is a little of everything and a lot of some things. Ken's huge inventory of album supplements is a big part of his store, but he carries worldwide stamps and even a selection of recent used U.S. commemoratives, with an emphasis on the se-tenant sets like the Legends of the West and the Civil War issues of the 1990s.

I asked Ken if he did much business in recent used U.S. stamps. "A fair amount," he replied. He pointed out that a declining use of commemoratives on mail makes it a lot harder for collectors to complete longer sets.

Even though he has three people who work soaking and sorting such stamps, Ken adds, "I can sell more of them than I can get my hands on."

A general stamp store gives the collector an opportunity to look over and examine the many varieties of supplies that are available, from stamp mounts to tongs, album pages and more.

Many stamp dealers buy and sell collections as well, providing a couple of services for the collecting community. Those who have decided to begin collecting in a new area can sell their older collections to a local dealer. The convenience of dealing locally can make the transaction a little easier.

An individual interested in beginning a collection in a certain area may find a collection at the store that he can take up and continue with ease at a reasonable price.

The stamp store continues to be a mainstay of the stamp hobby, but keeping the store going can be challenging. Rent, utilities, alarm systems and insurance are just a few of the overhead costs the stamp store owner must bear.

While most dealers who operate a stamp store have a regular group of customers, many things can affect the amount of business in the store.

Ken noted that when a teacher in the Grand Rapids area tries to start up a stamp-collecting group, his business in beginner albums and supplies increases. "There has to be somebody to spark the interest first," Ken said. "You have to have something to get them looking in that direction to start with."

The advantages of visiting a retail stamp store are obvious. The comfortable surroundings allow the collector a chance to look over stamps and supplies at his own pace. Making a selection from the multitude of choices is easier with the help of someone who has years of experience in the field.

Stamp stores usually are easy to find and open five or six days a week. That lets the collector do his stamp shopping when it's convenient for him to do so.

How can you find a stamp store near you? Most can be found in the yellow pages of the telephone directory under the heading "Stamps for Collectors" or "Hobbies." Many collectors have found out about stamp stores by asking clerks at the local post office.

Groups like the American Stamp Dealers Association or the American Philatelic Society can provide information about local stamp stores as well.

If you're already a customer of a local store, think about the first time you stepped into that shop full of treasures. Isn't there a youngster somewhere that you know who might enjoy the experience?

Stamp collectors develop one at a time. For some young collector, you may be the one who can spark that interest with a visit to the stamp store. At the same time, you may be helping the local stamp dealer whose occupation has been providing a showcase for the greatest hobby in the world.

Use your want list to find stamps you need

What do you want?

There are thousands and thousands of different stamps out there, and remembering which ones you want to fill the empty spaces on your stamp album pages can be quite a task.

Did you need the 3¢ Abraham Lincoln flat-plate printing of 1923 (United States Scott 555) or the 3¢ Lincoln rotary-press printing of 1925 (584)? Or was it the 3¢ Lincoln rotary-press issue of 1927 (635)?

How about your collection of U.S. Celebrate the Century postally used singles? Are you missing the 33¢ Video Games stamp from the 1980s set (3190l) or the 33¢ Virtual Reality stamp from the 1990s set (3191j)?

Can't remember? Don't feel bad. There are so many different varieties of so many different stamps that keeping them all straight is darn near impossible.

What do you want? You probably want a want list.

Stamp collectors have created and used want lists since about the time the second postage stamp was issued in 1840.

A want list is simply a handy way to remember the stamps that you need, so you don't accidentally buy or trade for duplicates of stamps that you don't need.

Shown at right in Figure 62 are a couple of pages from a specialized want list of stamps sought for a U.S. collection.

A want list can be complete and actually list every stamp that is missing from your collection, or it can be abridged and list only a limited number of stamps that you want to look for right away.

For example, if you're collecting the stamps of Switzerland, you may be missing hundreds of stamps, from the earliest cantonal issues of 1843 to the latest commemorative that was issued last week.

You can either create an extensive want list that shows every single stamp you need to complete your collection, or you can simply record only the stamps you need from a specific area, such as Swiss semipostals (all 650 of them). Or you can list the missing regular issues from, say, the 1934 definitive series onward.

A want list can be handwritten, typewritten or created on a computer. It can consist of a simple list of catalog numbers, or it can be created from the illustrated pages of a published stamp catalog.

The type of want list you need depends in part on the

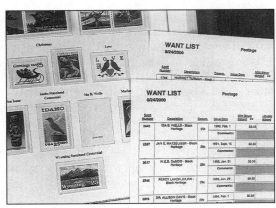

Figure 62. A stamp collector keeps track of stamps that are missing from a collection by creating a want list.

way you plan to use it.

Let's say you are going to contact a certain stamp dealer for the first time, to ask if he carries the type of material you are looking for.

You can include with your inquiry a want list that gives him some idea of the stamps you want to buy. You may want to start out by sending a shorter list of the stamps you most want to find, but mention that you have a longer list if the dealer wants to take a look at it.

By the way, it's always a good idea to enclose an addressed, stamped envelope anytime you are writing to someone for information. It shows that you are willing to help with the trouble and expense of the reply. After all, you're the one asking the person on the other end to devote some time to answering your question.

Your want list to the stamp dealer can be very simple. Print the words "WANT LIST" clearly across the top and include the country name and catalog numbers of the stamps you need. If you're using the Scott catalog, mention that on your list as well.

And don't forget to neatly print your name and address at the top of every page of your list, just in case the pages get separated while the dealer is looking them over.

Don't send your original list in the mail. Send a photocopy instead, to avoid extra work for you if the list gets lost or you never hear back from the dealer.

Any time you are sending a copy of your want list to someone, make sure it is neat and easy to read. No one wants to spend a lot of time trying to decipher illegible numbers scrawled on a sheet of paper. Besides, if the numbers are hard to read, the dealer may send you the wrong stamps.

Typing or computer-printing your want list will help reduce or eliminate the problems a dealer can have discerning what you want.

A number of different computer programs are available that can help you create your want list. However, you don't have to use a computer to create a useful want list. Many collectors simply keep a pocket notebook with lists of the stamps they need.

A topical collector, for example, often learns about stamps relating to his collection while looking for other information in a stamp catalog. It's easy to keep an ongoing list of suitable stamps by jotting the new information in the notebook.

Remember to cross off the notation when the stamp is found and added to the collection. The same is true for computer-generated inventory lists, which generally can be updated with a few simple clicks and a revised printout of the information.

Collectors who enjoy looking through mixtures or inexpensive selections at stamp dealers' tables at shows may find that a want list containing only catalog numbers is inadequate. Many dealers may have large quantities of stamps they sell for about 5¢ or 10¢ each, often as mixtures, but they rarely bother to list and catalog such inexpensive stamps. The collector may encounter an inexpensive stamp that he thinks he needs for his collection, but if the stamp is not identified by the dealer, looking at a long want list of catalog numbers alone probably won't be much help.

Some collectors carry with them a pocket catalog that is marked up to indicate the stamps the collector already has. Figure 63 shows an example, using the Scott

U.S. Pocket Stamp Catalogue. By carrying the catalog, the collector can refer to the illustrations to positively identify the stamp he finds at the dealer's counter.

Always remember to keep your want list up-to-date, or you could wind up with extra stamps that you don't need.

You'll find that your want list is something you'll take with you wherever you go looking for stamps: at the stamp shop, at a stamp show, at your local stamp club meeting, or browsing the ads.

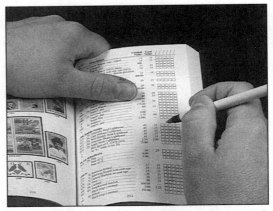

Figure 63. Notations in a pocket catalog remind the collector which stamps he already has and which he still needs to find.

Chapter 4
What to Collect

There's no limit to the ways you can collect

A "cover," as described previously, is any mailed or postmarked item that can be studied or added to a collection. Most often this refers to an envelope with a stamp on it that has traveled through the mail, but it might also refer to a post-card, a wrapper from a parcel, an aerogram or any other mailed item.

Less frequently the word "cover" is used to describe an envelope or postcard that has a stamp on it but has not been mailed.

Although the hobby that you enjoy is most frequently referred to as "stamp collecting," many collectors prefer to save intact covers with the stamp, post-mark, addresses and so on all kept together for study and enjoyment.

As you start out in what we like to call the "stamp hobby," your first collection might be one each of the stamps of a single country, such as the United States or Canada.

Many collectors want or need nothing more than the pleasure of building a single-country collection. One could say that this method of collecting is the foundation upon which the hobby grows.

Other collectors look for a second collection, or an alternate way of collecting, or just something different to do. When they look around, they often find that the stamp hobby provides more choices and collecting possibilities than anyone could imagine. Whether your interest is in stamps or covers, you certainly ought to be able to find something that keeps you busy, keeps you entertained, and holds your attention for as long as you wish.

Many collectors concentrate on the stamps of a single country. Figure 64 shows a recent stamp from the United States at left and another from India at right.

Choosing a country is often easy. It may be the country of your birth, or per-haps you are interested in another land where your family originated.

The most popular way to collect a country is to save one of each stamp issued, but what if you're looking for something different?

One easy choice is to look for a specialty. This means focusing your atten-tion on part of a country's stamp output instead of the entirety of it. You might find an interest in what's known as the back of the book: stamps such as air-mails, semipostals, Offi-cials and so on. These spe-cial-duty stamps are some-times listed after regular-

Figure 64. Collectors often choose to save the stamps of just one country. In the United States, the choice is often U.S. stamps (such as the 1999 Jackie Robinson stamp at left), although some collectors prefer stamps from a different country (such as the 1998 stamp from India shown at right).

issue stamps in standard postage stamp catalogs, which explains why they're called "back-of-the-book."

Even a regular stamp series can be the focus of a specialty collection. Instead of collecting a single stamp or a pair of U.S. coil stamps, for example, some collectors save strips of three or five with a plate number on the center stamp in the strip.

Figure 65 shows a plate number strip of three U.S. 17¢ Electric Auto stamps, Scott 1906, from the 1981 Transportation coil series. A small plate number "1" can be seen near the bottom of the center stamp in the strip.

Reference works such as the Durland *Standard Plate Number Catalog* or the Scott *Specialized Catalogue of United States Stamps & Covers* list seven different plate numbers on this issue, 1-7. Collectors may look for examples of each number, either in mint strips, postally used singles, or on cover.

Figure 65. Instead of collecting one each of every stamp from a country, some collectors save varieties such as this 1981 plate number strip from the U.S. Transportation coil series.

Similar plate number collecting challenges exist with booklet stamps and sheet stamps that yield plate number blocks with the number in one or more corners of the pane. A pane is the standard unit of stamps sold at post office windows, often 15 or 20 stamps together. Panes are cut from larger press sheets before they leave the stamp printing facility.

There are many other interesting stamp-collecting specialties.

Perfins are stamps that have small holes punched into the design to identify the authorized user of the stamp. It's possible to build collections of stamps showing a number of different perfin designs.

Going beyond the single-country collection, worldwide stamps offer a new range of possibilities.

One of the most popular worldwide specialties is the topical or thematic collection. A topical collection consists of stamps that all share a common design element. For example, the stamps illustrated in Figure 66 all show birds, and birds are one of the most popular collecting topics. A thematic collection is a lit-

Figure 66. These stamps from Jersey, the United States and Tonga show birds. One collecting option is to save stamps whose designs show a specific topic.

New Sweden Settlement
Natives of Sweden and Finland crossed the ocean to America 350 years ago.

FIRST DAY OF ISSUE

Figure 67. First-day covers include a stamp, a postmark showing the issue date for that stamp, and often a design related to the topic of the stamp. The covers shown are from the United States (top) and East Germany (bottom).

tle different, in that the collector uses the designs on the stamps to tell a story about a chosen subject. In such cases, the stamps may show different topics, but the topics relate to a single theme.

Postmarks and postage meter stamps also can be important additions to topical or thematic collections.

Some collectors look only for worldwide stamps issued during a specific time period, such as a single year. Many of these specialties lead to collecting on-cover examples that show where and when the stamps were used.

A popular cover-collecting specialty is first-day covers (FDCs). Figure 67, top, shows an FDC from the United States and, at bottom, another FDC from East Germany.

Most postal administrations around the world create special postmarks for use on the day a stamp is first issued. These agencies either sell special commemorative covers or allow collectors to prepare their own covers for postmarking on the issue date.

The decorative design at the left of each of the two covers pictured in Figure 67 is called a "cachet" (pronounced "ka-SHAY"). It is a prominent feature of many first-day covers.

Collecting covers that carried the daily mail can be a challenging choice, but it also is one of the most interesting collecting areas. This type of collecting often involves research and study, and leads the collector into the field of postal history.

A collector who is interested in a specific stamp series may begin collecting covers that show different ways stamps from that series were used to carry the mail. Take the 17¢ Electric Auto stamp shown in Figure 65 as an example.

When it was issued in 1981, the 17¢ stamp fulfilled the second-ounce rate for first-class postage. In later years, however, the Electric Auto stamp could be

Figure 68. Collectors of postally used covers often research the details of the stamps and postmarks found on the cover.

found filling other rates, often in combination with another stamp, and it was also adapted for presorted first-class mail.

The German postal card shown in Figure 68 serves as an example of how covers start collectors on the road to research. Mailed in Berlin in 1935, the card has a stamp imprinted upon it. That's what makes it a "postal card" rather than a "postcard." A postcard needs to have a regular stamp affixed to it before it can be mailed.

A cover collector may ask many questions about such a cover. When was this particular postal card first issued? How long did it remain on sale? Were many created or just a few? Does the postage paid by the imprinted stamp meet a special rate?

The unusual pictorial cancel on the stamp raises more questions. What does it signify? Was it only used in Berlin or in other cities as well? How long was it used?

To answer these questions, the postal historian looks through reference books, journal articles, post office records and other sources. It's a little different than buying a new stamp and placing it on a stamp album page, but as you can see, it is just one of many collecting options this hobby has to offer.

What area will you collect next: U.S. plate number coils, topicals, postal stationery, first-day covers or postal history?

Pick a country, any country, and collect it

A lot of stamp collectors like to concentrate their efforts on collecting the stamps of a single country. Some choose to accumulate stamps from the country where they were born, while others have an interest in stamps from a foreign land. Stamps from another country may appeal to the collector because of ancestral ties or because the collector spent some time visiting or living there. Others find that collecting stamps from another country is like opening a new book and learning as much as possible.

Developing the foreign collection can be a very satisfying educational experience, as each stamp tells a little bit about the country's people, its history and its culture.

Printed album pages are a starting point for many single-country collectors, because the pages provide a logical layout for the stamps. Most albums begin with spaces for the earliest issues and continue to the most recent, with stamps in sets usually grouped together. Regular supplement pages picturing the newest stamps are issued every year or so and can be added to keep the album up to date. This arrangement makes it easy for the collector to see which stamps have been obtained and which are still missing.

Shown in Figure 69 are Scott specialty album pages for the country of Denmark, located in northern Europe. Albums and album pages are available by mail from stamp collector supply dealers, from local retail stamp dealers or direct from Scott Publishing Co.

Finding the stamps to go on the pages is what makes this a lifelong hobby. The collector interested in the stamps of Denmark has more than 1,200 stamps to track down, not including minor varieties, airmails, semipostals, Official stamps, postage dues and more.

An ancient Chinese proverb states that the journey of a thousand miles begins with a single step. In a similar way, the collection of a thousand stamps can begin with just one. It also can begin with a bunch.

Collectors have been accumulating stamps for a long time, and often the collections formed are sold by their owners and bought by other collectors. Complete collections can cost a fortune, and buying one really eliminates the adventure of building your own.

The purchase of a smaller, unfinished collection, however, can give you a jump-start as you begin to assemble your own single-country collection.

Figure 69. Stamp collectors often use preprinted album pages to keep their single-country collections organized.

Such collections are often advertised by stamp dealers or sold at stamp shows.

An early decision the collector might make is whether to collect stamps in mint condition (unused) or postally used. Some collections combine the two, particularly when a stamp is hard to find or considerably more expensive in one condition, but easily available or reasonably priced in another.

For example, an unused set of Denmark's 1907-12 stamps depicting King

Frederik VIII is listed in the 2003 Scott *Standard Postage Stamp Catalogue* at $86.25, while the same set postally used is valued at $8.65.

Current new issues, such as the recent Danish booklet stamps shown in Figure 70, often can be purchased at face value directly from the postal service of the issuing country, from an authorized agent or from a new-issues dealer.

Figure 70. New issues, like these booklet stamps from Denmark, can be obtained, often at face value, from a variety of sources.

Older issues, used or unused, may be purchased from stamp dealers and auction houses. Many prominent stamp and auction dealers advertise regularly in *Linn's*. Each week *Linn's* Auction Calendar provides details of the type of stamps that are being offered and information about how to request auction catalogs.

Many collectors begin with packets and mixtures that contain only stamps from the country that interests them. Figure 71 shows a selection of 300 different stamps from Denmark. Each stamp is off-paper and postally used. These carefully sorted selections are called packets. A mixture is a large group of stamps that may include duplication.

Figure 71. Packets of stamps may help build the foundation for a collection of stamps from a single foreign country.

Some collectors enjoy buying stamps from circuit books, such as those offered by the American Philatelic Society and other stamp clubs. Circuit books are one way collectors can view and purchase stamps in the privacy of their own homes. Each book contains many stamps for sale, priced and sorted by catalog number.

As explained in Chapter 2, some stamp dealers also provide what are called approvals — an offering of stamps sent to the collector's home for examination. The collector must return the stamps within a certain time, including payment for any stamps he decides to purchase. Approval dealers continue to send new selections regularly until the collector requests that the approval service end.

Many stamp dealers have set up shop using computers, posting their business on the Internet's World Wide Web.

As a collection grows and the album spaces are filled, the collector may find that mixtures and approvals contain mostly duplicates of the stamps already in his collection.

To obtain the stamps he is missing, the collector may send "want lists" to dealers.

As previously stated, a want list usually is simply a description of difficult-to-find stamps that the collector is looking for, often listed by catalog number.

For instance, a collector may write to a dealer requesting unused

Figure 72. Specialist collectors often look for covers, such as this envelope from Denmark, to expand the collection.

copies of Denmark Scott 212 and 215, two less common stamps from the 1930 King Christian X set.

Some collectors eventually decide to specialize in a single stamp or series of stamps. They may seek out multiple copies of the same stamp, to look for different printing varieties, for instance. Often these collectors also begin to look for covers that show uses of the stamp that interest them.

Figure 72 shows Denmark Scott 4, the 4-skilling brown stamp from 1854, on an 1858 cover sent from Assens in the northeastern part of the Jutland peninsula to Flensburg, a city that is now part of northern Germany.

Covers can range in cost from a few cents to hundreds of dollars or more. The scarcity of the stamp, the rarity of the usage, the condition of the piece and collector demand for the cover are all factors that can affect prices.

First-day covers from many countries, bearing postmarks that show the first day a stamp was placed on sale, also are actively collected.

Specialty collections go beyond printed album pages and standard stamp catalogs,

Figure 73. Auction catalogs, specialized stamp catalogs and other published studies help the collector learn more.

and the collector begins a journey of research and study that may result in new discoveries and information that can enrich the collecting community.

All collectors can benefit from literature published about the area of interest. As shown in Figure 73, this can include auction catalogs and specialized stamp catalogs as well as books that document research in different specialty fields.

Collector organizations are particularly helpful to the single-country collector. Most groups publish regular journals to keep members informed about new discoveries, publications, auctions, dealer offerings and more.

It's a good idea to be thoughtful about the country you wish to collect. Consult catalogs and published literature to see what kind of stamps have been issued, if there are interesting historical areas to pursue, and if there is a specialty group that can help you as you get started.

The topical collector has many different options

One very popular way to collect stamps is by topic.

Instead of looking for stamps from just one country, the topical collector looks for stamps and related postal items showing a subject that reflects a specific topic or theme. For example, a stamp collector who also has an interest in tigers may want to accumulate as many stamps as possible that show tigers, such as the four issues shown together in Figure 74.

The country of issue does not matter to many topical collectors, as long as the pictured subject fits into the collection.

In the book *Adventures in Topical Stamp Collecting*, George Griffenhagen and Jerome Husak suggest that topical collectors can choose to create either subject collections or thematic collections.

Subject collecting involves finding stamps that picture the subject of interest and organizing the stamps in whatever way pleases, whether by country, chronologically or by subtopics. Thematic collecting expands the subject collection to include additional postal items that tell a story about the topic.

Stamps and other philatelic items in a tiger thematic collection may show ways mankind has threatened the extinction of tigers with hunting, traps and the destruction of habitat. The collection may include stamps showing circuses and zoos where tigers are held in captivity. Other relevant stamps could tell where and how tigers live in the wild and what they eat. Stamps depicting authors who have written about tigers, such as Rudyard Kipling, also could be included.

Therefore, while the thematic collection about tigers would certainly include many tiger stamps, it also would include stamps and related items that do not show tigers but that help illustrate the story of tigers in a logical sequence.

The collector may design and create his own album pages and describe his topic on each page of the collection, fitting in appropriate items to illustrate the theme. Many thematic collectors prepare their collections as exhibits that are displayed at stamp shows.

How does a collector choose a topic?

Often the choice is a personal one based on the collector's inter-

Figure 74. Tigers are just one of many possible collecting topics. The stamps shown here are from South Korea (top left), Malaysia (top right), East Germany (bottom left) and Macau.

Iowa Territory, 1838   USA 15

Figure 75. Postal stationery is a good source for topical collecting material. Farming is represented on a 1988 U.S. postal card marking the Iowa Territory sesquicentennial.

ests. Some collectors choose to look for stamps related to their occupations. For example, a stamp-collecting doctor may decide to collect medical themes on stamps.

Others select favorite sports, literary themes, animals and so on. A topical collection can show anything that has been pictured on stamps. Some topics, such as birds or butterflies, literally comprise thousands of stamps. These are very popular topics, but the collector must concede that such a collection will never be complete.

One alternative is to specialize within such a large topic by looking for items related to a specific species, such as the cardinal or the monarch butterfly. Smaller topics can be equally challenging, for it may be difficult to find enough stamps to create an interesting collection.

Postage stamps are not the only collectible objects that are sought by topical collectors. Postal stationery items from all over the world often feature interesting topics. Figure 75 shows the imprinted stamp image from a 15¢ U.S. postal card commemorating the sesquicentennial of the Iowa Territory. The design shows a harvesting scene and would be an important addition to a collection on the topic of farming.

Along with postal cards, collectors can look for stamped envelopes and aerograms to add to the topical collection. These prestamped items all pay postage for mailing, which is an important element in the topical collection. Most collectors do not include items like picture postcards for the sake of the picture alone, because the picture really has no correlation to how the mail is processed and carried.

Of course, a picture postcard mailed with a stamp that ties in with the collecting topic would fit nicely into the topical collection.

Some collectors also avoid items like nonpostal labels and revenue stamps.

Of course, the collection is created to please the collector, not the experts (except, perhaps, in the case of judged exhibits). It's completely up to the collector what he does or does not want to include.

Many stamp collectors complain about the prevalent use of postage meter stamps on daily mail, but for the topical collector the meter stamp can be another source of interesting material.

For many years meter stamps have been created that include pictorial or slogan elements, such as the example shown in Figure 76. This 1961 meter stamp

Figure 76. Many postage meter stamps contain pictorial elements. The airplane shown on this 1961 U.S. meter stamp would be a fine addition to an aviation topical collection.

from Des Plaines, Ill., includes the image of a jet in the slogan imprint at left, a fine addition to a topical collection with an aviation theme.

Postmarks and pictorial cancels also provide ample material for topical collectors. These can include pictorial or slogan standard machine cancels, as well as commemorative postmarks honoring special events.

Two such postmarks are shown in Figure 77. At top is a fairly common Danish postmark from the 1980s reminding everyone to use postal codes properly when addressing mail. A busy bee wearing a mailman's cap is pictured on the cancel.

Figure 77. The Danish postmark at top includes the image of a cartoon bee in flight. Below it, a commemorative cancel from the United States includes images of hot-air balloons.

Pictorial postmarks appear from time to time on daily mail in the United States. Lexington, Ky., for instance, has used a machine cancel that shows a galloping horse.

Some countries, like Great Britain, sell advertising space on their postmarks, which usually adds a topical element to the cancel.

At the bottom of Figure 77 is a 1997 commemorative postmark from Reno, Nev., to mark a local balloon race. Many postmarks like these are offered each week in communities all across the world. Information about obtaining current U.S. postmarks is found in stamp-hobby publications such as *Linn's Stamp News*.

Meter stamps and postmarks are best kept intact on an undamaged cover (an envelope, postcard or parcel wrapper), rather than clipped off the paper. The intact cover is more interesting and tells more about the postal history of the marking.

First-day covers are another source of interesting topical material. The topic may be represented in the design of the stamp, the postmark or the cachet, or even all three.

Figure 78 shows a 1999 first-day cover

Figure 78. Ships are shown on both the stamp and the postmark on this 1999 first-day cover from India's Department of Posts. A lighthouse is the main feature of the cachet at left.

from India's Department of Posts commemorating 125 years of Mumbai Port Trust. The 3-rupee stamp and the first-day cancel both show ships, while the cachet (the pictorial envelope design at left) features a lighthouse.

Many topical collectors don't care if their stamps are mint or postally used, but most try to collect items that are in the best possible condition. Heavy cancels that obscure the stamp design usually are avoided unless the object is particularly scarce.

As the topical collection grows it can turn into a delightful display of many different postal objects.

With a great array of collectibles to choose from, many topical collectors happily maintain a number of different topical collections at the same time.

Here's what you can do to save the world

There are so many different ways to develop a stamp collection that it's probably impossible to think of them all.

Many collectors intentionally limit their interests in one way or another, often by topic or by country. By defining a collection in this way, the collector has fewer items that he must look for, and he can concentrate on finding items pertaining to the subject of his choice.

For some collectors, though, that way of doing things is simply too limiting. Those folks are worldwide collectors; they enjoy collecting all of the stamps in the world.

Every stamp in the world? How many is that?

The editors of the Scott *Standard Postage Stamp Catalogue* can only estimate, but at the end of year 2003, they figured that number exceeded 450,000, with about 1,300 new stamps being issued every month. Those rough figures count only stamps that are listed with major catalog numbers. Keep in mind that a new pane of 20 stamps may be assigned just one major number.

Obviously the worldwide collector is never going to fill every space in every album.

Fortunately for most collectors, that's not the point. They simply are interested in all aspects of stamp collecting, and they don't want to deny themselves any part of it.

In a scientific survey of *Linn's Stamp News* subscribers conducted in 2000, 24 percent of readers described themselves as general worldwide collectors. To some degree, many of us start out as worldwide collectors, but it looks like three out of four collectors give up that ambition and choose to specialize in one area or another.

Most of those who remain worldwide collectors realize that organization is a key to keeping things all together. That means choosing a way to store stamps so that the next time you get a stamp from Luxembourg to add to your collection, you'll be able to find the album where the stamp belongs.

Even when saving the whole world, collectors have many different ways to keep stamps arranged. Many use preprinted stamp albums and supplements that are updated each year with spaces for every new stamp that has been issued.

One of these albums, the Scott International Postage Stamp Album, is shown in the picture at the left of Figure 79. The album shown open in the illustration

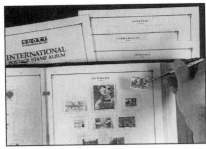

Figure 79. A number of different stamp albums are suited for the worldwide stamp collector, but be aware that any large worldwide collection is bound to take up a lot of shelf space.

has spaces for the stamps issued by the countries of the world during 1986. Two albums are required to complete that single year.

As you can imagine, collecting this way year after year means that you buy a lot of binders and pages. The picture at the right of Figure 79 shows about 10 binders holding International album pages. Sixty binders are needed to hold the complete world collection through 2001. A collection that size is out of the question for some collectors. They choose to limit their worldwide accumulations to a specific era, such as the first century of postage stamps (from 1840 to 1940). For other collectors, 60 binders are just a start.

Scores of worldwide stamp collectors dedicate entire rooms to hold their collections. Walls are lined with bookcases filled with albums, stock books, catalogs and supplies, while stamps yet to be sorted reside in storage boxes, glassine envelopes and filing cabinets.

Many worldwide collectors prefer to keep their albums divided by country, so they have all of their German stamps in one set of binders, all of their French stamps in another, and so on.

The six-volume Scott catalog lists several hundred stamp-issuing countries, so you can imagine that this method of collecting also can take up a lot of space.

A number of collectors use a combination of different albums to house their collections. General worldwide albums may not hold spaces for minor varieties, souvenir sheets and the like, so collectors sometimes print their own album pages or create new space by adding blank pages to the preprinted ones.

The choice of collecting mint stamps or used stamps is often unimportant to general worldwide collectors. Any stamp that will fill the space usually meets with the collector's approval.

Some collectors save both mint and used examples of the same stamp when they can, either by hinging both stamps on the same page, or by obtaining a second set of stamp pages so that they have one set for mint and one for used.

While most collectors keep a close eye on condition and always look for the best possible example of a needed stamp, many will accept a damaged stamp to fill an album space if a sound one is not available for a reasonable price. Such damaged stamps are known as "space-fillers." The collector remains aware of the faulty stamps in his albums and watches for better ones to replace them.

Collectors may start out in the worldwide collecting game when they inherit a collection-in-progress from a parent, grandparent or some other source. Other collectors have established their worldwide interests by purchasing entire collections from retail stamp dealers or at auction. Often these collections are not complete, but they make a good starting

Figure 80. On-paper stamp mixtures (left) and off-paper packets (right) are two ways the worldwide collector can try to fill album spaces. Duplicate stamps can be used for trading.

point for the person who wants to collect the world. In many cases, the collection already comes mounted on album pages, so the collector obtains both stamps and supplies with one purchase.

The next step may be filling in the empty spaces on the album pages.

Buying stamps one by one from retail dealers can be costly if you're working on a worldwide collection, so many collectors look for bargain methods to obtain those missing stamps.

There are many ways to obtain stamps at well below catalog value, including mixtures and packets (Figure 80 shows each) and approvals selections. These offers are readily available with stamps for virtually every collecting area. Dealers in these selections regularly advertise in the pages of *Linn's Stamp News*.

Collectors who buy stamps in packets often get a large number of all-different stamps for a low cost per stamp. Stamp mixtures may provide a large number of stamps, but collectors often encounter a lot of duplicate stamps as well. The collector simply selects his favorite from all of the duplicates to add to his collection, and then he trades his duplicate stamps with other worldwide collectors for other stamps that he needs.

Figure 81. Many worldwide stamp collectors engage in stamp trading to build their collections. Stock books help keep duplicate stamps organized and ready for trading.

Shown in Figure 81 is a typical collector's stock book filled with duplicate stamps of Iceland. Once again, organization is an important factor in worldwide collecting. Keeping duplicate stamps neatly organized helps the collector when it comes time to make those trades.

Trading partners can be found in many ways. Local stamp clubs almost always have a number of members who enjoy collecting worldwide and swapping with others to build their collections. Stamp exchange groups also advertise in the Trading Posthorn at the beginning of

Linn's classified advertising.

Many worldwide collectors purchase stamps in much larger lots to work into their expanding collections. Some stamp dealers offer box lots and complete mounted collections that appeal to the worldwide collector. Larger lots are regularly available from auction houses that are dispersing estates or collections from similar sources.

Collectors who think saving all the stamps of the world would be fun should remember that completing the world is impossible. The collector has to have the patience to understand that not every space will be filled and that the worldwide collection may be a commitment that will last a lifetime.

Stamp album binders, pages, hinges and other supplies can be a little pricey, and putting together enough for a worldwide collection can take a lot of money.

Planning the way you want to organize your collection will probably help you avoid large purchases you may later regret. Be careful about what you purchase so that you can keep up with maintaining your collection and disposing of your duplicates.

Stamp collectors who choose to save the world really don't have a set of rules they have to follow. The goal is to collect as many worldwide stamps as possible and to have fun doing it.

There are many ways to collect new stamps

Many stamp collectors like to build collections of new issues from one or more specific countries. When it comes to obtaining those new stamps, several options are available for the collector. Some methods offer tremendous convenience, while others offer a wide selection of specialized options.

Let's take a look at how collectors obtain mint new-issue stamps for their collections. The term "mint" refers to unused stamps that also are undamaged in any way. Mint stamps from Canada and the United States are shown in Figure 82.

So, where does the collector go to buy mint new-issue postage stamps?

1. The post office. Most people think of the post office when they want to buy new stamps, and that certainly can be an important source. There are times, however, when a post office cannot supply the specific stamps that a collector needs.

Figure 82. Collectors who wish to purchase new issues for their collections have several options. Shown are mint stamps from Canada (left) and the United States (right).

In the United States, collectors visiting the post office can buy stamps at a standard service counter, at a philatelic window, from a postal store or from a vending machine. Similar options exist for collectors in many other countries as well.

Many U.S. post offices serving smaller communities have a limited selection of stamps for sale, and they don't offer specialized philatelic services. Some post offices may carry new-issue commemorative stamps when they are first released, but they may not have them on hand for very long. The stamps that the post office clerk has on hand also may not be the best stamps to add to a collection.

Because those stamps are being offered primarily as postage to customers who have items to mail, they may not be in true mint condition. Postal clerks often paperclip or rubber-band bundles of stamps together, creating creases and folds that may not bother a postage customer but that a stamp collector would look at as damage.

If the clerk has several customers waiting, he may not have time to display his stamp stock to cater to the needs of a stamp collector looking for different varieties.

Some larger post offices have a philatelic window where the clerk carries a broader stock of stamps to fulfill requests from stamp collectors. Philatelic clerks usually have on hand most of the stamps that currently are available from the United States Postal Service. Some clerks make an extra effort to locate plate number varieties on any coil, booklet and sheet stamps that are issued so they can offer these to their customers as well. In general, philatelic clerks also handle their stamp stocks more carefully, so that the stamps are not creased or damaged in any way.

Postal stores are retail units located within selected post offices or at special locations, such as an airport. Postal stores offer prepackaged stamps and postal stationery items in various formats. These products usually are displayed in a plastic-wrapped package, resting on shelves or hanging from pegs. For example, a collector may be able to find numerous blocks of 10 recent commemorative stamps, with attached selvage (margin paper) that includes plate number markings. He can select the specific block he prefers to buy from the items on display.

Another benefit of the postal store is that the customer can leisurely examine the available stamp stock to find the items he wants to purchase. The collector is not likely to find coil stamps at the postal store, though, and the selection of booklet stamps and other varieties is sometimes limited.

Post office vending machines sometimes offer collectibles that may be otherwise hard to find. Collectors report from time-to-time that they find scarce plate numbers on coil stamps or new booklet discoveries through vending-machine purchases.

2. Postal administrations and agents. New-issue stamps of the United States and many other countries can be purchased directly from the issuing postal authority. Most postal services sell only the stamps of their own country. A few may offer limited numbers of stamps from selected other countries as well, but usually only by mail order.

Some countries offer collectors the opportunity to buy new-issue stamps by computer though Internet sites on the World Wide Web. Many postal authorities, however, have web sites that describe the available stamps, but they require collectors to make their stamp purchases by mail. The United States Postal Service

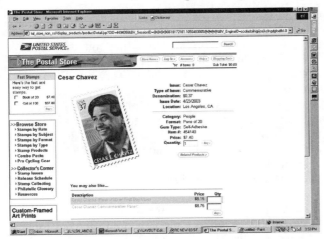

Figure 83. Collectors may purchase new U.S. stamps on the Internet, but the range of formats offered may be limited.

has an Internet site where collectors can buy stamps directly. A small part of the USPS Stamps Online Internet site is shown in Figure 83.

Although many different stamps are listed at the site, the format selection is limited to full panes and coil rolls of stamps only, which usually means 20 stamps of each issue, or 100 for coil stamps.

Many postal authorities offer their stamps for sale through mail-order catalogs or newsletters that describe the products available. The catalogs *Details* from Canada Post and *USA Philatelic* from the United States Postal Service are shown in Figure 84. Both of these postal authorities offer most of their current stamps through these catalogs in a variety of different formats.

For many countries other than Canada and the United States, collectors can write directly to the postal administration or, in some cases, to its representative agent in the United States.

The various postal administrations around the world operate in many different ways. Some offer standing-order deposit accounts, meaning the collector can obtain all the new issues of the country by providing advance payment. The stamps are then sent to the collector as they are released or at regular intervals.

Figure 84. Canada and the United States offer philatelic catalogs describing new issues that are available for purchase.

Many countries allow the collector to purchase just the stamps they are interested in through catalogs such as those shown in Figure 84.

A collector interested in new issues from another country should write to the postal administration or its U.S. agent to learn what options are available. Some postal authorities have very limited philatelic services and may not provide direct mail-order service.

3. Stamp dealers. Stamp dealers specializing in new-issue service provide customers with another way to purchase new stamps. Most new-issue-service dealers offer stamps from many countries around the world. Figure 85 shows how in some cases collectors can select from a large list of countries or stamp topics advertised by the dealer.

Figure 85. Some stamp dealers offering new-issue services to collectors provide a wide range of collecting choices.

Many new-issue stamp dealers advertise regularly in the pages of *Linn's Stamp News*, either with display advertising throughout the publication or in classified advertising in the back pages.

Specialized dealers in U.S. stamps also advertise regularly. Listings for U.S. coil and booklet stamps include many dealers offering new issues in formats and varieties not specifically available from the United States Postal Service.

Stamp dealers must charge an additional fee for their expanded services, but many collectors prefer the convenience of working with a knowledgeable dealer who can alert them to important new varieties.

Local retail stamp dealers and dealers who participate in stamp shows can also be important partners in your new-issue collecting strategy. For local dealers, look in the telephone yellow pages under the headings "Hobbies" or "Stamps for collectors."

Stamp shows take place every week in cities all around the country. Check *Linn's* Stamp Events Calendar regularly for shows in your area.

Cover collecting is a part of postal history

The postage stamp was created more than 160 years ago to serve as proof that a fee was paid to deliver the mail.

For many collectors, this function of the postage stamp is its most important feature.

Instead of clipping postage stamps from envelopes, postcards, parcel wrappers and other mailed items, these collectors save such "covers" intact, study them for information about how they carried the mail, and look for other characteristics that reveal information about postal history.

The term "cover" is used to describe any mailed or postmarked item, such as an envelope, but it also can be used to describe any prepared item before it is mailed.

First-day covers, one of the most popular forms of cover collecting, provide the most basic information about the history of an individual postage stamp.

FDCs have enjoyed considerable popularity for years. These envelopes or cards are marked with a special cancellation that includes the official issue date for the stamp used. Official first-day covers are marked with a specially designed cancel, such as the example shown in Figure 86, which includes the city where the stamp was issued. Unofficial first-day covers have a conventional postmark

Figure 86. First-day covers may include a special design that relates to the featured stamp and a postmark that shows where and when the stamp was issued.

indicating the issue date, but they are canceled in a different city.

Modern FDC collectors often prefer envelopes with a special design called a "cachet" (pronounced "ka-SHAY") that tells more about the issued stamp or somehow complements its design.

In Figure 86, the cachet on a FDC for the 20¢ Metropolitan Opera stamp of 1983 features musical notes and information about the Met's centennial year.

There are many other types of FDCs, from historic examples that show the earliest-known use (EKU) of a postage stamp to combination covers that use a variety of stamps with subject themes similar to that of the new stamp issue.

The postmark or cancellation on a cover often adds special interest to the item. It may indicate a special mailing use, reveal a significant date or mailing location, or feature other historical detail.

The postcard shown in Figure 87 was mailed in 1934 from the Century of Progress international exposition in Chicago, Ill., using the 1¢ Century of Progress stamp issued by the United States to celebrate the show.

Not only is the stamp used on a postcard that celebrates the show, but it is also postmarked with a Chicago slogan machine cancel that reads "A CENTURY OF PROGRESS STATION."

This type of cancel, used with the Century of Progress stamp, is listed in the Scott *Specialized Catalogue of United States Stamps & Covers*. It is an historical feature that enhances the mailing use of this particular 1¢ stamp.

If the stamp were soaked free of the postcard to place it in an album, the historic aspect of its use would be lost.

Modern commemorative postmarks often contain topical elements that are of interest to many collectors. Sometimes the cancel may feature a design that does not specifically relate to the stamp being used.

The cover from Austria pictured in Figure 88 bears a postmark showing a hot-air balloon, though the stamp celebrates the bicentennial of the Linz diocese. The cover also has a cachet that celebrates the 1,000-year anniversary of the town of Garsten, while other markings on the envelope indicate that the cover was flown by hot-air balloon during delivery.

The United States Postal Service provides commemorative cancels on a regular basis. Many are listed in stamp-hobby publications. By writing to the addresses provided, collectors can obtain these commemorative cancels for a limited

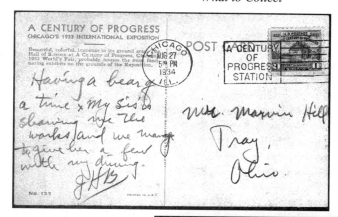

Figure 87. The machine cancel on this 1934 postcard is from Chicago's Century of Progress station. The 1¢ stamp celebrates the same international exposition.

period after they are first issued.

Many collectors look for covers that show the different ways that stamps are used to carry the mail. While examples of covers that traveled by first-class letter mail may be common, other postal services are often harder to find.

The envelope shown in Figure 89 is not a rarity, but it shows a proper use of the U.S. 13¢ blue special delivery stamp of 1944 combined with the 3¢ violet Thomas Jefferson stamp from the 1938 Presidential series. When the envelope was mailed March 30, 1948, the combined postage paid for special delivery of first-class matter less than 2 pounds in weight. It has the additional feature of being mailed from Vonnegut Hardware Co., a family business operated in Indianapolis, Ind., by relatives of novelist Kurt Vonnegut Jr.

Though this particular cover bears no postal service markings other than the machine cancellation, many covers will include handstamped or handwritten indications of special handling.

Collectors will encounter markings or labels requesting airmail service, registration, priority or express handling, or delivery by certified mail, to name but a few.

Other markings may show postage due, attempted delivery, rerouting, military handling, censorship and so on. The list of special-mail features is nearly endless, and it extends to all countries around the world.

How does one choose to collect one type of cover and not another? It depends in part upon the interests of the collector.

Many specialists concentrate on a single postage stamp or series and then look for covers that properly use those stamps in various ways.

Someone who specializes in the 1938 Presidential series may add the special delivery cover in Figure 89 to his collection to show how the 3¢ stamp was used in combination with the special delivery stamp.

That same collector may also look for covers using stamps from the same series to obtain domestic or overseas airmail delivery, fourth-class library parcel delivery, return receipt service, and so on.

Another collector may take the same Figure 89 cover in a different direction, by adding it to a study of U.S. special delivery services. Such a collector would use a variety of covers to illustrate the different rates that were imposed for special delivery services from the time the service was first initiated in 1885. Or he may look for examples mailed to different destinations.

Collectors also look for modern examples that request similar delivery services or feature interesting stamp usage.

Figure 90 shows a cover mailed to *Linn's Stamp News* using a plate number single from the 1997 booklet of 32¢ Statue of Liberty self-adhesive stamps. The plate numbers can be seen along the bottom of the stamp.

Though the stamp on its own would make a nice postally used example of the

Figure 88. A commemorative cancel from Austria is used on this 1985 cover sent by hot-air balloon.

Figure 89. Different collectors may have an interest in a special delivery cover: one for the specific stamps used upon it, another for the service it fulfilled.

Figure 90. Modern covers worth saving include those bearing plate number singles. This example is franked with the 32¢ Statue of Liberty booklet stamp of 1997.

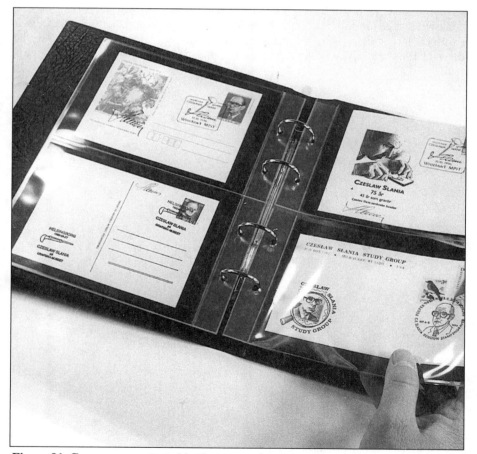

Figure 91. Covers are protected in the pages of a cover album but can be viewed and studied by the collector.

issue, the cover with the stamp affixed provides the additional information of where and when the stamp was mailed and where it was delivered, information that would be lost if the stamp were soaked off it.

The collector value of the plate number single is enhanced slightly by the fact that it has not been removed from the cover.

Just as stamps need to be handled carefully to avoid damage, covers also should be handled with care. First-day covers with smudges, bent corners or worn edges are far less desirable than cleaner, crisper examples.

Some collectors use special cover albums to protect and display their favorite items. One example of a cover album is shown in Figure 91.

Transparent plastic sleeves are used by many collectors to keep dirt and fingerprints off. The protected covers can be stored in a sturdy box. It's best to look for a box that is constructed of acid-free or archival materials.

Collectors also keep an eye on condition when purchasing covers from dealers or other collectors. The value of an item declines if it has suffered damage, such as grime, tears (including rough opening) and so on.

Keeping a cover collection organized can be a challenge, because each item is so much larger than a single stamp. However, many collectors have found that there is a lot to study and enjoy when you save the cover and not just the stamp.

Chapter 5
Condition

What to look for when looking for stamps

When you decide you need a stamp for your collection, there are many different ways to go about obtaining it. Among the possibilities for finding or buying stamps are a visit to the retail stamp store, a trip to a stamp show, or a purchase from a mail-order stamp dealer. Unless you're in the market for a great rarity, you're likely to find what you're looking for.

In some cases, adding a stamp to a collection is as easy as finding a copy that was used to mail a letter, carefully soaking it free of the paper and letting it dry.

Most of the time, collectors are presented with a selection of similar stamps from which they can choose. The stamp dealer may have a stock book holding a dozen copies of the desired stamp. Or 10 copies of the same issue may show up in a stamp mixture.

Instead of simply picking out one stamp at random, the collector should study the available copies, choosing the best example to add to his collection. This is true whether the desired stamp is in mint condition — meaning it is unused and the stamp gum is undisturbed — or postally used — meaning it was used as postage on a mailed item.

What qualifies a stamp as the best? Some guidelines are very clear cut, while others depend on the preferences of the collector. Here are some suggestions of where the collector should look when deciding to select a stamp for his collection. Figure 92 shows areas to examine on a typical stamp.

Perforations. The small holes between stamps that make it easy to separate them are called perforations. Whether the stamp is mint or used, the condition of the perforations can vary quite a bit. When stamps are separated from one another, they leave points of paper all around called perforation "teeth." If the stamp has been separated carefully and cleanly, the teeth should be well defined and even in length.

A stamp with perforation teeth that are very short (nibbed) or missing altogether is considered damaged. A similar hazard to watch for is perforation teeth that have been accidentally trimmed off when the stamp is cut from

Figure 92. Different factors affect the quality of a stamp in many different ways. Often, the personal preference of the collector may determine which stamp should be added to the collection.

envelope paper. If a stamp's perforations are very uneven (some longer and some shorter), it detracts from the overall appearance of the stamp.

Although it may seem that carefully cutting stamps through the perforations with scissors or a razor would eliminate this problem, this method of separating perforated stamps is not accepted by collectors. They demand stamps that are separated by tearing by hand rather than cutting.

Because the perforation teeth are small and stick out from the main part of the stamp, they are easily damaged by accidental bending or folding. The teeth at the corners of stamps should be examined closely.

Paper. Just as perforation teeth can be bent or creased so can the main body of the stamp. Once stamp paper is bent to a certain degree, the minute paper fibers begin to crease and break. As a result, the stamp retains a crease that cannot be repaired. Even when a stamp is bent, but not creased, it will often hold the shape of the bent section, instead of lying flat or having its natural slight curve.

Small tears in the stamp paper are sometimes difficult to detect with a quick glance. For this reason, the stamp should be looked at closely to make sure the paper is not torn in any area. Sometimes this is easier to do by looking at the back of the stamp, where there is no design to distract from possible paper damage.

On an unused stamp, the back of the stamp may also reveal marks where a stamp hinge was removed. A hinge mark usually appears as a small area measuring roughly 12mm by 6mm where the gum has been disturbed by the light moisture of the hinge. It appears near the top of the design but on the reverse of the stamp. Though hinge marks are not a fatal flaw, many collectors prefer unused stamps that have undisturbed gum.

Hinges do have the potential to cause more serious damage to the stamp paper. Although many hinges are advertised as "peelable," some are more forgiving than others. Hinges that are roughly removed from the back of a stamp can cause a "thin," which is an area where a layer of paper has actually been peeled off the back of the stamp.

"Toning" or "foxing" are two terms to describe the discoloration of stamp paper. Toning is a gradual darkening of the stamp paper, often caused by a combination of age and some external chemical element. Foxing is a more concentrated reddish-brown spotting on the stamp paper that is caused by bacteria that can spread to other nearby stamps.

In some cases these paper discoloration problems can be remedied, but given a choice between a stained stamp and a more pristine copy, collectors should choose the one without the built-in problems.

Fingerprints on the design are usually permanent, and the body oils and chemicals that are part of the fingerprint will cause more damage as time goes on. This type of damage can be avoided by using stamp tongs, but stamps that already have fingerprints on them should be avoided altogether.

Postmark. Here's where a collector's personal preferences play a big role. On postally used stamps, some collectors prefer a cancel that is barely visible on the stamp, while others hope to read without difficulty the date and location where the stamp was postmarked.

Most collectors agree that they don't want heavily canceled or pen-canceled modern stamps. At the other extreme, some collectors think a used stamp that has no postmark is a failure, for it shows no evidence of having passed through the mail.

Each collector should decide what suits him best. The finicky collector may want to assemble stamps that have postmarks that are similar in appearance. And there's nothing wrong with being finicky. If you're going to have a stamp collection, you certainly should create it in a way that will satisfy you.

Printing. Because stamps are printed using several different methods, there are different kinds of problems that may result.

Some stamps that are line engraved may have less depth to them than others, resulting in paler colors or weaker lines in the printing. The 1980 Great Americans definitive series of stamps from the United States has shown several examples of this.

Closely compare just a few stamps with the same design from this series, and printing differences will become noticeable.

To print the stamp design image clear and sharp, multicolor offset- and gravure-printed stamps need excellent color registration (where the colors on the stamp are all precisely lined up with one another). This isn't always easy to find. When the colors are just a little out of alignment, the design on offset-printed stamps may look muddy or blurry, while examples of the same issue with proper color alignment are vivid and well-defined.

Gravure-printed stamps, like the 1996 32¢ James Dean and 1997 32¢ Humphrey Bogart commemoratives from the United States, sometimes show tiny pale flecks in the design instead of smooth, constant colors.

Some combination-printed stamps from the United States have had some common problems, with bits of intaglio lettering or highlighting missing from offset-printed stamps. Some of these problems may be attributed to variations in papers or paper coating.

Misregistration of the two printing processes has resulted in intaglio printing appearing in different locations on the stamp, causing an odd variety that may not be wanted.

Color. Color is a printing problem all its own. While collecting color varieties is a very interesting field of specialization, a collector who is looking for one example of a stamp to add to a standard collection should find one example that has the right colors.

Both unused and used stamps can suffer from color change caused by exposure to outside chemicals (like cleaning agents) or light (sunlight or room light).

The color misregistration previously described can cause a color on a stamp design to appear odd or unusual, not the best selection for a one-each collection.

Centering. The Scott *Standard Postage Stamp Catalogue* refers to the "grade" of a stamp, and values those that have a grade of very fine. The grade of a stamp is a description of how well-centered the central design is within the edges of the stamp. The collector should keep an eye out for stamps that have margins of equal size all around the design.

If the design is printed quite close to the perforations on one side, the stamp gets a grade of fine, which for most collectors of modern stamps is not fine at all.

The Scott catalog ranges in description from fine to extremely fine, the latter term describing stamps that are "close to being perfectly centered." The word "perfect" can cause a problem for stamp collectors, because with a little close examination, flaws can be found in virtually every stamp.

If the selection is limited, a collector may have to give up one quality to obtain another. A stamp that has great perforation teeth may have centering that would grade at less than very fine.

Looking for the perfect stamp, therefore, is not the goal. However, before a stamp is added to a growing collection, it should be examined by the collector to make sure that it's a worthy addition.

Watch for damage you can (or can't) see

Building a stamp collection involves searching for the right stamps that will make your accumulation something you can be proud of. A collector should always keep a close eye on the quality of the stamps he is adding to the collection.

Stamps that are faulty should be passed by unless no other alternatives are available.

The different kinds of faults collectors encounter are not always immediately visible. Whenever a collector contemplates acquiring a new stamp, he should closely examine the stamp to make sure it doesn't suffer from one or more of the problems described here.

Perforation damage is one of the most common faults that collectors find on postage stamps. When perforated stamps are separated from one another, the

paper points all around the design are called the "perforation teeth."

If stamps are carefully folded along the line of the perforation holes before they are separated from one another, the perforation teeth usually will be tall, sturdy and even. Sometimes, however, one or more of the teeth will get pulled right off the stamp during separation, leaving little stumps or nothing at all where the perforation teeth should be.

Figure 93. Perforation damage may come as short or pulled perforations, as seen along the left edge of the stamp at left, or torn corners, as on the Japanese stamp at right.

When one tooth is considerably shorter than the rest, it is called a "short perf." When one tooth is completely missing, it is called a "pulled perf."

At left in Figure 93 is a 10¢ stamp from Zanzibar's engraved definitive set of 1936. The stamp is in fairly good shape except for the lower portion of the left edge. There you can see at least three perforation teeth that are short or pulled. Others are missing from the right side and the bottom of the stamp.

Do you think this is a tiny defect not worth worrying about? The fact is that when you're collecting stamps you're dealing in very small items, so small defects actually make up a big part of what is being collected.

Most collectors would prefer to add to their collections a stamp with sound perforation teeth all around. The illustrated Zanzibar stamp is common enough that the collector should pass this example by and look for one that is in better shape.

Another more drastic separation problem is illustrated by the stamp shown at right in Figure 93. The 1½-sen Wedded Rocks stamp from Japan was issued in 1936. At the lower right in the pic-

Figure 94. Creases often affect the corners of stamps. At left the crease is obvious in the lower-left corner, but at right the same stamp, with the crease unfolded, appears undamaged.

tured example, the corner of the stamp is torn off. Most likely this happened as the stamp was being removed from the sheet. This type of damage sometimes occurs when an attempt is made to remove a single stamp from a pane without creasing or tearing along any other stamps. To accomplish this, the individual doing the tearing actually has to negotiate the corner of the stamp while separating along the perforations. The success rate for this maneuver is low, and the missing corner on the Wedded Rocks stamp illustrates a common result.

Creases are caused when stamp paper is bent to such a degree that the structure of the paper fibers is changed — and not for the better. Creases are permanent. They can be hidden sometimes, but where the crease exists, the paper is weakened.

At left in Figure 94 is the 1952 50-centavo Eva Peron stamp from Argentina. The paper has been creased along the lower-left edge, leaving the corner folded underneath the stamp. At right in Figure 94 is a photo of the same stamp, but with the creased corner carefully folded flat and smoothed over. You really can't see the crease at all, but it's still there.

If it's so hard to see the crease, how can a collector watch for them?

The corners of stamps are what get creased most often. One way to check a stamp for creases is to hold the stamp with one pair of tongs, and very lightly apply pressure near the corners with another pair. If the corner flops over, you've found a crease. If you get a little resistance, the stamp is probably sound.

Creases also become much more apparent when the stamp is immersed in watermark fluid. It's easier to see the crease with the stamp face down, so you're looking at the back of the stamp. The watermark fluid will make the crease look like a straight dark line in the paler paper of the stamp.

A tear in the stamp paper sometimes can be difficult to see if there isn't any paper removed.

Figure 95 shows the $1 Fruit Growing parcel post stamp issued by the United States in 1913. A postally used example has a Scott catalog value of $35. The design on the illustrated stamp is a little off-center, so its value would be discounted.

The off-center design is the least of this stamp's problems, however. While it may look like a sound stamp in the illustration at left in Figure 95, a close examination of the stamp shows it has a jagged 5-millimeter tear starting at the lower edge of the right side.

Some collectors try to patch up such a problem with a little homemade stamp gum or even the remnant of a stamp hinge. If the stamp is your own space-filler, the hinge repair isn't a bad idea. It is a bad idea if it's being used to deceive a potential buyer. It's also something to watch for as you examine stamps, particularly as the stamp's catalog value increases and the price starts to climb.

Figure 95. Damage to this U.S. $1 parcel post stamp is not immediately evident in the photo at left. A careful examination of the stamp reveals a tear that begins along the right edge.

With the use of high-speed sorting and canceling machinery, scrapes in stamp paper have become a more common fault. As envelopes rocket through these metal mazes, stamps can get snagged on anything and everything. Another U.S. stamp helps to show this kind of scrape. The 25¢ Mail Delivery stamp of 1989 pictured in Figure 96 has a 7.5mm horizontal scrape extending left from the center of the right edge.

Almost all scrapes from mechanical sources begin along the right edge, which is the leading edge as sorted envelopes travel through the machines.

Stains on stamps can come from a lot of different sources, including chemicals and residue from foreign substances. Chemicals in tape and glue are deadly to stamps, often creating a stain that cannot be removed. That's why most collectors use stamp hinges and stamp mounts that are specially made for affixing stamps to pages.

Other stains can be the result of something as simple as a food spill or as seemingly innocent as soaking the stamp off paper. If the paper is brightly colored, as some greeting card envelopes are, that color can soak free as the stamp is taking its bath, and once-white stamp paper can turn a completely different hue.

Color changelings are another form of stamp damage. Again, the damage can be the result of chemical contamination or even environmental factors, such as exposure to light.

Both light and chemicals can fade or alter ink colors to make a stamp look like it is a different color than it's supposed to be. That sometimes makes for an interesting stamp, but not one that you want as the representative example in your stamp collection.

While you're keeping your eyes open for damage, don't forget the back of the stamp. What looks like a mint stamp in perfect condition may

Figure 96. The surface scrape near the right edge of this stamp's design most likely occurred during a journey through sorting machinery.

Figure 97. A mint stamp that appears undamaged on the front (left) may be hiding faults on the back. The arrows point to a hinge, bacterial foxing and a severe paper thin.

be something less.

A charming semipostal stamp from Belgium is shown at left in Figure 97. The young fellow on this 1937 stamp is Baudouin, who 14 years later became Belgium's king. This semipostal, the high value of an eight-stamp set, looks just about perfect when viewed from the front. No scrapes or gouges, no bends or tears, the design is wonderfully centered, and the color isn't faded or changed.

This stamp's problems are all behind it. Four faults can be spotted on the reverse of this stamp. There's a tenacious stamp hinge at the top that apparently was affixed with a lot of moisture, because the stamp paper is slightly bowed at the contact point. While many collectors don't mind a light hinge mark on a mint stamp, this particular hinge, when removed, will probably leave substantial evidence of its stay.

At the other end is a nasty thinning of the stamp paper. Several layers of paper were skinned from the surface, leaving a section so thin that light can shine through.

Much of the adhesive on the stamp is glazed. Instead of having an even texture, the gum appears pasty and mottled in a lot of places, evidence that the stamp was actually lightly affixed to something, perhaps an album page and then pried off. Most likely the paper thin mentioned earlier occurred when this prying event took place.

Finally, there are some rust-colored spots known as "foxing" in at least two places on the back. Such spots are caused by bacteria that grow on the stamp paper or adhesive and turn it the approximate color of reddish fox fur.

The foxing, glazing and thinning all point to a likelihood that this stamp was stored under pressure in a humid area, which activated the adhesive and invited in the bacteria.

Stamps should be kept in low humidity, never in basements or other areas where humidity is uncontrolled.

If you were buying this Belgian semipostal from a circuit book, approval packet or a stamp dealer, you would be wise to turn it over and inspect the back.

Even the least expensive stamp in your collection deserves to be one that you will enjoy looking at in years to come.

Stamp grading describes design centering

The value of a stamp often is determined by its scarcity and by the demand for the stamp among collectors. A stamp that is difficult to find and that many collectors would like to own often has great value in the marketplace.

There are two other important general features that affect the value and desirability of any collectible stamp: condition and grade.

Terms of condition apply to the physical state of the stamp. Damage, such as creases, scuffs, tears, holes, paper thins, stains, gum disturbance and so on, affect the condition of the stamp. The worse the damage is, the less desirable the stamp. The grade of a stamp is determined primarily by its centering.

Some authorities also add that the appearance of a cancellation may affect the

Descriptions of stamp grades

Stamp collectors and stamp dealers use grading terms to describe the centering of the printed design on collectible postage stamps. Grading is not an exact science, and these examples provide approximate descriptions only. Very early issues may be graded higher than similarly centered stamps from a more recent era. For issues that are rarely found well-centered, a grading may be qualified as appropriate for the specific issue. The images shown in this chart were computer-altered by digitally manipulating the image of a single stamp.

Extremely Fine (XF): The design of the stamp is almost perfectly centered within the boundaries of the outer edge. The designs of very early perforated stamps are completely clear of the perforations and appear balanced.

Fine (F): The grade of Fine applies to stamps that are noticeably off-center in two directions. The design will be very close to the perforations on modern issues, or touching the perforations or outer edges on very early issues.

Very Fine (VF): The design on the VF stamp will be slightly off-center on one or two sides, but overall the stamp presents a well-balanced appearance. Values provided in the Scott catalog apply to stamps with a grade of Very Fine.

Average (Avg.) or Very Good (VG): Perforations will cut into the outer edge of the design on a stamp with the grade of average. Classic stamps with more narrow margins around the design will have perforations cutting into the design on one or two sides.

Fine-Very Fine (F-VF): The design is visibly off-center on a stamp with a grade of F-VF. The shift may be moderate in one direction, or less so on two sides. The design remains clear of perforations on modern issues.

Fair: A stamp with the grade of fair will have perforations that cut substantially into the design on at least one side and that show significant imbalance in the overall appearance of the stamp. The grading may deeply affect value.

Figure 98. The various terms used to describe stamp centering are known as "grades." Stamp grading is not a precise art.

grade of a postally used stamp.

The centering on a stamp is determined by the position of the design of the stamp in relation to the outer edges of the stamp. On most individual postage stamps, there is an unprinted area of margin around the outside of the stamp design. A stamp is perfectly centered when the space in this margin is exactly the same at left and right, and exactly the same at top and bottom.

The chart shown in Figure 98 explains the terms that are most commonly used to describe the grade of a stamp.

The stamp used in the illustration is a 1928 10-krone definitive from Denmark depicting King Christian X. Because the stamp design has a rectangular shape, it is easy to check the centering of the design. To show the differences in stamp centering more clearly, the image of a single stamp was digitally manipulated on computer to

Figure 99. Imperforate stamps are graded by how balanced the stamp margins are in relation to the cut outer edges of the stamp.

create the images used on the chart. The chart begins with the top grade of stamp, extremely fine, which is often abbreviated XF.

Many stamp dealers and some collectors also use the term "superb" to convey that a stamp is perfectly centered.

Each level of stamp grading below the grade of XF indicates that the design is a little less perfectly centered than the previous grade. The very fine (VF) stamp, therefore, is a little more off-center (and therefore, a lesser grade) than the XF stamp. The stamp with a grade of fair is significantly off-center, to the point where the perforations cut into the design on at least one side.

Even lesser grades of poor or bad may be encountered by the collector, but dealers rarely sell and carry stamps that fall into these categories.

The range of stamp grades is not an exact science. It is possible to measure the margin areas of a stamp and determine that the design is perfectly centered, but from that point there is often some subjectivity involved in describing the grade of a stamp. Several factors must be taken into consideration when determining the grade of a stamp.

Figure 100. Many early perforated stamps, such as this 1880 issue from Great Britain, have narrow margins. The perforations often cut very close to the design.

Most stamps will be graded by comparing the centering of the design to the edges of a stamp's perforations.

Imperforate stamps, such as United States Scott 15, the 1855 10¢ green type III shown in Figure 99, also can be graded. Because many classic imperforate stamps were printed close together on the sheet, it can be difficult to find examples that are neatly trimmed and present a well-balanced appearance.

The 1855 10¢ Washington shown in Figure 99 would be graded XF because the outer edges of the stamp are quite clear of the outer edge of the printed design and the stamp presents an overall balanced appearance.

The designs of many early perforated stamps also were

printed close together on the sheet, making it difficult to find examples where the perforations do not cut into the design. The perforations on Great Britain's 1-shilling pink stamp of 1880 (Scott 65), shown in Figure 100, are very close to touching the bottom line of the design frame, but obviously the margins of the stamp are so narrow that there is not much leeway in any direction.

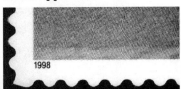

Figure 101. Collectors who purchase new issues should seek out examples that present a balanced appearance.

While some of the stamps shown in these illustrations are rare issues with lofty catalog values, all collectors should take the factors of grading into consideration when selecting stamps for the collection.

Because most modern stamps are created in enormous quantities, the collector often may find new issues that have undesirable centering. Since most of these stamps are readily available, the collector should always take time to examine each stamp he is considering for purchase to make sure he is obtaining a well-centered example. If he is offered an unsatisfactory example by a postal clerk or stamp dealer, the collector should hold out for a better grade of stamp.

Figure 102. The year date in the lower-left corner of U.S. stamps is one factor to consider when examining the appearance a stamp.

The $3.20 Shuttle Landing stamp from the United States was issued Nov. 9, 1998. A well-centered example is shown in Figure 101.

Some collectors have wondered about the small year dates printed in the lower-left corner of U.S. stamps. Does the placement of that date affect the grade of the stamp? An enlargement of the date on the Shuttle issue is shown in Figure 102.

Certainly the date should not be touched by the perforations at the bottom of the modern stamp, and the design of the stamp should be well-balanced in relation to the perforations. If anything, the design should be only slightly higher on the stamp to accommodate the tiny year date, but the difference between the top and bottom margins should be very minimal.

Finally, collectors need to understand that grading is only one factor that affects the desirability of a stamp.

Figure 103. Though the centering of a stamp's design may present a balanced appearance, other factors, such as the physical condition of the stamp, will affect its value.

Figure 103 shows the unwatermarked 1894 15¢ Henry Clay stamp, Scott 259, which postally used has a catalog value of more than $50. This value is given for a sound copy of the stamp with a grade of very fine.

The example in Figure 103 does not meet this description. Though the centering has the appearance of a VF stamp, the torn upper-right corner and the terribly heavy cancellation that obliterates much of the design reduces the value of this stamp to a small fraction of the catalog listing.

Postage stamps that are canceled-to-order

When a stamp is used on a mailed item to pay for postage, it usually receives a postmark to prevent anyone from using the stamp again.

But why do stamp collectors find postmarked stamps that have full, unused gum on the back? Such stamps are canceled-to-order and are known among collectors as "CTO."

There are several reasons why CTOs exist.

For the governments of some countries, selling canceled, unused stamps at a discount directly to stamp dealers has provided additional income. Such countries print mint, uncanceled stamps for use as postage, to be sold at the post office. They also have created canceled-to-order versions of the same stamps for sale to stamp dealers or stamp wholesalers.

Stamp dealers use the supply of canceled stamps to create packets to sell to collectors. The postal authority profits from the sale of the stamps without having

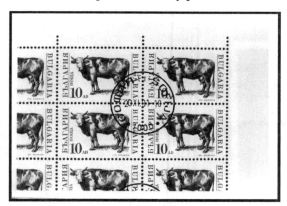

to provide postal delivery services. The stamps can never be used for postage in the future because they are canceled with a postmark.

The postal authority prints sheets of stamps with postmarks placed to mark every stamp on the sheet. An example is shown in Figure 104. Bulgaria Scott 3591 is a 10-lev definitive stamp from 1991 depicting a cow. The stamp

Figure 104. While printing sheets of stamps for postage, some postal authorities have also printed sheets of canceled-to-order stamps like these for eventual sale to stamp collectors. Shown above is an enlargement of a corner of the sheet.

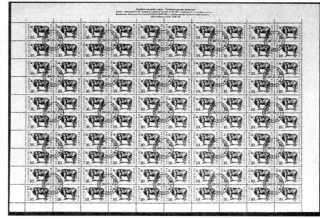

was printed in sheets of 100. A circular cancellation mark is printed 25 times on the sheet. Each mark covers four stamps, as shown in the enlarged illustration. This unused sheet has stamp gum on the back, just like any new stamp issue.

In some cases, the postmarks are applied to the stamps during the stamp printing process.

Other countries have postmarked CTO stamps by hand or by machine after printing. The stamps sent to be canceled may be remainders that were not sold for postage.

Figure 105. Each CTO stamp in this 1990 set from Yemen has a cleanly printed postmark on the upper-left corner and full gum on back.

The presence of stamp gum on the back of a canceled stamp is the easiest way to identify a CTO. A crisp sharp cancel perfectly marking the corner of one stamp is another clue that a stamp might be a CTO. This is particularly true for stamps that have cancels printed on them.

Figure 105 shows six stamps from a 1990 set issued by Yemen. All of the stamps have precisely printed cancels in the upper-left corner. Each stamp also has full gum on the back.

In other cases, the CTO may look more like a stamp that traveled through the mail. The postmark on Czechoslovakia Scott 1740, a 1971 definitive stamp shown in Figure 106, is paler than the crisp bold marking on the Yemeni stamps, and it bears a pair of wavy cancellation bars trailing the circular marking. The Czech postmark more closely resembles the kind of mark one might expect to find on a stamp that has journeyed through the mail. A look at the back of the same stamp, however, shows that it has full gum and never fulfilled postal duty.

Figure 106. From the front a stamp may look like it was used on mail, but gum on the back shows it is a CTO.

An enterprising collector could easily soak off the gum in water, dry the stamp and flatten it, and the result would be a Czech stamp that appears to have been used to deliver mail. The effort probably would not be worthwhile, however. Though a specialist collector may prefer a postally used stamp to a CTO, it's likely he would want his example of the stamp to be on cover, that is, on a mailed envelope to prove its usage. And postmarked stamps from countries like Czechoslovakia, Bulgaria and Yemen, all known CTO producers, are suspect when found off-paper. Even without gum on the back, many collectors can spot the familiar placement and marking of a CTO cancel.

Figure 107. Ras al-Khaima is one of the Trucial States that began manufacturing and distributing CTOs during the late 1960s.

Figure 108. A U.S. stamp with full gum and marked with a favor cancel resembles a CTO.

The Scott catalog listings for Bulgaria also include a notice about canceled-to-order stamps of that country:

"Beginning about 1956, some issues were sold in sheets canceled to order. Values in second column when much less than unused are for 'CTO' copies. Postally used stamps are valued at slightly less than, or the same as, unused."

A similar notice appears among the Scott listings for stamps from Czechoslovakia and other entities that create and sell CTO stamps.

Many of the countries that have issued CTO stamps are former Eastern European communist bloc nations, including Albania, East Germany, Hungary, Romania and Russia, as well as Bulgaria and Czechoslovakia. Most of these countries began marketing CTOs during the 1950s and stopped after 1991.

During the 1960s, the stamp market was flooded with CTOs from the Trucial States of the Arabian peninsula. Many of the stamps produced by these entities — Ajman, Dubai, Fujeira, Manama, Ras al-Khaima and Sharjah — are not recognized in the Scott catalog because evidence suggests that actual postal use of these stamps was negligible. A CTO issue from Ras al-Khaima commemorating the 1968 Grenoble Winter Olympic Games is shown in Figure 107.

Other countries that have issued CTOs include Costa Rica (during the 1910s), Spain (from 1854-82), Liberia (beginning in 1885), and several more.

In the April 29, 1996, issue of *Linn's Stamp News*, Michael Schreiber reported on mint U.S. stamps that were marked with a roller-cancel by a local postmaster for use as a receipt of a major stamp marketing firm's postage due bill payment. The firm then sold the stamp, with full gum on the back, to customers requesting used copies of recent U.S. commemoratives.

The customer who wrote to *Linn's* provided the 1995 32¢ Winton Automobile stamp, Scott 3022, shown in Figure 108. She was concerned that the stamp might be a CTO.

In this case, the stamp actually fulfilled a postal function. As the article explained, the use of postage stamps as a receipt for a postage due bill payment is an approved postal-service procedure. Though with full gum on the back the stamp resembles a CTO, it is, in fact, what is known as a favor cancel. Whenever a collector or postal customer specifically requests a cancel or postmark, the result is known as a favor cancel.

Another example of a favor cancel is shown in Figure 109. The Paris Disneyland postmark from France applied to the 1997 Happy Birthday stamp (France Scott 2556) is not a standard machine-applied cancellation one normally finds on mail. Instead, it is carefully struck by hand on a postcard souvenir for the benefit of a collector.

Figure 109. This pictorial postmark from Paris, hand-applied to a 1997 French stamp, is another type of favor cancel.

Favor cancels may be applied to stamps used on mail as well. The block of four 1996 Homeopathic Medicine stamps from Germany (Scott 1946) shown in Figure 110 was used to mail a large envelope from the headquarters of the German postal service.

The clean marking in the center of the four stamps closely resembles the canceled-to-order markings described in previous paragraphs, but Germany (previously West Germany) was never known to create CTOs. The postmark was carefully applied to please a stamp-collector customer.

From time to time, customers of Denmark's postal service use removable paper note stickers with diagrams that instruct clerks how to properly place a favor cancel on a mailed philatelic package (one going to or sent from a collector).

For some collectors, only cancels created by normal mail-processing procedures are acceptable. Other collectors notice that CTOs and favor cancels are neatly applied and usually do not physically damage the stamps, which is a hazard of machine-applied cancels.

CTOs packaged in packets have been used for many years to introduce new collectors to the hobby. Though the CTO stamps may never have fulfilled a postal function, they are inexpensive collectible items that have been used to help promote the growth of the hobby.

Figure 110. Sometimes stamps that were used on mail may resemble CTOs.

Chapter 6
Proper Handling and Storage

Even stamp collectors need the right tools

Stamp tongs: Stamp tongs are an essential tool for every stamp collector. In many different ways, tongs help collectors handle stamps safely and reduce the chances of damage. Stamp tongs resemble tweezers that are sold for beauty care or first-aid service. They generally are made of two flat metal legs welded together at one end to create a spring action that allows the free ends to pinch together.

Figure 111 shows stamp tongs being used to hold British definitive postage stamps. Stamp tongs have

Figure 111. Stamp collectors use tongs to hold stamps without harming them. Shown are tongs with pointed tips for precision work (left) and spade tips to hold larger items (right).

rounded, polished tips that make them safe for use with stamps. Standard tweezers have sharpened edges that can easily cut into stamp paper. Tweezers designed for beauty care should never be used to handle stamps.

You'll find more information about stamp tongs in the next section.

Stock pages and stock books: The stock page is a firm sheet with horizontal compartments that can hold your stamp inventory safely. Most stock pages have holes punched along one edge so they can fit into a three-ring or similar binder.

Stock books are bound volumes containing stock pages that cannot be removed from the book. Figure 112 shows a simple manila card stock page at left and a small open stock book at right. The pages of the stock book in the illustration have horizontal strips of glassine affixed to the page to act as pockets that support and hold stamps. The book also has glassine interleaving to protect the stamps on facing pages. Glassine is a thin, semitransparent paper that has several uses in the stamp hobby.

Some stock pages are made of black plastic or vinyl manufactured specifically to be free of harmful chemicals that can damage stamps. Stock pages and stock books hold stamps firmly in place, yet the stamps

Figure 112. Stock pages (left) and stock books hold stamps in place, yet allow them to be easily moved or rearranged.

can be moved easily from one location to another as a collection grows and evolves.

The collector must be careful when placing stamps into a stock page to avoid bumping the edge or corner of the stamp against the top of the holding strip. Some collectors use tongs to pull back slightly on the holding strip while placing the stamp (held with a second pair of tongs) into position.

Stock pages are made with as many as 12 rows to hold stamps or as few as one (for full panes or larger souvenir sheets). Some stock pages are double-sided, providing extra storage space.

Most stock books have a set number of rows per page. Stock books come in different sizes with pages made of different materials, including manila card, or black or white board.

Several styles are available for less than $10, while fancier versions with extra pages and padded leather covers can cost as much as $40. Stock pages are usually sold together in packs of five or 10, with prices ranging from 25¢ to $1 per page or more, depending on the style.

Glassine envelopes and cover sleeves: Many collectors use glassine envelopes to keep together small groups of stamps. The semitransparent glassine paper makes it possible to see the stamps inside the envelope, but the material is strong enough to provide some protection from damage. Figure 113 shows a number of glassine envelopes at left.

Glassines can be used to hold postally used stamps that have been soaked and dried until the collector has an opportunity to sort them and put them into a stock book or album. Collectors can write identifying information on glassine envelopes, but any writing should be done before stamps are placed in the envelope, to keep from impressing the writing onto the stamps inside.

Figure 113. Glassine envelopes (left and top right) and polybag sleeves (lower right) provide inexpensive protection.

Large glassine envelopes can be used to hold covers, which are envelopes or cards that are stamped or postmarked. At top right in Figure 113 is a first-day cover from the Czech Republic that will fit into the glassine envelope behind it.

All stamps or covers that are placed into glassine envelopes will need additional protection from creasing or other damage. Many collectors use sturdy storage boxes that hold their glassines in place. If glassines are simply tossed into a drawer with other objects, such as stock books or stamp catalogs, the heavier objects can easily crumple the glassine envelope and the items inside.

Some collectors prefer inexpensive transparent polybag sleeves to enclose the covers they save. A first-day cover is shown in a polybag sleeve at lower right in Figure 113. Packages of 100 sleeves are generally available from 3¢ to 5¢ per sleeve. Glassine envelopes may be slightly more expensive.

Magnifying glass: Stamp collectors rely upon magnifiers to see important details in stamp designs and to detect faults in the stamps they are examining. Though a magnifier doesn't protect stamps from damage, it can protect you from buying a damaged stamp. Because stamps are so small and fragile, even a tiny defect can substantially detract from a stamp's quality. A collector can use the magnifier to examine a stamp before he purchases it to make sure the stamp is sound.

Most collectors begin by looking over the outer edges of the stamp. The points extending from the edge of a perforated stamp are known as perforation teeth. As previously stated, they are one of the most vulnerable elements of a stamp, and collectors should avoid stamps that have bent or missing teeth. Stamp edges also should be examined for minute tears or cuts into the stamp paper.

Figure 114. Magnifying glasses help collectors spot defects in stamps. They also provide a better view of stamp designs.

Many different kinds of magnifiers exist, ranging in price from a couple of dollars for small hand-held lenses to precision illuminated models that sell for a couple hundred dollars. A glass with four- or eight-power magnification (symbolized as 4x or 8x) will help the beginner collector get a good close-up view of stamp details. With higher power magnification the details will appear even larger.

Figure 114 shows three magnifiers commonly used by collectors.

The object in the center of the illustration is a magnifying loupe with a fixed focal point. This magnifier can be placed carefully over the stamp, and the details of the stamp will be enlarged and precisely focused.

All of these important stamp-collecting tools are available from local stamp dealers or from mail-order stamp supply dealers. Visiting a stamp dealer at his shop or at a stamp show gives you the option of seeing first-hand the many different kinds of products that are available.

Once you have the right tools in hand, you can feel confident that you are handling and protecting your stamps and covers properly.

Choose the stamp tongs that are best for you

Before you pick up a stamp, you'd better pick up stamp tongs.

One important step you can take to keep your stamps in the best possible condition is learning to use stamp tongs when handling your stamps. Stamp tongs are simple tools that allow you to pick up and examine a stamp without ever touching it with your fingers.

Why is this important?

Everyone's skin has a small amount of natural oil on the surface. If you pick up a stamp with your fingers, the oil transfers to the stamp. On mint stamps, the damage may be obvious almost immediately. Dark offset or lithographed stamps may show a stain that cannot be removed. The gum on the back of the stamp will be permanently marked with a fingerprint. Over time, the effects may become worse and include discoloration of the stamp design.

Because stamp tongs are a precision grasping tool, they are much better than fingers for picking up stamps without damaging them. With your fingers, you can bend or crease a stamp very easily while trying to pick it up off a smooth flat surface or out of your album or stock book.

Stamp tongs are considerably different from the tweezers that can be bought at drug stores and are used for beauty care. Tweezers have sharp edges at the tips that are used for grasping. Those sharp edges, if used on a stamp, can cut or permanently indent stamp paper. You should never use tweezers to hold stamps.

Stamp tongs are created with specially rounded and polished tips. Although they can slide easily under a postage stamp, the rounded, finished edge on the tips will not cut through the stamp paper.

If you've ever shopped for stamp tongs, you may have been surprised by the variety of lengths, shapes and tips that are available. And you also may have wondered what the differences were. Stamp tongs generally are available in two lengths,

Figure 115. Although shorter stamp tongs are well suited for younger collectors, they are also chosen by some adults who find that the shorter length provides more versatility.

as shown in the photo in Figure 115. The shorter pair in the photo is slightly more than 4½ inches long and is well-suited for younger collectors. The longer pair, at 6 inches, is designed primarily for adult use.

Some adult collectors prefer the shorter tongs, particularly for working out of smaller stock books and for frequent removal of single stamps from glassine envelopes. The shorter length makes them a little more handy for this type of hobby work in narrow settings.

There are in-between lengths as well, and length can be one factor that helps you decide if a particular pair of tongs is right for you. If you have smaller hands, you may find the smaller tongs are more comfortable.

Almost everyone finds stamp tongs a little awkward when first using them. Fortunately, it doesn't take long to get comfortable handling stamps with them.

Most stamp tongs have a serrated or ridged area on each outer side. You can grasp that area between your thumb and forefinger, a little like holding a pen: the tips of your tongs point down, like the tip of a pen. Tongs have a bit of a spring-action, so they are normally in an open position. When you lightly squeeze with your thumb and forefinger, you can close the tong tips on a stamp.

Some collectors hold tongs between their thumb and middle finger, using the forefinger to hold the tongs stable. You'll certainly find one method that is most comfortable for you.

One of the most noticeable differences among stamp tongs is the shape of the tips. In Figure 116 there are four different types of tips illustrated. These are not all the types that are available but represent the most common types.

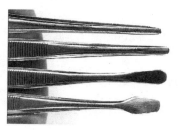

Figure 116. There are a number of different styles of stamp tong tips. Each style has a different specific use.

Starting from the top of the illustration, the tips shown first and second are very similar. The upper tip is very pointed, and the second tip is slightly more rounded. Both of these pointed-tip styles are used often by stamp dealers and professional philatelists. The taper of the tip is very gradual.

The tapering ends have one specialized use, and that is to remove peelable hinges from stamps. Because the taper is gradual and even, a collector may grasp the hinge and carefully roll the tongs so that the hinge evenly peels off the back of the stamp. This method distributes the stress on the stamp paper so that there is less chance of creasing. It can only be used with completely peelable stamp hinges. Hinges that are not peelable will damage the stamp paper if you try to remove them this way, so another method must be found.

Either of the top two tongs are for precision use, like placing stamps in stamp mounts or picking up a single stamp out of a glassine envelope that also contains several other stamps.

The third pair of tongs in Figure 116 has rounded tips, often referred to as paddle tips. Though pointed tips on quality tongs will give you a good grasp on your stamp, some collectors feel that the paddle tip provides a more secure hold of the stamp. The paddle tip is not as precise as the pointed tip and requires a little extra care when selecting a single stamp from a group of stamps.

Because the grasping area is even more wide on the spade-tip tongs, shown at the bottom of Figure 116, it takes that security of grasping the stamp one step further, making it a recommended style for younger collectors. Spade tips also provide a little more stability for handling full mint panes and souvenir sheets. The spade tip also is useful for picking up larger quantities of stamps, such as from inexpensive approvals and packets.

Collectors who prefer to remove stamps from a soaking bath with tongs should also use spade tips rather than the other, more pointed styles. Tongs with pointed tips can pierce the wet stamp paper. With a small amount of care, it is unlikely that you will damage your wet stamp with your spade-tip tongs.

If you do use tongs in water, make certain that you thoroughly dry them after use, to prevent corrosion of the polished finish.

Specially angled tongs are also available, usually with a spade tip. As shown in Figure 117, the angled tongs work particularly well for removing stamps from stock books or stock pages.

The angle of the tips allows the collector to approach the stock book with the tongs without having to bring fingers uncomfortably close to the other stamps in

Figure 117. Angled stamp tongs make it easier to remove and replace stamps from stock books and stock pages.

the book. With regular straight tongs, you might brush against stamps with your knuckles, potentially bending perforation teeth or knocking a stamp out of the holding pocket.

The quality of the tongs that are available for purchase may vary depending on the manufacturer. Collectors use some of the more popular brand names because they provide a better quality, with rust-resistant metals and finely polished tips that meet precisely without gaps or misalignment.

If you're in the market for new stamp tongs, you might examine the tips with a magnifier to make certain they meet and close precisely, and that the tips are smooth and polished.

Deluxe tongs are available with a gold plating that helps to further prevent corrosion of the surface. The gold plating is also better for individuals whose skin is sensitive to the polished nickel-plating of conventional tongs. To protect any type of stamp tongs, keep them in a plastic or leather case when not in use.

Once you are accustomed to using tongs, you will find they are handy for many common stamp-collecting procedures. It is much easier to apply a stamp hinge in the correct position with a pair of pointed tongs than it is with 15mm wide fingertips. Some collectors use two pairs of tongs in such instances — one pair to hold the stamp and one to apply the hinge.

While there are many uses for stamp tongs, there are even more things for which you should not use tongs. Among these are any type of repair or mechanical use that will potentially damage the tongs. Even if you don't notice the damage immediately, it can cause harm to stamps you handle. A damaged tong tip is shown enlarged in Figure 118. The sharp edge caused by the gouge in the metal will slice through a stamp (or even a layer of skin) without any difficulty.

Examine your tongs from time to time to make sure they are smooth and free of corrosion or rust. Most tongs will work very well and last many years, but if you find they are not in tip-top shape, it's time to retire them and buy new ones.

Stamp tongs are sold by most stamp dealers and range in price from about $3.50 to $7 for the more common styles.

With a good pair of stamp tongs in your hands, you show that you have respect for the stamps that you've decided to collect.

Figure 118. A stamp tong tip that is damaged (shown under magnification) can cause damage to stamps.

Stock books and sheets help organize stamps

One common concern among stamp collectors is keeping the stamps they have accumulated properly organized and protected. Stock books and stock sheets (or stock pages) can be vital tools in this important effort.

It's easy to fall into the trap of amassing a huge quantity of stamps, either in mint condition or postally used, without taking time to find a safe way to store them. The end result can be stamps that are creased, dirty, stuck to each other or stuck to something else. That makes the effort of collecting stamps of quality rather meaningless.

Stamp collectors are notoriously fussy about the condition of the stamps they collect and with good reason. Stamps that have suffered even very minor damage generally have substantially less value than undamaged stamps.

If you buy a terrific stamp in excellent condition from a stamp dealer, it makes sense to be careful about preserving that condition as you include the stamp in your collection. Many collectors will immediately add the stamp to an album page, using either a stamp hinge or a stamp mount. Properly mounted stamps are usually safe in a stamp album of good quality.

There are times, however, when it's not possible or convenient to add new stamps to your album right away. For example, collectors usually have to wait several months for album supplement pages to be released after they have purchased the newest stamp issues.

Collectors of postally used stamps often accumulate many duplicate stamps that they set aside for trading purposes.

In such instances, many collectors make use of stock books and stock sheets to organize their stamps and keep them safe. Stock books consist of several pages of firm material, usually a heavyweight paper or card stock, bound between two covers. The number of pages may range from eight to 64. Most stock books have pages measuring approximately 8½ inches by 11 inches, but smaller sizes are also available.

Two standard-size stock books are shown open in Figure 119. Each page of the stock book has long horizontal pockets that run from one edge of the page to the other. The pockets are created by strips of acetate, glassine paper or other suitable material affixed in horizontal rows. Stamps fit into these pockets easily and are held in place by the fixed horizontal strips.

Figure 120 shows a close-up of several German stamps held in place

Figure 119. Stock books come in many different styles. All are designed to hold stamps safely and aid in organization.

on the page of a stock book. Reflected light on the clear acetate strips shows how the stamps are held in place.

Most stock books also have glassine paper interleaving between each page to protect facing pages of stamps from one another.

The terms "stock sheet" and "stock page" are used interchangeably to describe any number of different loose-leaf pages that are specially made to hold stamps securely. Each stock sheet is made out of a firm material: either heavyweight paper, chemically safe plastic or manila-style card stock. Stock sheet sizes may vary, but most are 8½ inches by 11 inches.

Figure 120. Each page of the stock book has rows of horizontal strips creating long pockets to hold the stamps in place. In this example, each strip is made of clear acetate.

Examples of two different stock sheets are shown in Figure 121. Both styles have punched holes along the left edge of the page so they can be kept easily in a binder. The manila-style stock sheet shown at right in Figure 121 is one of the more inexpensive versions that can be purchased. Many collectors like to use this style because it is easy to make notes directly on the page identifying specific stamps.

In Figure 121 is a black stock sheet with only four pockets. The deeper pockets are convenient for holding blocks of stamps. In the example, several U.S. plate blocks are placed on the stock sheet.

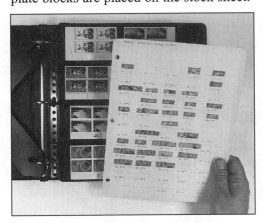

Figure 121. Loose-leaf stock sheets (also known as stock pages) can be stored in a binder. Stock sheets are created with many different pocket sizes to accommodate collectors' needs.

Many different stock-sheet formats are available, ranging from pages with just one pocket to pages with eight pockets. Some pages are available with two or three different-sized pockets on a single page for specialized uses.

It's usually best to keep stamps separated from one another on the stock page so they do not overlap. This is particularly true for mint stamps that have gum on the back. The closed pages of a stock book will apply some pressure upon the stamps on the page. If the stamps are exposed to humidity, they may adhere to other stamps they are touching.

To help prevent this problem,

stock books should always be stored upright, never lying flat, and they should be kept in an environment with low humidity. The books should not be squeezed into a tight spot on the shelf, because the added pressure may activate some of the stamp adhesive. Though it must be stored standing upright, the book should have at least a little bit of wiggle room.

Along the same lines, when the collector carries the stock book or stock sheets from one place to another, care must be taken to ensure that the stamps and pages are upright, so that none of the stamps can fall out and be lost or damaged.

Some collectors choose to overlap postally used stamps on the stock page because such stamps no longer have gum on the back. This saves space when a large number of loose stamps are being stored.

However, the collector should take care not to overstuff the horizontal strips that create the stock-page pocket. The pressure of many overlapped stamps bulging in a single pocket can loosen acetate strips or rip out glassine strips, making it easier for individual stamps to fall out.

Figure 122. To prevent possible damage from mishandling, collectors use stamp tongs to place or remove stamps from the stock page. Tongs with angled tips provide easier access.

When adding stamps to the stock page or when removing or rearranging stamps, the collector should use stamp tongs rather than fingers. It is hard to grab hold of a stamp on a stock page with fingers, and the stamp or the stock page may be damaged in the attempt. Besides, fingers can also harm stamps by contaminating them with dirt or skin oil.

Figure 122 shows a collector placing a stamp on a stock page using stamp tongs with angled tips. The angle at the end of the tongs gives the collector a little easier approach to stamps arranged on a flat page. Any style of stamp tongs may be used for this purpose, however.

Other temporary stamp storage options for collectors exist.

Figure 123 shows a smaller stock card, a dealer sales card and a glassine envelope. While these items do provide some protection for the stamps they hold, they

Figure 123. Collectors may choose from other temporary stamp storage options including smaller stock cards (top left), dealer sales cards (top right) and glassine envelopes (bottom).

are susceptible to damage themselves under certain circumstances. These smaller storage options should be kept secure in a location that will protect them from creasing or sudden contact with heavy items that can harm the stamps they hold. Stamps in these smaller holders should not be placed loose in drawers or kept in large boxes with books, magazines or other large objects.

Keep your stamps away from these hazards

The choice to become a stamp collector means a chance to enjoy a satisfying hobby for a lifetime.

There are responsibilities that come with the hobby, however, in some ways similar to the responsibilities that come when you decide to have children or adopt a pet. Your stamp-collecting responsibilities include the proper careful handling of your stamps and providing a good home for your collectibles.

Postage stamps are handled every day by millions of people all over the world. Most of these people are using stamps to mail items, though a few will be saved by collectors like you and me.

All of the casual handling of stamps for postage may make us inattentive when we're handling stamps for our collections. Mint stamps in particular are subject to easy damage from careless handling and storage. Mint stamps are those that have never been used for postage, have full undamaged gum on the back, and are in the same condition as when they arrived at the post office.

While working with or storing your stamps, you should always avoid a number of hazardous conditions.

Skin oil. There are many times when you need to handle your mint stamps with your hands. For example, if you separate a single stamp from a block of stamps, or if you separate a block of stamps from a full pane, you need to hold the stamps with your hands. Everyone has some residue skin oil on the surface of their fingers, and the components of this natural oil can actually deface the stamps that you handle.

Dark-colored lithographed or photogravure stamps, like the 1996 32¢ James Dean stamp from the United States, are particularly susceptible to damage from skin oil.

You can reduce the effects of skin oil on the design of your stamps by thoroughly washing and drying your hands before handling stamps. Some collectors use clean cotton gloves when handling mint stamps, to avoid touching the gum or the design surface with their fingers.

Being aware that skin oil can harm your stamps will help you handle them in a way that will save them from damage. Using stamp tongs whenever possible to handle your mint stamps also will help to avoid the damage that may occur through contact with skin oil.

Food and beverages. A collector working with a stamp collection may want to partake of a snack or a drink while enjoying his hobby, but these items pose a threat to stamps and albums. It's always a good idea to take snacks and meals in a location completely separate from the area where the stamps are being enjoyed.

There are a number of reasons for this. Beverages can spill, immediately rendering irreparable damage to stamps or album pages. Foodstuffs may crumble or drip, staining stamps and pages forever. The moisture and grease from food and

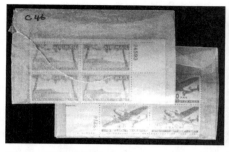
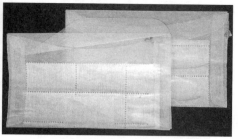

Figure 124. Although they were stored in glassine envelopes to keep them safe, the U.S. plate blocks shown here were damaged when they came into contact with water.

drink are dangerous around stamp collectibles. Always enjoy these items far from your collection, and carefully wash and dry your hands before returning to your hobby.

Moisture, water and humidity. Once again, mint stamps are particularly susceptible to damage from these elements. Moisture of any kind can damage mint stamps. Simple humidity (moisture in the air) can affect the adhesive on mint stamps and cause them to curl up. If you live in a humid part of the country, you need to find a safe way to counter the humidity when you work on your stamp collection.

The basement is often the most humid area of a residence. If you're not certain of the humidity levels in your home, a hygrometer may help you determine the best area to store your collection. Storing your collection in a cool, dry place is a good guideline.

Water is a natural enemy of mint stamps, and the illustrations in Figure 124 go far to prove this point. The two glassine envelopes in the illustration hold what once were two mint plate blocks of U.S. airmail stamps. Glassine envelopes are semi-transparent envelopes made for stamp storage.

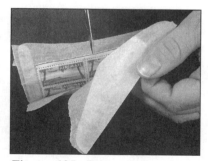

Scott C46, the Diamond Head 80¢ airmail of 1952, has a catalog value of $22.50 as a mint plate block. Scott C30, the Transport 30¢ airmail of 1941, has a catalog value of $11 as a mint plate block. Both of these plate blocks were damaged when they came into contact with water. Figure 125 shows how the Diamond Head block is affixed to the inside of the envelope.

The stamps could be separated from the envelope by soaking in water, but that will remove all the adhesive from the stamps. Of course, the stamps will no longer be in mint condition, and the value for them will be considerably less.

Figure 125. Because the stamp gum was moistened by contact with water, these stamps have bonded with the inside of the glassine envelope. Soaking the whole mess in water will separate the stamps from the envelope, but the mint condition of the stamps has been destroyed.

 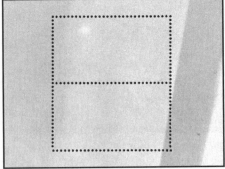

Figure 126. At first glance these Icelandic stamps seem undamaged, but an inspection of the back shows creasing. They were damaged when they were improperly stored.

The lesson to be learned is always keep your mint stamps away from water and humid conditions.

Improper storage. Glassine envelopes are helpful for storing stamps, but they can only do so much. The envelopes are not very sturdy, and stamps can be damaged by creasing if the glassine is not kept in a safe place.

In 1992, Iceland issued a handsome two-stamp pane, Scott 751, honoring explorers Leif Eriksson and Christopher Columbus. The example shown at the left in Figure 126 looks fine in the illustration. The reverse of the pane is shown at right in Figure 126. With the light aimed at an angle, a severe crease in the stamp paper is evident.

Although this item was in a glassine envelope, it was stored loosely with other items. At some point, it was creased and permanently damaged by a heavier object stored next to it.

Glassine envelopes of stamps should be stored carefully to avoid damage. Keep such envelopes upright and away from possible harm. If the glassines can slide around and lay flat, the stamps they contain may be damaged by creasing.

Pressure. The effect of pressure can activate the adhesive on many mint stamps, causing them to adhere to other stamps or the pages of albums or stock books.

Stamps in glassine envelopes that are stored between the pages of books or stamp catalogs can become stuck together. The three stamps shown in Figure 127 show what can happen. Although all are common canceled stamps, the stamp stuck on top is an East German Official stamp with full gum. It is firmly stuck to the other two stamps because they were

Figure 127. Stamps with gum that are stored together under pressure can adhere to one another. The 10-pfennig East German stamp on top has full gum on the back, and it is stuck to the two postally used stamps underneath it.

all stored together under pressure.

Mint stamps in albums or stock books can become stuck to pages if they are stored under pressure. For that reason, all albums and stock books should always be stored upright. Laying them flat causes the weight of the pages to create the pressure that can damage the stamps.

A number of hazards can combine to damage your stamps. Heat and humidity combined with pressure can permanently affix mint stamps to pages or the inside of glassines. Once the adhesive on a mint stamp is activated, it is disturbed. Even if the collector can easily peel the stamp from the item to which it is stuck, the gum will show signs of disturbance, and the stamp will no longer be in mint condition.

To properly save your collectible items, you need to keep them away from danger. For mint stamps and other collectibles, there are more than a few hazards that you need to watch for. By taking good care of your stamps, you'll get plenty of enjoyment from them for years to come.

Collectors use albums to display their stamps

One of the most familiar components of the stamp hobby is the stamp album, a book filled with pages that have designated spaces to mount and display stamps.

Stamp albums with printed pages appeared in the United States as early as 1863, just 16 years after the first U.S. stamps were issued.

For many years, stamp albums were manufactured much like ordinary books, with the pages bound into a spine between two hard covers. A postage stamp album from the 1930s is shown in Figure 128.

Early bound albums had several drawbacks. As years went by and new stamps were issued, there was no way to update the album with new pages.

The slim volume in the illustration boasts that it "contains spaces for postage stamps from every stamp-issuing country in the world," but many countries in the album are represented by just a handful of spaces on a page, even though they may have issued hundreds of stamps before the album was produced.

Most stamp albums today are designed to hold the stamps of just one country or geographic region. Larger countries that have issued many stamps, such as the United States, may even require more than one album to hold all the pages needed to accommodate each stamp. The spaces on album pages often include images of the stamps that are supposed to fit in the space.

Some album pages provide catalog numbers along with the illustrations to further help the collector identify the proper stamp. Figure 129 shows an illustration from a Scott album page for the stamps of Austria.

Figure 128. Some older stamp albums have pages bound as a book. Pages unfortunately cannot be added or removed from such bound albums.

Figure 129. The spaces on some stamp album pages show the design of the stamp and a catalog number or similar identifying information.

Scott Publishing Co. is a major distributor of postage stamp albums in the United States. Like *Linn's Stamp News,* Scott is a division of Amos Press of Sidney, Ohio.

As the stamp collector obtains stamps, he adds them to the album pages. On Scott album pages, the stamp fits within the framing border of the designated space and covers the illustration and catalog number.

The preprinted album pages are neatly organized and help the collector create an attractive display for his collection. The spaces generally are arranged on each page in the order the stamps were issued. That means the earliest stamps are shown on the first pages, with later stamps following.

Stamps with special designations, such as airmail, semipostal and postage due, may appear on separate pages near the back of the album.

Stamp albums come in all sizes. Some are very comprehensive, with spaces for virtually every stamp issued by a certain country or geographic area. Others are less complete, or they offer fewer spaces for the beginner collector.

The pages in albums differ as well. Some basic albums have pages printed on white paper similar to standard office paper, while more expensive albums have pages printed on heavyweight archival-quality paper. These two types are represented by the Scott *Minuteman* album of U.S. stamps shown at left in Figure 130, and the more advanced Scott Specialty album shown opened up in the same illustration.

The *Minuteman* album is sold complete with pages and binder, but the com-

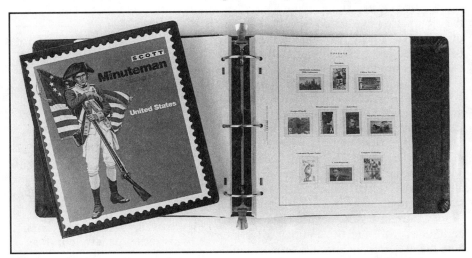

Figure 130. Different albums fulfill varying collector needs. The opened Scott Specialty album has heavier pages than the more basic Scott Minuteman album at left.

Figure 131. The components of many albums are sold separately. Shown are the album binder (left), three sets of album pages (center), and packages of annual supplement pages (right).

ponents of the Specialty album are sold separately.

Figure 131 shows how a specialty album of Great Britain is made available to the collector. At left is a sturdy binder that holds the pages of the album. In the center of the illustration are three sets of album pages for stamps of Great Britain. Depending on the size of the country, the pages may come in one, two, three or more sets. Those specialty pages for Great Britain are sold for the years 1840-1973 (part I), 1974-96 (part II) and 1997-99 (part III).

To bring the album up-to-date, the collector can purchase annual supplement pages that match the album page sets and contain spaces for stamps issued in recent years.

The 2002, 2001 and 2000 Great Britain supplement packs are shown at right in Figure 131.

Some album manufacturers also offer a boxlike slipcover that protects the binder and its pages from dust.

As collectors begin to seek out special varieties of stamps, such as some perforation or tagging varieties, they often find that preprinted pages may not have spaces for all of the stamps that interest them.

To help such collectors, many album manufacturers offer blank pages or pages with a lightly printed grid pattern with borders that match the preprinted pages. The collector can use these pages to design his own album supplements. The grid pattern helps the collector align the stamps on the page.

Although many different album styles are available, some collectors prefer to design their own page layouts using blank pages. Matching stock pages, with rows of transparent sleeves that hold many stamps, also are available in some cases.

Some collectors choose not to use preprinted pages, and instead, they create their own albums using blank paper and standard notebook binders. This method is fine if the collector uses high-quality materials.

Some plastic-coated binders may include chemical softeners that can damage stamps if they come into contact with them. Paper that is not of archival quality may discolor, and this chemical change can affect stamps as well.

Stamp albums, supplement pages, binders and similar stamp-collecting supplies are available from most stamp dealers. Many dealers in stamp supplies advertise weekly in popular stamp-hobby publications.

Hinges help you show off your collection

Stamp albums are great for showing off a stamp collection, but the collector has to be careful about affixing his stamps to the album page. Over the years some terrific stamps have been ruined because collectors used glue, paste or tape to stick the stamps onto album pages. The chemicals in these adhesives will stain stamps, and of course, it is just about impossible to remove a stamp that's been glued to an album page.

Other collectors have simply used the gum on the stamp to stick the stamp to the page. That's not a good idea, either. You can't remove the stamp from the page without damaging the page, and quite possibly the stamp as well.

Don't use glue, don't use tape, and don't lick the back of the stamp. Just how do you stick stamps in an album?

Collectors use two popular methods. Stamp mounts are plastic see-through stamp holders with adhesive on one side. Mounts enclose the stamp so it can be placed onto the page. Mounts are attractive and they do a great job of protecting the stamp, but they can be expensive. A very common stamp could have less value than the stamp mount holding it.

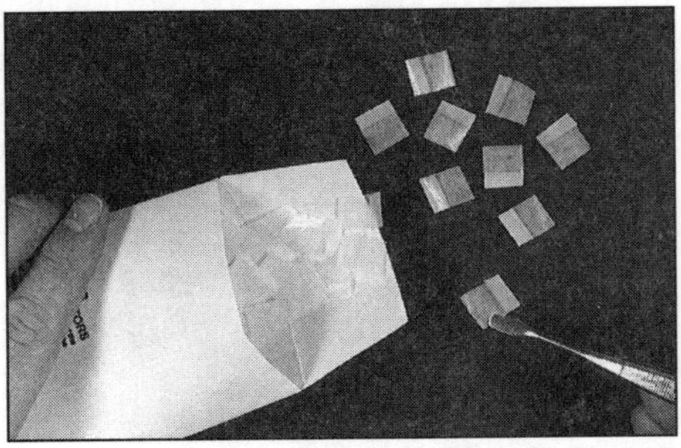

Many collectors use inexpensive stamp hinges to affix stamps onto album pages. Hinges are small bits of glassine paper about ¾ inch long and ½ inch wide with a light adhesive on one side. Most hinges are prefolded: about one-fourth of the paper is folded under, with the adhesive on the outside. Stamp hinges are shown in the photo in Figure 132. A package of 1,000 hinges usually costs a dollar or two.

Figure 132. Prefolded adhesive stamp hinges are often sold by stamp-hobby suppliers in packages of 1,000 for less than $2. Hinges can be used to affix stamps to stamp album pages.

Some collectors use stamp mounts for mint stamps (stamps that never have been used and have undisturbed gum on the back) and hinges for postally used stamps (stamps that have no gum or unused stamps that were previously hinged). As you learn more about hinges, you'll discover why.

There are four easy steps to using a stamp hinge.

The first step is to very lightly moisten the short folded side of the hinge with the tongue, as shown in the photo at the top of Figure 133. Don't apply too much moisture to the hinge. You'll actually dilute the adhesive if you do, and the hinge won't hold your stamp very well.

An overly moist hinge also will wind up moistening the back of the stamp,

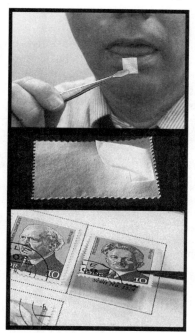

Figure 133. The short part of the folded hinge is lightly moistened with the tongue (top) and then applied to the back of the stamp with the fold close to the top of the stamp (center). Next, the bottom one-third of the long part of the hinge is lightly moistened, and the stamp is positioned in the album space. When the hinge is dry, the stamp remains attached to the page, but the stamp can be lifted to see its reverse (bottom).

causing that part of the stamp paper to expand or bow.

The second step is to position the moistened short side of the hinge on the back of the stamp, as close to the top of the stamp as possible without touching the perforation holes. The photo in the center of Figure 133 shows a stamp face down with a hinge affixed to the back. Notice that the long part of the hinge is sticking out.

The third step is to moisten the bottom one-third of the long part of the hinge. Once again, just touch the hinge lightly to the tongue: don't get the hinge too wet. Take care as well not to moisten the back of the stamp in the process.

When the long part of the hinge is moistened, it's time for the fourth and final step: placing the stamp onto the album page. Position the stamp where you want it on the page and smoothly press down the rest of the stamp. The hinge will cling to the page where it makes contact.

Once the hinge adhesive dries, you'll be able to lift the stamp to examine the back, if you wish, as shown in the photo at the bottom of Figure 133. Notice how the stamp swings up as though it is attached to the page with a tiny door hinge.

If you don't like the way you placed the stamp on the page, or if you accidentally put the stamp in the wrong spot, don't pull it up right away. That may damage the page or the stamp. Give the hinge about 15 minutes or so to dry completely. Then you should be able to gently remove the hinged stamp from the page, remove the hinge from the stamp, and start from the beginning.

Most hinges on the market are advertised as peelable, meaning the hinge can be peeled from the stamp after it is dry without harm to the stamp. Unfortunately, this description too often cannot be relied upon, so test your hinges first before mounting important stamps.

One way to remove a hinge from a stamp is to grasp the hinge at the top, near the fold, using stamp tongs. Gently tug the hinge off, either by pulling it smoothly from one side to another, or by rolling it down the back of the stamp. Stop if you meet any resistance, or you may begin to damage the stamp.

Anytime a stamp hinge has to be removed from a stamp, proceed with great care. With any luck, a gentle tug on the stamp should pop it off without undue stress on the stamp. That's the beauty of a truly peelable hinge. If the hinge is at all stubborn,

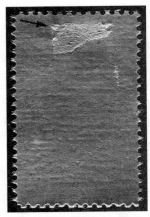

Figure 134. When a stamp hinge is removed from a gummed stamp, the gum shows a disturbance called a hinge mark. The removal of a stamp hinge created the roughly triangular mark at the top of this stamp.

you run the risk of damaging the stamp while trying to remove the hinge.

When a hinge is used on a mint stamp, the moisture from the hinge disturbs the stamp gum. That disturbance may be slight or it may be considerable. It will become apparent when the hinge is removed.

Figure 134 shows a once-mint stamp with a serious hinge-mark near the top of the stamp. Not only is the gum disturbed, but some of the stamp paper fiber has pulled up as well.

It's easy to create a thinned area of paper on your stamp by tugging on a stubborn hinge. Once the paper is thinned, the stamp is considered to be damaged.

If you need to remove a hinge from a stamp but it just won't let go, you have a couple of options. Some hinges will respond to the firm but gentle application of pressure using a blunt edge, such as the welded end of a pair of stamp tongs. Figure 135 illustrates this method.

With the stamp face down on a smooth, hard table, slowly and carefully press down on the hinge where it is attached to the stamp and rub back and forth, as though you were trying to scratch off the coating from an instant lottery ticket. Don't press so hard that you'll mar the stamp paper, and don't go so fast that you might bend the stamp.

Work on the entire area of the hinge where it is attached to the stamp. This action loosens the adhesive, and within a few seconds you may be able to roll the hinge off the stamp.

If this method doesn't work, dabbing at the contact point with a lightly moistened cotton swab or a small, clean, damp artist's brush may loosen the hinge enough that it can be removed.

Here is a warning, though: If used on a gummed stamp, the moisture method may also activate surrounding gum, and it can cause a moisture bump in the stamp paper.

Another option is to remove all unattached hinge paper by carefully trimming the hinge, leaving a small remnant of the hinge on the back.

Stubborn stamp hinges on postally used stamps can be removed by soaking the stamp in water until the hinge floats free. The stamp is then simply dried and flattened as usual.

You can see why some collectors don't care for using stamp hinges on mint stamps. The hinge disturbs the mint stamp gum and can be

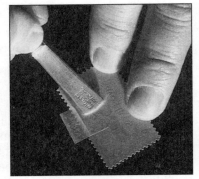

Figure 135. The application of gentle pressure with a blunt edge (the welded end of a pair of stamp tongs) on the surface of a stamp hinge is one way to loosen a hinge that won't peel off.

difficult to remove. For other collectors these problems are unimportant. They use hinges on all of their stamps.

Stamps that are hinged onto album pages don't get a lot of protection, so it is important to handle the pages with care. It is possible for stamps to fall off their hinges and for a hinged stamp to fall off the album page. Album pages always should be turned gently to reduce the chance of stamps flying from the page.

The album binder should not be stuffed with pages because this makes it easier for stamps to suffer damage or fall off because of pressure.

Although there are some problems associated with using hinges, they remain one of the most popular ways to affix stamps to album pages.

Hinges are available from local stamp dealers and from mail-order stamp-hobby suppliers.

Stamp mounts protect and display stamps

Stamp collectors have used many different methods to show off their stamps. A large number of collectors prefer to display their stamps in stamp albums. Some create their own albums using blank pages or pages they have designed, while other collectors use pages specially prepared by album manufacturers.

One important step is to place stamps on these pages in such a manner that they will be safe, undamaged and easy to see.

Stamp hinges often are used to keep postally used stamps in place on an album page. Some collectors also use hinges for mint stamps (unused, undamaged stamps with undisturbed gum), but many do not, because the moisture used to apply a stamp hinge permanently mars the gum on the back of a mint stamp.

For those who prefer a different method to show off mint stamps, stamp mounts provide easy viewing and do not disturb the gum on the stamp the way a stamp hinge will. Stamp mounts are specially constructed of a safe, flexible, lightweight plastic that is clear on the front so that the face of the stamp can be seen through the mount. Yet the mount is sturdy enough to hold and protect your stamps.

In Figure 136, you can see three stamps that are inside stamp mounts, along with an unmounted stamp and some loose stamp mounts. The mount is like a small envelope or pocket that holds the stamp in place. The clear front is solid. Many mounts have a back made of black plastic with a split in the middle. The split creates flaps that open up so the stamp can be easily inserted.

Figure 136. Stamp mounts are available in precut sizes that fit virtually every size of stamp.

A block of stamps is shown being inserted into a stamp mount at the left of Figure 137. The bottom back flap of the mount is opened by the collector, and the bottom part of the stamp is placed inside, positioned so that the face of the stamp shows through the clear front of the mount.

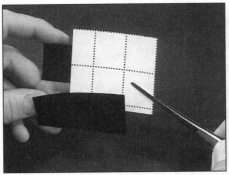

Figure 137. Stamps are placed in the mount through the split in the back (left). When the bottom part of the stamps has been properly positioned, the top part can be put into place. The back flaps close when released.

The top part of the stamp then can be positioned inside the top part of the mount, as shown at the right of Figure 137, and the back flaps close. The mount returns to its flat form, the stamp can be viewed from the front, and it has some protection from dirt, dust and damage.

Some other stamp mounts are clear all around, and the stamp slides into the mount through an opening on one side.

The mount has a moisture-activated adhesive coating on the back side that holds it to the album page. When the back of the mount is moistened it doesn't affect the stamp in any way, because the stamp is securely inside the transparent pocket of the mount.

Stamp mounts are attached by lightly moistening only a small part of the backing, along one complete edge, usually at the top of the mount. Do not use a lot of moisture when attaching the stamp mount to the page. Excess moisture will cause the page to lose its firmness. Also take care that the moisture does not get inside the mount, where it can touch and damage the stamp.

Once the adhesive is moistened, the mount can be placed on the album page, as shown in Figure 138.

The stamp mount also has been referred to as a "pochette," which in French means "little pocket."

Most modern stamp mounts allow the stamp to be removed easily and returned to the mount. The mount remains in place on the page as the stamp is inspected.

Stamp mounts are available in many precut sizes. Some are as large as entire stamp panes,

Figure 138. A block of four stamps is shown in a mount affixed to an album page.

while others are as small as the individual stamps shown in Figure 136. Mounts can be purchased in longer strips for coil stamps and cut to the length needed to create an attractive display.

Using many stamp mounts can be expensive, and there are some collectors who continue to use stamp hinges on common mint stamps because the cost is less than buying stamp mounts. There are also many collectors who put their most prized used stamps in stamp mounts because they feel more comfortable with the added protection of the stamp mount.

Many stamp album manufacturers offer albums and supplement pages that are described as hingeless. This means the page already has a perfectly sized stamp mount affixed to each spot, ready to accommodate a stamp. Figure 139 shows stamps on a hingeless album page, as a collector inserts a stamp into one of the permanent mounts.

With hingeless pages, the collector is saved the time and trouble of buying and sizing stamp mounts, but the hingeless pages also cost more money.

Here are a couple of pointers when using stamp mounts.

Most collectors mount stamps on only one side of the page. If stamps are mount-

Figure 139. Hingeless album pages protect stamps and eliminate the need for stamp mounts or hinges.

ed on both sides of the page, the edges of the mounts can snag on one another and damage the stamps when the album is closed. Mounting stamps on both sides of the page also gives the stamp album an overstuffed appearance.

Mounts are a little more difficult than hinges to remove from album pages, but sometimes it can be done with a little patience. Wait until the mount is completely dry. Remove the stamps from the mount, then slowly try to take the mount off the page by sliding a letter opener or dull knife between the page and the mount.

If you need to attach a stamp mount to a page with the split on the back of the mount positioned vertically, moisten the edge of the mount that will be nearest the outer edge of the page. That way, when the page is turned, the mount is less likely to swing open and potentially damage the stamps inside. An example of this mounting procedure is shown in Figure 140.

Choose a mount that is the

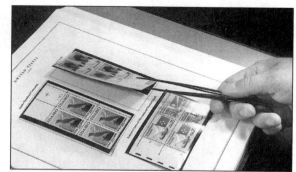

Figure 140. Only one side of the stamp mount is affixed to the album page. The adhesive along the edge of the mount nearest the outer edge of the page is lightly moistened.

right size for the stamps you are saving. If the mount is very snug, the pressure can damage the stamp perforations. If the mount is loose, the stamp is less secure and could slide out.

Most stamp mount manufacturers have descriptive size guidelines available to help you select the right size mount for your stamps. Your local stamp dealer should be able to help you with stamp mount information, and will probably have a good selection of stamp mounts and stamp hinges available for purchase.

By properly hinging or mounting your stamps, you can show off the items you've collected in a safe and attractive way.

There is a right way; here's the wrong way

Let's review the wrong way to save stamps.

You may have heard before that there is no wrong way to build a stamp collection, and in one sense that is true. You can create a stamp collection any way you please. You can choose to collect whatever stamps you like.

But there is a wrong way to save stamps. In fact, there are several wrong ways.

Postage stamps are pretty fragile items. Even the slightest bump or bend can sometimes damage the paper of a stamp. For that reason, it's always a good idea to use stamp tongs to carefully handle any of the stamps that you save.

When it's time to put stamps into a collection, there are several ways to properly protect the stamps you've saved. Stamp hinges and stamp mounts can be used to safely attach stamps to album pages. Collectors also can choose to use stock pages, stock books or spe-

Figure 141. Most of the stamps in the two albums at top left were affixed with transparent tape. Chemicals in the tape adhesive stained all the stamps, including the two German issues in the top right photo. The page containing the German stamps and many others is shown at bottom left.

cially designed glassine envelopes to hold stamps safely until they are placed into an album or on an exhibit page.

All of these important collector tools are available from retail stamp dealers or from mail-order stamp supply dealers. These items have all been around for many years, but all too often, new collectors don't learn about them until it's too late.

Years ago I was given some older preprinted stamp albums, shown in the photo at top left of Figure 141. I was eager to page through the albums, but I was quickly dismayed by the sight of rectangular brown stains on almost every stamp in both albums.

Although the albums contained some fascinating stamps, they were nearly all damaged by residue from aging transparent tape. You can see the damage yourself on the examples shown in Figure 141. In the top right illustration are two stamps from Germany, Scott 796 from 1959 (left) and Scott 810 from 1960. Both stamps have dark-brown stains in the center, where the stamps were taped to the page of the album.

The entire page is shown at bottom left in Figure 141. Every stamp on the page has the same kind of damage. There are a few spaces visible where the stamp fell off the decaying tape, but the tape remains on the book.

The tape was rolled and affixed to the back of each stamp. On some others, the tape was applied to the face of the stamps to hold them in place on the page.

All of the stamps that were touched by the tape are damaged. They have little or no value to most collectors or dealers because of the chemical stain from the tape.

The first wrong way to save a stamp: using tape of any kind. All tapes have chemicals in the adhesive that will stain and damage stamps. Often the taped stamp cannot even be removed from the book where it is attached.

Most of the stamps in these albums were postally used. A few were unused stamps that would have been classified as being in mint condition if the tape had not done its dirty work. One example is shown at left in Figure 142. The stamp is Japan Scott C40, an 80-yen airmail stamp from 1953.

On this stamp, the stain is not visible on the front of the stamp, and at first I thought perhaps it had been properly attached with a stamp hinge. Although hinges usually leave a small disturbance on the gum, they do not otherwise damage unused stamps.

Figure 142. Although the Japanese airmail stamp does not look damaged on the face of the stamp, the tape affixed to the back has disturbed the gum and left a telltale stain.

When I lifted the stamp with my tongs, however, it came off the page, and the tape on the back was quite visible (Figure 142, center). I was able to easily pull the dried-up tape off the back of the stamp and discovered the distinctive brown stain that remained (Figure 142, right).

Even though the stain appears only on the gum side, the stamp is still considered damaged, and as such is not a desirable collectible. It is also possible that the chemical in the stain will continue to damage the stamp paper, eventually appearing on the face of the stamp.

Undamaged, a mint copy of Japan Scott C40 has a catalog value of $5.50. With the tape stain, it serves as a minimum-value space filler.

There were many other similar sad stories in those two stamp albums.

Another collection that I came across recently was a pocket notebook filled with dozens of stamps from around the world.

From information penciled on the first page, I gathered that two fellows from Iowa maintained this pocket collection during the first decade of the 20th century. Those were the days before transparent tape, and many collectors unfortunately used another form of adhesive to place their stamps on pages: glue.

In a few cases, when the glue was water soluble, a stamp might be saved by soaking it in water. Much more frequently, however, the glue damages the stamp, not unlike the transparent tape shown previously.

In Figure 143 are two Portuguese stamps from the Iowa collection. The upper stamp is an apparently unused copy of Azores Scott 58; the faint red overprint "ACORES" is across the chin of King Luiz in the illustration. The lower stamp is Portugal Scott 71.

On the lower, postally used stamp, there are glue stains all around the edges of the paper. It's possible the stamp could be soaked off the paper, but the stains would most likely remain.

The second wrong way to save a stamp: using glue on any kind of stamp. Even new

Figure 143. These two stamps were both improperly attached to a page of a notebook. The collector licked the back of the unused stamp at top and pressed it onto the page. Glue was used on the lower stamp, staining the edges of the stamp paper.

"glue sticks" using a so-called "removable" adhesive are not recommended. It is possible that chemicals in the adhesive could damage stamps.

Apparently, to affix the top stamp in the Figure 143 illustration to the page, the collector simply licked the back of the stamp and attached it to the paper. The good news is that since chemical adhesives were not used, the stamp almost certainly can be soaked off the page and saved as an unused stamp with no gum. The bad news is that with full gum the stamp has a catalog value of $20. Without gum, its value is considerably less.

The third wrong way to save a stamp: licking the gum on the back and sticking it on a page. Mint or unused stamps with full gum are best saved in a stock book or stock page, or in glassine envelopes. If the stamp is placed in an album, stamp mounts will display the stamp without disturbing the gum. Stamp hinges can be used, but may decrease the stamp's value by disturbing the gum.

A few other wrong ways to save stamps have been tried by collectors throughout the years.

When "magnetic" style photo albums appeared on the market years ago, some collectors thought that the clear plastic pages provided a perfect way to show off a stamp collection. Unfortunately, the albums hold photos in place with thin lines of adhesive on the page, and the clear plastic cover applies additional pressure to keep the photos in place.

Most stamps that were saved this way have been ruined. In Figure 144 you can see one stamp from Czechoslovakia at right, and the tattered remnants of another at left. Both stamps were affixed to one of the "magnetic" style photo album pages. When the collector attempted to remove the stamp on the left, the adhesive on the album page wouldn't give it up, and the stamp came off in shreds.

The fourth wrong way to save a stamp: keeping it on an adhesive photo album page.

The truth is that many supplies and pages that are perfectly fine for other everyday uses are quite hazardous to postage stamps. Many papers and plastic page covers contain chemicals that can discolor stamps, causing damage that cannot be repaired.

Although high-quality stamp supplies may cost a little more in some cases, they will treat your stamps right. By saving and storing your collectibles in the proper environment, you'll be able to enjoy them for years to come.

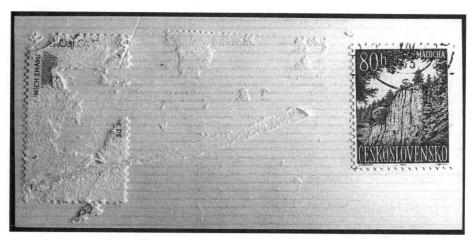

Figure 144. An album with adhesive pages designed to hold photographs proves deadly for postage stamps. Attempts to remove the stamp at left resulted in shreds of paper.

Ways you can save your self-adhesive stamps

In 1989 the United States Postal Service issued only one self-adhesive stamp. By 2000, that number had increased to 60 a year. Many countries began using self-adhesive stamps in the 1990s, and collectors began to wonder how these new-fangled postage stamps would fit into their collections.

In many ways, collecting self-adhesive stamps is not much different from collecting perforated stamps that have a lick-and-stick adhesive.

The first U.S. self-adhesive stamps appeared just before Christmas 1974. These experimental stamps were not without their problems, and it was 15 years before the next U.S. self-adhesive was issued.

The 1989 incarnation of the self-adhesive stamp was a pane of 18 25¢ Eagle and Shield stamps, Scott 2431. These stamps initially sold for $5, or 50¢ more than the face value of the stamps. The surcharge for the pane was explained as a way to pay for the extra cost of producing a self-adhesive stamp.

Customers also could order coil strips of the new self-adhesives from the USPS philatelic center for the same surcharged price.

Customer resistance to the idea of paying more than face value for stamps resulted in the Postal Service eliminating the surcharge.

The majority of early U.S. self-adhesive coil strips were sold only by special order through the Postal Service's Philatelic Fulfillment Service Center in Kansas City, Mo. Because many mailers now prefer self-adhesives, the Postal Service has since made self-adhesive coils available for purchase at most post office windows.

Self-adhesive coils come in roll sizes ranging from 100 stamps to 10,000 stamps. In most cases, collectors can buy single stamps, pairs, or multiples of coil stamps from the Postal Service. Collectors who wish to obtain a plate number example that appears at regular intervals on the coils usually are required to buy longer strips, as shown in the top photo in Figure 145.

For coil strips with a single design, most collectors prefer a strip of five stamps with the single stamp bearing the plate number positioned in the center. This is called a plate strip of five, or PS5. Some specialist collectors save strips of seven stamps or more.

When you purchase your coil stamps, ask the clerk to sell you a length that includes at least one more stamp than you intend to save. For instance, if you want to save a plate strip of five, ask for three stamps past the plate number. You will save the strip with two regular coil stamps on either side of the plate number single and remove the stamps that are on either side of this strip of five (Figure 145, center left).

If you put these removed stamps on another piece of backing paper, you may have trouble removing them a second time, so it's a good idea to have a couple of pieces of outgoing mail ready for those two stamps.

By removing those two stamps, you have plenty of room on either side of your strip of five stamps to carefully cut it from the rest of the strip. You can use scissors or a razor and straight edge (Figure 145, center right).

A good way to trim this kind of strip is to leave a length of backing paper on either side of the strip that is at least one-half the width of a single stamp. Your taste may be different, but don't trim the backing paper so closely that you might damage the stamps in the strip.

At the bottom of Figure 145 you can see two different plate strips of the 32¢ Flag Over Porch self-adhesive coil stamps that were issued May 21, 1996, and June 15, 1996. Similar methods can be used to save single stamps, pairs, or strips of any size.

Self-adhesive stamps have been issued in panes of various sizes. Shown in Figure 146 are a pane of 20 32¢ Pink Rose stamps, a pane of 10 32¢ Flag Over Porch stamps, a pane of 20 32¢ Riverboats stamps in commemorative format, and a pane of 18 32¢ Flag Over Field stamps. The pane of 18 stamps are specially manufactured to be the same size as a U.S. dollar bill. The stamps can be vended through automatic teller machines and are sold over the counter at philatelic windows.

Most U.S. self-adhesive panes include small paper strips that can be removed so the pane can be folded, creating what the U.S. Postal Service calls a convertible booklet. These removable strips may include plate numbers that identify the cylinders that were used to print the colors on the stamps. Collectors can search

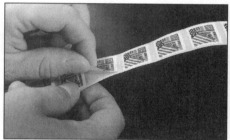
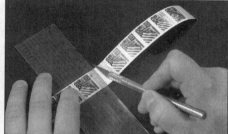

Figure 145. Long strips of coil stamps (top) can be trimmed to shorter lengths by removing single stamps from either side of the desired strip (center left) and trimming the strip carefully (center right). The plate numbers on these coil strips are located in the bottom margins of the center stamps on each of the two illustrated strips of five (bottom).

Figure 146. Self-adhesives in panes are issued in various sizes, with either commemorative or definitive stamps.

out varieties of these plate numbers for individual issues and try to collect an example of each.

Some of these number combinations have been difficult to locate and are sold by stamp dealers for higher prices. Of course, in such instances collectors keep the panes complete and intact, unfolded, with no strip or stamps removed.

Some collectors who prefer to save only a single unused example of these self-adhesives remove surrounding stamps from a central example, as shown in Figure 147. The remaining stamp can then be trimmed from the pane, again using scissors or a razor. The trimmed stamp is shown at bottom right in Figure 148.

Some self-adhesive panes include slits through the backing paper that make it possible to remove single stamps or blocks to add to the collection.

Coil strips, full panes, single stamps and multiples all can be saved and displayed in many different ways. Many collectors use stock books to keep track of recently issued items that have been purchased. Mint items can be saved in stamp mounts, as shown in Figure 148. The manufacturers of such mounts provide them in a wide variety

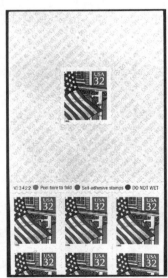

Figure 147. By isolating one stamp from a self-adhesive pane, the collector can trim the backing paper and save the single stamps, as shown at bottom right in Figure 148.

116

of sizes and widths to accommodate almost any item. Stamp mounts protect your self-adhesive stamps from dust and damage.

Postally used examples of self-adhesive stamps are also fine collectibles. The corners of two different covers are shown in Figure 149, each bearing a variety of Scott 2920, the 32¢ Flag Over Porch self-adhesive of 1995. The lower example is Scott 2920b, the small date variety.

U.S. collectors also

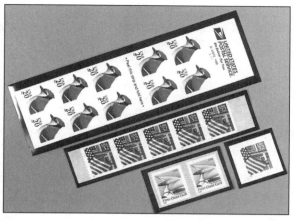

Figure 148. Stamp mounts help preserve and display the different sizes of panes, strips, pairs and singles.

watch for plate number singles on mail from coil stamps and selected booklet issues.

Postally used self-adhesive stamps can be saved on cover or off cover in albums or stock books. Self-adhesives with die-cut simulated perforations often have a straight edge on one or more sides, and collectors can search for varieties from

Figure 149. Shown here are two postally used varieties of the 1995 32¢ Flag Over Porch self-adhesive. The top stamp has the large year date near the lower-left corner of the stamp, and the bottom example has a small year date. Varieties like these can be saved on cover, or in albums and stock books.

various positions on the pane.

Soaking self-adhesives from stamp paper usually is no different from soaking stamps with water-activated adhesive, but some self-adhesive stamps from a number of countries, including the United States, can be nearly impossible to soak free.

Collectors have used a number of different methods to ease this problem, but have found only limited success. Unfortunately, it is possible for the stamp to become damaged when treated with one of these experimental methods.

A drop or two of dishwashing liquid in the stamp bath sometimes helps break down the tough adhesive. Longer soak times and warmer water have been used by others to remove self-adhesives from paper.

When a problem stamp shows up in your soaking, separate it from the rest and decide what you would like to do with it.

Stamps can be saved "on piece," which simply means you stop soaking. Dry and flatten the stamp still on paper, and mount it in your album with the neatly trimmed envelope paper all around it.

You can try one of the methods previously mentioned, but watch carefully for problems.

Most of the soaking problems associated with self-adhesive stamps affect the earliest issues. Postal authorities in many areas have tried to make their stamps more user-friendly for collectors by improving the ability of the adhesive to break down in water.

Collectors of modern postage stamps are learning that self-adhesives can coexist peacefully with the more traditional stamps in their collection. As postal authorities change the way they create postage stamps, collectors learn to adapt and sometimes change the ways they create their collections.

Show your collecting pride with an exhibit

If you've been collecting stamps for a while, you probably know that it can be fun to show your collection to another stamp collector or to family or friends who express an interest in your hobby.

Every stamp collector who loves pulling out his collection and talking about his stamps should seriously consider becoming an exhibitor.

Exhibiting a collection is the highest form of show-and-tell for someone who enjoys the stamp hobby. Developing an exhibit can help you become a more disciplined and informed collector.

Now, don't run away from the idea just because you think you can't put together an exhibit unless you own the greatest stamp rarities in the world. That line of thinking is totally wrong. Exhibiting is something that anyone can do, from the novice to the most advanced collector.

Let's look at what exhibits are all about.

The philatelic exhibit is a display created from a collection of stamps or covers (mailed envelopes, postcards and so on) or a combination of these and similar items, such as postmarks or meter stamps.

Exhibits are shown publicly at stamp shows all around the world, from the smallest local club gathering to the most prestigious international competitions.

Many exhibitions are competitive; that is, the exhibits at the show are judged.

Usually the exhibits receive awards or medals at various levels, and one exhibit may be selected as the best overall for that show.

For national and international competitions there are some pretty strict rules about the format of the exhibit and what kind of material can be shown. Exhibitors who compete at these levels have to know and follow the rules to attain the finest prizes.

The American Philatelic Society publishes the *Manual of Philatelic Judging* (Figure 150), which outlines specifics rules and guidelines for exhibits shown in APS competitions in the United States. This contains important information for exhibitors as well as judges.

For a collector just having some fun with his collection or who wants to create an exhibit just to show family and friends, the exhibit can be anything at all that he wants it to be.

In many ways, the exhibit is similar to the pages of a stamp album, except that you decide how things should be ordered.

The stamps and covers in an exhibit are arranged on pages, usually 8½ inches by 11 inches or thereabouts, but the exhibitor includes on the pages written explanations and descriptions of the items being shown.

The exhibit should tell a story, like you might tell a friend about your collection if he was sitting in a chair next to you. What is the significance of the stamps and covers you collect? Do they represent the activities of a specific country's postal service in a certain time or place? Can you help the person who looks at your collection learn something more about your collecting area?

It is a good idea to select a specific topic to address with your exhibit. Consider where your collection is the strongest, and try building your exhibit on that.

To get an idea of the diversity of exhibits, look at the partial list in Figure 151 of many exhibits displayed at the 2000 Philadelphia National Stamp Exhibition.

Manual of Philatelic Judging
How Exhibits Are Judged
Fourth Edition

Figure 150. The American Philatelic Society's *Manual of Philatelic Judging* can help an exhibitor learn the rules of competitive exhibiting.

FRANCE: SES ÉMISSIONS DE SEPTEMBER 1870 À 1875.	167-171
Presents the 1870-75 issues and evolution of their postal use in accord with historic events.	
Klerman Wanderley Lopes (Brazil)	
POSTAL FRENCH CAMEROON 1915-1958	172-181
Stamps & covers showing rates, routes, cancellations and special markings during W.W.II.	
Thomas O.Taylor (PA)	
CHILE 1900 SURCHARGE 5	182
Chile 1900 Surcharge 5 is the first surcharged stamp of Chile. This exhibit will acquaint you with its history, varieties, and usage.	
Alvaro Pacheco (FL)	
FIRST U.N. ISSUE, 1951	183-192
Comprehensive study of the first U.N. issue: printings, errors, varieties and uses - including precancel.	
Anthony F. Dewey (CT)	
CRACOW POSTAL HISTORY 1549-1849	193-198
300 Years of development and evolution of Krakow (old capital of Poland) mail service under various administrations.	
Frank M. Wiatr (CT)	
MEXICO POSTAL STATIONERY	199-207
Envelopes, postal cards and wrappers: 1876 to 1920.	
Richard Colberg (PA)	
● UNITED STATES PHILATELY	
FEDERAL MIGRATORY BIRD HUNTING STAMPS	208-214
The Federal Duck Stamp series shown with all known plate# singles, usages, and most errors and varieties.	
Charles Ekstrom (CT)	
U. S. BEER STAMPS 1866-1919	215-219
A chronological history of the stamps used to pay tax on beer from 1866 to 1919.	
Alan Cimiano (CT)	

Figure 151. Exhibits are listed in a stamp show program. Each exhibit shows a specific subject, but the subjects are quite varied and are presented in different ways by different collectors.

For example, one collector described and showed 300 years (1549-1849) of the development of the mail service in Krakow, Poland. Another built an entire exhibit around just the 1951 first stamp issue of the United Nations.

Obviously you can choose a large topic or a small one. The size of your exhibit can be large or small as well.

Most competitive exhibits are 16 pages or more, with some covering as many as 200 pages. Many stamp shows display exhibits in 16-page frames, so a four-frame exhibit presents 64 pages.

Before you start building your exhibit, consider going to a stamp show to look at how other collectors put their exhibits together. You may find that the presentations that you see will give you some great ideas about how you would like to handle displaying your own favorite stamp topic.

Each week *Linn's Stamp News* publishes a list of stamp shows taking place all over the United States and Canada. You can find a show near you by checking the weekly Stamp Events Calendar.

Most exhibits begin with a title page that acts as an introduction and lets the viewer know why the exhibit was created. The title page should tell specifically what is being exhibited and provide an outline of the exhibit. It can also point out the most significant items in the exhibit.

That way, the person looking at the display can start out with a good idea of what he will see and how it will be presented.

Figure 152 shows the title page from Ken Martin's exhibit "Blood, the Gift of Life." This exhibit has won several awards in national competitions. It is displayed on 79 pages.

Martin's title page includes two interesting items from his collection showing subjects related to his exhibition topic of blood donation: a postmarked stamp and an unused postal card. His title page also specifically describes how the philatelic items in the exhibit help tell the story of blood donation.

After your exhibit is outlined in the title page, the rest of the exhibit should present your collected material in a logical sequence that both informs the viewer and holds his interest.

Does it sound like a lot of planning has to go into the exhibit? It often takes exhibitors a long time to

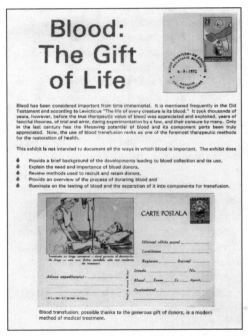

Figure 152. Many exhibitors prepare a title page that acts as an introduction to describe what will be shown. As shown here, it may include some material of the type that will appear in the body of the exhibit, or it may have only text to begin.

decide exactly how to arrange each page. Collectors prepare preliminary pages, make notes and outlines, consider how the exhibit will flow from one page to the next, and so on.

The exhibitor uses materials similar to those found in high-quality stamp albums: acid-free papers and safe philatelic mounts, all of which are available from stamp-hobby supply dealers.

The information on each exhibit page can be neatly hand-lettered, typed or computer-printed.

Every page of the exhibit should show philatelic items, such as stamps or covers, postmarks and the like. The best exhibits include original research and have a concise narrative.

As shown in Figure 153, judges look over the exhibits in competition and use many criteria to make their decisions, based on the guidelines in the APS judging manual.

After the awards have been decided, the judges often hold a critique session where exhibitors may ask the judges about their observations. The critique is open to anyone who would like to attend and is a very useful tool for any exhibitor, for it provides great insight into how judges view the exhibits and the type of details they look for.

More than 30 annual stamp shows around the country are known as APS Champion of Champions qualifying competitions. The grand-award winners of these particular shows participate in the once-a-year World Series of Philately, and the best exhibit of the year from a U.S. national exhibition is chosen from among those qualifiers.

For these national shows, exhibitors pay frame fees to help cover the expenses of producing the show. All of the fee and deadline information can be found in the show's exhibition prospectus, a printed list of guidelines that includes the application to exhibit. The prospectus is usually available from the show chairman several months before the show takes place.

Whether you decide to create an exhibit just for your own pleasure or if you plan to be declared the APS Champion of Champions some day, there is no doubt that as you create your exhibit you will learn more about the subject you've chosen to collect.

Every stamp exhibitor has to start somewhere, and the sooner you start, the more time you'll have to develop the skills to become a champion.

There are many great resources to help the prospec-

Figure 153. Stamp show judges carefully review each exhibit and base their decisions on established guidelines. They also answer questions from exhibitors at the exhibition critique.

tive exhibitor, and among these is membership in the American Association of Philatelic Exhibitors. Members receive a quarterly journal filled with very helpful suggestions from many exhibitors who share their experiences.

Plan to spend a little time looking through the exhibits at a stamp show some time soon. You'll find you will learn a lot about the stamp hobby, and you may learn that you, too, would like to become an exhibitor.

Chapter 7
Information for the Collector

Stamp identification

Have you ever visited Helvetia? Have you ever even heard of Helvetia? How about Shqiperia, Éire or SWA?

These are all countries around the world that have issued stamps. You can see examples in Figure 154. However, you probably know these lands better by the names Switzerland, Albania, Ireland and South-West Africa (which in 1990 became known as Namibia).

If you aren't familiar with the name Helvetia, you may wonder why the stamps of Switzerland don't have the name Switzerland printed on them. That's because many countries call themselves by names we might not recognize. Switzerland is one of them.

Three of Switzerland's official languages are German, French and Italian. The name of the country is "Schweiz" in German, "Suisse" in French and "Svizzera" in Italian. Helvetia is the Latin name for Switzerland, and it is used on the country's postage stamps and coins.

As if that isn't confusing enough, the name of Albania in the Albanian language is Shqiperia, as shown on the 1975 stamp at top right in Figure 154. However, 10 different spellings of that name have appeared on various Albanian postage stamps and overprints. Fortunately, they all begin with the unusual letter combination "Shq," which makes the stamp a little easier to identify.

Identifying postage stamps from around the world can be a monumental task.

Some stamps are very easy for Americans to identify because they come from countries that speak English, or because the names on the stamps closely resemble the English-language names used to identify the country.

At the top of Figure 155 are two stamps that have easy-to-identify names: At left is an issue from Canada, and at right is a stamp from New Zealand. Some of the other countries whose names on stamps match the English-language spelling include Argentina, Bahamas, Chile, Costa Rica, Malta and Mexico.

Can you figure out which

Figure 154. Can you identify these stamps with unusual inscriptions? At top are issues from Switzerland and Albania. The bottom stamps are from Ireland and South-West Africa.

Figure 155. Stamps from Canada and New Zealand (top) bear names that are familiar to English speakers. The three issues at bottom may be puzzled out with a little guesswork.

countries issued the three stamps shown at the bottom of Figure 155? The stamp at bottom left is inscribed "Belgique-Belgie." The name is close to the English-language name "Belgium," and that's where the stamp is from. The stamp in the center bears the name "Ceska Republika," which some collectors will recognize as the Czech Republic. The stamp at right is a pretty easy one if you know your Baltic nations: "Latvija" on the stamp is the name for Latvia in northeastern Europe.

Other country names that are spelled in a way that is similar to their English-language names are "Danmark" (Denmark), "Italia" (Italy) and "Romana" (Romania). Although these names are fairly easy to interpret, there are plenty of names like "Shqiperia" and "Éire" to trip us up.

Fortunately, stamp collectors can find some helpful resources to figure it all out. Sometimes the answers are available in general desk references. The *Merriam Webster's Collegiate Dictionary*, for example, identifies "Helvetia" and "Eire" in its Geographical Names section, but it doesn't list "Shqiperia" or any of its nine varieties.

The Scott *Standard Postage Stamp Catalogue* lists many unusual spellings in the Index and Identifier section near the end of each volume. The Scott catalog index lists some of the 10 spelling varieties of "Shqiperia" and identifies the country as Albania.

One reference work is particularly helpful for identifying worldwide stamps: *Linn's Stamp Identifier*, published by *Linn's Stamp News*.

Linn's Stamp Identifier, shown in Figure 156, is a 130-page softcover reference guide to the stamp inscriptions and overprints found all over the world.

It starts with a seven-page introduction that defines what a postage stamp is, because many of the items collectors try to identify are actually something different. The book cites as examples revenue stamps, local stamps, postal stationery

imprints, essays and proofs, cinderellas (which are stamplike labels), charity seals and similar items. A number of these nonpostage stamps are illustrated and described throughout the book, and there are sections listing locals, seals and labels, and telegraph stamps.

One 54-page section of the book provides an alphabetical listing of stamp inscriptions, including overprints.

The collector who encounters a large stamp bearing no country name but including the inscription "OFF. SAK" will learn that the stamp is an Official (government-use) issue from Norway.

Figure 156. *Linn's Stamp Identifier* **is a reference book that helps collectors identify where their stamps are from.**

A stamp bearing only the word "POST" and a number also can be identified using the alphabetical listing. Under "POST" the listing states "with posthorns in the four corners — Germany, Russian issue for East Saxony."

There are hundreds of other listings that help the collector figure out where his postage stamps are from.

The last two pages of the alphabetical listing include inscriptions in Greek and Cyrillic characters. The letters of the Greek and Cyrillic alphabets are quite different from the Roman letters used in the English alphabet. Greek letters are used not only on the stamps of Greece but also on the stamps of the Aegean Islands, Crete, Epirus and Eastern Rumelia. Cyrillic letters are used in many Slavic countries, including Russia, Ukraine, Bulgaria, Serbia, Yugoslavia and Montenegro.

Linn's Stamp Identifier also includes a 65-page section illustrating difficult-to-identify stamps. This section is particularly helpful for locating stamps with Arabic and Asian inscriptions.

Both of the stamps shown in Figure 157 are illustrated in the book. They may seem impossible to identify at first look, unless you're a specialist collector in these

areas. The stamp at left in Figure 157 is an issue of Saudi Arabia, according to the *Stamp Identifier*, while the stamp at right is from Japan, although it doesn't have on it the inscription "Nippon" that normally identifies modern Japanese issues.

Figure 157. English-speaking collectors often have difficulty with stamps bearing Arabic (left) or Asian inscriptions.

Overprints and surcharges on stamps can also be confusing, and *Linn's Stamp Identifier* provides a key to many of these as well.

One overprint example is shown in Figure 158. Many 1918 issues from Ukraine are stamps of Russia overprinted with a trident shape that appeared in the arms of the Grand Duke Volodymyr. A note in the Scott catalog lists Ukraine as one of a dozen countries that overprinted these Russian issues in one way or another, but the *Stamp Identifier* concisely pins down the proper country.

Linn's Stamp Identifier and the Scott catalogs are available direct from the publisher or from many dealers in philatelic literature.

Figure 158. Stamps of Russia bearing this trident overprint can be identified as early issues of Ukraine.

Many sources exist to determine stamp values

Many stamp collectors will tell you they collect stamps for the fun of it, but most are aware that those little pieces of gummed paper they save have at least some intrinsic value.

Determining that value can be significant for the collector who wants to buy a stamp at auction, from a dealer or a fellow collector. How do you know what you should pay for that stamp? Are you paying too much?

The Scott *Standard Postage Stamp Catalogue* assigns each stamp a minimum retail value of 20¢ for any listed postage stamp. Does this mean every common stamp you own is worth at least 20¢? Probably not.

The Scott catalog value reflects the retail price that you can expect to pay for a stamp in the grade of very fine with no faults. Generally, a stamp grade of very fine means the design is well centered within the margins of the stamp.

For common stamps, the minimum catalog value takes into account stamp dealer expenses for handling common stamps and preparing them for resale.

If you walk into a stamp store and request a common older commemorative stamp, such as the U.S. 4¢ Higher Education stamp of 1962, the stamp dealer is likely to charge you about 20¢ for the very fine grade stamp that he has in stock. The few pennies profit he makes on the sale won't go far toward paying the rent on his store, his insurance, his employees' salaries or his utility bill.

There's a chance you might encounter that same stamp for sale in a big box marked "FACE VALUE" the next time you go to a stamp show.

The fact is there are plenty of these stamps to go around. The stamp you find in the face-value box may not grade very fine, or it may sport some fingerprints or bent perforations. It's even possible it will be in great shape, and you can use it to fill an empty space in your album.

Some dealers can sell minimum-value stamps for just face value because they aren't catering to a customer's specific need. They don't have to watch for condition, they don't have to organize and carefully store the stamps, and they don't have to worry about replenishing their stock if they run low.

When a collector seeks out stamps that sell at retail for well beyond the catalog's minimum value, determining the proper value becomes more important.

Let's say a collector is putting together a nice mint-stamp collection of the

126

1922 definitive series from the United States. These are the stamps some collectors refer to as the "Fourth Bureau issue" because this issue was the fourth full definitive series printed by the U.S. Bureau of Engraving and Printing.

To begin with, our collector should determine the grade of stamp that he wishes to collect. While a stamp grading very fine (VF) is superior to a stamp grading fine very-fine (F-VF), it is also likely to be more expensive. The collector must determine what his budget can afford while planning a collection that he will enjoy.

A mint ½¢ Nathan Hale stamp, Scott 551, will probably cost no more than 25¢, even in very fine grade, but the cost of other stamps in the series is substantially more.

For example, Figure 159 shows the 25¢ yellow-green Niagara Falls stamp (Scott 568) from the 1922 series. In the 2003 Scott *Specialized Catalogue of United States Stamps & Covers*, the 25¢ Niagara Falls stamp lists for $18 unused and $32.50 never-hinged. The catalog listing for Scott 568 is shown in Figure 160.

Figure 159. The 25¢ Niagara Falls stamp of 1922. How much should you pay to add this stamp to your collection?

Why is there such a difference between the unused and never-hinged values? It's a matter of condition and a matter of supply and demand.

The term "unused" often describes a stamp that has gum on the back but gum that has been disturbed in some way. Even the small mark left by a removed stamp hinge will change a stamp's condition from mint to unused.

A collector who insists that the stamps in his collection have undisturbed gum often will have to pay more for the condition he demands. A collector who is unconcerned with minor gum disturbance can enjoy paying the smaller of the two amounts.

Remember that the Scott catalog lists retail prices that you may expect to pay if you purchase a VF grade stamp without faults from a stamp dealer. If you

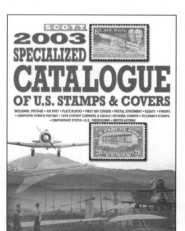

568	A171 25c **yellow green**, *Nov. 11, 1922*	18.00	.60
	green	18.00	.60
	deep green	18.00	.60
	Never hinged	32.50	
	On contract airmail cover		27.50
	Block of 4	75.00	4.00
	P# block of 6	240.00	
	Never hinged	360.00	
	Double transfer	—	—
	Plate scratches ("Bridge over Falls")	—	—
b.	Vert. pair, imperf. horiz.	2,000.	
c.	Perf. 10 at one side	5,000.	11,500.
	No. 568b is valued in the grade of fine.		

Figure 160. Catalogs provide detailed price listings for basic stamps and known varieties. Collectors need to understand what these prices represent to use the information wisely. Shown are price listings for U.S. Scott 568, the 25¢ Niagara Falls stamp shown in Figure 159.

want to sell the same stamp to a dealer yourself, he'll normally pay you considerably less than catalog value. If he didn't, he'd have no way to make a living.

The stamp catalog is just a starting point for determining values, however. Other resources can help you decide if the price you're looking at is too high, too low or just right.

Collectors also can consult dealer price lists, auction listings, advertisements and other resources when researching stamp values. After all, the more pricing information the collector has about the stamp he wants to buy, the better chance he has to make an informed buying decision.

For collectors of foreign stamps, the values listed in specialized catalogs from other countries can be useful, but it's important to understand if the values are compiled from retail price listings, if they are theoretical market prices, or if the catalog publisher is also a stamp dealer and the catalog is doubling as a retail price list.

When it's time to spend money carefully on stamp purchases, it's important to research the many differences between stamps. Often it is possible for collectors to find examples of similar stamps that sell for prices that are substantially different.

Consider all of the factors that are involved — grade, condition and scarcity — when evaluating your information. The stamp catalog is an important starting point for determining stamp values, but the knowledgeable collector uses additional information to find the best value for his money.

Stamp values are affected by many factors

What should you pay for that stamp?

There are a lot of different variables that affect the value of a collectible postage stamp. Every time a collector thinks about buying a stamp, he should keep several factors in mind. Otherwise, he may wind up paying more than he should.

Buying a stamp is not the same as buying, say, a can of coffee. If Store A sells your favorite brand of coffee for $9 and Store B sells the same brand in the same size can for $7, you'll probably buy that coffee at the lower price.

Figure 161. The $1 Woodrow Wilson definitive has a Scott catalog value of $6.75. There are many factors that can affect that value.

If you're in the market for the $1 Woodrow Wilson definitive, U.S. Scott 832, shown in Figure 161, you may encounter a similar situation. Dealer A may offer an unused copy for $9, while Dealer B has an unused copy for $7. A smart collector won't simply go for the lower price. Perhaps the stamp that Dealer A is offering is perfectly centered, while Dealer B has a stamp for sale with a slightly off-center design. Or, Dealer B's stamp may have a small fault that the collector needs to look out for.

The collector may decide that Dealer A's price is acceptable for the higher-quality example. Or he may feel that Dealer B is offering a better value, though the stamp is not quite as pristine. It is certainly possible that both dealers have stamps that are virtually identical in all respects, but Dealer B simply offers his stamp at a lower price.

Even before the collector looks at the different copies of the stamp that are available, he can begin to learn about the approximate value of the stamp. This will give him information he needs when selecting the stamp he would like to buy.

There are a few different ways that collectors can go about finding stamp price information. Stamp catalogs like the Scott *Standard Postage Stamp Catalogue* and the Scott *Specialized Catalogue of United States Stamps & Covers* provide values for stamps that have been issued by the United States and other countries. Scott Publishing Co. is not a retail stamp dealer, so the values listed in its catalogs are not prices for specific items. Instead, they are approximate retail values for the stamps described in the catalog.

The origins of the values that are given in the Scott catalogs are described very clearly in the introduction for each volume.

"The Scott Catalogue value is a retail value; that is, an amount you could expect to pay for a stamp in a grade of very fine with no faults.

"The value listed for any given stamp is a reference that reflects recent actual dealer selling prices for that item.

"Dealer retail price lists, public auction results, published prices in advertising and individual solicitation of retail prices from dealers, collectors and specialty organizations have been used in establishing the values found in this catalogue."

The catalog introduction also explains that "stamps that are of a lesser grade than very fine, or those with condition problems, trade at lower prices than those given in this catalogue. Stamps of exceptional quality in both grade and condition often command higher prices than those listed."

The Scott catalog value for the unused Woodrow Wilson definitive is given as $6.75 in the 2003 Scott specialized catalog. This is for an example with a grade of very fine and no faults.

The grade of a stamp is a description of how well-centered the design of the stamp is. In the Scott catalog, the grade of very fine is described in part this way: "may be slightly off center on one side, but the design will be well clear of the edge. The stamp will present a nice, balanced appearance."

A note within the United States listings also states that the catalog values from Scott 772 onward are for never-hinged items, so that attribute also would apply to the catalog value for the Woodrow Wilson definitive. A never-hinged stamp is one that has never had a stamp hinge applied to its back, so the stamp gum is original and completely undisturbed.

The factors that first influence what a stamp is worth begin with two familiar concepts: supply and demand. The supply of a stamp is determined by how many copies are available to the collector market. The demand is determined by how many collectors want to own a copy of the stamp.

The two stamps shown in Figure 162 help to illustrate this concept. At left in Figure 162 is U.S. Scott 359, a 3¢ George Washington definitive that sold April 18, 1997, for $1,400 at a Shreves Philatelic Galleries auction. At right in Figure 162 is U.S. Scott 529, another 3¢ George Washington definitive that is similar to the Scott 359 next to it. It sells, however, for about $3.

What's the difference? Technically, there are some small differences in the designs of the two stamps, in the way they were printed, in the paper on which

Figure 162. Though similar in appearance, the values of these two stamps are considerably different. One reason for the difference is the basic law of supply and demand.

they were printed, and in their perforation measurements.

The biggest difference, though, is supply and demand. There are fewer copies of Scott 359 available to collectors than there are of Scott 529. The supply of Scott 359 is low, making it rarer and more valuable than the more common Scott 529. As a result, more collectors are looking for a copy of Scott 359. This increase in demand for the stamp drives the price even higher.

After the collector reviews the published values for the stamp he wishes to purchase, he can use that information to look at the stamps that various dealers have to offer.

A number of other factors, along with supply and demand, can influence the price of a specific stamp.

The condition of the stamp includes any faults that may appear on the stamp. The more serious the fault, the greater the decrease in value.

Figure 163 pictures an example of the 1¢ Benjamin Franklin stamp issued in 1857. Under scrutiny, it appears to be the type IV variety, which is listed as Scott 23. A postally used copy, as described by the 2003 Scott catalog, is valued at $700.

The illustrated stamp is not worth anything near that amount, however. The stamp has a number of significant faults. Most obvious is the fact that the lower-right corner of the stamp is torn away. The perforation teeth along the left side of the stamp are worn short. The paper of the stamp is discolored and stained in several areas. The lower-left corner of the stamp is creased diagonally. The back of the stamp is heavily hinged, possibly covering a thinned area or some other fault.

Though U.S. Scott 23 has a catalog value of $700 used, the illustrated copy of the stamp has very little value at all, perhaps a couple of dollars, because it is riddled with faults.

These variables in value change from stamp to stamp, but major faults usually mean major reductions in value.

Figure 163. When a stamp has serious damage, its value may be dramatically reduced. Even small faults lower the value of a stamp.

Faults and condition problems that are far less noticeable still can reduce significantly the value of a stamp. Evidence of repair on a stamp usually lowers the value, as does thinned paper on the back or scuffs on the front. Pinholes or tears through the stamp paper also reduce the value.

Postally used stamps with heavy cancels marring the design often have lesser value.

Many collectors prefer that the mint stamps they purchase have no disturbance of the adhesive on the back. Detracting elements include hinge remnants or gum that has been disturbed because a hinge was previously attached. Often, a never-hinged stamp sells for more than one that was previously hinged.

The condition of a stamp also can be improved by various factors. For instance, the presence of a Steamboat cancel on a postally used VF grade Scott 23 increases the stamp's value; the Scott catalog adds $135 to the stamp's value for such examples.

The Scott catalog notes that "exceptionally wide margins, particularly fresh color, the presence of selvage, and plate or die varieties" also can increase the value of a stamp.

Even factors such as a dealer's overhead expenses can affect the price he will charge for a stamp.

The collector always should inspect stamps carefully before buying, looking for factors that make the stamp a good buy, or that might be reason to continue looking for an example that is a better value.

Different collectors have different feelings about what is acceptable and what is not when it comes to stamp buying. One collector may accept a lesser grade of stamp if the stamp has no faults. Another collector may be able to live with a nibbled perforation tooth if the stamp design is perfectly centered.

Comparison shopping is common for stamp collectors, but eventually the price that is acceptable is the one agreed upon by the seller and the buyer, and not necessarily what is listed in a catalog.

If the collector wants to purchase a specific stamp, he needs to determine for himself what price is acceptable for the stamp he is considering, using the information he has accumulated in research and an examination of the stamp in question to form that decision.

Where to start looking in the stamp catalog

Collectors use stamp catalogs to help identify specific postage stamps and learn more about them. Because so many stamps have been issued, though, the process of finding the information in the catalog at times can be challenging.

Stamp catalogs often follow similar formats. Stamps are basically grouped chronologically by country: The first stamps ever issued are listed first, and the most recently issued stamps are listed at the end.

If stamps from one set or series are issued over a period of time, however, they may all appear together following the first stamp in the series that was issued.

For example, let's say a country has a series of Flower stamps, where all the stamps have similar designs. The Rose stamp was issued in 1990, the Daffodil stamp in 1991, the Daisy stamp in 1992 and the Carnation stamp in 1993.

Instead of placing these four stamps far apart from each other in the catalog, the catalog publisher may list them together in one group, with consecutive catalog numbers, among the 1990 stamp listings.

Why do collectors need catalogs? There are several reasons.

Many collectors want to arrange their collections in a specific order, often chronological. To help with this process, the catalog tells when each stamp was issued.

Collectors who have a goal of collecting all the stamps of one country, or at least all the stamps from a certain era, use the catalog to determine which stamps they already have and which stamps they still need.

The catalog also provides some idea of stamp values, to guide the collector who purchases his stamps from a retail stamp dealer or who trades with other collectors.

Specialized catalogs help collectors determine the differences between stamps that may look identical at first but which actually have characteristics that set them apart from one another.

Looking up a stamp in the stamp catalog is often like looking up a word in the dictionary to find its proper spelling. You have to have some idea where to begin before you can find what you're looking for.

Let's use as an example the stamp shown in Figure 164. The first step is to identify the country that issued the stamp.

The central design of the stamp shows a crab. Along the bottom of the stamp is the inscription, "ÍSLAND 800."

Numbers on a stamp often represent the postage value, and that is true for this stamp. But what of the "ÍSLAND" inscription?

Figure 164. When faced with an unfamiliar postage stamp, the collector can turn to the stamp catalog to learn more about it.

Some catalogs, including the Scott *Standard Postage Stamp Catalogue*, include an identifying index that will help you narrow your search. As shown in Figure 165, the index informs the collector that stamps inscribed "Island" are listed in Vol. 3 of the catalog.

A look in the Vol. 3 index of the Scott standard catalog directs the collector to the page where the listings for the country we know as "Iceland" begin.

...aq [British Occupation]	.. vol. 4
Ireland	Vol. 3
Ireland, Northern	Vol. 3
Irian Barat	760
Island	Vol. 3
Isle of Man	Vol. 3
Isole Italiane dell'Egeo	Vol. 3
Isole Jonie	Vol. 3
Israel	Vol. 3
Istria	825
Itaca ovptd. on Greece	Vol. 3

Figure 165. A check of the catalog index points the collector in the right direction.

Why do the stamps of Iceland have "ÍSLAND" printed upon them? The official name of the country in the Icelandic language is "Lyðveldið Ísland," which in English means "Republic of Iceland."

Some other resources can help collectors identify the country of issue for various stamps, including *Linn's Stamp Identifier*.

We've traced the Crab stamp to the chilly reaches of Iceland, but we still

Figure 166. Some stamps, including Figure 164's Crab stamp, bear a small year date that helps to further the identification process.

don't know much else about it. Sometimes the stamp itself will help with a few clues.

In the lower-right corner of the Crab stamp, the numbers "1985" are printed in tiny type. This represents the year of issue for the stamp. The corner of the stamp is enlarged in Figure 166.

Many countries now include this issue-date information as part of the design, most frequently near the bottom of the stamp.

Although the catalog has numerous designs illustrated in the Iceland listings for stamps issued in 1985, unfortunately, none of them looks anything like our Crab stamp.

There is, however, a listing of three stamps with no illustration, which is reproduced here at the bottom of Figure 167. The listing bears the heading "Animal Type of 1980," which tells us we may be on to something.

Turning back to the 1980 section of the Icelandic listings, we discover a stamp shown with a design that is similar to our Crab stamp but picturing a dog rather than a crab. That 1980 listing is reproduced at top in Figure 167.

The Crab stamp is not illustrated in the standard catalog because it is part of a series that follows a set design format.

Just one representative design is shown the first time issues from the series are listed, in this case, a 10-krona stamp depicting the dog identified as "Canis Familiaris."

Following the dog's name next to the design is an illustration number, "A162." Other stamps in the same series that are listed but not illustrated in the catalog will include the same illustration number.

Look at the bottom of that 1980 listing. The catalog suggests, "See Nos. 534-536, 543-545, 552, 553, 556-558, 610-612."

Now let's look back at the original listing we discovered for the 1985 issues. Sure enough, the stamps listed there are 610, 611 and 612, the

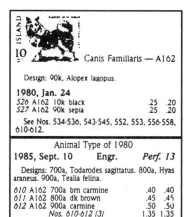

Figure 167. Stamp catalog listings provide information about the stamp, including the date of issue, value and catalog number. The listing at top directs the reader to check additional listings for stamps of similar design (bottom).

last three from the suggestion printed at the end of the 1980 listing.

The three stamps shown have postage values of "700a," "800a" and "900a." The little "a" in this case stands for "aurar," which you could think of as the Icelandic equivalent of "cents."

Our Crab stamp, remember, has the number "800" inscribed on it, and a check of the design descriptions in the listings shows the 800a stamp followed by the name "Hyas araneus."

To identify our Crab stamp, we can find the same name, apparently a Latin sci-

Figure 168. When the date of issue does not appear on the stamp, the collector must look for other helpful clues.

entific name, inscribed along the right side of the Crab stamp design.

Take another look at the listings for those three stamps. Each has the illustration number, "A162," but to the left of the illustration is an individual number for each of the three stamps. These are the catalog numbers — in this case, the Scott catalog numbers — that help identify the stamp.

The 800a Crab stamp issued by Iceland in 1985 is identified as Iceland Scott 611.

This may seem like a lot of effort to track down a single stamp, and sometimes finding a stamp in the catalog requires a little detective work.

Other times, you may locate the stamp listing easily without having to check back and forth.

It was helpful to find a year date printed on the Crab stamp, but more stamps exist without the year date than with one. Sometimes other characteristics can help with identification.

Shown at top in Figure 168 is a Swedish stamp that has no issue date printed on it, but it does have birth and death dates for the honored subject, physician J.J. Berzelius. Those dates are 1779 and 1848.

Sweden didn't issue stamps until 1855, so neither of the two dates on the stamp are the issue date. However, many countries issue stamps on some significant anniversary of the birth or death of the subject.

Since the stamp looks fairly modern, one might guess that it celebrates the 200th birth anniversary of the subject, which would have taken place in 1979. And a quick check in the 1979 listings for Sweden finds the stamp identified as Scott 1293.

Shown at bottom in Figure 168 is another stamp that needs to be identified, but in this case we have no dates whatsoever to help us. It's easy to tell the 4¢ stamp showing Walter F. George was issued by the United States, but when?

Sometimes it's possible to narrow down stamp identification using the denomination, which in this case is 4¢. The postage rate for first-class letter mail in the United States was 4¢ for 1 ounce or less between Aug. 1, 1958, and Jan. 6, 1963.

You don't have to know those dates to help you find the Walter F. George stamp in the catalog, but you can page through the U.S. listings until you find a lot of stamps with 4¢ face values.

Because the first-class rate is the one most commonly used, you'll find the Walter F. George stamp listed among the other 4¢ stamps. It was issued Nov. 5, 1960, and is identified as U.S. Scott 1170.

This method doesn't always work. For instance, the stamp listed as U.S. Scott 1169, just before the George stamp, is an 8¢ stamp showing Giuseppe Garibaldi. If you go looking for that stamp in the period when the first-class rate was 8¢, you'll come up empty-handed.

Some catalogs, including the Scott *Specialized Catalogue of United States Stamps & Covers*, include an alphabetical listing of the stamp subjects that can help you locate details about a specific stamp.

Most catalogs include a great amount of introductory information that is very useful for navigating the listings. Reading through the introduction to the stamp catalog is bound to increase your knowledge about stamps and stamp collecting. By making you more familiar with the catalog, it will also make it easier for you to locate the listings for the stamps you want to identify.

Perforations make stamp separation easier

I'm so old that I can remember when stamps didn't have perforations.

No, I'm not as old as the oldest U.S. postage stamps; they were first issued in 1847. But if you read on, you'll learn how I can remember when stamps didn't have perforations.

You may already know that perforations are the little holes that are punched into stamp sheets to make it easier to separate one stamp from another.

If you look at Figure 169, you'll see a single $5 Bret Harte stamp that is still part of a full pane. All around the stamp are perforation holes. With careful tearing along the lines of holes, a stamp can be individually separated from the pane. That's pretty easy.

Figure 169. The $5 Bret Harte stamp was issued in a pane of 20 stamps. The holes surrounding each stamp in the pane are the perforations.

In 1847 the story was a little different. The first U.S. stamps, a 5¢ stamp showing Benjamin Franklin and a 10¢ stamp showing George Washington, didn't have any perforations. This type of stamp, with no perforations, is called "imperforate."

These early stamps, and several others that followed them, were printed in sheets of 200 stamps. The sheets were cut in half and sold as panes of 100 stamps. When a postal customer bought stamps, or a mailer needed to use a single stamp, the stamp had to be cut from the pane using scissors.

Three 1847 5¢ Franklin stamps are shown in Figure 170. There are no perforations between the stamps, and if you look at the bottom edge of the stamps, you can see that they were cut from the pane.

Sometimes the person cutting out the imperforate stamps did a sloppy job, trimming off part of the stamp design. Some of these early stamps can be quite valuable, but if part of the design has been cut off, the stamp loses much of its value.

Figure 170. Early U.S. stamps, like these 1847 5¢ Franklin stamps, did not have perforations. They had to be cut with scissors or torn apart by hand.

Scissors can still cause trouble with stamps even today. Most collectors do

135

not like stamps that have been cut through the perforations with scissors or a razor. They prefer stamps that have been neatly separated by hand.

The first perforated U.S. postage stamps were produced in 1857, and since that time the majority of U.S. stamps have had perforations.

When perforated stamps are separated from one another, the stamp design is surrounded by points of paper that are called the perforation "teeth."

There have been many different types of machines used to create perforations. Rotary perforators are mounted on revolving cylinders. Line perforators punch the perforation holes first in one direction (for instance, vertically) and then in the opposite direction (horizontally).

Comb perforators punch out one row of perforations at a time. Each stroke of the perforator creates the top and side perforations for one row of stamps. With the next stroke in the following row, the top perforations also act as the bottom perforations for the adjoining first row, and the perforator continues through the full sheet.

Harrow perforators, used mostly on smaller sheets, punch all of the holes in the sheet with one stroke.

Sometimes stamps with the same design are perforated using different machines, creating a collectible variety. How can a collector tell the difference?

Using a special tool called a perforation gauge, collectors can actually measure perforations. The gauge is like a ruler that tells you on a given stamp how many perforations there are within the space of 2 centimeters. If the perforations are closer together, they will measure at a higher number on the gauge.

For example, in 1925 the United States issued a 17¢ Woodrow Wilson stamp, Scott 623. The perforations all around the stamp measured "perf 11," meaning that on this stamp, you would find 11 perforation holes in the space of 2 centimeters.

For easy measurement, the stamp is placed on the gauge, as shown in Figure 171, and moved up or down until the teeth of the perforations are all centered on the vertical indicator lines. The measurement is then shown by the numbers at the side of the scale. The perforations at the top of the stamp are being measured in Figure 171.

A 1931 printing of this same stamp design, cataloged as Scott 697, has slightly different perforations. While the side perforations still measure 11, the perforation holes along the top and bottom of the stamp are slightly farther apart from one another and measure 10½.

If you look for this 1931 stamp in the Scott *Specialized Catalog of United States Stamps & Covers*, you will see it is described as "Perf. 10½ x 11." Such catalog descriptions always list the horizontal per-

Figure 171. A special tool called a perforation gauge is used to measure perforations. The paper tips, called perforation teeth, at the top of the stamp are perfectly lined up with the vertical lines at the perf 11 indicator on the gauge.

foration (10½) first and the vertical perforation (11) second.

With some stamps, the difference in perforation can mean a tremendous difference in value.

Figure 172. The perforations are different on a sheet stamp (left), booklet stamp (center) and coil stamp (right).

Another factor that contributes to value is the condition of the perforation teeth on a stamp. If one tooth is bent, missing or torn short, it detracts from a stamp's value.

To remove a stamp from a pane or booklet, carefully fold the pane along the perforations of the stamp that you wish to remove. You can apply some pressure by running your finger along the fold, on the side of the pane that you do not intend to save. Avoid excessively touching new stamps that you intend to save, so you do not leave skin oil or fingerprints on the stamp or the gum. Reverse the fold and again apply light pressure. Repeat this procedure a couple of times, and then gently separate the stamps along the perforation.

The type of perforation that you find on a stamp can give you specific information about the stamp.

Three U.S. stamps depicting wildlife are shown in Figure 172. The 30¢ Cardinal stamp (Scott 2480) at left has perforations all around the stamp. It comes from a pane of 100 stamps. The 25¢ Pheasant stamp (2283) in the center has perforations at the top and left side of the stamp, and straight edges at the bottom and right side. The Pheasant stamp comes from a booklet. It is also found with three perforated edges and one straight edge. The 25¢ Honeybee stamp (2281) at right has straight edges at top and bottom, and perforations at left and right. It is a coil stamp.

These identifying perforation features usually are dependable, although there are a number of exceptions. For example, some U.S. booklet stamps in commemorative format are tall with straight edges at the top and bottom, and perforations only on the left and right sides, so they resemble oversized coil stamps.

Two other forms of stamp separation that all collectors should be familiar with have been used on U.S. stamps. One form of the 29¢ Flower stamp depicting a tulip was issued in

Figure 173. The 29¢ Flower coil stamps at left are separated by rouletting, a series of linear slits. They were issued by the United States in 1991.

1991 as a coil with a type of separation between each stamp called "rouletting." Figure 173 shows a pair of the Flower coil stamp with roulette separations at left and a perforated version of the same stamp at right.

Figure 174. Die cuts on U.S. self-adhesives can be straight, as seen on the 1995 stamp at left, or cut to simulate perforations, as seen on the 1996 stamp at right.

Unlike perforating, which punches out holes, rouletting does not remove paper from the stamps. Rouletting consists of a series of linear slits piercing the paper. The stamps separate from one another in a manner similar to perforation.

A single coil stamp with rouletted separations may look like it has straight edges all around. A closer examination of the sides of the stamp will show that the rouletted separations leave evidence of where the stamp has been detached from the adjoining stamps.

You can also find the 1994 G-rate coil stamp with rouletted separations.

Another form of stamp separation that has become very common is die-cutting, which is used to separate stamps on self-adhesive panes and coils. U.S. self-adhesives started out with straight-edge cuts between stamps on panes, but later issues have die cuts in a shape simulating perforations.

In Figure 174, you can see the 1995 nondenominated (32¢) self-adhesive Love stamp with straight die cuts at left and the 1996 32¢ self-adhesive Love stamp with die cuts simulating perforations at right.

And now you know why I'm old enough to remember when stamps didn't have perforations. Although some of the die cuts look like perforations, they are not. Again, no paper is removed when the die cut is created, so it is not a perforation.

I can show you additional examples of modern U.S. stamps intentionally issued without perforations, such as the 1989 souvenir sheets for the 20th Universal Postal Congress. The sheet shown in Figure 175, Scott 2438, has four 25¢ stamps that could be used intact for $1 postage or could be cut apart so each stamp could be used for 25¢ postage. An imperforate airmail sheet (C126) was issued during the same week, with four 45¢ stamps upon it.

If you find completely imperforate stamps today, check your Scott catalog carefully. If the

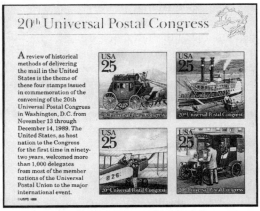

Figure 175. An imperforate souvenir sheet was issued by the United States in 1989 to commemorate the 20th Universal Postal Congress.

stamps were supposed to be perforated, you may have found a valuable error.

As the number of self-adhesive stamps increases worldwide, perforations may disappear from modern stamps before we know it. However, perforated or not, we will always have plenty of stamps to enjoy and keep in our stamp collections.

Overprints fulfill many different functions

When a new postage stamp is needed in a hurry, postal authorities sometimes alter an existing stamp to suit their needs. This commonly is done by applying an overprint.

An overprint is any printed marking or text (other than a postal cancellation) that is applied by postal authorities to unused postage stamps with the intention of modifying the original.

The most common form of overprint is one that changes the face value of the stamp. This specific type of overprint is called a surcharge. The two stamps shown in Figure 176 illustrate a typical surcharge.

In 1979 the island nation of Barbados issued a set of definitive stamps showing birds. The 28¢ stamp at left in Figure 176 depicts a blackbird and is cataloged as Barbados Scott 503. Nearly three years later the same stamp was overprinted (or surcharged) with a new denomination of 15¢. The new surcharged stamp, Scott 570, is shown at right in Figure 176. Postal authorities printed the new denomination to the right of the original denomination and added a large black block to obliterate the original 28¢ denomination.

Stamps overprinted with surcharges to fulfill a sudden need for a new postage denomination also are known as provisional issues. Some stamps are overprinted to reduce waste by giving new life to stocks of otherwise obsolete issues.

Some stamp collectors have complained that certain countries surcharge or overprint stamps simply to sell additional issues to collectors, but often there is a genuine postal need for the overprinted stamp.

Note that the surcharge on the Barbados stamp in Figure 176 is less than the original value. Overprints are often simple in design and easy to counterfeit.

Most postal authorities choose to surcharge stamps by overprinting a high-value stamp with a lesser value to discourage counterfeiters from creating fake overprints that illegally increase the face value of the stamp. There are, however, many surcharged stamps that properly increase the face value of the stamp.

Many of these overprints were created during the 1920s, when rampant economic inflation took its toll on some European nations. Germany surcharged dozens of stamps

Figure 176. The 28¢ stamp of Barbados from 1979 (left) was surcharged in 1982 to change the value to 15¢. A surcharge is any overprint that changes the face value of the stamp.

in 1923 with ever-increasing values as inflation overwhelmed the country and postage rates skyrocketed. As an example, stamps originally printed with a 30-pfennig denomination were surcharged at a face-value of 8,000 marks.

Because overprints can be easy to duplicate or alter, collectors should use caution when purchasing overprinted stamps of great value. Such items should be authenticated by an expert to verify that they are genuine.

Envelopes and postal cards also are known with surcharges. The United States began surcharging stocks of 3¢ envelopes in 1920 to meet reduced postage rates that went into effect the year before. U.S. postal cards also were surcharged in 1920, changing their value from 2¢ to 1¢.

Another common use of overprints is to authorize the use of postage stamps originally printed for use in another area, region or country.

During the period 1904-79, the Canal Zone was under the jurisdiction of the U.S. government, but mail from that region was sent using stamps bearing a Canal Zone inscription. On several occasions, U.S. stamps were overprinted for use in the Canal Zone.

Figure 177. Numerous U.S. stamps were overprinted for use in the Canal Zone. Shown is the 1922 $1 Lincoln Memorial issue (top) and an overprinted example.

The top illustration in Figure 177 shows the $1 Lincoln Memorial definitive stamp (Scott 571) from the 1922 fourth Bureau issue. Below it is the overprinted stamp created for use in the Canal Zone. The latter stamp is cataloged as Canal Zone Scott 95.

This overprinting technique also has been used when one country maintains post offices within another country. An example are Germany's stamps for its post offices in China from 1898 to 1913. The name "China" is overprinted on numerous German stamps of that period.

Country names overprinted on stamps can proclaim new independence (such as the Estonian issues of 1919) or reflect military occupation (such as Germany's stamps for its 1940 occupation of Alsace and Lorraine in France).

Overprints are regularly used to designate a new function for a previously issued stamp. Most often, this change is reflected by the imprint of a single word.

Figure 178 shows two stamps

Figure 178. Overprints are sometimes used to change a service designation. The 1973 50¢ Butterfly stamp of Tanzania saw use as a regular issue (left) and as an Official stamp.

from Tanzania issued during December 1973. At left is the 40¢ definitive postage stamp (Scott 40) and at right is the same stamp overprinted for Official use by government departments (Scott O20).

Overprints that name service designations sometimes can be difficult to interpret.

Figure 179. Overprinting may be used to add a commemorative inscription to an issued stamp. Shown are 1984 issues from the Cayman Islands. Both were issued for postage.

Danish stamps overprinted "PORTO" and Ethiopian stamps overprinted "T" are postage due stamps. Parcel post stamps of Belgium overprinted "JOUR-NAUX DAGBLADEN" are intended for use as newspaper stamps. Regular postage stamps of Spain from 1909-10 overprinted "CORREO AEREO" were used as airmail issues in 1920.

There are many other examples of how overprints can change the intended purpose of a stamp's use.

Some countries have used overprints to commemorate a recent event when there may not be time to create a new postage stamp. In such cases, existing postage stamps are marked with a message that announces the new subject.

Cayman Islands used this method in 1984 to note the meeting of the Universal Postal Union Congress in Hamburg, Germany. Shown in Figure 179 is the 50¢ Lloyd's List stamp released May 16, 1984, and cataloged as Scott 525. The overprinted issue at right appeared one month later and is listed as Scott 527.

Collectors of U.S. stamps will recall that this method was used in 1928 to remember Molly Pitcher on the 150th anniversary of the Battle of Monmouth. U.S. Scott 646 is a 2¢ carmine George Washington regular-issue stamp with the words "MOLLY PITCHER" overprinted in black.

Some collectors consider U.S. precanceled stamps to be a form of overprinting, while others argue that it is actually a form of cancellation and therefore not properly an overprint. Figure 180 shows U.S. Scott 1054A, the 1960 1¼¢ Palace of the Governors coil stamp in unprecanceled form at top, and bearing a Grand Rapids, Mich., precancel at bottom.

Figure 180. Some collectors consider U.S. precanceled stamps to be overprints.

The precancel is applied either by a local post office or by the stamp printer. Stamps with a precancel are intended for use by volume mailers. With precancels, a post office can avoid passing large quantities of mail through canceling machinery.

Overprint errors are an interesting collecting specialty. Some are scarce and can be quite costly.

In December 1995 Greenland surcharged its 0.25-kroner Queen Margrethe II issue with a new value of 4.25kr. Just a few of the stamps were accidentally overprinted with the surcharge upside down, as shown at right in Figure 181. The stamp with the inverted surcharge is a highly prized error that many collectors seek.

Some similar overprint errors from other countries are quite common and are not particularly valuable.

Figure 181. An inverted overprint is one type of error. A few of Greenland's 1995 surcharged stamps (left) were found with the overprint printed upside down.

Another type of overprint error is the omitted overprint. In many cases, this can only be verified if the error stamp is attached to a properly overprinted example.

In some cases, though, the stamp is only known in its overprinted form. When the overprint is omitted, the error can be verified because no stamps without the overprint were regularly issued.

The 1922 inflation issues of Germany again provide an example. Three of the surcharged stamps issued with roulette separations were never issued without an overprint, so examples of the overprint-omitted error of these otherwise common stamps sell for hundreds of dollars.

There are numerous other examples of how overprints are used by postal authorities to alter postage stamps, and varieties of overprints can make an interesting collecting specialty.

Details about many overprints and overprinted stamps can be found in the Scott *Standard Postage Stamp Catalogue* or in specialized catalogs for specific countries.

Check watermarks to identify valuable stamps

The watermark found in postage stamp paper can make a big difference in the process of properly identifying a stamp.

Some postage stamp varieties occur when identical stamp designs are printed on different kinds of stamp paper. One identifying feature of some stamp papers is a watermark. Collectors who encounter two otherwise identical stamps with different watermarks consider each stamp to be a separate identifiable issue.

A watermark is a translucent impression in paper that allows more light through the affected area. It is created during the manufacture of the paper by the impression into the moist paper of a molded wire form known as a dandy roll.

Elegant stationery items often bear a watermark that features the name or insignia of the paper manufacturer. This type of watermark usually can be discerned simply by looking at the paper with a light behind it. Watermarks also appear in some currency, including the redesigned paper money of the United States first issued in 1996.

Stamp paper watermarks show various designs, letters, numbers and pictorial elements.

Figure 182. Watermark patterns can include pictorial elements, letters or numbers. Shown from left to right are watermarks on stamps of Denmark, Trinidad and Tobago, and Italy.

Sometimes a watermark in stamp paper can be seen just by looking at the unprinted back side of a stamp. More often, the collector must use a few basic items to get a good look at the watermark.

Figure 182 shows actual photographs of watermarks in stamp paper. Each photo shows the back side of a printed postage stamp. At left is an 1895 stamp from Denmark, showing a watermark design of a single crown. The center stamp was issued by Trinidad and Tobago in 1936. It features multiple crowns and the cursive letters "CA" (standing for the stamp bureau Crown Agents). The stamp at right was issued by Italy in 1980. It pictures multiple five-point stars.

Each of these three photographs was taken while the stamp was placed in a black tray and saturated with a few drops of watermark detection fluid. Watermark fluid and trays can be purchased from stamp hobby dealers, either locally or by mail order. The fluid ranges in cost from $6 to $20 for a 3-ounce or 4-ounce bottle, depending on the brand purchased. Trays are inexpensive, usually costing no more than $2.

The chemical solvent in some watermark fluids must be handled carefully. Although most watermark fluids are nonflammable, prolonged breathing of the vapors can be harmful and ingesting the fluid can be fatal. All warnings printed upon the label of the watermark fluid container should be followed carefully. Children should use watermark fluid only with the supervision of a responsible adult.

The process of bringing out the stamp watermark is fairly simple.

Place the dry stamp face down in a clean tray or dish made of black glass or plastic. Apply a few drops of watermark fluid directly to the back of the stamp, just enough to fully saturate the paper.

Because the fluid evaporates quickly, look at the back of the saturated stamp and take note of the watermark pattern. Within moments, the fluid will evaporate, the stamp will be dry and you will not be able to see the watermark. If you need to review the watermark, you can apply a few more drops of the fluid to the same stamp, repeating the process.

The illustration in Figure 183 shows the application of watermark fluid. The bottle shown in the illustration is open because the fluid was being used at the moment the photograph was taken. Because the fluid evaporates quickly, bottles and containers of watermark fluid should be tightly capped whenever they are not in use.

Watermark fluid can be applied to either used or unused postage stamps.

Although a stamp will have the appearance of being wet when saturated with watermark fluid, it will be unchanged after the fluid evaporates, which generally

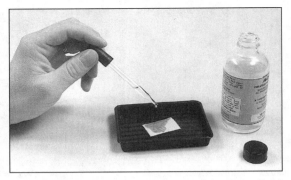

Figure 183. A few drops of watermark fluid applied to the back of the stamp will bring out the details of the watermark.

takes less than a minute. The watermarking process does not affect mint stamp gum. Watermark fluid can also be helpful in detecting damage to stamps, such as thins in stamp paper, tears, creases or repairs. When saturated with the fluid, these flaws are much easier to spot.

The solvent in some early watermark fluids could damage the designs of some gravure-printed stamps manufactured with fugitive inks (ink that runs when immersed in certain liquids). Most of these issues, such as the 1933-37 series from Netherlands Indies, are so identified in stamp catalogs. Today's fluids generally describe themselves as safe for watermarking all stamps.

Not all stamps are printed on watermarked paper. In fact, most stamp papers today are unwatermarked. Most U.S. postage stamps issued after 1917 do not have watermarks. The last U.S. postage stamps to bear watermarks were issued in 1938. Major stamp catalogs provide individual listings for stamps of similar designs printed on papers with different watermarks.

There are many examples where the value difference between two similar stamps with different watermarks, or a watermarked stamp and an unwatermarked stamp, can be quite substantial. The stamp illustrated in Figure 184 provides one example.

The £1 black Windsor Castle stamp from Great Britain was originally issued in 1955 as part of a four-stamp set. Each stamp in the set bears the St. Edward's Crown and E2R multiple watermark, identified as watermark number 308 in the Scott *Standard Postage Stamp Catalogue*. The 1955 £1 issue, Great Britain Scott 312, has a 2003 Scott catalog value of $110 in unused condition.

A second variety of the same stamp issued in 1959 was printed on paper with a different watermark, the St. Edward's Crown multiple (Scott 322). The 1959 issue is Great Britain Scott 374, and the unused stamp has a catalog value of $7.50.

A final issue of the Windsor Castle stamp (528) appeared in 1967 on paper with no watermark. It catalogs unused at $3.25.

The catalog illustrations of the two watermarks and the catalog listings for all three stamps are shown in Figure 184. The colors, printing method and perforation measurements for all three stamps are identical. To positively identify the £1 black, the watermark must be checked.

The word "multiple" used to describe the British watermarks in Figure 184 means the paper has a repeating watermark design that appears across each stamp. When just one watermark design appears on each stamp, as shown on the Danish stamp at left in Figure 182, it is simply known as a single watermark.

There are also "sheet watermark" stamps, where a single design covers an entire sheet, and each stamp bears only a portion of that one design (or sometimes no portion at all).

Watermarks are most frequently read from right to left, meaning that symbols or text, when viewed in the watermarking tray, will look backward. That accounts for the reversed "CA" lettering on the Trinidad and Tobago stamp shown in the center of Figure 182.

Errors and varieties of watermarks include reversed watermarks that read from left to right, watermarks that are inverted, watermarks that are both inverted and reversed, and watermarks that are sideways that are supposed to be upright.

Even using the simple watermarking method described here, it can be difficult to distinguish some watermarks.

Watermarks on stamps printed in yellow and orange can be particularly difficult to see. Viewing the saturated stamp through a transparent colored filter can help in some instances. Some experts recommend using a filter that closely matches the color of the stamp design. Other watermarks are simply very faint and are difficult to distinguish under any circumstances.

The watermarks on some U.S. stamps appear on only a small corner of the stamp and can be hard to spot.

Some collectors have used cigarette lighter fuel to detect watermarks, claiming that the fluid is less expensive and causes no harm to the stamps. There are several drawbacks, however. Lighter fuel is a flammable product manufactured with the chemical naphtha. It may leave a filmy residue on stamps, and its smell is awful. While it is inexpensive,

1955	Engr.	Wmk. 308	*Perf. 11x12*	
309	A133	2sh6p dark brown	10.00	2.00
310	A133	5sh crimson	35.00	3.25
311	A133	10sh brt ultra	70.00	11.00
312	A133	£1 intense blk	110.00	32.50
		Nos. 309-312 (4)	225.00	48.75

See Nos. 371-374, 525-528.

1959	Engr.	Wmk. 322	*Perf. 11x12*	
371	A133	2sh6p dark brown	.40	.20
372	A133	5sh crimson	.75	.40
373	A133	10sh bright ultra	2.50	1.75
374	A133	£1 intense blk	7.50	4.25
		Nos. 371-374 (4)	11.15	6.60

1967-68		Engr.	Unwmk.	
525	A133	2sh6p dk brown ('68)	.30	.30
526	A133	5sh crimson ('68)	.70	.60
527	A133	10sh brt ultra ('68)	3.75	*5.00*
528	A133	£1 intense black	3.25	*4.00*
		Nos. 525-528 (4)	8.00	9.90

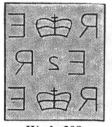

Wmk. 308   Wmk. 322

Figure 184. Although the £1 stamps identified as Great Britain Scott 312, 374 and 528 look alike, they are distinguished by different watermarks. The difference in value is substantial.

lighter fuel is not designed for detecting watermarks on stamps, and it is not recommended for that purpose.

A few mechanical devices also are used by collectors to detect watermarks on stamps. Such devices may be handy to have at stamp club meetings and shows, for they can be used without the application of watermark fluid, which is best done at home.

Collector reactions to these devices vary. While some prefer them because they eliminate the need for watermark fluid application, others have said that they are less reliable than the fluid method for revealing the watermark design.

Watermark detection is a very basic part of stamp identification. Your stamp catalog will serve as a guide to distinguishing similar stamps that are marked with different watermarks.

Most postage stamps have security features

As the use of traditional security printing procedures declined in the 1990s, postal authorities worldwide added a number of interesting features to postage stamps that are intended to foil attempts at counterfeiting.

Postage stamps are considered to be security documents of the countries that issue them. They are, after all, marked with a face value and are negotiable for specific services.

The early revenue stamps and postage stamps of the United States shared many characteristics with U.S. currency, from their portraits of honored statesmen to the fine line engraving used to create intricately detailed designs.

Shown at left in Figure 185, for example, is the 15¢ black Abraham Lincoln memorial postage stamp of 1866, U.S. Scott 77. The portrait of Lincoln on the stamp is not terribly different from the portrait of Lincoln that appeared for many years on the U.S. $5 bill, shown at right in Figure 185.

One important similarity is the detailed engraving that creates the portrait and was used in each case to print it. If you take a close look at the portrait on either document, you will see that it is created by carefully incised fine raised lines that show remarkable detail in Lincoln's face and in the shaded background behind him.

Printing presses are abundant, and creating counterfeit currency would be a fairly simple procedure if not for the special printing process used to create paper money. That same security process, intaglio printing (pronounced in-TAL-yo), was once the only way that U.S. postage stamps were printed.

The image of the stamp design was engraved in recess into a small piece of steel known as the die. Through a

Figure 185. The engraving on the U.S. 15¢ Lincoln memorial stamp of 1866 (left) is similar to the engraving on U.S. currency, such as on the $5 bill detail at right.

process of repeated image transfer, the recess design in the die was reproduced on a large printing plate that was fitted onto a special press. This process was used to create the elaborate fine detail and raised designs characteristic of intaglio printing.

It was nearly impossible to convincingly fake such intricacy, and postage stamps and revenue stamps resembled the security documents they were intended to be.

By 2000, many postal authorities, including the U.S. Postal Service, had mostly abandoned the craft of intaglio printing for their postal issues, being either unable or unwilling to invest in the quality and skill that their predecessors were able to accomplish more than 130 years before them. A few countries, including Sweden, Denmark, Slovakia and the Czech Republic, continued to create and issue intaglio-printed stamps with great pride.

Many postal authorities now opt to use the cheaper, faster and easier process of offset lithography, which transfers an inked image from various printing plates to rubber blanket cylinders and then onto stamp paper that whizzes through the press from a giant roll called a web.

Because these modern stamps have very little to distinguish them from decorative stickers that can be purchased at the greeting card store, postal authorities have looked for different ways to apply an element of security to the colorful postage labels they now produce.

Some of these security characteristics seem on the surface to have little genuine utility. The U.S. Postal Service, for example, claims that printing panes of stamps with multiple designs is considered to be a security component. Presumably it is more difficult to reproduce 20 different stamp designs than just a single design.

Many of the security features now employed in postage stamp printing are difficult to produce illicitly, but they are also difficult to detect without the help of special equipment.

As an example, some countries imprint special designs on their stamps using luminescent ink that can only be viewed with ultraviolet light. Indonesia is one country that has used this technique for a number of years.

Figure 186 shows a 1000-rupiah stamp, Indonesia Scott 1853, issued June 5, 1999. The image of the stamp at top shows how it appears under normal light. At bottom is an image of the same stamp exposed to longwave ultraviolet light. The insignia of POS Indonesia, the Indonesian postal service, appears several times on the single stamp.

Luminescence and phosphor tagging are used by postal authorities to trigger sensing devices in mail-sorting machinery, but the taggant also serves as a security device to thwart potential stamp counterfeiters.

Someone intent on counterfeiting Indonesia's stamps probably would not be dissuaded

Figure 186. A 1999 Indonesian stamp viewed with normal light (top) and under ultraviolet light.

by the presence of the POS Indonesia insignia, but if the bogus stamps do not contain the proper marking, it makes the case for prosecuting the counterfeiters much easier.

A number of other characteristics just as subtle are intended to serve as security features on postage stamps.

Microprinting is used by postal authorities in the United States, Canada and a few other countries. Letters or numbers are printed in type so tiny that it is virtually impossible to read the text without using a magnifying glass or microscope.

Figure 187 shows the 33¢ John & William Bartram stamp (U.S. Scott 3314) issued May 18, 1999. The word "BOTANISTS" is microprinted upon one petal of the flower in the stamp design.

If the design of the stamp is improperly reproduced by photocopying or some similar means, the microprinted text is rendered illegible in the process, making it easier to tell a counterfeit stamp from the genuine article.

During the 1990s, the United States also made use of technology that allowed a hidden image to be printed within the stamp design. To see the hidden feature that was encoded into a few selected stamp designs, a special acrylic decoder lens must be placed on the stamp and tilted at a prescribed angle.

Figure 188 shows two views of the 32¢ Wisconsin Statehood stamp of 1998, Scott 3206. At left is the stamp as it appears when viewed normally. At right is the same stamp photographed through the special decoder lens. A large badger appears to be floating in the blue sky above the farm scene.

As with microprinting, the hidden image cannot be precisely reproduced on a bogus stamp by using photographic techniques.

Some other security features used on stamps are less complicated and more obvious. A few nations, including Great Britain and the Netherlands, use syncopated or elliptical perforations

Figure 187. Tiny letters or numbers known as microprinting can be seen only with magnification. Microprinting is hard to reproduce.

Figure 188. Hidden images can be detected in select U.S. stamps using a special decoder lens. The lens reveals a badger on the 1998 32¢ Wisconsin Statehood stamp (right).

Figure 189. Several security features were incorporated in Britain's £10 Britannia stamp issued in 1993 (left). The German semipostal at right includes a hologram in its design.

that interrupt the normal pattern of perforation holes. Large oval-shaped syncopated perforations can be seen along the top and bottom of Britain's 1993 £10 Britannia high-value stamp, Scott 1478, pictured at left in Figure 189.

This same stamp uses granite paper, which contains visible colored threads or fibers. The paper is specially made to print stamps and is not readily available to potential stamp fakers.

The Britannia stamp also uses an optically variable ink to print the queen's profile in the upper-right corner. When the stamp is tilted slightly, the metallic color of the queen's image appears to change from one color to another.

This stamp also includes multicolored microprinting, embossed braille lettering and phosphor tagging. Some of these security features, including embossing and granite paper, have been used by various stamp printers for many decades.

Some other traditional forms of security, including watermarks in stamp paper and the precise measurement of perforation holes, also are used by some of today's stamp contractors.

New technology has created perhaps the flashiest security feature of them all: the holographic image, which uses lasers to convey a silvery three-dimensional image on a two-dimensional stamp. Shown at right in Figure 189 is a hologram stamp issued by Germany in October 1999. The 300-pfennig+100pf semipostal stamp is identified as Scott B859. The holographic effect is lost in the reproduction shown here, which demonstrates how the hologram, while being a fascinating decorative element, also serves to make counterfeiting the postage stamp much more difficult.

While the security features of most postage stamps are not as obvious as a gleaming holographic image, nearly all postal adhesives can claim some added measure of security.

Though our stamps may no longer convey the noble dignity of security documents of the 19th century, postal authorities continue to use different means to protect the integrity of the stamps they produce today.

Buyer beware: the fake stamps are out there

Beware. They're out there. Without your knowledge, they may already be in your own collection. They are fakes and forgeries, counterfeits, altered stamps

149

and covers. Some collectors call them album weeds.

If you think the problem of phony stamps and covers is small and can't affect you, think again. Even experienced stamp collectors can be swindled by a more experienced scam artist, one who alters a common stamp or cover to make it seem much more valuable than it really is. And many veteran stamp dealers don't realize that some of the inexpensive stamps they're carrying in their stock books aren't genuine.

There are so many different kinds of alterations, stamp forgeries and counterfeit issues that dozens of books and hundreds of articles have been written about them.

Stamp collectors are affected by fakes and forgeries in two very different ways. First of all, the collector has to be aware these items exist to avoid being deceived into buying fake stamps that are offered as the real thing. And secondly, many fakes and forgeries, when properly identified, can make an interesting addition to a stamp collection.

Yes, a number of collectors, at an appropriate price, add forgeries to their albums intentionally, not for purposes of fraud but to study the continuing history of the stamp hobby in one of its more unusual areas.

To begin with, let's dispel the common notion that only expensive stamps are faked. A swindler may be able to make an illegal profit by creating a fraud that looks like a valuable stamp, but that's not the only reason fakes are created.

In the introduction to *Linn's Focus on Forgeries*, author Varro E. Tyler notes that stamps cataloging for $50 or less "have been most commonly forged, usually to supply different varieties

Figure 190. *Linn's Focus on Forgeries* by Varro E. Tyler provides comparisons of forged common stamps and genuine issues. Shown here are a forgery of Uruguay's 1926 20¢ airmail issue (left) and a genuine stamp.

for the packet trade." Tyler even notes that one obstacle he sometimes encounters in his study of forged stamps is that he has difficulty finding the genuine stamp he needs for comparison, because the forgeries abound and the genuine stamps are scarce.

Tyler's book compares the genuine stamp side-by-side with the forgery. Tyler points out with clear illustrations and a precise description exactly how a collector can tell the difference.

One deceptive forgery from the 321 different examples scrutinized in the book is illustrated in Figure 190. It is an imitation of the 1926 20¢ airmail issue from Uruguay. Can you tell the difference between the fake and the actual stamp?

In the illustration (shown here reduced in size), the forgery is shown at left and the genuine stamp at right. The description that accompanies the photographs in the book points out that in this case, the forgery includes a distinct notch of color in the upper edge of the wing of the albatross shown in the design. A photographic enlargement of the important area, also shown here in Figure 190, points out the difference.

There are two basic types of stamp forgeries, created for two different reasons.

A philatelic forgery, such as that of the stamp from Uruguay in Figure 190, is usually created with the intent to defraud or deceive the stamp collector.

In addition to these deceptive items, some stamp dealers of decades ago created what they called "facsimiles," unofficial reproductions of postage stamps that collectors could purchase to fill the empty spaces on their album pages. Many of these facsimilies included some type of inscription or marking to indicate they were not true stamps, such as the words "facsimile" or "falsch" (German for "false"). The word may be part of the stamp design, or it may be found stamped somewhere on the front or back.

The second type of forgery is the postal forgery, which is a stamp forgery created with the intention to defraud the government or postal administration. Postal forgeries are commonly referred to as counterfeit stamps, and often they

Figure 191. Postal forgeries are generally not created to defraud collectors. Like this counterfeit stamp from Nigeria, many postal forgeries are used to avoid paying postage fees.

are discovered on mailed envelopes and parcels.

Examples of counterfeit stamps are uncovered regularly.

In the April 2000 issue of *German Postal Specialist*, the monthly journal of the Germany Philatelic Society, Rudolf Anders reported on several postal forgeries of recent German stamps.

During the 1990s, a flood of mail promoting a mail-fraud scheme was sent to addresses around the world in similar brown envelopes franked with forgeries of Nigeria Scott 560B, the 50-naira Rock Bridge stamp released May 23, 1990. One such envelope bearing a counterfeit stamp is shown here in Figure 191.

Some collectors who received such a mailing have saved the envelope and its contents, knowing full well the stamp on the cover is a crude fake, probably created on a color photocopier.

A dangerous problem for stamp collectors the world over is that of genuine common stamps altered to look like something more rare and valuable. Often this deception is created either by adding or removing characteristics from the common stamp to make it look like a rarity.

Any single common perforated stamp with wide margins, for example, may have its perforations trimmed away by a faker to create the impression that the stamp is a scarce imperforate error.

Collectors always need to be wary of this type of scam and should proceed cautiously when considering purchasing a single stamp promoted as an imperforate error. For this reason, stamp dealers selling genuine imperforate errors often offer them as unsevered pairs or blocks that more clearly show they are genuine.

Figure 192 shows a dangerous altered stamp on a fairly

Figure 192. Altered stamps and covers are often created from a common, inexpensive genuine item. This 18¢ Flag coil has a small "6" falsely added to the bottom of the stamp design, making it resemble a scarce plate number coil stamp.

common first-day cover.

The 18¢ Flag coil of 1981 was the first U.S. coil stamp issued under a new U.S. Postal Service policy that added plate numbers at the bottom of individual stamps at established intervals. Before long it became obvious that plate number 6 of the 1981 Flag coil was quite a rarity.

A first-day cover bearing a single plate number 6 of this coil would be a terrific find, so one faker decided to create some on his own, using a plain, unnumbered stamp of the same issue. A small "6" was simply added to the bottom of the stamp at the position where a genuine plate number would be found.

Police experts examining one of these covers brought to their attention discovered it was a fake and took steps to halt production of more.

What can the collector do to protect himself from dangerous fakes and forgeries?

It's important to read about faked items whenever such news stories appear, for similar techniques often are used repeatedly to create different kinds of fakes.

Stamp collectors always should closely examine the stamps they are buying, particularly as the value or rarity of the stamp increases. On valuable items, collectors should insist on receiving a certificate of authenticity from an established expertizing firm or organization. In the United States, major expertizers include the American Philatelic Expertizing Service, the Philatelic Foundation, and Professional Stamp Experts.

Stamp experts associated with these organizations render opinions on the authenticity of stamps and issue a certificate with an accompanying photograph that describes the stamp and identifies any flaws that are found. They may note alterations to stamps, such as the addition of new gum to make the stamp appear never-hinged, the reperforation of one or more sides to make the stamp seem like a scarce variety, the hidden repair of damaged areas, the removal of a cancel from a stamp to make it look unused, or the addition of a faked scarce cancel or other postal marking on a cover to make the item appear more valuable.

Experts of the Royal Philatelic Society of London in 1999 examined a stamp purported to be an 1856 1¢ Magenta from British Guiana. Only one existing stamp in the world has been accepted as a genuine 1¢ Magenta; it is shown at top in Figure 193. The contender that hoped to share the title is shown below it.

After submitting the more recent find to high-powered microscopic examination, the expert committee of the Royal declared the stamp was a fake bearing characteristics of an altered 4¢ Magenta printed around the same time.

Of course, there are fees associated with highly specialized work such as expertization. Collectors interested in learning more should contact the

Figure 193. Are they real or fake? Only the experts can say. At top is the genuine British Guiana 1¢ Magenta, and at bottom is a very similar stamp described by experts as a forgery.

expertizing groups for additional information.

There are far too many ways for stamps to be faked for the collector to accept every item at face value. Armed with knowledge and ready to give careful scrutiny, the collector has a chance to avoid the album weeds and accept only the genuine articles for his collection.

Stamp hobby offers a lot of good reading

Why spend good money reading about stamps when you could spend that money buying stamps instead? Here's one reason: The money you spend to read about stamps can save you a lot of money when you do your stamp shopping.

Reading about stamps can also profit you in another way: You'll know a lot more about what you're collecting. Your collection will turn out better as a result, and you're bound to get more enjoyment out of your hobby.

Brothers L. Norman and Maurice Williams once wrote in *Stamp Review* that "more journals are devoted to philately than to any other hobby." That statement still may be accurate, as dozens of stamp societies large and small create a wide range of publications for collectors to enjoy. The Williams brothers rank among the pre-eminent stamp writers in history. Maurice Williams died in 1976, and his brother Norman died in 1999.

In the *Stamp Review* article, the Williamses reported that the first philatelic periodical was "a small monthly of eight pages, published at one penny. The paper was called *The Monthly Advertiser*, and it was published by Edward Moore & Co., of Liverpool. The first number appeared on December 15, 1862, and the first editorial stated that 'Postage Stamp collectors and dealers have long felt the want of a publication which should devote itself entirely to their interests, and serve as a medium for their advertisements.' "

This kind of commercial publication continues today in many forms. One example is the weekly stamp hobby newspaper *Linn's Stamp News*.

More commercial stamp hobby publications are shown in Figure 194. The illustration pictures monthly magazines from Germany and Great Britain, as well as *Scott Stamp Monthly*, which like *Linn's* is published by Amos Hobby Publishing of Sidney, Ohio. All of these publications provide news and feature articles about the stamp hobby, though each presents the information with a different perspective.

News articles often provide readers with information that can save them money while they are shopping for stamps. *Linn's* readers regularly learn of new stamps being issued by U.S. and worldwide postal authorities long before such items are announced in mail-order catalogs

Figure 194. Commercial periodicals report on general-interest collecting topics. Shown are monthly and weekly publications from around the world, including *Linn's Stamp News.*

and other publications. Often this gives them an opportunity to pick up hard-to-find items while they are still available.

Collectors also enjoy looking through a great selection of advertisements from stamp dealers. By reading the ads in *Linn's*, *Scott Stamp Monthly* and other stamp-hobby publications, the collector can find the best stamp deals and learn about collectibles that may not be advertised elsewhere.

Journals published by stamp-collecting societies provide the collector with details of new research and discoveries in specialized collecting fields.

Figure 195. Stamp-collecting societies publish many journals or newsletters that contain articles on specialty areas of the stamp hobby.

Many different collector groups exist within the stamp hobby. Most of these groups publish regular journals, such as those shown in Figure 195. The valuable specialized information found in these journals is often not available in general-interest publications.

Stamp catalogs are another valuable resource for the collector. General world-wide catalogs provide basic listings for stamps issued by countries all over the globe. Specialized catalogs present in-depth details about stamps issued by a single country or within a single specialty area. Many stamp catalogs, including those shown in Figure 196, are published commercially. Others are created by postal authorities or specialty stamp societies.

Collectors can find a wealth of information in stamp catalogs, including where and when a stamp was issued, approximate retail values, descriptions of varieties and much more.

Catalogs are generally available from stamp dealers and specialty dealers who advertise in philatelic literature. Some catalogs are available for purchase direct from the publisher.

Many dealers in stamp-hobby literature also carry reference books

Figure 196. Stamp catalogs are important reference works for collectors. Catalogs can be general or specialized in nature.

Figure 197. Books on the subject of stamp collecting are available from stamp-hobby literature dealers. The subjects range from specialized research to general historical references and more.

and other publications for the stamp collector. Just a few are shown in the photo in Figure 197. Some of these books include research compiled by a single collector or a group and provide background and details on a specific collecting area. Others may give historical perspectives or simply provide basic stamp-collecting information. There are many books for beginner collectors as well as for experts.

A number of books published by *Linn's Stamp News* are available from dealers or direct from the publisher.

Auction catalogs are yet another type of philatelic literature. Auction catalogs list stamps and covers that are being sold through auction at a set date. A collector can learn a lot by reading through various auction catalogs and the listings of the prices realized.

Auction catalogs, such as those pictured in Figure 198, often show which stamp varieties are bringing high prices at auctions and give the collector a broader view of the many stamps and covers that are available. Some auction houses specialize in stamps of a specific area, such as Great Britain, Asia, early United States, and so on.

Occasionally a special auction catalog will be produced when a highly prized collection is placed on sale. Some of these catalogs are known as the definitive reference work for some of the world's great stamp gems.

Two such sales were the 1995 Honolulu Advertiser sale of Hawaiian rarities and the 1998 auction of the Robert Zoellner collection of United States stamps, which included the sale of the only example of the 1868 1¢ blue Benjamin Franklin Z grill in private hands.

While some auction catalogs are provided free of

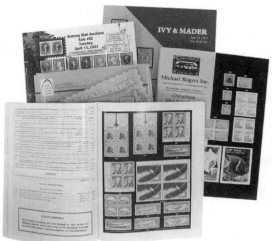

Figure 198. Auction catalogs are created to describe stamps that are offered for sale, but they are also useful for learning more about the many types of stamps that are available.

charge to prospective buyers, many are sold for a fee to cover the costs of printing and distribution. Auction houses regularly advertise throughout the pages of *Linn's*.

A quickly growing source of stamp-hobby information is the World Wide Web on the Internet. Computer users tap into this network of information sites to view details about everything imaginable, including stamps and stamp collecting. Collectors can find many specialized stamp-hobby sites on the Internet, as well as information direct from postal authorities.

With this incredible wealth of information available, the collector has to decide what he wants to read and what he wants to save.

Auction catalogs, newspapers, magazines and journals can pile up quickly, leaving little space for anything else.

Many collectors create clipping files by cutting out articles and pages that are of interest to them. They keep a number of files with relevant headings, such as "Swedish booklet stamps," "Trans-Mississippi issue of 1898" or "Stamp printing techniques." This method saves space and keeps information organized and easy to find. Other collectors keep articles or photocopies in loose-leaf notebooks.

Stamp collectors are often inquisitive individuals, and reading about stamps and the stamp hobby gives the collector an opportunity to fulfill that desire for knowledge.

Stamp societies exist for many specialties

So you're a stamp collector? Join the club.

And you can believe that there are plenty of clubs to choose from. To start out with, local stamp groups can be found in cities throughout the world. These neighborhood clubs give collectors a chance to regularly meet with others who enjoy the hobby as much as they do.

Something many collectors don't realize is that there are also a tremendous number of specialty groups that accept members from just about everywhere. While many of these groups hold meetings from time to time at different locations, most of their members never attend those meetings. Instead, they learn about the group's activities through regular journals or newsletters.

These journals provide news and articles that specifically appeal to collectors with a specific area of interest.

If you're a collector of the stamps or postal history from Germany, for instance, the Germany Philatelic Society provides its members with a journal, *German Postal Specialist*, which is published six times per year. Members read about new stamps from Germany, specialist studies on new and classic issues, new postal history discoveries and much more.

The November-December 1998 issue of *German Postal Specialist* shown in Figure 199 includes an article by Gunter Bechtold describing a very rare use of Germany's perforated 50 million mark stamp of 1923. The postcard that prompted the feature is shown here at right in Figure 199.

Local GPS chapters hold regular meetings at locations all around the United States and in Canada, but many members live far from the meeting sites and can't regularly attend.

The Germany Philatelic Society is just one of dozens of groups that specialize

Figure 199. Many societies provide members with news and information about specialized areas. The Germany Philatelic Society, for instance, publishes *German Postal Specialist* (left) for its members. One article in that publication featured the postcard shown at right.

in one country or geographic area. There are groups for collectors of Canada, Great Britain, Haiti, Italy, Japan, Mexico, Scandinavia, Switzerland and many other areas, including Earth's polar regions.

For collectors of U.S. stamps, the United States Stamp Society (formerly known as the Bureau Issues Association) publishes its monthly journal, the *United States Specialist*, "for the collector of postage and revenue stamp issues of the United States," as the journal says.

Another U.S. group is the U.S. Philatelic Classics Society. Its quarterly journal, the *Chronicle of the U.S. Classic Postal Issues*, presents important studies of the earliest U.S. stamps and postal history.

Stamp collecting isn't just about accumulating the issues of individual countries, however, and collectors with other interests can often find groups that help them as well.

For example, the United Postal Stationery Society was established in 1945 for collectors with an interest in worldwide postal stationery items: stamped envelopes, postal cards, aerograms and so on. A copy of the journal *Postal Stationery* is shown at left in Figure 200. Articles cover a range of topics on U.S. and worldwide issues, including highlights of new items, specialized studies of classic items and much more.

Like many groups, UPSS also pub-

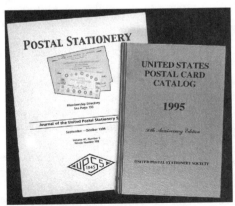

Figure 200. Some groups, including the United Postal Stationery Society, publish regular journals as well as books, such as this journal (left) and postal card catalog.

lishes reference materials for the benefit of its members. Shown at right in Figure 200 is the *United States Postal Card Catalog* from UPSS. The society also holds club auctions that allow members to buy and sell items of interest. Auctions are a feature that many different specialty groups provide for their members as an easy way to help them build their collections.

A number of other societies exist that appeal to collectors with interests in similarly specialized areas. For example, there are groups that cater to collectors of airmail items, perfinned stamps

Figure 201. Shown here are four stamps featuring bicycles. Topical collectors look for stamps with a subject in their area of interest.

(those with initials or designs punched through the face of the stamp), precanceled stamps, postal history, cinderellas (stamplike labels and bogus issues), revenues, postage meter stamps, U.S. plate number coils, postmarks and many others.

One very popular collecting society is the American Topical Association, a group of collectors who are interested in building collections that focus on the subject shown on the stamp rather than the country of origin.

Many who are interested in topical issues build one or more collections based on the stamp's subject. Thematic collectors look for stamps with related subjects as well, to help tell a story about the main subject — such as a stamp showing honey to be used in a thematic collection about bees.

Other topical collectors just keep an eye out for any stamp that shows their favorite topic. Figure 201, for instance, pictures four different stamps that would appeal to the bicycle topic collector.

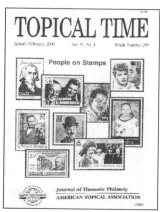

The ATA has nearly 50 separate study units that further specialize in varied topics such as astronomy, chess, lighthouses, music, railroads and sports. There's even a Bicycle Stamp Club that is an ATA study unit. Members of the ATA receive its journal, *Topical Time*, 10 times per year, and have access to many handbooks and checklists of popular collecting subjects. Figure 202 pictures the cover of an issue of *Topical Time*.

Different groups offer their members different benefits, and as a result, the membership dues can vary considerably, from just a few dollars annually to $25 or more. Stamp-society dues are a very worthwhile investment for collectors who are serious about their hobby.

Figure 202. The journal *Topical Time* is published six times per year by the American Topical Association.

The information that comes from belonging to a specialty society can more than make up for the money spent. Many club members find information that helps them save money in their stamp purchases. Others find great deals in club auctions they might not see anywhere else.

Remember, too, that every group has to pay for costs associated with mailing and journal production.

Some clubs maintain libraries that allow members to check out reference works and other research materials. Others offer stamp circuits, so that members may view and purchase stamps at home.

One group that provides all of these benefits as well as many others is the American Philatelic Society. The APS has the most extensive public-access philatelic library in the United States. Its sales division gives APS members an opportunity to buy and sell stamps by mail in more than 150 categories of countries and topics.

Members also receive the monthly journal *American Philatelist*, which keeps members up to date on APS-sponsored shows, activities and other hobby events, and includes numerous interesting feature articles in each issue.

Many collectors around the world enjoy these and many other benefits of APS membership. The APS also maintains a list of its many specialty society affiliates, so if you're looking for a special group to join, the APS will probably be able to help you.

Varieties are the spice of stamp collecting

Why is stamp collecting such a magnificent hobby? For one thing, it offers incredible variety. Collectors have an unlimited number of specialty areas from which to choose, and anyone with an interest in the stamp hobby can find something appealing to collect.

Variety is an important characteristic of the stamp hobby, and it is also a descriptive term that has some very specific meanings for collectors.

One philatelic definition for the term "variety" is "a variation from the standard form of a stamp." Examples of such variations include stamp errors, such as one or more missing colors on a stamp, full rows of perforations between stamps that are missing, parts of the stamp design that are inverted, and fluorescent tagging that is inadvertently omitted.

Other variations are minor design changes, deviations in the standard perforation gauge for an issue, specific multiples (such as blocks of four or booklet panes), distinct paper differences (like the China Clay paper varieties of the 1908-09 definitive series), distinct color differences and many others. All of these things are called "varieties."

In the Scott *Standard Postage Stamp Catalogue* and the Scott *Specialized Catalogue of United States Stamps & Covers*, varieties like those just mentioned are given a minor catalog listing, which is usually the same Scott number as the standard form of the stamp, followed by a lowercase letter.

Here's an example. The 20¢ Medal of Honor stamp was issued June 7, 1983. In the Oct. 10 issue of *Linn's Stamp News* that year, a report was published announcing the discovery in New England of a variety of that stamp missing the engraved red color. The Scott catalog editors make sure that such items are true errors; that is, they make certain there is absolutely no trace of the missing color on the stamp. Then the item appears in the Scott catalog as a minor listing.

The complete Scott catalog listing for the Medal of Honor stamp is shown in Figure 203, along with the standard form of the stamp (Scott 2045, shown at center) and the color-omitted error that received the minor listing (Scott 2045a, shown at bottom). As you can see, the Medal of Honor color-missing variety is listed with a 2003 catalog value of $240. But not all stamp varieties are valuable. There are other varieties that list as low as the Scott catalog minimum value. Such lower value varieties are usually items produced normally or intentionally.

The color-missing error of the Medal of Honor stamp was, of course, an accidental printing error that occurred at the Bureau of Engraving and Printing. The error was not noticed before the stamp was sent to post offices, and the color-missing stamps were sold and eventually got into collectors' hands. The *Catalogue of Errors on U.S. Postage Stamps* by Stephen R. Datz reports that the number of Medal of Honor stamps known with the color-missing error is estimated to be between 320 and 400.

The 25¢ Ring-necked Pheasant stamp variety illustrated in Figure 204 has the same type of minor catalog listing as the Medal of Honor stamp, but it came into being in quite a different way and has a considerably different value.

Color is again the reason for the minor catalog listing, but the difference between the Medal of Honor variety and the Pheasant variety is that the latter was created intentionally.

In *Linn's U.S. Stamp Yearbook 1988*, author

Figure 203. The listing in the Scott U.S. specialized catalog for the 1983 Medal of Honor stamp includes a minor listing at the bottom for the color-omitted error. The lowercase letter "a" before the description is considered part of the catalog number for the variety, which is identified as Scott 2045a. The normal stamp is shown at center, and the variety is shown at bottom.

Figure 204. The light-sky variety of the 25¢ Pheasant booklet stamp was created intentionally in 1988. The sky in the original printing of the stamp (left) was considered too dark by the USPS, so screened red dots were removed from a later printing (right) to make the sky lighter.

161

George Amick explains that in the first printing of the Pheasant booklet stamps, the details of the pheasant in the design were difficult to distinguish in the small stamp, particularly against the dark blue sky. The U.S. Postal Service asked American Bank Note Co. to make the color of the sky a little lighter in its later printing of the stamps so the pheasant design would be more prominent. ABNC removed screened red dots from the sky color to fulfill this request, and the subsequent printings were quite distinguishable from the earlier ones (though the effect is less visible in the illustration here).

In the Scott catalog, the standard form of the Ring-necked Pheasant stamp is cataloged as Scott 2283. The variety is Scott 2283b. The catalog value of the variety is a few dollars more than that of the standard issue.

Exact print quantities are not available, but it is likely that thousands and thousands of the Pheasant variety booklets were created, as opposed to the couple of hundred color-missing Medal of Honor stamps. This accounts for the big difference in the comparative value of the two varieties.

James E. Kloetzel, editor of the Scott catalog, helps to clarify why Scott 2283b received a minor catalog listing, while other design differences may receive a major listing. He notes that because the red color was removed from only part of the design on Scott 2283b, the stamp is a minor variety of the same design as the original issue, not a major alteration of the stamp.

"If all the red were omitted," Kloetzel stated, "that would likely give it a major listing. A major variety is a stamp that has a significant and easily discernible design difference."

The 29¢ Elvis Presley stamp of 1993 provides an excellent example for this type of major catalog listing variety.

Most U.S. stamp collectors are aware that in 1993 the U.S. Postal Service issued a 29¢ stamp depicting popular singer Elvis Presley. The stamp was issued Jan. 8 of that year, and more than 500 million copies of the stamp were distributed and sold.

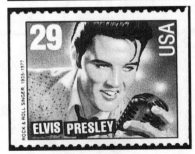

What some collectors do not know is that there is not just one U.S. Elvis stamp — there are three. The three major varieties are shown in Figure 205. The differences between the three stamps are considerable enough that each variety has been assigned an individual Scott catalog number.

Figure 205. Because each of the three 29¢ Elvis Presley stamps was created by a different printer and can be distinguished from the others, each is assigned a different major catalog number.

Shown at top is the famous original stamp, printed by the Bureau of Engraving and Printing and sold by the Postal Service in panes of 40 stamps. As mentioned earlier, this stamp was first issued Jan. 8, 1993.

Five months later, on June 16, the Postal Service issued its Rock 'n' Roll//Rhythm & Blues stamp set in panes of 35 stamps. These stamps were printed by the firm of Stamp Venturers, and each pane contained seven different stamp designs featuring musicians, including one depicting Presley. The Presley stamp from this pane is shown in the center of Figure 205. The most noticeable difference between the first and second stamps is that the second stamp bears Presley's first and last names, while the earlier stamp is only inscribed "Elvis."

June 16 was also the issue date for the Rock 'n' Roll/Rhythm & Blues booklet stamps, manufactured by Multi-Color Corp. for ABNC. Each booklet contained 20 stamps, among them a third Presley stamp shown at bottom in Figure 205. This third stamp is very similar to the second, though the booklet stamp design has a thin dark framing border, and each stamp has straight edges on two or three sides.

The first Presley stamp is cataloged as Scott 2721. The second stamp is 2724, and the booklet stamp is 2731.

Another factor that distinguishes 2724 (the June 16 stamp from the pane of 35) from 2731 (the booklet stamp) is a major change in the perforation gauge. Scott 2724 has a perforation gauge of 10, and 2731 has a perforation gauge of 11, meaning the perforation holes are closer together on the latter stamp.

Another form of minor listing is shown in Figure 206. Stamp issues with different designs from the same pane, like the 13¢ Butterfly stamps issued in 1977, are called se-tenant. Blocks of se-tenant stamps receive minor listings by Scott and are saved by collectors in the order that they are cataloged. For example, the four butterfly stamps in Figure 206 are Scott 1712 in the upper-left corner, 1713 in the upper-right corner, 1714 in the lower-left corner, and 1715 in the lower-right corner. The full block of four stamps is listed as 1715a.

Stamp collectors can use their knowledge of varieties to help shape their collections. Some may wish to find as many varieties as possible to fill out their collections. Others may believe that some varieties are insignificant and not worth pursuing, or are too costly to try to collect.

As always, such decisions are up to the collector, who can look for the best way to enjoy the abundant varieties of stamp collecting.

Figure 206. Some minor catalog listings describe collectible multiples for specific issues. Scott 1715a refers to the four 13¢ Butterfly stamps, Scott 1712-15, collected as a single block of four, in the positions described by the catalog.

Counting stamps helps to pinpoint varieties

The hobby of stamp collecting dates back to the 19th century, and since that time collectors have found many ways to share information with one another. Sometimes that means using special terms that have a specific meaning in the stamp hobby. Collectors also have developed a simple but significant method to describe the location of one specific stamp on a pane.

Every stamp in a given pane is designated by a number, beginning with the stamp in the upper-left corner, which is identified as position 1. Each stamp in the pane is counted, from left to right. When the last stamp in the top horizontal row is counted, the numbering continues with the first stamp at left in the second horizontal row, and so on, until the last stamp in the lower-right corner of the pane has been assigned a number.

Figure 207 shows a pane of the 20 Classic American Aircraft stamps issued July 19, 1997. The stamps on the pane all have different designs.

At top left is a stamp showing the P-51 Mustang, in position 1 on the pane. The next stamp to the right shows the Wright Model B Flyer in position 2.

There are four stamps in the top row, so they are in positions 1 through 4. Position 5 is the stamp showing the Northrop Alpha, which is the first stamp in the second horizontal row. In position 6, continuing to the right, is the Martin B-10.

As you continue counting, the last stamp in the pane, in the lower-right corner, ends up being in position 20. That stamp shows the Grumman F4F Wildcat.

One collector can say to another, "The Curtiss Jenny is in position 19 on the Classic American Aircraft pane." Each collector will know that as they count down the stamps on the pane, the Jenny will be found as the next-to-last stamp in the bottom row of the pane of 20 stamps.

This method of numbering stamps is commonly used to describe where a stamp containing a plate variety can be located. Often, additional information is needed to point out the location.

A plate variety is a variation in a printing plate that results in some element of the stamp design being identifiably different from a normal issue of the same stamp. Plate varieties are repeated over and over again during the stamp-printing process. Therefore, when someone finds an unusual mark on a postage stamp, it can be confirmed as a plate vari-

Figure 207. Collectors can refer to the 20 stamps on this 1997 issue by the position each stamp has on the pane.

Figure 208. The "snowball" plate variety is visible in front of the skier's forward hand on the stamp shown at right.

ety if other collectors find an identical mark in postage stamps that they have examined.

Sometimes a plate variety occurs when the printing plate is accidentally damaged in some way. Other plate varieties may be caused by the intentional retouching of a stamp engraving, to strengthen design lines that have become worn through excessive use.

Fine printed lines on stamps and in the margin selvage caused by cracks in the printing plates are evidence of another form of plate variety.

Look at the two stamps shown in Figure 208. They are both examples of U.S. Scott 716, the 1932 2¢ Olympic Winter Games issue. There is a plate variety on the stamp on the right. Directly in front of the skier's forward hand is a small spot in the same carmine (reddish) color as the rest of the stamp. The spot is a plate variety called the "snowball" by some collectors. On certain panes of 100 stamps, this variety appears on only one of those stamps. The spot is caused by an indentation in the printing plate, possibly a small gouge. As sheets of these stamps were printed, the spot was printed over and over again, each time on one stamp only.

This variety is identified in the Scott *Specialized Catalogue of United States Stamps & Covers* under the catalog listing for Scott 716. The listing for this stamp from the Scott specialized catalog is reproduced in Figure 209. At the

Skier — A222

OLYMPIC WINTER GAMES ISSUE
3rd Olympic Winter Games, held at Lake Placid, N.Y., Feb. 4-13, 1932.
FLAT PLATE PRINTING
Plates of 400 subjects in four panes of 100.

1932, Jan. 25		*Perf. 11*
716 A222 2c **carmine rose**	.40	.20
carmine	.40	.20
Never hinged	.50	
P# block of 6	10.00	—
Never hinged	12.50	
Cracked plate (20823 UR 41, 42;		
UL 48, 49, 50)	5.00	1.65
Recut (20823 UR 61)	3.50	1.50
Colored "snowball" (20815 UR 64)	25.00	5.00

Figure 209. The Scott *Specialized Catalogue of United States Stamps & Covers* listing for Scott 716 notes the "snowball" variety.

bottom of the listing is the phrase, "Colored 'snowball' (20815 UR 64)." This information tells the collector exactly where the plate variety is located on a full sheet of these stamps. Other information in the listing helps to decode this identification.

First of all, the number 20815 refers to the plate number that was used to print this 2¢ stamp. Other reference works, like the Durland *Standard Plate Number Catalog*, reveal that 12 different plates, numbered 20815 through 20826, were used to print the stamp. The specific plate

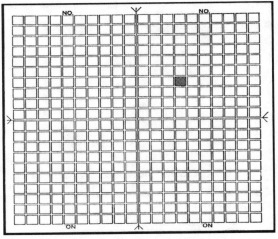

Figure 210. The press sheet for Scott 716 contained 400 stamps. The sheet was divided into four 100-stamp panes.

number was printed in four positions in the margin selvage of the press sheet.

As the Scott specialized catalog listing notes, the stamps were printed from plates of 400 subjects (individual stamps), which were then divided into four panes of 100 stamps each.

The diagram in Figure 210, modified from the Scott specialized catalog, shows how this is laid out. With close inspection, it is possible to see that there is a thin line down the center of the sheet vertically and another across the center of the sheet horizontally. These guidelines are printed on the sheet and indicate where the press sheet is cut into four separate panes, each containing 100 stamps. After the cutting is completed, the same plate number appears in one position on each pane, indicated in the diagram with the notation, "NO."

Now, back to figuring out where the stamp with the plate variety is located.

In the listing (20815 UR 64), the letters "UR" stand for "upper right," meaning the plate variety appears in the upper-right pane of the four panes that came from press sheets with plate number 20815. The "64" in the catalog listing means the flaw appears on stamps in position 64 on those specific panes.

Look again at the diagram in Figure 210. Remember, the upper-right (UR) pane consists of the upper-right one-fourth of the full press sheet shown in the diagram. To count the stamps in that UR pane, you must begin in the top row to the right of the horizontal center guideline and count to the right, returning to the center guideline when you reach the end of the first row. The stamp in position 64 of the upper-right pane is shaded in the Figure 210 diagram.

When that upper-right pane was cut from the sheet and sold in the post office, it looked something like the diagram shown in Figure 211.

From that pane of 100 stamps, how can the collector tell it was the upper-right pane? There were at least two ways to tell for this issue. The plate number appears above the stamp in position 6 on the upper-right pane. The upper-left pane has the plate number appearing over the stamp in position 5. The two lower panes show the plate numbers at the bottom of the panes. Also, the top-right plate number for the 2¢ Winter Games issue was preceded by the letter "F."

Remember, there were 12 different plates used to print these stamps. Eleven of those plates did not contain the snowball in any position. That means out of 4,800 engraved designs that were repeatedly reproduced for this issue (400 stamps x 12 plates), only one had the snowball variety.

That may explain why an unused stamp with that plate variety has a catalog value much higher than the normal issue.

Additional information for this section was found in *Encyclopedia of Plate Varieties on U.S. Bureau-Printed Postage Stamps* by Loran C. French, and *The United States Commemorative Stamps of the 20th Century, Volume 1*, by Max G. Johl.

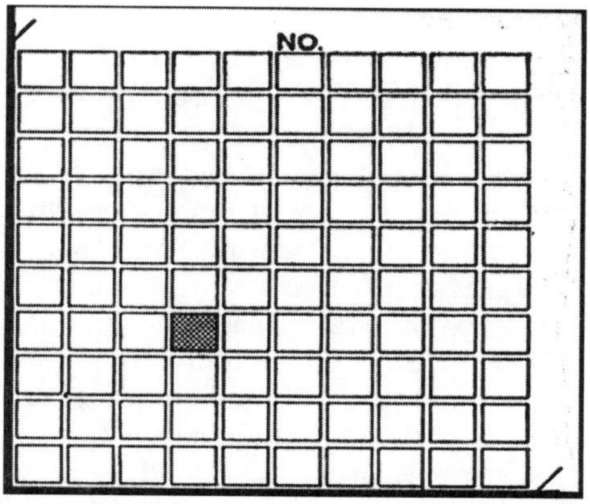

Figure 211. The "snowball" variety appeared in position 64 (marked with shading) on the upper-right pane from press sheets that were printed with plate number 20815.

Production errors and freaks add excitement

Inverts occur when at least one element of the stamp design is printed upside down in relation to the remainder of the design.

Color-missing errors occur when one or more colors are completely missing from the stamp design.

For a stamp to qualify as a perforation error, the perforations or die cuts separating one stamp from another must be completely missing from at least one side.

Notice how the word "completely" often plays a role in describing these major errors. For a stamp to qualify as a major error, there must be an absolute production failure at some point.

Following are some additional errors that are recognized by stamp collectors.

Errors of color occur either when the wrong ink is used by the printer during stamp production or the wrong design element is entered into the printing plate.

About a year before the Inverted "Jenny" was discovered in 1918 by stamp collector William T. Robey, collectors learned that the U.S. Bureau of Engraving and Printing had accidentally printed panes of 100 2¢ carmine red George Washington stamps that contained either one or two 5¢ stamps by mistake. The 5¢ designs, normally printed on separate sheets in blue, had been entered mistakenly into the 2¢ printing plate to correct earlier faults.

As is often the case, this stamp error commands a substantial premium, many times greater than the normal stamp.

Watermark errors are classified by some collectors as paper errors because the stamp is clearly printed on a paper other than the one intended for the issue. Two

U.S. stamps of 1895, the 6¢ (Scott 271) and the 8¢ (272), were discovered printed on paper watermarked "USIR" (United States Internal Revenue) intended for the production of revenue stamps.

Because these stamps were normally watermarked "USPS" with about one letter appearing on each stamp, only those single stamps clearly showing the "I" or "R," or blocks of stamps including those letters, are counted as errors.

Double impressions are identified when a second impression of the stamp design is applied on top of a stamp that has been printed once already. Such errors are quite rare. They occur among some U.S. issues of the 1850s, 1860s and 1870s, including the 3¢ dull red of 1853, Scott 11.

A second type of double impression occurs when the stamp design is printed once on both sides of the paper. Again, this type of error is very unusual and on U.S. stamps can only be found on a few 19th-century issues.

On such an error, the impression, which should appear only on the front on a normal stamp, is printed instead on both sides.

A different variety known as an offset freak occurs when a reverse-image of the design is inked upon the back of the stamp. Offsets are not errors, but they are still very collectible.

The Scott U.S. specialized catalog describes errors as "stamps having some unintentional major deviation from the normal."

For nearly every type of stamp error that exists, there is some kind of production variety that a collector might mistakenly believe to be an error. Some of these varieties are still quite collectible and may have premium value, but in some cases what is believed to be an error turns out to be nothing more than a shoddy printing job or a normal stamp altered by some means.

It may be hard to believe, but there's one U.S. invert that is actually a normal stamp — and it may not be the stamp issue that you're thinking of.

When the 4¢ Dag Hammarskjold memorial stamp was released in 1962, a collector named Leonard Sherman discovered the stamp with the background yellow color inverted. When the U.S. Post Office Department learned of the mistake, a new printing of the stamp with the background color intentionally inverted

Figure 212. When inks are not placed properly during the printing process, unusual varieties can occur. The normal 8¢ Tom Sawyer stamp is shown at left; printing freaks with misaligned colors are shown at center and right.

was ordered by Postmaster General J. Edward Day, destroying any potential premium value of the error.

The color invert, listed as Scott 1204, has the same minimum value as the normal printing of the same design, Scott 1203.

In 2001 the U.S. Postal Service issued a pane of seven stamps that included three stamps that resembled the Pan American invert errors of 1901. But the newer stamps are not invert errors at all, even though their central designs are printed upside down, for that is precisely how the Postal Service intended them to look. Is that the issue you thought of as the U.S. invert that was a normal stamp?

Collectors often find multicolor stamps that they believe are either color-missing errors or errors of color that are actually stamps with poorly registered inks. When stamp inks are properly registered, each color of the design is correctly placed and the design appears sharp and clear.

Even the smallest shift of a color printing plate or cylinder can create designs that look blurred or even doubled.

The 8¢ Tom Sawyer stamp of 1972, Scott 1470, provides an example of this problem.

At left in Figure 212 is shown a normal, proper printing of this multicolor commemorative. Each element of the design appears correct.

In the center of Figure 212 is a stamp of the same design but with some colors shifted slightly. Notice the name "Tom Sawyer" across the top is moved to the left, the lines defining the slats of the house extend into the left margin, and the two boys in the design appear to be doubled.

This stamp is not missing any colors, nor is it a double impression. It simply suffers from poor color alignment.

The stamp at right in Figure 212 shows the same problem taken to an extreme. The name and design elements are severely out of alignment, creating an almost abstract stamp design.

Even though they look very unusual, these are not error stamps because all of the colors are present.

Even though they are considered freaks rather than errors, misaligned colors may be of interest to specialist collectors of errors, freaks and oddities, or to specialist collectors of the Tom Sawyer commemorative stamp.

The third stamp in the illustration will probably fetch a premium on the stamp market.

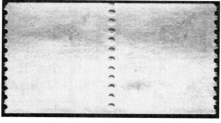

Figure 213. Blind perforations are a production freak that occurs when perforation holes are not fully punched through stamp paper. Traces of the holes are seen on the back (right).

Minor color shade differences also catch the eyes of many collectors, but unless there is an actual incorrect color used in the printing, these are classified as either freaks or oddities.

The freak, in this case, is a normal variation in the printed color as created by the printer. The oddity could be a color changeling, such as a stamp that has faded in color because of extended exposure to light.

There are also many different varieties of perforation freaks.

Figure 213 shows a phenomenon known as "blind perfs." While this pair of 15¢ Flag coils from 1978 (Scott 1618C) may appear to have no perforations between them, a closer examination proves otherwise.

Viewed from the back (Figure 213, right), the stamps show perforation holes cut into the paper, but the holes are not removed from the paper. Since evidence of perforation exists, the coil pair is not considered an imperforate error.

Figure 214 shows the 32¢ Marilyn Monroe stamp of 1995. This issue was created with star-shaped perforation holes in each corner of each stamp, but the example shown has one such perforation completely missing at upper left.

A single unpunched hole does not qualify the stamp as an error, but this variety is recognized and sought-after by collectors.

Shifts in perforations are also encountered on many issues. They can be very minor, cutting slightly into the stamp design, to severe, as shown in Figure 215 on the 1¢ Thomas Jefferson coil of 1968 (Scott 1299).

Because the perforation holes on the illustrated Jefferson coil split each stamp almost in half, it makes a more interesting variety. Because these freaks are easy to find, they have a premium of only a few dollars.

Figure 214. Although a single missing perforation is not considered an error, the missing-star variety of the 32¢ Marilyn Monroe is still worth adding to a collection.

There are many other types of production varieties in addition to the few described and illustrated here.

Everyone who finds an error, freak or oddity wonders about its value.

The value of an error is usually tied to its scarcity. A new discovery may command great prices at first, but those prices can drop like a stone if additional examples are found.

On the other hand,

Figure 215. Perforation shifts can cause dramatic changes in the appearance of the stamp, but if the freak is fairly common it will probably command only a modest premium value.

the value of a new error discovery has also been known to increase as it becomes apparent that no other examples are known.

The values of other freaks and oddities are generally less than all but the most common errors. Collectors are often attracted by varieties that show a dramatic or unusual change in the stamp design, and the attractiveness of a freak may increase its value on the collector market.

In any case, errors, freaks and oddities make an interesting addition to any stamp collection. They tell us a little about how stamps are produced and how mistakes can be made during stamp production.

Collectors keep an eye out for stamp errors

If you're dining at a restaurant and there's something wrong with the meal you ordered, you'll probably send it back and ask for a replacement. When you go to the post office and ask for postage stamps, if there is something wrong with the stamps you get, you may want to take them anyway.

From time to time, stamps or postal stationery items are discovered that are different from normal issues because of a mistake made during production.

Although stamp printers are very careful about creating only properly manu-factured postage stamps, there are times when something goes haywire during production and the mistakes are not caught before the stamps are distributed. The most prominent of these inadvertent varieties are known as "errors," and many have a value to collectors that is far greater than the value of a normal example of the same item.

In the stamp hobby, there are specific guidelines that determine what qualifies as a major error. Some stamps that look wildly unusual still may not be errors because they do not fit specific descriptions.

Production varieties that do not qualify as major errors are usually called "freaks" or "oddities." Although they usually have less value than errors, they still can be of interest to collectors and regularly trade for more than face value.

The Scott *Specialized Catalogue of United States Stamps & Covers* lists U.S. stamp errors, assigns each a minor number designation and often a retail value. The values of errors can vary wildly depending on factors such as scarcity, demand and the attractiveness of the error. Some major errors can be purchased for only a couple of dollars. Others sell for $100,000 or more.

Modern production varieties properly described as freaks or oddities also may be described in the Scott U.S. specialized catalog, but they are not assigned an identifying catalog number.

Because freaks and oddities are far more numerous than errors, many are not noted in the Scott U.S. specialized catalog at all.

Let's start by looking at the different types of stamp errors that exist. Although the examples shown here are all varieties of U.S. stamps, foreign issues released unintentionally with the same characteristics also are regarded as errors.

Inverts are probably the most dramatic type of production error. An invert is created when one part of a stamp design is printed upside down in relation to the remainder of the design. One of the most famous stamp errors in the world is an invert.

In 1918 the United States issued a 24¢ airmail stamp showing an airplane known

171

as the Curtiss "Jenny." A few of the stamps were placed on sale in Washington, D.C., May 13. The following morning a 29-year-old stamp collector named William T. Robey went to a branch post office in Washington to buy a full pane of 100 of the new issue. When Robey received his stamps from the window clerk, he immediately noticed that the blue airplane in the center of the design was printed upside down.

A normal example of the 24¢ airmail, identified in the Scott catalog as C3, is shown at left in Figure 216. The invert error, Scott C3a, is shown at right in Figure 216.

Robey's original 100 stamps are the only ones ever discovered and sold.

In the book *Jenny!* (now out of print) published by *Linn's Stamp News*, George Amick points out that "it is the Jenny invert that the layman thinks of when he thinks of a stamp rarity."

Figure 216. One of the world's best-known stamp errors is the Inverted "Jenny," a 1918 24¢ airmail stamp from the United States with the center of the design printed upside down (right). A normal example of the same stamp is shown at left.

This production mistake occurred because the blue airplane and the red frame were printed in two separate actions. Amick notes that after the red frame was first printed on the pane, it is likely that the blue printing plate was unintentionally inserted upside down, creating the inverted image on the stamp.

A single unused example of the Inverted "Jenny" is listed in the Scott catalog with a value of $170,000. The normal stamp usually sells for a little less than $100 in hinged condition.

However, Scott C3a is neither the first U.S. stamp invert, the scarcest, nor the most valuable. Inverts of the 15¢ and 24¢ issues of 1869 take those honors. There is a grand public fascination with the Inverted "Jenny" that exceeds the interest in those other notable rarities, however, and that has made it one of the most cherished stamps in the world.

Another type of invert is less dramatic but is still considered a major error.

From time to time, postal administrations apply overprints to stocks of unused stamps, changing the denomination or even the name of the issuing country, or sometimes commemorating an event of some sort. When this overprint is accidentally applied upside down, it is considered an inverted-overprint error.

Color-missing errors range from startling varieties that immediately catch the eye to errors that are nearly indistinguishable from the normal issue. Figure 217 shows an intriguing color-missing error of the 20¢ Science & Industry commemorative of 1983.

As with the Inverted "Jenny," the printing of the Science & Industry stamp involved two different printing steps. In this case, however, different printing processes were involved. The colorful background of the stamp design was printed by offset-lithography, a process that transfers an inked design from a printing

Figure 217. Color-missing errors can be very dramatic. The 1983 20¢ Science & Industry issue from the United States is known with all intaglio black printing absent (right). A normal stamp of the same issue is shown at left for comparison.

cylinder to a rubber blanket roller and then onto paper.

The lettering and gridlike pattern in the same stamp design was printed in black by the intaglio method, where ink from the recesses of an engraved plate is deposited directly onto the paper. The black intaglio printing is entirely absent on the stamp at right in Figure 217, which qualifies it as an error.

Sometimes stamps are discovered with part of a color missing but still showing some evidence of the ink on the stamp. These are considered freaks, not major errors. On a color-missing stamp error at least one color that is supposed to be present in the design must be absent without a trace.

Tagging-omitted errors are considered by most specialists to be very similar to color-missing errors. The term "tagging" describes luminescent material that is applied to printed stamps or to stamp paper to make it glow when exposed to certain ranges of ultraviolet light. Often it is impossible to see tagging on a stamp in normal light.

One method of applying tagging to a stamp is to cover all or part of the design with a luminescent compound similar to invisible ink.

Some U.S. stamps in the 1960s were intentionally printed in two varieties: with and without tagging. Those stamps printed intentionally without tagging are identified in the Scott catalog as "untagged" and are not considered errors.

For many later issues, the entire print run of the stamp would be tagged. Examples of those later tagged issues that have been found with absolutely no tagging present on the stamp are considered

Figure 218. This block of four 29¢ Wonders of the Sea stamps should have perforation holes separating each of the four stamps. Without them, the item is an imperforate error.

"tagging-omitted" errors and are listed in the Scott catalog as "tagging omitted."

Imperforate stamp errors are issues that are supposed to have perforation holes separating individual stamps but do not. The term sometimes is used to describe self-adhesive stamps that are missing the straight or wavy-line die cuts that separate individual stamps, though the more-specific term "die-cut omitted" is also used.

There are several different kinds of perforation errors.

Stamps that are fully imperforate do not have any perforations on any side. Figure 218 shows a corner block of four stamps from the 29¢ Wonders of the Sea issue of 1994. There are no perforation holes anywhere on this block. Because very few of these errors have been found, these imperforate stamps are likely to sell for a substantial amount of money. The block in the illustration is actually a plate number block — the plate number appears at top in the margin paper — so it may have additional premium value.

Sometimes stamps are discovered where horizontal rows of perforations are missing and vertical rows of perforations are present, or the reverse: horizontal rows of perforations present but vertical rows missing. If a single vertical row of perforations is missing from a pane, it can create an error known as a "horizontal pair imperf between." That means a side-by-side pair of stamps are normally perforated on all sides, except that no vertical perforations separate the two.

Figure 219 shows a horizontal pair imperforate-between of the 14¢ Sinclair Lewis stamp of 1985.

If all vertical rows of perforations are missing, a pair of side-by-side stamps would be called "horizontal pair imperf vertically." The two stamps would have perforations at top and bottom but none between them or on either side.

Similar configurations occur if one or more horizontal rows of perforations are absent and all vertical perforations are present.

Because some perforation errors can be faked simply by trimming off the

Figure 219. Otherwise normal stamps that are missing perforations between them are created when a single row of perforations is missing from the pane. The error shown is an imperf-between horizontal pair of the 1985 14¢ Sinclair Lewis stamp.

edges of a normally perforated stamp, collectors usually choose to save imperforates in pairs, strips or larger blocks to fully show the extent of the error.

Chapter 8
Stamp Classifications

Recognizing definitives and commemoratives

The terms "definitive" and "commemorative" are used regularly by stamp collectors to define specific types of postage stamps. For many years these terms seemed very clear and very separate, but lately some definitives and commemoratives have become harder to tell apart with certainty.

The general guidelines for distinguishing definitives and commemoratives are still useful, but exceptions to these guidelines are becoming more common.

The stamp world began with a definitive issue, Great Britain's "Penny Black," a black 1-penny stamp issued May 6, 1840 (Figure 220, left). The stamp is small and of a fairly plain design. It features the face of a world leader, Britain's Queen Victoria, who had been crowned less than two years earlier and was only 20 years old when the stamp was issued.

Figure 220. The first stamp issue of the world, Great Britain's Penny Black (left), and the first stamp issued in the United States (right) are both definitives.

The first U.S. stamps were also definitives. U.S. Scott 1, issued July 1, 1847, is a small 5¢ reddish brown stamp on bluish paper and features the face of Benjamin Franklin, the first U.S. postmaster general. The stamp is shown at right in Figure 220.

Even today, definitive stamps are generally small in size and plain in design, issued at the first-class postage rate or some other useful denomination.

Many nations issue definitive stamps picturing their former or current leaders, prominent citizens, or the nation's flag. Sometimes definitives may show the value of the stamp as a main element of the design, such as Norway's Posthorn definitives. Some definitives are from a series with a specific theme, such as the U.S. Transportation coil definitives. Examples of both are shown in Figure 221.

Figure 221. Stamps that are in a series look similar to one another but have different denominations. Norway's Posthorn issues (left) and the U.S. Transportation coils (right) are two well-known definitive series.

Definitives like these two are from series that include different denominations to pay for different rates or to be used as "makeup" postage (added to other stamps to pay for a more expensive postal service).

Definitives are printed in large quantities, to remain on sale for an indefinite period of time. In most cases, a definitive stamp at the first-class rate will remain on sale until that rate finally changes. For that reason, a definitive stamp may be sent to press several times, meaning the same design is printed again and again whenever more stamps are needed.

Commemorative stamps are generally larger in size, about twice the size of an average definitive. Many collectors consider the first U.S. commemorative stamp set to be the original Columbian Exposition issues of 1893. Sixteen different stamps were issued, in values from 1¢ to $5. Each stamp was a different single color. The 1¢ value of the set, Scott 230, is shown at the top of Figure 222.

Commemoratives are usually issued in limited quantities, either as single issues or in sets.

Some commemorative sets may be small, like the two-stamp 29¢ Recognize Deafness/American Sign Language set issued by the United States in 1993.

Figure 222. The 1¢ Columbian issued in 1893 (top) is the low value of what many consider the first U.S. commemorative set. Commemoratives often serve as reminders, like the 1995 POW & MIA stamp shown at bottom.

Other sets may be larger, like the 50-stamp 29¢ Wildflowers stamps from the United States issued one year earlier.

A commemorative issue is almost always printed in one press run, though on rare occasions, a highly popular commemorative may be returned to press for an additional printing.

Commemorative stamps are most frequently issued to fulfill the postage rate for first-class letters. Most of today's commemoratives are in full color and depict a special event, a person, a feature of the issuing country, an anniversary or simply a topical design of some sort.

The word "commemorate" means to remember with a special observation. The 32¢ POW & MIA commemorative issued in 1995 and shown at the bottom of Figure 222 is a good example of how such stamps can be used to remember something special. Commemorative stamps are usually on sale only for a limited time. In the United States, commemorative stamps are customarily taken off sale within about one year of their issuance, sometimes less.

If you look at the two stamps in Figure 223, you probably can now tell which is the definitive and which is the commemorative. The 29¢ Flag Over White House coil stamp on the left is a definitive. The 29¢ Cherokee Strip Land Run stamp on the right is a commemorative.

So what's the problem?

For starters, consider the two stamps shown in Figure 224. At left is a 1912 issue depicting U.S. President Abraham Lincoln. At right is a 1995 issue featuring U.S. President James K. Polk. Small stamps, single-color, depicting a world leader — must be a definitive, right?

Wrong.

Although both of these stamps seem to fit the description of a definitive stamp, they are actually commemoratives. The 2¢ Lincoln stamp, Scott 367, was issued on the 100th anniversary of Lincoln's birth as a special memorial issue. An imperforate variety and a special paper variety of the same stamp also were issued.

Figure 223. The 29¢ Flag Over White House coil is a good example of a definitive stamp. The 29¢ Cherokee Strip Land Run stamp is a good example of a commemorative.

The 32¢ Polk stamp, though first called a definitive even by the Postal Service, has been redefined as a commemorative. According to USPS, the print run for this stamp was only 105 million. Although that may seem like a lot of stamps, it's a fairly small amount compared to the original quantity ordered for a definitive like the 29¢ Flag Over White House coil first issued in 1992 that was shown at the left in Figure 223. *Linn's U.S. Stamp Yearbook 1992* reports that more than 5½ billion of the first eight plate numbers of the Flag Over White House definitive originally were distributed. That's more than 50 times the quantity distributed of the Polk stamp — and the Flag Over White House coil was eventually printed with an additional seven plate numbers.

Other commemoratives that look like definitives include the Champions of Liberty stamps issued 1957-61, the 13¢ Indian Head Penny stamp of 1978 and the 15¢ Dolly Madison stamp of 1980.

The opposite type of confusion also exists. There are U.S. definitive stamps that look like commemoratives, including the $2 Bobcat issued in 1990 (shown at the top of Figure 225).

Collectors have discovered that foreign countries often use colorful pictorial stamps for their definitive sets. Among the countries whose modern definitive sets look like commemoratives are Mexico, Australia, Cook Islands and Tuvalu.

The high value of Mexico's Tourism definitive series, Scott 1801, is shown at the bottom of Figure 225.

To help you determine if a stamp like the Mexico Tourism issue is a definitive, you can check the Scott *Standard Postage Stamp Catalogue*. Foreign definitive stamps are often in extended sets with a wide variety of face values. There are 12 different denominations for the 12 Tourism stamps, which were issued in 1993.

Commemoratives, on the other hand, are usually at a single rate, or at two or three commonly used rates. If the catalog listing shows a long list of differently

Figure 224. They may look like definitives, but they're really commemoratives: the 1912 2¢ Lincoln memorial stamp at left and the 1995 32¢ James K. Polk stamp at right.

177

denominated issues under a single stamp design, it is more likely that the group consists of definitive stamps.

A third category of stamp that is issued less frequently has been commonly called "special stamps." These are stamps printed in higher quantities at a first-class rate, with a special significance to the design. Christmas stamps and Love stamps are the two types of stamps that are categorized as "special stamps." They are neither definitive nor commemorative.

Special stamps stay on sale for longer periods than commemoratives, and they may be printed several different times to replenish stock when post office stocks run low.

The general rules for definitives and commemoratives are still valid, though exceptions exist for U.S. and foreign stamps.

The stamps in Figure 223 are good examples of what collectors consider definitive and commemorative stamps.

Figure 225. They may look like commemoratives, but they're really definitives: the U.S. 1990 $2 Bobcat stamp at top and Mexico's 1993 6-peso Tourism definitive shown below it.

Souvenir sheets come in all shapes and sizes

Postal authorities worldwide have issued souvenir sheets to commemorate any number of different special events, from royal births to major stamp exhibitions. Although the main purpose of any postage stamp is to show that postage fees have been paid, it often serves a second purpose: to commemorate a past event or a well-known place or person.

The designs of most commemorative stamps are developed with this aim in mind. Even a definitive (regular-issue) stamp, which generally remains on sale for a longer period, may show a past or present political ruler or some other prominent figure.

Souvenir sheets take this commemoration one step further, by announcing or promoting a present-day event.

Definitions of what constitutes a souvenir sheet have varied considerably, causing some confusion within the stamp hobby. Because different postal authorities create different kinds of souvenir sheets, there are no set guidelines that define a souvenir sheet.

Many souvenir sheets are small and contain relatively few stamps, sometimes as few as one. Such is the case for what is considered by some collectors to be the world's first souvenir sheet.

On Dec. 22, 1922, Princess Elisabeth of Luxembourg, the younger sister of that country's eventual ruler (from 1964 to 2000), Grand Duke Jean, was born. Just 12 days later, on Jan. 3, 1923, Luxembourg issued a special small sheet that contained a single green 10-franc stamp with perforations all around and a wide border of margin paper. The souvenir sheet, Luxembourg Scott 151, is shown in

Figure 226. There is no inscription in the margins, but the special sheet was prepared specifically upon the occasion of the royal birth.

In *Prifix*, the specialized stamp catalog published in Luxembourg, the Princess Elisabeth sheet is described as "der erste Block der Welt." In German stamp collecting terminology, "Block" often describes what is known in English as a souvenir sheet, so the description can be interpreted as "the first souvenir sheet in the world."

Figure 226. Is this the world's first souvenir sheet? Luxembourg Scott 151, a small pane containing just one stamp, was issued in 1923 to commemorate the birth of a princess.

However, this was not the first small sheet issued to commemorate a royal event. Two years earlier, when Prince Jean was born, Luxembourg issued a sheet of five stamps depicting Grand Duchess Charlotte. The sheet containing these stamps is listed in the Scott *Standard Postage Stamp Catalogue* as Scott 125a.

A sheet of 10 stamps issued by Luxembourg even earlier honored the ascension of Grand Duke William IV to the throne in 1906. In the Scott catalog, this sheet is listed as Scott 82a and is described as a "souvenir sheet."

Since these previous Luxembourgian issues exist, why is the Princess Elisabeth sheet considered by the *Prifix* catalog to be the world's first souvenir sheet?

The catalog description doesn't really provide any clues. Perhaps the answer is because the Princess Elisabeth sheet bore only one stamp, which certainly was a novelty at the time. Or it may be because the stamp in the small sheet had never been issued previously.

Surprisingly, the *Prifix* catalog makes no special note of the two earlier commemorative panes. Unfortunately, it's all part of the confusion that surrounds the use of the term "souvenir sheet."

Some collectors avoid the term altogether, choosing instead to use the terms "miniature sheet" or "sheetlet" to describe such smaller items.

The first souvenir sheet issued by the United States, however, measures more than 6 inches across and contains 25 stamps, more than most panes that are issued by the United States today.

In 1926 the United States released a 2¢ stamp commemorating the 1776 Battle of White Plains, N.Y. The stamp was printed using two different plate arrangements. A standard pane of 100 (from divided sheets of 400 stamps) was sold at post offices across the country.

A second pane of 25 was created with wide margins all around bearing the inscription, "INTERNATIONAL PHILATELIC EXHIBITION, OCT 16TH TO

23RD 1926" across the top of the pane and "NEW YORK N.Y. U.S.A." across the bottom. This second pane, the souvenir sheet shown here in Figure 227, was sold only at the stamp show announced in the inscription and through the Philatelic Agency then located in Washington, D.C.

Souvenir sheets frequently are issued to commemorate major stamp shows and exhibitions, making those issues all the more appealing to stamp collectors.

In 1997 the United States Postal Service issued two souvenir sheets to commemorate the Pacific 97

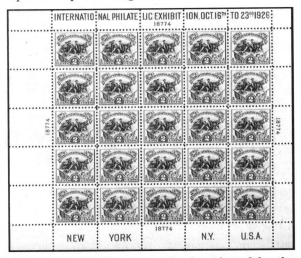

Figure 227. The first souvenir sheet issued by the United States commemorated the 1926 International Philatelic Exhibition with 25 stamps remembering the 1776 Battle of White Plains.

world stamp exhibition in San Francisco, Calif. Each sheet contained 12 stamps: one with 50¢ Benjamin Franklin stamps, the other with 60¢ George Washington stamps (Scott 3139-40). Each issue included a bold inscription across the top of the pane naming the show and the dates of its duration. The sheets were sold only during the 10-day run of the show, at the show and by mail order. After that time, most of the unsold stamps were destroyed by the Postal Service.

The Scott *Specialized Catalogue of United States Stamps & Covers* does not list this issue as a souvenir sheet, however. Instead, the stamps are each described and listed as a "pane of 12."

For World Stamp Expo 2000, which took place July 7-16 in Anaheim, Calif., the Postal Service created one mammoth issue of 15 high-value stamps. Although all 15 stamps could be obtained on a single uncut press sheet, the stamps also were sold individually and in smaller groups as four souvenir sheets measuring 5 inches by 7.25 inches, and a single round souvenir sheet measuring 3.65 inches in diameter. Figure 228 shows the round sheet.

Figure 228. A round souvenir sheet from the United States is one of five issued during July 2000 to commemorate World Stamp Expo 2000.

Most of the souvenir sheets issued by the United States to honor national and international philatelic exhibitions are clearly described in the Scott U.S. specialized catalog.

In some cases the stamps on these philatelic souvenir sheets are imperforate; that is, there are no perforations around the stamps to allow them to be removed from the souvenir sheet. An example is the 1947 Centenary International Philatelic Exhibition issue (Scott 948) shown in Figure 229. The souvenir sheet contains two stamps reproducing the designs of

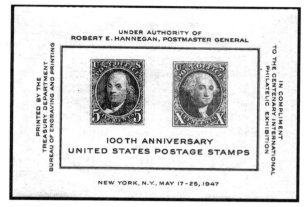

Figure 229. Souvenir sheets sometimes contain imperforate stamps. This 1946 U.S. issue may be used for 15¢ postage, or individual stamps may be cut from the pane.

the 1847 first issue of the United States: the 5¢ Franklin and the 10¢ Washington. The entire souvenir sheet could be used for 15¢ postage, or mailers, if they wished, could cut the stamps from the sheet and use them individually to pay 5¢ or 10¢ postage.

Souvenir sheets have been issued to commemorate other national and worldwide events including the 25th anniversary of Walt Disney World (Canada Scott 1621b, issued in 1996) and a 1999 solar eclipse (Hungary Scott 3639).

Some collectors look at souvenir sheets as a strategy by postal authorities to sell more stamps to collectors by creating an issue that appears to have some special significance.

A number of nations have regularly issued small single-stamp panes with high-value stamps as part of traditional stamp sets. Often these small panes do not mark any kind of event, yet many have also been labeled as souvenir sheets.

As an example, in 1996 St. Vincent issued a small pane bearing one perforated $6 stamp as part of its Birds set. The Scott catalog lists this item as a souvenir sheet, Scott 2292, though there is no commemorative inscription upon it, only the words "BIRDS OF ST. VINCENT." The single-stamp pane is shown in Figure 230.

Some collectors would argue that this small pane is not a souvenir sheet, because it is clearly not a souvenir of

Figure 230. Although it is listed as a souvenir sheet in the Scott catalog, this 1996 $6 issue from St. Vincent does not appear to be a souvenir of any event.

any event at all. Instead, they would simply consider it a small pane bearing one stamp.

Although the terminology is not as precise as most stamp collectors would prefer, the souvenir sheet is an interesting part of the stamp hobby.

Collectors may choose to collect only souvenir sheets that promote stamp shows and exhibitions, or they may look for souvenir sheets related to another type of event or some specific topic.

Many collectors enjoy souvenir sheets because they fit easily on a stamp album page. Some modern souvenir sheets contain interesting artwork as part of the decorative selvage.

Most major stamp catalogs provide descriptions that help the collector determine if the souvenir sheet has a commemorative purpose. As always, it's up to the collector to decide if any given issue is appropriate to include in his collection.

Back-of-the-book stamps have specific uses

The many postage stamps of the world fit into different classifications, depending upon the specific postage needs they are intended to fulfill.

Most postage stamps are created for use as regular postage. The majority of regular postage stamps pay the most popular letter rates, while others may fulfill rates for postcards or other types of postage fees. Stamps for regular postage usually have no special designation inscribed upon them, and they may be used alone or in combination with other stamps to pay postage fees.

Figure 231 shows a 50-lira regular postage stamp issued by Italy in 1973 to honor opera singer Enrico Caruso. In the Scott *Standard Postage Stamp Catalogue*, the stamp in Figure 231 is assigned the catalog number 1137, so a stamp collector may describe it as Italy Scott 1137. Anyone who uses the Scott stamp catalog can open to the Italy listings, look for the stamp identified as 1137, and find a description and illustration for the Caruso stamp shown in Figure 231.

The listings for each country in the Scott catalog begin with stamps classified as regular postage. Like the 50-lira Caruso stamp, they are identified with a simple number, or less frequently, a number followed by a capital letter.

The listings for regular postage stamps usually begin with the number 1 for the earliest issue and continue numerically to include the most recent stamps issued before the catalog was published.

Of course, there are exceptions to this rule. For example, the very first stamps of the kingdom of Italy begin with Scott 17. Long ago it was decided that the numbering of Italy's stamps should begin with 17 so that they could follow the 15 stamps of the kingdom of Sardinia, which preceded the 1861 establishment of the Italian kingdom. The stamps of Sardinia are now listed separately under the heading of Italian States.

Figure 231. Italy issued a 50-lira stamp honoring singer Enrico Caruso in 1973. The stamp is listed as Scott 1137 among Italy's regular issues in the Scott *Standard Postage Stamp Catalogue*.

Within any given country section of the Scott catalog, there are often other classifications of stamps following the listings for the regular postage stamps. The most common of these special stamp classifications, according to the Scott catalog, are airmail, military, newspaper, occupation, Official, parcel post, postage due, postal tax, semipostal, special delivery and war tax.

Because these classifications appear following the regular stamp listings in the Scott catalog, they are known as back-of-the-book stamps, sometimes abbreviated BOB. A BOB stamp usually can be identified by inscribed or overprinted wording that indicates the special rate, fee or purpose it is intended to fulfill.

In the Scott catalog, such stamps are listed with a special letter prefix before the Scott number. For example, airmail stamps are listed with the capital letter C followed by a number.

Some countries still issue many stamps with special classifications. Germany, Belgium, the Netherlands and many other countries regularly issue semipostal stamps. Occupation stamps and war tax stamps, however, rarely or never appear today.

Following are brief descriptions of the most common classifications listed by Scott.

Airmail (Scott prefix C): Airmail stamps pay specific rates for mail carried by airplane, either from one location in a country to a destination in the same country, or from one country to a different country. The designs of airmail stamps often feature aviation themes or show some symbolic figure of flight.

The 50-lepton airmail stamp shown in Figure 232 was issued by Greece in 1933. It depicts an aviator and the front of an airplane. In the Scott catalog it is identified as Greece Scott C8.

Many, but not all, airmail stamps from English-speaking countries can be identified by the word "airmail" appearing as part of the design.

Figure 232. The design of this 1933 Greek airmail stamp, Scott C8, includes an aviator and the front of his airplane.

Stamps from other nations use other words to identify their stamps, such as "Aereo" from Spanish-speaking lands, "Flugpost" or "Luftpost" from Germany, "Poste Aerienne" from France, and so on. The Greek words "ΕΝΑΕΡ. ΤΑΧΥΔΡ. ΣΥΓΚΟΙΝ" on the stamp in Figure 232 indicate it is intended for airmail use.

Military (Scott prefix M): Many countries have issued stamps for use by their military personnel, usually when stationed in locations outside of the home country. Often, these military stamps are simply regular postage stamps overprinted to indicate their intended use by the military. During World War II, for example, Italy issued regular definitive stamps overprinted "P.M." (for "Posta Militare") in black letters.

Some countries, including Austria, China and Finland, have created military stamps that are of a different design than any of their regular issues.

Newspaper (Scott prefix P): Different countries have had different uses for their newspaper stamps. In Denmark, newspaper stamps were attached to accounting forms. Other countries have used newspaper stamps to indicate prepaid postage for bundled or individual newspapers.

In the United States, newspaper stamps were initially used in 1865 for postage prepayment. By 1875 the stamps were being used for accounting purposes.

Figure 233. Official stamps from India (left) and some other countries include the word "SERVICE." Recent Official issues of the United States (right) are inscribed "Official Mail."

Occupation (Scott prefix N): A nation whose armed forces occupy another nation may issue stamps for use in the occupied territory. In many cases this type of occupation occurred during or after the two World Wars. The issued stamps often are the stamps of the occupying nation, overprinted to indicate where the stamps are being used.

When Germany occupied the French regions of Alsace and Lorraine early in World War II, German definitive stamps picturing Paul von Hindenburg were overprinted with the names of the French regions for use as postage in the occupied territories. Those stamps are listed in the Scott catalog as France N27-58.

Official (Scott prefix O): Official stamps are issued by governments to pay for postage on mail sent by authorized government representatives and officials. Official stamps are used by some postal services to pay for their own postage as well.

A 1984 50-paisa Official mail stamp from India, Scott O220, is shown at left in Figure 233. The inscribed word "SERVICE" indicates its Official status. A 1995 20¢ Official mail stamp from the United States, Scott O155, is shown at right in Figure 233.

Parcel post (Scott prefix Q): The Universal Postal Union established international parcel post service in 1878 for the purpose of mailing parcels or merchandise. Individual countries also have developed domestic parcel post services, and many, including the United States, have created stamps specifically for parcel post use.

Postage due (Scott prefix J): Many countries have used postage due stamps to indicate that payment is required from the intended recipient of a letter because the sender did not apply enough postage.

Figure 234 shows at left a 1934

Figure 234. Postage due stamps from Denmark (left) bear the word "PORTO." Most postage dues from Great Britain (right) are marked "TO PAY," though some say "POSTAGE DUE."

1-øre postage due stamp from Denmark, Scott J25, inscribed "PORTO." At right in Figure 234 is a 1970 20-penny postage due stamp from Great Britain, Scott J88, inscribed "TO PAY." The earliest British postage dues included the phrase "POSTAGE DUE."

Postal tax (Scott prefix RA): Some countries have raised money for government projects by instituting a postal tax. During specified periods, every piece of mail sent within the country has to pay the postal tax by using a special stamp created for that purpose, as an addition to the regular postage fees required for mailing.

Semipostal (Scott prefix B): A semipostal stamp (sometimes called a charity stamp) pays for postage and also collects funds for a specified charity or government project. Most semipostals show two denominations separated by a plus (+) sign. The first denomination indicates the postage fee, and the second tells how much is being donated to charity. Semipostal stamp use is usually voluntary.

Figure 235 shows a German 100 pfennig+50pf semipostal issued in 1995 to raise funds for the German Youth Stamp Foundation. The charity value of the stamp (in this case 50pf) is known as the surtax.

Figure 235. This German semipostal stamp was issued in 1995 to help raise funds for a youth stamp-collecting charity, indicated by the surtax amount shown as "+50."

The first U.S. semipostal stamps are simply inscribed "First Class." They are also sold for a specific amount more than the first-class postage amount, with the surtax assigned to a specific cause.

Special delivery (Scott prefix E): In the United States, special delivery service once provided for a mailed item to be delivered promptly to the addressee, even after the scheduled daily delivery for that customer had passed. Similar services were offered in other countries. The first U.S. special delivery stamp, Scott E1 from 1885, is shown in Figure 236.

War tax (Scott prefix MR): War tax stamps were used primarily during World War I to help pay the expenses of war by raising additional revenue. War tax stamps are mostly previously issued definitives with the overprinted message "war tax." The United States has not issued any war tax stamps.

Figure 236. U.S. special delivery stamps, such as this 10¢ issue of 1885, Scott E1, were used by mailers to ensure prompt mail delivery.

There are many interesting stamps that actually combine two or more of the stamp classifications described here. In such cases, the Scott number letter prefix is a combination of the appropriate letters. For example, Greece issued postal tax semipostal stamps in 1943. These mandatory issues are listed as Scott RAB1-3.

Iceland issued numerous stamps Jan. 1, 1930, including an airmail stamp overprinted for Official mail use. The airmail Official stamp is listed as Iceland Scott CO1.

These stamps have all played different roles in the history of mail delivery. Finding them in the catalog can sometimes be a challenge, if the collector is looking among the regular postage issues.

The collector who learns and recognizes the inscriptions that often identify back-of-the-book stamps will find it easier to track down the facts about them.

Semipostals pay for postage and more

Though semipostal stamps have been created and sold by postal services in other countries for more than a century, the first to be issued by the United States made its debut in 1998.

In 1897, the good people of the British colony New South Wales (now part of the country of Australia) came up with an interesting idea. Money was needed to fund a facility in Sydney to care for consumptives — men and women who were suffering from the debilitating effects of pulmonary tuberculosis, which was then a critical public health concern. At the same time, new postage stamps were being planned for the diamond jubilee of Queen Victoria, to celebrate her 60th year as Britain's monarch.

It was decided to offer for sale to the public two large and very colorful postage stamps marking the anniversary, to be sold for a special price. The 1-penny stamp, with the queen's portrait in the upper-right corner, was sold for 1 shilling. The 2d stamp was sold for 2/6d.

If you're not familiar with the predecimal monetary abbreviations of Great Britain and its colonies, the small letter "d" stands for "penny" and the slash ("/") after a numeral stands for "shilling." Therefore, "2/6d" stands for "2 shillings and 6 pence." For stamps issued after Britain's 1971 changeover to decimal currency, the small letter "p" is used to designate "penny."

Each of the New South Wales stamps was printed with both of the applicable values upon them. The designs featured allegories of charity, images of stronger women helping the weak. The extra money accumulated from the sale of these so-called charity stamps was accepted as a donation from the stamp buyer and was used to help maintain the desperately needed medical facilities.

According to the 24th edition of *The Australasian Stamp Catalogue*, the money raised was added to a fund that helped create the Queen Victoria Home for Consumptives, Thirlmere, and a second home at Wentworth Falls.

Figure 237. The world's first semipostal stamps, issued in New South Wales to benefit a much-needed medical facility, frank this 1897 cover addressed to London, England.

As the 1897 cover from Aberdeen, NSW, to London, England, shown in

Figure 238. Like most semipostal stamps, this 1998 issue from Germany shows two value figures: the 220-pfennig postal value and the 80pf donation value. The combined total results in a 300pf cost to the customer.

Figure 237 demonstrates, both stamps could be used for postage. However, despite the high cost of the stamps, their postal values were still only 1d and 2d. This innovative fund-raising method was the first use of charity stamps, which in the United States came to be known by the name "semipostals."

The word "semipostal" implies that only part ("semi") of the cost of the stamp is valid for postage.

Throughout the next 100 years, many other countries began to use this method to provide an easy and inexpensive way for its citizens to donate to charitable causes while purchasing postage stamps.

Among the countries that have issued semipostal stamps are Albania, Austria, Belgium, Canada, Denmark, France, Japan, Russia and many others.

Some countries, such as Great Britain and Cuba, have issued very few semipostals and have not pursued an active semipostal program. Others, including Belgium, Germany and Switzerland, continue to issue several semipostals every year for the benefit of various charities.

The two charity stamps from New South Wales each are inscribed with both the full cost of the stamp and the postal value. The modern method for indicating these values is shown on the 1998 German Youth stamp shown in Figure 238, from a set of five stamps that show various cartoon film characters. Figure 238 shows the high value of the set, depicting the goblin Pumuckl. The value of the stamp is inscribed in the upper-right corner of the design as "220+80." The purchase price of the stamp was 300 pfennigs (which adds up to three German marks). The postal value of the stamp is 220pf.

While the stamp was on sale, the German postal service donated the additional 80pf of payment to the German Youth Stamp Foundation, to promote the well-being of young people. The donation amount is also known as a "surtax," a word that simply means an extra charge or tax.

Almost all semipostal stamps around the world are marked in this fashion to indicate the value of the stamp for postage plus the amount of the charitable donation.

Germany's various semipostal stamps issued each year benefit a number of different charities, including the National Sports Promotion Foundation, the Foundation for Promotion of Philately and Postal History, and public welfare organizations.

The first semipostal stamp from the United States was

Figure 239. The surtax collected from sales of the first U.S. semipostal benefited breast cancer research efforts.

issued July 29, 1998. The design of the stamp is shown in Figure 239.

The stamp came about as the result of a Congressional effort to benefit breast cancer research. A bill signed into law by President Bill Clinton required the Postal Service to issue the stamp. The surtax collected from the sale of the Breast Cancer Research semipostal stamp was earmarked for the National Institutes of Health and the Defense Department. Both agencies are engaged in research to stop the disease.

The stamp, as you can see from the illustration, is nondenominated, in part because it was issued not long before an increase in first-class postage rates. The stamps initially sold for 40¢. For the first five months, the postage value was 32¢, and 8¢ was designated for research. When U.S. postage rates went up by 1¢ on Jan. 1, 1999, the postage value of the stamp increased to 33¢, and the surtax was subsequently reduced 1¢ per stamp, to 7¢.

Another rate increase Jan. 7, 2000, changed the stamp to a 34¢ stamp with a 6¢ surcharge. On March 23, 2002, the cost of the stamp was revalued at 45¢, making the surcharge 11¢ for just a few weeks. Postage rates increased to 37¢ on June 30, 2002, and the surtax value of the Breast Cancer Research semipostal was reduced to 8¢.

In the Scott *Standard Postage Stamp Catalogue*, collectors can find semipostal stamps listed immediately following the regular issues for any given country. Regular issues normally appear first in a country's listing, usually with

SEMI-POSTAL STAMPS

Allegory of Charity
SP1   SP2
Illustrations reduced.

1897, June   Wmk. 55   Perf. 11
B1 SP1 1p (1sh) grn &
         brn   37.50   37.50
B2 SP2 2½p (2sh6p) rose,
         bl & gold   200.00 *200.00*
Diamond Jubilee of Queen Victoria.
The difference between the postal and face values of these stamps was donated to a fund for a home for consumptives.

Figure 240. Listings for semipostal stamps appear separately in the Scott *Standard Postage Stamp Catalog*.

Scott catalog numbers beginning with No. "1." After the listings for the most recent issues, semipostal stamps are listed, with Scott catalog numbers prefixed by the letter "B." For example, shown in Figure 240 are the Scott catalog listings for the two New South Wales semipostals. The stamps are assigned Scott catalog numbers B1 and B2 for New South Wales, and a brief description of the two stamps is also provided.

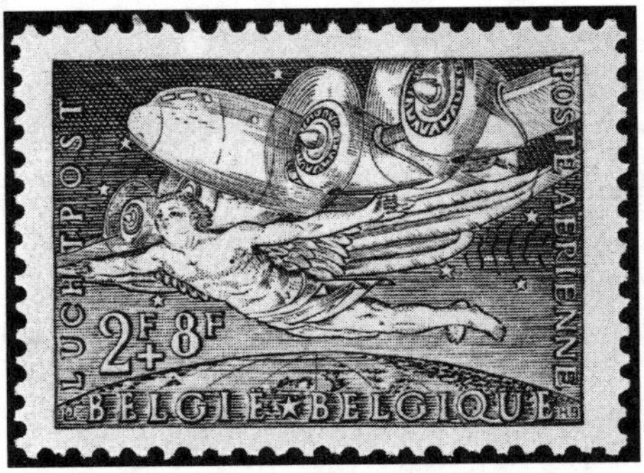

In a few instances, stamps designated for other tasks, such as airmail, also work as semipostals. The example shown in Figure 241 is Belgium Scott CB3, a 1946 airmail semipostal stamp. The stamp sold for 10 francs. Of that, 2fr paid for postage and 8fr was collected as a surtax for the National Aeronautical Committee.

Figure 241. An airmail semipostal stamp from Belgium, Scott CB3, issued in 1946.

Stamp collectors are clearly divided on the issue of semipostals, with many expressing a dislike for the surtax concept.

When the U.S. Breast Cancer Research semipostal bill was sent to President Clinton, Randy Neil, then-president of the American Philatelic Society, wrote a letter asking the president to veto the bill.

In part, Neil noted: "Stamp collectors see semipostal stamps as a tax that falls disproportionately and unfairly on our hobby. Stamp collectors will buy a substantial percentage of these stamps and as a consequence pay a substantial portion of the premium."

Linn's Stamp News editorial director Michael Laurence in his Editor's Choice column also spoke out against semipostals as an unfair tax on collectors. He cited a report from the U.S. General Accounting Office that noted that collectors in other countries have voiced objections to "supporting causes against their will when they collect a complete set of stamps issued by the country."

Other collectors have little opinion or they favor the idea of semipostals, choosing to believe that collecting a 40¢ semipostal is hardly different from collecting, say, the 1990 40¢ Claire Chennault stamp issued in the Great Americans series.

Not long before the Breast Cancer Research semipostal stamp was issued, collector Laurence Gross wrote to *Linn's*, "I applaud the prospective issue of the Breast Cancer Research semipostal," noting that many thousands of dollars may be raised for "this worthy cause."

In fact, after five years, more than 475 million stamps had been sold, raising nearly $34 million for research.

As with all stamps, collectors always have the freedom to choose whether or not they wish to add semipostals to their stamp collections.

Airmail collecting can take you anywhere

When Wilbur and Orville Wright made the first power-driven, controlled, heavier-than-air airplane flights on Dec. 17, 1903, they envisioned that their efforts could someday lead to passengers and mail being transported by air. Eventually others saw the benefits of using airplanes to carry the mail, and it was only about a decade after the Wright brothers' experimental flights at Kitty Hawk, N.C., that airmail service became a reality.

Airmail has been an important element of the stamp hobby for many years. The interests of the airmail collector can easily go back to the 1859 mail-carrying balloon flight of John Wise in Indiana, or at least to the 1870s, when mail was sent from Paris by manned balloon and pigeon post during the Franco-German war. There is even a record of messages sent by French balloon from a fortress at Conde in 1793.

The airmail collecting community acknowledges many forms of air transportation besides the airplane, including catapults, zeppelins, helicopters, rockets and manned spacecraft.

Some of today's collectors focus on assembling collections of stamps that have been created for airmail service, while others look for the envelopes, postcards and aerograms that have been sent through the mail and document airmail postal history.

Figure 242. The first airmail stamp in the world (left) was an overprinted special delivery stamp issued by Italy in 1917. The first U.S. airmail stamp (right), issued in 1918, was the first stamp specifically printed for airmail use.

The first airmail stamp is generally acknowledged to be the overprinted 25-centesimo issue from Italy placed on sale in May 1917. The stamp was originally an Italian special delivery stamp that was overprinted with three lines of text in black type:

ESPERIMENTO POST AEREA
MAGGIO 1917
TORINO-ROMA • ROMA-TORINO

The overprint translates as "Air post experiment, May 1917, Turin-Rome, Rome-Turin." An example of Italy Scott C1, the world's first airmail stamp, is shown at left in Figure 242.

The letter C that appears as a prefix of the Scott catalog number for this stamp designates a stamp intended for airmail use. Such stamps often have the word "airmail" or the foreign language equivalent printed upon them.

The Italian airmail stamp was created for an experimental flight that took place May 20, 1917, and returned May 27. The plane carried 440 pounds of mail and 200 newspapers.

The world's first airmail stamp doesn't show an airplane, but it does mention "air post" in the overprint.

The first stamp specially printed for airmail doesn't say airmail anywhere on it, but it shows an airplane well known to collectors of U.S. stamps: the Curtiss JN4H, also known as the "Jenny."

The United States issued three airmail stamps in 1918. The first, placed on sale May 13, has a denomination of 24¢ and was printed in two colors: a carmine-red frame around a blue vignette (the central part of the design) of the Curtiss Jenny in flight. The stamp is shown in Figure 242.

The reason that stamp collectors know this stamp so well is that one of the world's greatest stamp errors was created with this issue. Known as the "Inverted Jenny," the error stamp shows the airplane flying upside down instead of right side up.

Only 100 examples of the error stamp were ever found, bought as a single pane the day the stamps first went on sale by a stamp collector named William T. Robey.

In *Airmail Antics*, a book published by *Linn's Stamp News*, author Fred Boughner points out that the very plane shown on the first U.S. airmail stamp was also the very first plane used May 15, 1918, to carry the nation's first organized airmail delivery — right down to the five-digit identification number, 38262, that appears on the side of the plane on the stamp.

Although *Airmail Antics* is now out of print, it still may be available from some dealers in philatelic literature.

The cost of the first U.S. airmail stamp met the price for airmail delivery of a letter along a route between Washington, D.C., Philadelphia and New York City.

Even though the 24¢ Jenny airmail stamp was the first U.S. airmail issue, it was not the first stamp to show an airplane. That honor goes to the 1913 U.S. parcel post stamp issued in 1913 (and shown here in Figure 243). Below the vignette is printed the phrase, "Aeroplane Carrying Mail."

Figure 243. This 1913 stamp from the United States is a parcel post stamp, not an airmail, but it was the first postage stamp in the world to picture an airplane.

Many countries have issued airmail stamps over the years, often with various denominations to fulfill postage rates for domestic or international delivery, or mail of varying weights.

U.S. airmail was for many years divided into two basic categories, domestic and international, with additional rates for other airmail services (such as airmail special delivery and airmail postcards). As a very basic example, domestic airmail letter service in 1964 was available for 8¢ per ounce, while international airmail service to Europe during the same year was 15¢ per half-ounce. Appropriate airmail stamps were available to fulfill either rate.

This seemingly simple rate explanation belies the fact that airmail rates were far more complex during the early years of air service, and specialist collectors often engage in substantial research to understand the postage fees paid for the delivery of letters in years past.

The U.S. domestic and international airmail stamps are listed together as one group in the Scott *Specialized Catalogue of United States Stamps & Covers*. Immediately following the listings of the airmail stamps are separate listings for airmail special delivery stamps (a 16¢ blue stamp from 1934 and a 16¢ red and blue stamp from 1936), and two airmail semiofficial stamps (a 5¢ balloon post stamp issued in 1877 and a 25¢ privately issued airmail stamp from 1911).

The United States and many other countries also have issued postal stationery items that were specially designed for airmail purposes. One of the more common of these items is the aerogram or air letter sheet, which consists of one lightweight sheet, normally imprinted with a stamp. The message is written on one side of the sheet, which is then folded into the shape of an envelope, sealed and addressed.

Stamped envelopes and postal cards for airmail use were also sold at post offices in many countries. An unused 1985 airmail postal card from the United

Figure 244. This 1985 postal card from the United States is an example of airmail postal stationery. Similar airmail items include stamped envelopes and aerograms (air letter sheets).

States is shown in Figure 244. The 33¢ value imprinted on the card fulfills the international postal card rate in effect from Feb. 17, 1985, to April 2, 1988.

A stamp collector may collect the airmail stamps and postal stationery items of a specific country as part of the general country collection, or he may develop a specialty interest in airmail stamps from one or more countries.

Another collecting interest for airmail enthusiasts is the field of cover collecting. Covers are mailed envelopes, postcards, wrappers and similar items, and they are collected for the way they document certain rates or specific airmail flights.

A simple envelope bearing one 15¢ U.S. airmail stamp mailed in 1964 from the United States to an address in Germany might not be particularly valuable, but it would be a legitimate example of the half-ounce international airmail letter rate then in effect.

As cover collectors build their collections, they are continually challenged to find examples that represent rates that are more complex, which often means that legitimate examples are scarcer. Many collectors are also intrigued by souvenir covers created years ago by their predecessors in the airmail-collecting specialty.

The cover pictured in Figure 245 was sent by zeppelin mail on the first Europe-Pan American round-trip flight of Germany's *Graf Zeppelin*. The envelope is marked with a 1930 New York City postmark and two circular cachets (in this case, stamped markings) documenting the zeppelin journey. Added to all of this is the presence of three cherished U.S. airmail stamps: the 1930 Graf Zeppelin set issued specifically to commemorate the round-trip flight. These three stamps, with denominations of 65¢, $1.30 and $2.60, were available at post offices for only 73 days. They were withdrawn from sale June 30.

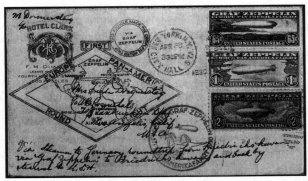

Figure 245. Many factors can affect the value of an airmail cover, including the stamps franking the envelope, mailing date, postal markings, private cachets and the flight itself.

The cover shown in Figure 245, with a few minor faults, sold for nearly $1,000 during a 1990 auction.

Some airmail covers sell for much more than $1,000, and of course, there are many that also sell for far less.

Just consider the many airmail collecting areas that exist: Charles Lindbergh flight covers, contract airmail covers (flown by private carriers under contract to the U.S. federal government) including first flights, airport cancellations, interrupted (crash) mail, historic flights, military flights, space covers and much more.

Many airmail collectors rely upon philatelic references that help them research and understand the items they collect. For example, the airmail rate information quoted earlier in this article comes from two important books by Henry W. Beecher and Anthony S. Wawrukiewicz: *U.S. Domestic Postal Rates, 1872-1993* and *U.S. International Postal Rates, 1872-1996*.

The five-volume *American Air Mail Catalogue* published by the American Air Mail Society is a truly remarkable record of many significant airmail-collecting areas, including documentation of contract airmail routes and many other topics that have been mentioned in this article.

Postage dues can take many different forms

Postage due stamps have been used by many nations to ensure that proper payment is made for the delivery of mail.

When postal authorities find a piece of mail that does not show full postage payment, they usually try to collect the postage amount that is owed, either from the sender or the addressee.

To begin this process, the short-paid item is marked in some way to identify it as postage due. Often, postage due stamps are used for this purpose, applied directly on the item to show the amount due. Hand-stamped and handwritten markings also serve notice that postage payment is incomplete.

A 10-centime postage due stamp created by French authorities in 1859 is considered to be the first such issue in the world. Unused examples of the stamp, shown in Figure 246, are quite scarce today.

Figure 246. This French stamp from 1859 is considered to be the world's first postage due.

This early French postage due stamp is identified in the Scott *Standard Postage Stamp Catalogue* as France Scott J1. Scott editors use the prefix "J" to identify postage due stamps, which appear in each country's listings following regular postage stamps, semipostals and airmails.

There is, in fact, a postage due listing in the Scott catalog for Netherlands Indies J2 that dates from 1845, 14 years before the French postage due. However, this typeset, fill-in-the-blank label is listed separately from postage due stamps in the Dutch stamp catalog *Speciale Postzegelcatalogus*. It is classified there as an overland mail marking, and it likely served a somewhat different purpose than that country's regular postage due stamps. Figure 247 shows the stamp as it is illustrated in the Dutch catalog.

Postage due stamps may look quite plain to some collectors, but generally they are utilitarian stamps, manufactured for function rather than for beauty.

Of the three worldwide postage due stamps pictured in Figure 248, the 5-penny 1984 stamp at left from Gibraltar (J15) shows just how basic these stamp designs can get.

At least it has a design all its own, which is not true for the other two

Figure 247. This 1845 stamp from Netherlands Indies is listed as a postage due stamp in the Scott catalog, but the Dutch catalog *Speciale Postzegelcatalogus* describes it differently.

stamps in the same illustration. The 1921 Austrian postage due (J102) in the center and the 1987 issue from Suriname (J63) at right are simply previously issued regular postage stamps overprinted with words that convert them into postage dues.

The United States issued its first postage due stamps in 1879. It discontinued using postage dues in 1985. Over the course of more than 100 years, the United States issued more than 100 postage due stamps with just four basic designs. For all of these issues, the colors range only from brown to red, and the central design for all of them is just a numeral of value.

In 1913 the United States also issued parcel post postage due stamps, a set of five green stamps, again prominently featuring the numeral of value. Before the year was out, these stamps, originally intended for exclusive use on parcel post mail, were allowed to be used as regular postage due stamps.

The cover shown at the top of Figure 249 illustrates one way regular U.S. postage due stamps were used on short-paid mail.

Mailed March 16, 1968, from Incline Village, Nev., to Rockland, Maine, when the domestic letter rate was 6¢, this envelope bears the 6¢ Illinois Statehood stamp issued just one month before.

The postage due assessment of an additional 6¢ is marked on the cover in two ways: by the handstamped message "POSTAGE DUE" applied below the postage stamp with the value "6¢" written in by hand, and by the two postage due

Figure 248. The 1984 Gibraltar postage due at left shows a fairly plain design. The 1921 Austrian postage due in the center and the 1987 issue from Suriname at right are both regular-issue postage stamps overprinted with postage due messages.

Figure 249. U.S. postage due stamps are used on the 1968 cover at left, an overweight first-class envelope sent at letter rate. The postcard below, mailed from Austria in 1982, was also short paid. The "T" marking to the left of the stamps includes information used by the delivery office to determine the amount of postage the recipient must yet pay.

stamps from the 1959 series to the left of the postage stamp, Scott J89 (1¢) and J93 (5¢).

The envelope, with its "DO NOT BEND" handstamp near the bottom, almost certainly carried more than 1 ounce in weight. In 1968 each additional ounce of postage was also assessed 6¢, which accounts for the 6¢ postage due marking and stamps.

Postage due stamps were used in addition to handstamped markings to provide some accountability for the funds collected while processing this mail. As use of the stamps declined in the 1970s, post offices more frequently used specially marked postage due meter stamps.

Because of the many different world currencies, analyzing short-paid mail coming in from foreign countries can be much more complex, but the countries of the world have devised a system to determine how much should be collected to process a short-paid item.

The Universal Postal Union was established in 1874 to foster postal cooperation among the many countries of the world.

Not long after, it was agreed that short-paid mail sent internationally would be marked with a stamped letter "T" (for the French word "taxe") and assessed the amount due in French centimes, which each country could then convert to its own currency.

The "T" marking is still in use today, though the method of assessing postage due on international mail has changed.

The postcard shown at the bottom of Figure 249 was mailed in 1982 from Austria to the United States. The letter "T" appears in a box with two numbers: 100, which represents the short-paid amount in the currency of the sending office (Austria), over 700, which in this case represents the Austrian overseas surface rate.

That fraction, 100 over 700, is multiplied by the U.S. foreign surface rate in effect at the time, 30¢, which would round down to 4¢. Added to a 42¢ international handling charge put into effect in 1981, it totals the 46¢ postage due assessment marked on the postal card in the lower part of the address.

In recent years, U.S. postal authorities have used many different markings to indicate postage due on short-paid mail.

The postcard shown in Figure 250 was originally mailed in 1998 without any stamp on it. The mailer may have mistakenly believed the preprinted card was postage paid business reply mail.

The unfranked card was spotted en route and marked with a red pointing-finger "RETURN FOR POSTAGE" handstamp directing the item back to the mailer (whose name and address were carefully printed on the reverse of the card).

Figure 250. Originally mailed without a stamp, this 1998 postcard was struck with a red pointing-finger "RETURN FOR POSTAGE" marking and sent back to the sender (whose name and address are on the reverse of the postcard).

On his second attempt to mail the same card, the mailer overpaid the postcard rate by 12¢, applying a 32¢ letter-rate stamp instead, and the card was delivered successfully.

On some occasions, the mail carrier may deliver the short-paid item and leave an envelope requesting the amount of money due, as shown in Figure 251. The addressee then pays that amount and leaves it in the mailbox for the carrier to retrieve on the next visit.

Postal historians enjoy looking for various uses of postage due stamps. The example shown in Figure 252 is a 1950 due bill on a post office form assessing a Chicago postal customer $1.06 for postage due, most likely a day's worth of business reply mail or short-paid business mail.

Three postage due stamps are affixed to the form: a $1 (J77) from the 1930 series and two 3¢ (J82) from the 1931 series.

There are so many different domestic and international postage due stamps and markings that collectors interested in the field are likely to specialize in a

Figure 251. An envelope without a return address marked postage due, delivered with a payment envelope from the U.S. Postal Service for the addressee to submit the 23¢ due.

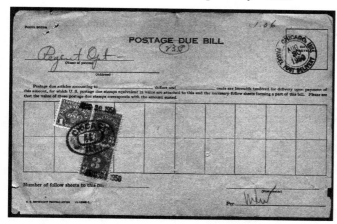

Figure 252. A 1950 postage due bill bearing $1.06 in U.S. postage due stamps. Such bills serve as invoices for payment of multiple short-paid pieces or business-reply mail accounts.

certain area, such as "T" markings, short-paid mail from or to one specific country, or domestic postage due.

Postage due stamps saved on cover are particularly interesting because they help to document the postal history of short-paid mail.

Some of the information on postage dues provided here was obtained from two books by Anthony S. Wawrukiewicz and Henry W. Beecher that are indispensable for understanding postage rates and the assessment of postage due charges: *U.S. Domestic Postal Rates, 1872-1999*, and *U.S. International Postal Rates, 1872-1996*.

What's so official about Official stamps?

Stamp collectors occasionally come upon postage stamps or postal stationery marked or overprinted with the word "Official." The term can be confusing, because it seems like all mail delivered by a postal authority would be considered official.

While that's true, the term "Official mail" is used to describe mail that is sent by employees and officials of selected government agencies, including postal authorities. Special stamps and postal stationery are created for use by these agencies, although most Official mail in the United States is paid for by postage meter stamps and permit imprints — much like what you find on most daily mail.

Postage stamps were first created for use on Official mail in the United States following an Act of Congress approved March 3, 1873.

It became apparent in the years following the Civil War (1861-65) that government officials were abusing the free-franking privilege that allowed them to send government mail using only their signature for postage. In an attempt to curb these abuses, Congress abolished the franking privilege in 1873 and authorized the manufacture of Official postage stamps with distinctive designs for nine government departments: Agriculture, Executive, Interior, Justice, Navy, Post Office, State, Treasury and War. The theory was that the designation of specific postage stamps would establish greater accountability for each department.

The first Official stamps were printed by the Continental Bank Note Co. using the same vignettes (central designs) as the regular-issue stamps of 1870. Shown at left in Figure 253, for example, is the 10¢ brown 1870 Thomas Jefferson stamp (Scott 139). At right is the 1873 10¢ carmine-red Official stamp (Scott O14) issued for the Executive Department.

Figure 253. The 1873 Official stamps from the United States used vignette designs of the 1870 regular issue. Shown are the 10¢ postage stamp of that series (left) and a 10¢ Official designated for use by the Executive Department.

In the Scott *Standard Postage Stamp Catalogue*, Official mail stamps are identified with the prefix letter "O" and appear in the catalog following regular postage issues and other stamps designated for specific uses, such as airmail, special delivery, postage due and so on.

The Official stamp in Figure 253 does not include the word Official in its inscription. Instead, it includes the name of the department authorized to use the stamp ("Executive") in an arch across the top of the portrait. There are also minor changes around the frame that make it different from the regular postage stamp.

The colors of the 1870 regular postage stamps were determined by the denomination of the stamp: the 1¢ was blue, the 2¢ was red brown, the 3¢ was green, and so on.

The colors of the Official stamps (or departmentals, as they have sometimes been called) were determined by the stamps' department designation: all Executive stamps were carmine red, all Navy stamps were blue, all Treasury stamps were brown, and so on.

The oddballs of the group, the stamps of the Post Office Department, were printed in black with no portrait. Within the oval vignette frame was only a large numeral of value and the words "OFFICIAL STAMP."

Official mail stamped envelopes were created at about the same time as the departmental stamps, first by the George H. Reay Co. of Brooklyn, N.Y., and then by Plimpton Manufacturing Co. of Hartford, Conn. The envelopes were created with several denominations and were designated for use by the Post Office Department and the War Department.

Figure 254 shows the stamped portion of Scott UO1, the 2¢ Post Office Department envelope that is the first Official envelope listed in the Scott *Specialized Catalogue of United States Stamps & Covers*.

In 1875, Continental Bank Note created a set of ungummed Official stamps with each issue overprinted with the word "Specimen." Some of these special printings are among the most valuable U.S. Official stamps. Some of the higher dollar value issues sell for thousands of dollars apiece.

In 1879, American Bank Note Co. printed selected values of the Official postage stamp series using the

Figure 254. The imprinted stamp from U.S. Scott UO1, the 1873 2¢ Official mail envelope for the Post Office Department.

same designs as the earlier set.

The practice of using Official stamps and envelopes was discontinued in 1884, though most of the stamps were supplanted by the use of penalty envelopes as early as 1879. Such envelopes bore a printed message declaring that they were intended for Official use only and that illegal use would result in a penalty (fine).

In 1910, Congress approved a new series of Official stamps for use by administrators of the U.S. Postal Savings program. The stamps bore no portrait but instead included the words "OFFICIAL MAIL" within a central oval. Six stamps were issued in denominations ranging from 1¢ to $1, along with three stamped envelopes in 1911 (Scott UO70-72) and a single 1¢ postal card in 1913 (Scott UZ1).

The use of Postal Savings mail stamps and stationery was discontinued in 1914, and 69 years passed before collectors saw new Official mail issues.

In 1983 a new style of Official mail stamp appeared, depicting the Great Seal of the United States and including the words "Official Mail USA" across the top of the stamp. Six values of sheet stamps and a 20¢ coil stamp were issued initially, with more stamps arriving following the Feb. 17, 1985, increase in domestic letter rates.

The design of the new Official mail stamp remained fairly consistent into the 21st century. Earlier issues were created by intaglio printing, which uses a recess-engraved die to create a plate that transfers a relief image directly to the paper. Beginning in 1988, Official mail stamps were printed by offset lithography, a process that indirectly transfers the plate image onto the surface of the stamp paper.

In 1993 a horizontal line of microprinted type was added just below the Great Seal design. Shown in Figure 255 is the $1 lithographed Official mail stamp of 1993, Scott O151.

Although modern Official mail stamps have been available since 1983, they are only infrequently found on covers from a limited number of agencies. It is much more convenient for most federal offices to make use of Official postage meters or Official

Figure 255. The $1 Official mail stamp, Scott O151, issued in 1993.

permit-imprint envelopes. As a result, collectors should save intact any covers bearing postally used Official mail stamps. Examples showing the agency where the mail originated and the date of mailing are of greater value than a single postally used stamp soaked off a cover.

Official mail postal cards and stamped envelopes with designs that matched the new series of stamps were also issued in 1983. The 1999 33¢ Official mail envelope, Scott UO89, is shown in Figure 256.

Many countries around the world have used official mail stamps and postal stationery.

Some nations create special designs for these items in the same way that the United States does. Many other nations have used overprints on regular-issue postage stamps to mark them for Official use only. Figure 257 shows Scott O3

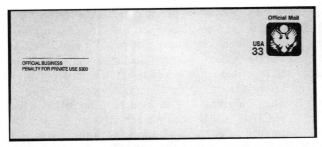

Figure 256. The imprinted stamp on the 33¢ Official mail stamped envelope of 1999, Scott UO89, resembles the design of the modern Official mail postage stamp.

from Basutoland, a scarce 2-penny red-violet Official stamp from 1934. The word "OFFICIAL" is printed across the stamp in black letters.

Similar overprints used by countries in the British Commonwealth also include such overprints as "O.S." (for "Official Service"), "Service," "O.H.M.S." (for "On His [or Her] Majesty's Service") and others.

The "O.H.M.S." initials are also found perforated through the designs of some Canadian Official stamps. Other Canadian Official stamps are overprinted with the single letter "G" in black.

Official stamps of South Australia from 1868-74 are overprinted with any of 55 abbreviations for various government departments, from "A" for "Architect" to "W" for "Waterworks."

Other nations around the world often use designations in their native languages to identify Official

Figure 257. Official stamps from countries around the world often are marked to indicate their status. Shown is Basutoland Scott O3.

issues. Official stamps from around the world are also listed in the Scott *Standard Postage Stamp Catalogue*.

Stamp collectors can purchase U.S. Official stamps and postal stationery items, when they are available, from the U.S. Postal Service, but because of the Official designation, such items cannot be used for regular postage by individuals.

Revenue stamps are proof that tax was paid

One way to describe what a revenue stamp is is to describe what it isn't. It isn't a postage stamp, though in some cases revenue stamps have been used to pay postage.

A postage stamp is actually a receipt to show that postage has been prepaid. The stamp you use to mail your letter is simply proof that you have paid the required amount to have your letter delivered.

In this way, a revenue stamp is similar to a postage stamp, as it also provides proof that a required fee has been paid. However, that fee is not for postage. Instead, revenue stamps act as receipts for fees usually levied on government-regulated transactions that are taxed to raise revenue.

Figure 258. Countries all around the world have issued revenue stamps to raise funds for government treasuries. The three North American examples shown here (left to right) are from the United States, Canada and Mexico.

As an example, the taxed sale in the United States of some controlled substances, such as alcoholic beverages, tobacco products or narcotics, all contributed to the issuance and use of revenue stamps documenting the transactions.

In the Scott *Specialized Catalogue of United States Stamps & Covers*, revenue stamps are listed beginning with the prefix "R." Revenue stamps for wine and beer are listed with the prefixes "RE" and "REA," respectively. Tobacco sales tax stamps are listed with the prefix "RJ," while narcotic tax stamps are found with the prefix "RJA."

Revenue stamps have been referred to as fiscal stamps from time to time to emphasize that they are used to obtain tax funds.

Revenue stamps are issued by many countries throughout the world. Three examples, from the United States, Canada and Mexico, are shown in Figure 258. Different nations have different circumstances under which revenue stamps are used.

Revenue stamps can be very difficult to identify for a number of reasons. In some cases, the stamps may not bear the name of the country of issue. In other instances, a revenue stamp may look like a postage stamp, and the collector can be frustrated when he is unable to locate it in a standard postage stamp catalog.

The Scott specialized catalog lists many U.S. revenue stamps, and the catalog editors have reviewed listings in the past and updated them with new information. However, not all U.S. revenue stamps appear in the catalog, and foreign revenue stamps generally are not listed in the Scott *Standard Postage Stamp Catalogue*.

Though revenue stamp collecting can be a very satisfying challenge for the collector, it is also an area that requires patience and study. Revenue stamp scholars continue to learn new information about the many issues that are known in the United States and worldwide.

Many U.S. collectors enjoy revenue stamps because they appreciate the engraved designs that appear on many issues.

The first revenue stamps used in what is now the United States were the 1755 colonial issues of Massachusetts, Scott RM1-RM4. These were typographed seals or embossed directly on documents. About 10 years later, other revenue stamps issued by Britain for use in the colonies were put into service.

In 1862, U.S. adhesive revenue stamps were created to help raise needed funds for the government during the Civil War. The Revenue Act of 1862, created by Congress, was devised to bring more money into the federal treasury. The Scott specialized catalog lists 102 stamps for this first revenue issue that were applied to bills of lading, bank checks, bonds and even playing cards.

The stamps that were created have "U.S. Inter. Rev." (U.S. Internal Revenue) or a similar phrase inscribed on them, a very helpful clue in identifying U.S. revenue stamps. The stamps often are found intentionally imperforate as well as partially perforated and fully perforated on two different kinds of stamp paper.

Scott R54, a 50¢ Conveyance stamp from the first U.S. issue, is shown at left in Figure 258.

A second issue of documentary stamps appeared in 1871, creating 31 new stamps, mostly with blue frames and black portraits. Ten proprietary stamps, listed with the Scott prefix "RB," also were issued during 1871-74.

Almost immediately, a third documentary issue was created, because the similarly colored second-issue documentary stamps were causing confusion among the users.

While some designs of the second issue were repeated with new colors, a new stamp appeared featuring a representation of "Liberty" (earlier issues had depicted George Washington).

Revenue stamps for beer were printed by the Treasury Department beginning in 1866. The denomination for these larger stamps varied depending on the size of the beer container. The 1871 beer tax stamp in Figure 259, Scott REA20, reflects the initial tax rate of 12½¢ for one-eighth of a barrel of beer.

Special stamps taxing miscellaneous customs fees were issued in 1887, and playing cards were issued new tax stamps in 1894. Over the years a number of other revenue tax stamps were created, including consular service fee tax stamps in 1906, cigarette tubes stamps in 1919 and silver tax stamps in 1934.

Figure 259. Beer is just one product for which U.S. revenue stamps have been created. Shown is an 1871 stamp taxing one-eighth of a barrel of beer for the sum of 12½¢.

As the many early revenue stamps were being issued by the federal government, a different group of revenue stamps was being created by the manufacturers of the goods that were being taxed. The Revenue Act of 1862 allowed manufacturers to have their own tax stamps created for the taxable items they sold, namely matches, medicines, perfumes, playing cards and canned fruit. These stamps are called private die proprietary revenue stamps.

Manufacturers enjoyed this option because the private die stamps were less costly than the stamps provided by the federal government. It also gave the manufacturers an opportunity to advertise on their own tax stamps, as the three examples in Figure 260 illustrate. At top left in Figure 260 is Scott RO43, a 1¢ black match stamp from the Brown & Durling Co. of Wadsworth, Ohio. The stamp at top right shows 2¢ tax paid for "Moore's Pilules Sure Cure for Chills" (Scott RS184). The bottom stamp is a 5¢ playing card stamp from Russell, Morgan & Co. of Cincinnati, Ohio.

Figure 260. Private-die proprietary stamps were used to pay taxes. They were created by the manufacturer of the taxed product and promoted the company's products.

Although the documentary and proprietary stamps listed in the Scott specialized catalog are shown uncanceled, collectors will find the earlier issues with either manuscript pen cancels, handstamp cancels or printed cancels. The collector may prefer a certain type of cancel, but in some cases the handcancels and printed cancels have a higher value than the pen cancels.

Examples of a pen cancel and a handcancel are shown in Figure 261. The stamps are Scott R169, a 25¢ documentary revenue from 1898 (left), and Scott RB21, a ¼¢ proprietary stamp from the same year.

Figure 261. A battleship was featured on many revenue stamps from the turn of the century. These two examples show a manuscript pen cancel (left) and a handstamp cancel (right).

The use of most federally issued revenue stamps in the United States has been discontinued, though firearms transfer tax stamps were issued during the 1990s and in 2001, and migratory bird hunting and conservation stamps (also known as "duck stamps") have been issued annually since 1934.

The 1990 duck stamp, Scott RW57, is shown in Figure 262. Because funds from the sale of these stamps are for a different government bureau, the stamps are inscribed "U.S. Department of Agriculture" (1934-38 issues) or "U.S. Department of the Interior" (after 1938).

Along with federal duck stamps, such as Scott RW57, collectors will come across state-issued

Figure 262. Federal duck stamps are issued by the Department of the Interior. Shown is the 1990 federal duck stamp, Scott RW57.

duck stamps as well. The Scott specialized catalog also lists these issues following the federal duck stamp issues.

Duck stamps aren't the only state-issued revenue stamps, though, and the array of collectible revenue stamp items becomes an extraordinary field when the collector begins to consider the many state-issued adhesives, including South Dakota's 1931 Lard Substitute tax stamp, Ohio's 1941 Bedding Inspection tax stamp and Michigan's 1959-63 Bear-hunting stamps.

The collector has a number of excellent resources to use to learn about revenue stamps, including specialized collector societies that provide information and publications about revenue stamps, and columns and articles in more general stamp-collecting periodicals.

U.S. provisionals, locals and carriers' stamps

Collectors of U.S. postage stamps know that the first federal postage stamps authorized by an act of Congress were the 5¢ red-brown Benjamin Franklin and the 10¢ black George Washington. Both stamps were placed on sale July 1, 1847. They are identified as U.S. Scott 1 and 2, respectively.

However, before these two historic stamps were issued, and for many years after, a variety of stamps other than the authorized federal issues were created by postal officials and by private companies and were applied to many letters mailed in the United States. In most cases, these stamps indicated that a delivery fee was paid by the mailer, and they served to carry the mail to its intended destination.

Some examples of these stamps are postmasters' provisionals, local stamps and carriers' stamps. All can be found in the Scott *Specialized Catalogue of United States Stamps & Covers*. They are listed in the catalog because they are important and valid early postal issues.

Postmasters' provisionals: In the United States, two important Congressional acts were instrumental in the development and use of federal postage stamps. These acts were created and went into effect exactly two years apart.

The Act of Congress of March 3, 1845, greatly simplified the tangle of postage rates that existed previously and made it less expensive to send letters by mail. The new rates were 5¢ for a half-ounce letter sent up to 300 miles and 10¢ for the same weight letter sent greater than 300 miles.

It wasn't until two years later, with the Act of Congress approved March 3, 1847, that Congress finally authorized the sale of postage stamps (effective July 1, 1847).

During that intervening two-year period, a number of local postmasters took it upon themselves to create postage stamps that reflected the new rates. These locally produced issues are known as postmasters' provisionals. When describing stamps, the word "provisional" means a stamp issued on a temporary or emergency basis until a regular issue becomes available.

The first postmasters' provisional stamp was offered in mid-July 1845 by Robert H. Morris, the postmaster of New York City. Featuring a portrait of George Washington, the 5¢ black stamp (Scott 9X1) is shown in Figure 263 on a folded letter sent to Lyon, France, in 1846. Additional postage due in this case was charged by the French postal authorities and is so marked on the letter.

Postmasters of other localities soon issued stamps of their own. Post offices issuing provisionals, as documented by the Scott U.S. specialized catalog, were Alexandria, Va.; Annapolis, Md.; Baltimore, Md.; Boscawen, N.H.; Brattleboro, Vt.; Lockport, N.Y.; Millbury, Mass.; New Haven, Conn.; Providence, R.I.; and St. Louis, Mo., as well as the New York City issues of Postmaster Morris. The catalog also lists an 1861 provisional envelope of Tuscumbia, Ala.

Figure 263. Cover to Lyon, France, franked with the 1845 5¢ postmasters' provisional stamp of New York City (Scott 9X1), issued two years before the first federal issues of 1847. The French post office charged additional postage due.

The postmasters of some of these cities, such as New Haven, sold envelopes marked with a special imprint or handstamp rather than postage stamps. Evidence shows that Postmaster Morris also created stamped envelopes, though no surviving examples are known.

As a group, the postmasters' provisionals are among the scarcest and most valuable U.S. stamps.

The 1845-47 issues were declared obsolete when the two federal stamps went on sale in 1847, so the longest any were in use was less than two years.

Provisional stamps were not used on all letters by any means. In most cases, a handwritten notation or handstamp upon the letter indicated if the postage was prepaid or due upon delivery. This practice was used on many letters even after the 1847 federal postage stamps became available.

Local stamps: Although the postmasters' provisional issue from Postmaster Morris appeared two years before the 1847 postage stamps, it was not the first stamp in the United States used to pay a mail-delivery fee. That distinction goes to the 3¢ 1842 local post issue of the City Despatch Post of New York, N.Y., Scott 40L1, shown in Figure 264.

The term "local post" is used to describe a number of different types of mail delivery services, principally private companies, that either functioned independently of federal services or in association with them.

Among these were city delivery services, independent mail routes and services, and express companies that were known for shipping parcels and letters long distances.

City delivery services were the most abundant of the U.S. local posts. They are what most U.S. collectors think of when the term "local post" is used. Many of these companies charged 1¢ or 2¢ to carry a letter to the post office when the Post Office Department did not provide such service, or locally from one location in a city to another.

For the delivery of a letter to a post office with deliv-

Figure 264. The 3¢ City Despatch Post stamp was the first stamp to pay a mail delivery fee in the United States.

ery to another city requested, the envelope would carry a local post stamp as well as a federal postage stamp.

D.O. Blood & Co. of Philadelphia, Pa., was one such company that carried mail during the 1840s and 1850s. Figure 265 shows a cover sent locally franked with the small 1850 1¢ Blood's One Cent Despatch stamp (Scott 15L13). Instead of postmarking, the Blood company marked its stamps with an acid that discolored both the stamp and the cover, as the illustration shows.

Blood's was one of the larger companies and therefore its stamps are among the more abundant of the U.S. local issues.

Issues from many of the smaller companies are terribly scarce, and in some cases, only a few examples are known.

Most of the city delivery services were

Figure 265. One of the larger local posts in the United States was D.O. Blood & Co. of Philadelphia, Pa. The local stamp at upper left is Blood's One Cent Despatch, Scott 15L13.

discontinued when an 1861 Congressional act bestowed the Post Office Department with the sole authority to carry letter mail on public thoroughfares.

The designs of local stamps range from relatively plain, such as the illustrated Blood issue, to more elaborate, with designs including bicycles, trains, eagles, statesmen and depictions of the mythological messenger Mercury.

Independent mail companies, such as Letter Express and Hale & Co., were successful in the 1840s because they offered less expensive rates for delivery to distant destinations than Post Office Department rates. That success was short-lived, however, as the postal reforms instituted by Congress in 1845 made Post Office rates more competitive. Aggressive actions by the Post Office to discourage railroads from carrying independent mail brought the independents to a quick end.

The most famous of the express companies was Wells, Fargo and Co., which began in 1852 and acted as agent for the well-known Pony Express in 1860. Its stamp issues include letter carriage stamps, newspaper stamps, a publishers' paid stamp and three envelopes.

The term "local post" has different meaning when applied to issues from countries other than the United States. Local issues of some countries, including Australia, New Zealand and Russia, are listed in the Scott *Standard Postage Stamp Catalogue*.

Carriers' stamps: Collectors often associate local stamps with carriers' stamps, and the two types of stamps do share similar traits. The carriers stamps paid a fee for the delivery of mail at a time when home delivery was not among the Post Office services. Instead, bonded mail carriers contracted with the Post Office to deliver mail for an additional fee of either 1¢ or 2¢ per letter. The money from these fees paid the carrier's salary in many cases.

Postal historian Calvet Hahn notes, "Carrier delivery to the homes was a post office provision from 1694 onward. This is the old 'Penny Post' where, if a letter was not picked up, the postmaster could send it out with a penny post from any post office and collect a fee.

"It was not until the 1840s that the fee was put into an account to pay carrier salary. Carrier post offices had both the Penny Post deliveries and the semi-official carriers."

Two official issues were created in 1851 under the authority of the postmaster general and were used in several cities. Scott LO1 is a nondenominated blue stamp depicting Benjamin Franklin, with the word "CARRIERS" across the top and "STAMP" along the bottom.

Scott LO2 is a 1¢ blue horizontal stamp showing an eagle within an oval that reads "U.S.P.O. DESPATCH PRE-PAID ONE CENT." Figure 266 shows a cover addressed to Philadelphia with the Eagle carriers' stamp and the orange-red variety of the 1851 3¢ federal issue, Scott 11, postmarked by a railroad route agent.

Figure 266. The 1851 1¢ blue Eagle carriers' stamp, Scott LO2, on cover to Philadelphia with the orange-red variety of the 1851 3¢ Washington, Scott 11, both tied by a railroad cancel.

Semi-official carriers' stamps were sanctioned by local postmasters for use in their particular city. Like the local stamps, these semi-official carriers' stamps showed a variety of designs, though most were small, fairly plain printed labels with ornamental borders.

By 1863, the Post Office Department eliminated the carriers' fees for mail delivery and retained mail carriers as government employees, thus ending the need for carriers' stamps.

One of the greatest collections of local stamps and carriers' stamps ever assembled was auctioned Nov. 15-17, 1999, in New York City. The David Golden collection, offered by Robert A. Siegel Auction Galleries, contained a wealth of rare historical stamps and covers documenting the period of the U.S. local posts and carrier operations. The items shown here in Figures 264 and 266 are among the many collectibles from that historic sale.

As with all stamps of value, collectors must be wary of fakes and forgeries that may be mistaken for genuine stamps.

Several books have been published documenting information about U.S. postmasters' provisionals, local stamps and carriers' stamps. The Scott U.S. specialized catalog also provides information on all three areas, with comprehensive listings of the issued stamps.

Why does my stamp have a lot of holes in it?

Most people know that perforations are the little holes that surround a postage stamp so that it can be separated easily from the other stamps around it. There also exist stamps that have little holes punched through the vignette — the picture area of the stamp — often in the shape of letters, but sometimes forming a design or geometric pattern. These specially perforated stamps are called "perfins." The name combines the words "perforated initials" or "perforated insignia."

A less common name for these same stamps is "spifs," with the five letters of the name standing for "Stamps Perforated with Initials of Firms and Societies."

In most cases, the perforations within the stamp design are created by the business or organization that purchased the stamps from the post office. Perfins identify the proper owner of the stamps and act as a security device to discourage theft or improper use.

Perfins are known on stamps from more than 200 countries. Though their use has decreased in recent years, they are still created and used by many groups.

Two examples of perfins are shown in Figure 267. The initials "A.D." are punched into the face of the Swedish stamp at left. The shadow below the stamp shows the lettering is face up on the design side of the stamp. The letters "AM. ICE" on the U.S. stamp in the center and at right of Figure 267 are punched so that they are right-reading on the reverse of the stamp, rather than on the face.

Perfins were used first on postage stamps in England when Joseph Sloper, the developer of a pin-perforating machine, obtained permission in 1868 from the General Post Office to perforate initials on postage stamps on behalf of his clients.

At the time, businesses were plagued by thefts of postage stamps from company stocks. Because stamps were easily stolen and resold, dishonest employees found them an attractive target. With the initials of the proper owner perforated through the design, it became easier to determine if the stamps were improperly used. For example, the letters "AM. ICE" on the perfin in Figure 267 identify that stamp as

Figure 267. Perfins are stamps with holes punched through the design. The letters identify the purchaser of the stamp.

 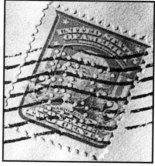

Figure 268. The earliest-known perfin on a U.S. cover was mailed May 26, 1908, by B.F. Cummins Co. of Chicago, Ill., a perforating machine manufacturer.

belonging to the American Ice Co. of Philadelphia, Pa. The only proper use of this stamp would be on business mail from American Ice Co. Any other use would raise suspicions that the stamp was stolen from the company.

Sloper's idea caught on throughout the British Commonwealth, and perfins soon appeared in other European countries as well.

The cover shown in Figure 268 illustrates the earliest-known use of a perfin in the United States. Postmarked May 26, 1908, the envelope was mailed from B.F. Cummins Co. of Chicago, Ill., a perforating-machine manufacturer. It bears a 2¢ George Washington and Shield stamp of 1903 with the perfinned initials "BFC CO."

Many collectors discarded perfins over the years because they thought the punched holes damaged the stamp. The perfins that were saved in collections usually were soaked from envelopes and placed in albums or stock books. Unfortunately, once the stamps were removed from the envelope, it became more difficult to identify the perfin pattern.

For example, with just the surcharged 30-øre Danish stamp and perfin pattern shown at the top of Figure 269, a collector might not be able to learn what the initials "F.D.B." stand for. However, since the stamp is actually still saved on a complete cover (Figure 269, bottom), the collector can see that the sender was Faellesforenin-

Figure 269. When perfins are kept on intact covers, it usually is possible to identify the sender and other interesting historical details.

gen for Danmarks Brugsforeninger, a cooperative association of Danish supermarkets. Because the postmark appears on the cover, the date and location of mailing also are known (Feb. 16, 1956, from Skive, Denmark).

Obviously it is more useful to save the entire cover rather than the single stamp alone. Many collectors now save perfins on cover to show how the stamp was used.

Collectors who come across perfins that have been removed from covers often can identify the pattern from listings in perfins catalogs. *Catalog of United States Perfins*, a several-hundred-page book edited by John M. Randall and published by the Perfins Club, illustrates patterns for thousands of perfins — most identified by name and location.

Catalogs help identify subtle changes in perfin patterns. Even though two patterns may appear nearly identical, slight differences help to pinpoint when an organization changed machines or its perfin pattern.

For example, the two stamps shown in Figure 270 both have perfin insignias of the letter "M" within a circle, representing the state of Michigan. The *Catalog of United States Perfins* identifies the insignia at left (on the 6¢ John Quincy Adams presidential issue of 1938, Scott 811) as pattern M9, used by the state from 1912-65. The slightly different version at right (on the nondenominated 29¢ F-rate stamp of 1991) is listed as pattern M9.7, in use from 1954.

Catalogs also illustrate the differences between similar perfin patterns used by different companies. The pattern "LL" over "C" in the United States, for example, was used by Lockland Lumber Co. of Lockland, Ohio, and by Lalley Light Corp., of Detroit, Mich. There is even another circled "M" perfin, for the Fred Miller Brewing Co. of Milwaukee, Wis. The catalog shows the distinction between the similar patterns.

Since the perforated letters are the focus of most perfin collectors, many exhibit their stamps face down, notes Kurt Ottenheimer, president of the Perfins Club. That way the punched-hole pattern is easier to read. "Thematic collectors may show their stamps face up," he adds.

There are a couple of different ways to collect perfins thematically. One is to relate the pattern of the perfin to the theme of the collection.

Railroads commonly used perfins on stamps that were supplied to various offices. Perfin covers or stamps with the railroad theme, such as "PRR" for the Pennsylvania Railroad, are a natural addition to such a collection.

Collectors of a specific topic also might seek out a perfinned stamp where the

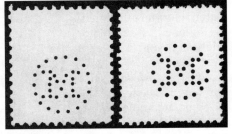

Figure 270. Collectors recognize subtle changes in patterns. These two insignia were used by the state of Michigan during two different eras.

Figure 271. Other types of holes through stamps may also identify the user or may serve to cancel the stamp.

vignette design fits the topic, though the perfin may not. There are more than 50 perfin patterns in the *Catalog of United States Perfins* that show a pictorial pattern, such as an anchor, hourglass, horseshoe, lighthouse, spinning wheel, star and so on.

Although the majority of perfins show letters to identify the proper user of the stamp, there are other stamps with holes punched through them that collectors may encounter.

At left in Figure 271 is a 4-peseta Spanish stamp from 1879 with a sizable hole punched through the design. This is a form of cancellation to indicate that the stamp was used for telegraph service. The center stamp is a privately perforated issue from 1908 with a Schermack control perfin that identifies the user of specific stamp-affixing machinery. The patterns of such stamps are also identified in the Perfins Club catalog. The stamp at right is a U.S. revenue stamp. On many revenues, perfins were used as a canceling feature, often identifying the user of the stamp as well.

Perfins also have been used for other purposes. Official stamps, intended for use by government agencies, are so designated by some countries through the use of a perfin pattern. Similar examples exist for postage due and specimen stamps.

An interesting use of perfins for decorative purposes was created in 1993 when Netherlands issued its two-stamp December Holiday set. The diamond-shaped stamps were issued with holes punched in a seemingly random pattern that actually repeated for each design: 16 holes for the Candles stamp and 14 holes for the Fireworks stamp. The holes created the illusion of snow when the stamps were affixed to white envelopes.

Perfin specialists continue to report new finds and pattern varieties. It is an active field of study that provides challenge and excitement for the collector.

It's not a stamp, but it looks a lot like one

Stamp collectors often encounter unfamiliar items that bear some resemblance to postage stamps, but the things they find may not be listed in any traditional stamp-hobby catalog. Some of these items can be identified very quickly, while the collector has to do considerable digging to learn about others.

Collectors use the name "cinderella" to categorize many stamplike labels and other items that are not genuine postage stamps, but which, for one reason or another, have an appeal that makes them collectible. The name "cinderella" comes from the fairy-tale character who looked like a princess though she was a poor neglected girl. Some cinderella stamp items look like genuine postage stamps, but they are really something else altogether.

Figure 272. With a regal eagle and fine line engraving, the EKKO verified reception stamp looks a lot like a genuine postage stamp. Instead it falls into the category of cinderellas.

Some of these items do have significant official functions, though they have no postal use. An example is the EKKO verified reception stamp shown in Figure 272.

During the 1920s, these labels were collected by radio listeners who would write to a distant radio station to let them know their broadcast was received in the collector's community. To thank the listener for providing the useful broadcast area information, many stations would send the correspondent a verified reception stamp. The stamps were sold by the EKKO Co. of Chicago, Ill. One of the four letters of the company's name appears in each corner of the illustrated stamp.

As a cinderella item, the EKKO verified-reception stamp holds a particular attraction for stamp collectors, because the line-engraved design of the label was printed by American Bank Note Co. using the intaglio process. Intaglio security printing was used extensively on U.S. postage stamps until the 1970s, and it is used to print U.S. currency as well. The scrollwork designs at the top and sides of the label, along with the engraved background pattern known as engine-turning near the bottom of the design, make this souvenir item seem like a very official document indeed.

Many collectors of cinderellas save these and other labels and stickers while they also maintain more traditional stamp collections.

A few cinderella collectors have no substantial interest in postage stamps, preferring instead to keep an eye out only for cinderella items that will be perfect additions to their very active collections.

There have been a few attempts to assemble cinderella catalogs and other reference works, but because the collecting field is so broad, it is virtually impossible to create a comprehensive listing. After all, one definition of a cinderella item could be the following: "If it looks like a postage stamp but it's not a postage stamp, it's a cinderella." That could include a sticker that arrived in the magazine promotion you recently received in the mail, or the popular promotional trading stamps that were handed out by retailers in years past.

Because preprinted album pages for most cinderella items don't exist, the collector may create his own pages, or save and organize items using stock books or other stamp-hobby supplies.

Many cinderella collectors concentrate their efforts within a specialty area. Some prefer to seek out items that were officially released by a government agency, such as tax (revenue) stamps issued for a specific type of product —

such as distilled spirits, for example.

Others may go into a completely different direction, looking for items that are blatantly bogus or counterfeit. These collectors are often particularly wary of stamplike labels created by private manufacturers with the intent to deceive collectors.

Following are just a few of the most popular cinderella collecting areas. The list is by no means complete, and any collector can add to it by choosing any item that suits him.

Bogus or phantom issues: Labels that intentionally bear resemblance to genuine postage stamps but do not have any recognized postal validity are known as bogus or phantom issues. Many of these are manufactured by private companies to sell to stamp collectors, despite the fact that the labels are not postage stamps.

The Universal Postal Union is an internationally recognized body to which most genuine stamp-issuing entities belong. Labels from genuine locations that are not recognized as stamp issuers by the UPU are often bogus. Other phantoms may be from locations that are altogether fictitious.

One of the many bogus issues collectors may encounter is inscribed "Principality of Thomond," as shown in Figure 273.

Figure 273. Stamplike labels that try to look like real stamps from nonexistent countries are known as bogus or phantom issues.

A report titled "Nonexistent Cities, States, Territories or Countries for which 'Stamps' or Overprints Have Been Printed" was published in 1996 by the Collectors Club of Chicago and the Arthur Salm Foundation. Within that report, issues purporting to be from the "Principality of Thomond" are listed relating to the "Dalcassian claim to Irish territory that is part of Shannon Airport.

The term "fantasy label" is used to describe the Thomond issues in *Linn's Stamp Identifier*.

Some bogus issues look like stamps from areas that once legitimately issued stamps, but no longer do.

Charity labels: Among the most well-known charity labels are Christmas seals (Figure 274), which are distributed in the United States and many other countries to raise funds to combat respiratory diseases.

Similar labels are created by other charities to encourage donations. Specialist collectors of these labels catalog all of the known varieties and often communicate with one another to exchange information.

Figure 274. Christmas seals are charity labels issued to encourage donations. Many charities' fund-raising programs use similar labels.

Christmas seals are sometimes listed in country-specific specialized catalogs, including the Scott *Specialized Catalogue of United States Stamps & Covers*.

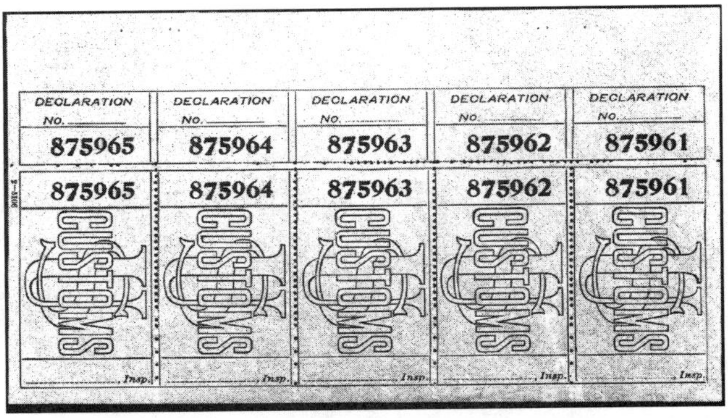

Customs and inspection labels: The United States and other governments often create special labels to indicate that imported items have undergone customs inspection. In some cases, a fee is paid for the customs

DECLARATION NO.	DECLARATION NO.	DECLARATION NO.	DECLARATION NO.	DECLARATION NO.
875965	875964	875963	875962	875961
875965	875964	875963	875962	875961

Figure 275. These Customs labels are from the United States, manufactured as a pane of five.

service, and the labels in those cases qualify as revenue stamps.

Customs labels from the United States are illustrated in Figure 275.

Essays and proofs: During the process of creating a postage stamp, artists create essays, which are proposals or preliminary designs for postage stamps. The essays may take the form of paintings, ink drawings, computer art or other renditions. Proofs are impressions of actual stamp designs created before stamp production begins. Proofs are often created to check for quality and appearance before actual stamps are printed.

Essays and proofs for many stamps are not available to collectors. Many that are available are relatively costly.

Essays and proofs are studied to learn more about the history of postage stamps. Early U.S. essays and proofs are listed in the Scott U.S. specialized catalog.

Etiquettes: The French word "etiquette" is related to the English word "ticket," which is defined as a notice attached to something. Simple labels that indicate a requested mail service are known as etiquettes. Among the more common are airmail etiquettes, such as the Austrian example shown in Figure 276.

On most airmail etiquettes, the word "airmail" appears in the native language of the country from which the label originates ("Flugpost" on the Austrian example), as well as in French ("Par Avion"). The label in the illustration also has the words in English.

Etiquettes have no postal value, but their great variety and common usage make them appealing to collectors.

Most of the labels also do not identify the country of origin. If the etiquette is used on cover, the origin of the label usually can be determined by examining the sender's address or the stamps used to frank the envelope.

Figure 276. Etiquettes are labels created to request a specific mailing service. The most common are airmail etiquettes, such as this modern example from Austria.

Other forms of etiquettes include labels indicating first-class or priority mail handling.

A similar area of cinderella collecting interest includes the labels and stickers from many countries used to mark registered or certified mail.

Exhibition promotional labels: In years past, stamp exhibitions would generate publicity by distributing handsome engraved and perforated labels that rivaled many postage stamps for style and quality. Many shows continue to create promotional labels, but most are now plain self-adhesive stickers printed by less-expensive methods. In other words, the exhibition label has followed the same basic evolutionary pattern as the postage stamp.

Facsimiles: Facsimiles differ from forgeries in that they are clearly marked reproductions of genuine postage stamps. The sale of facsimiles to collectors is done without deception, so the collector may possess and study a likeness of a stamp that may be very difficult to obtain.

The facsimile shown front and back in Figure 277 reproduces a 2¢ 1863 issue from the Confederate States of America.

Forgeries and counterfeits: There are two important types of stamp forgeries: those created to deceive stamp collectors and those created to deceive postal authorities. The latter also are

Figure 277. An unofficial postage stamp reproduction that is clearly marked as such is known as a facsimile. It is not intended to deceive collectors or postal authorities.

known as counterfeit stamps. Forgeries of older stamps are extremely widespread, and their existence is often noted in stamp catalogs.

Some collectors watch for forgeries and collect them along with an example of the genuine stamp they attempt to replicate.

In *Cinderella Stamps* by L.N. and M. Williams, forgeries of phantom stamps from Azerbaijan and other areas are described.

Forgery expert Varro E. Tyler authored books on the subjects of forged stamps, including *Focus on Forgeries*, a compendium of forged common stamps that compares single examples of forged stamps to the genuine item, and *Philatelic Forgers*, containing the stories of the world's most notorious stamp forgers.

Local stamps (private local posts): Though they usually are considered cinderella items, stamps from private local-post companies are often genuinely used to deliver mail, though within a limited area and under regulations. Local stamps from many countries are listed in various specialized catalogs.

Stamps from Herm Island in Great Britain, shown in Figure 278, are used to pay for the carriage of mail from the island to Guernsey, where the mail is then deposited into the British mail system (properly franked with British postage stamps).

Propaganda labels: Labels and stickers promoting causes that are usually political in nature are sometimes found on mailed covers. Propaganda labels resembling postage stamps have been created by many organizations, thereby increasing the appeal of the label to the cinderella collector.

Revenue stamps, fiscals: One of the more popular cinderella collecting areas is that of revenue stamps, also known as fiscals or tax stamps. The last term is probably the most accurate, for these are stamps created to indicate a tax has been paid.

Figure 278. Local stamps may pay for the carriage of mail from an area that has no convenient postal service to another area where mail service is available. The illustrated local stamp is from Britain's Herm Island.

Because revenue stamps are often created, printed and distributed by a governmental body, they enjoy the same air of legitimacy as postage stamps. Many are documented in postage stamp catalogs and in separate revenue catalogs.

Figure 279 shows a 24¢ Wines revenue stamp, series of 1916, from the United States.

Savings stamps: Postal savings stamps encouraged personal savings by establishing a regular method to set aside money. In the United States, stamps were issued as receipts for funds saved toward the purchase of war bonds, savings bonds and other similar savings programs.

Specimens: Though most specimen stamps begin life as actual postage stamps, the postal use of the stamp is voided with the application of the "SPECIMEN" overprint.

Specimens are distributed to publications for illustrative purposes, and they are sometimes used to demonstrate printing quality.

Figure 279. Revenue stamps such as this 24¢ Wines stamp are used to show payment of a required tax.

Figure 280 shows two specimens. The example at left from Nevis bears a "SPECIMEN" overprint. The stamp at right from Paraguay is marked "MUESTRA," the Spanish-language equivalent of "specimen."

Telegraph stamps: Labels issued to denote payment for a telegraph service were issued by private companies in the United States beginning around 1870. Similar services in other countries often were offered by the federal post office. In some cases, special telegraph stamps were issued, while in others, postage stamps paid the necessary fees.

Test or dummy stamps: To test the printing, perforating and coiling machinery

Figure 280. Stamps marked "SPECIMEN" (left) or "MUESTRA" (right) are not valid for postage. They are distributed for illustrative or examination purposes only.

Figure 281. By using test or dummy stamps, such as this Parrot design, instead of genuine stamps, printers don't have to worry about accounting for actual postage stamps when checking the operation of machinery.

used to make postage stamps, postal authorities and private security printers have made different varieties of test or dummy stamps. Because tight security is needed when working with genuine stamps, printers use test stamps to avoid security problems.

Often these labels are not available to the public, but many U.S. test stamps have appeared on the market and are listed in the Scott *Specialized Catalogue of United States Stamps & Covers*.

The example shown in Figure 281 is a self-adhesive test stamp depicting a parrot. It was manufactured by Banknote Corporation of America, a private security printer of U.S. stamps.

Unauthorized issues: There have been a number of cases where stamps purporting to be issues from genuine postal services have appeared on the market, only to be disputed by authorities as unauthorized stamps.

A well-known example is a set with the inscription "Republique d'Haiti" featuring illustrations of bird paintings by John J. Audubon.

According to the Scott *Standard Postage Stamp Catalogue*, "In 1975 or later various sets of bird paintings by Audubon were produced by government employees without official authorization. They were not sold by the Haiti post office and were not valid for postage."

A 5-centime value from this unauthorized set is shown in Figure 282.

The categories of cinderella issues provided here only begin to cover the enormous range of items that may be considered cinderellas.

Almost anyone who has been a stamp collector for any length of time probably has one or more of these cinderella items. For some collectors, the addition of cinderellas makes the standard stamp collection more interesting.

Topical or thematic collectors often like cinderellas for the way the labels broaden the scope of the collection. Certainly the Parrot label in Figure 281 would add a nice touch to a collection featuring birds or parrots.

Though in most cases they are not valid for postage, cinderellas make up a substantial and varied collecting field that many of us enjoy.

Figure 282. Although it looks like a 5-centime Owl stamp from Haiti, this is actually an unauthorized issue created without the approval of Haiti's postal service.

International Reply Coupons are collectible

International Reply Coupons have two uses for collectors of stamps and postal history. They can be saved as interesting collectible items, and they can be useful when conducting mail correspondence or transactions with people in other countries.

When you write to someone you don't know, it is considered polite to enclose an addressed, stamped envelope if you are requesting a reply. It's a nice gesture, for instance, if you ask for a price list from a stamp dealer who doesn't know you. This type of reply envelope is sometimes referred to in print as an "SASE" or "self-addressed stamped envelope."

That procedure works fine if the person to whom you are writing is in the same country as you.

What if you live in the United States, and you would like a price list from a stamp dealer in Great Britain? Sending an addressed envelope with U.S. stamps on it would not help the British stamp dealer because the U.S. stamps are not valid in his country.

It may surprise you to learn that this problem was solved in 1906 with the introduction of the International Reply Coupon.

Figure 283. International Reply Coupons from the 1990s from the United States (top) and Great Britain (bottom). The same type of form is used in both examples. Postmarks distinguish the issuing country.

IRCs can be purchased for a set amount in one country and can be redeemed for postage stamps in a post office in a different country. If you send the British stamp dealer an IRC with your request for his price list, he will be able to redeem the coupon for postage stamps that fulfill his minimum international postage rate.

Some stamp dealers and other businessmen request IRCs from customers in other countries who ask for information. They may request more than one IRC if the information requested costs more to mail than the minimum postage rate.

Figure 284. A 1983 stamp issued by Switzerland for official use of the Universal Postal Union shows a bird with International Reply Coupons as symbolic wings.

A standard IRC form is used in post offices internationally. Shown in Figure 283 are a 1995 IRC from the United States (at top) and a 1996 IRC from Great Britain (at bottom).

Just two add-on features differentiate them:

The U.S. coupon bears a U.S. postmark and an imprinted value in U.S. dollars. The British coupon bears a British postmark. The British example shown does not show a printed value.

Printed on the coupon is a message in seven languages (German, English, Arabic, Chinese, Spanish and Russian on the reverse, and French on the front): "This coupon is exchangeable in any country of the Universal Postal Union for one or more postage stamps representing the minimum postage for a priority [first-class] item or an unregistered letter sent by air to a foreign country."

Figure 285. IRCs can document aspects of postal history, as shown by this 1910 example from Germany offices in Turkey.

The Universal Postal Union is an organization created to encourage cooperation among postal services of the world. The IRC is a small example of this cooperation, as it is recognized in every UPU country. The UPU was formally established in 1874. During the 1906 Rome congress of UPU postal administrations, the concept of the International Reply Coupon was agreed upon.

For many years the front of the IRC was printed in yellow with the design of a bird carrying a letter in its beak, superimposed over the geographic grid of a world globe, with a background of vertical stripes.

Another bird, with IRCs as wings, was pictured on Switzerland Scott 9O14, a 120-centime stamp issued in 1983 for the official use of the international bureau of the Universal Postal Union. The stamp is shown in Figure 284.

Early coupons bore the printed name of the issuing country, with the message on the front appearing in a language relevant to the issuing country. Since they were created before the days of airmail, the earliest coupons could be redeemed for a stamp representing single-rate ordinary postage to a foreign country.

The first design showed an allegorical female figure delivering mail from one part of the globe to another. The example shown in Figure 285 displays this design. It is a 1910 IRC from Germany's offices in Turkey.

How collectible are these coupons? Well, the Figure 285 IRC is from the Corinphila stamp auction of the Cihanger collection that took place in April 2000. The example appeared in the lavish auction catalog with a preauction estimate of 300 Swiss francs (about $180). At left on the face of the coupon is a carefully applied postmark from the Turkish port of Smyrna (now known as Izmir).

If you refer back to the two coupons shown in Figure 283, you'll notice they also have postmarks at left on the face of the coupon. Most IRCs in collector hands are struck with one postmark, as the illustrated examples show. The postmark shows where and when the coupon was issued. When the coupon is taken to the post office to be redeemed, whether in the United States or in some other country, it is postmarked at right by the redeeming postal clerk, who then keeps

Figure 286. The use of added stamps to revalue IRCs following a rate change was authorized by the United States in 1995.

Figure 287. A new design for the IRC was revealed in 2001 and placed on sale in January 2002.

it and provides the correct amount of postage.

It may be possible to find a coupon with two postmarks that made its way into collector hands, or blank coupons with no postmark.

IRCs that demonstrate an intriguing aspect of postal history, such as the coupon from Germany's offices in Turkey, are particularly nice additions to a collection.

A different type of IRC postal history artifact is shown in Figure 286. When U.S. international postage rates were increased in July 1995, the cost of an IRC was increased from 95¢ to its present cost of $1.05. In the Dec. 18, 1995, issue of *Linn's Stamp News*, postal historian Terence Hines reported that a message was transmitted to all U.S. post offices July 11, 1995, stating in part, "Old rate international reply coupons (95¢) will continue to be sold in combination with the 10¢ Red Cloud [stamp] or its equivalent. The additional postage is to be affixed to the IRCs at the point of sale."

An example of this revaluation dated Sept. 9, 1995, by a post office in Chappaqua, N.Y., is shown in the Figure 286 illustration. Hines noted that the 1995 order was the first time the Postal Service authorized the use of stamps to revalue an IRC, though the unauthorized use of stamps for this purpose is known for an increase from 22¢ to 26¢ in 1974.

The Scott *Specialized Catalogue of United States Stamps & Covers* illustrates the four major coupon designs that have been issued by countries around the world, and it describes many different minor varieties that exist. Major design changes for the coupon were instituted in 1931, 1968 and 1975. A new design was created in 2001 and placed on sale at the beginning of 2002 (Figure 287).

The Scott catalog also describes and values the varieties of IRCs specifically issued for the United States. It lists and values coupons with one postmark only.

Collectors can look for IRCs from other countries to add to their specialized collections of those countries.

Collectors visiting foreign countries may purchase IRCs when they are visiting a local post office. Unlike postage stamps, which can be ordered by mail from postal authorities or from stamp dealers, an IRC will document the date and location of the visit, providing a personalized souvenir for a stamp collection.

Variable-denomination stamps used worldwide

Postal customers in the United States are accustomed to vending machines in post office lobbies that offer postage stamps in coils, booklets or small glassine packages. Many U.S. post offices leave their lobbies open after hours, making it possible for customers to complete their stamp purchases any time of the day or night.

In recent years, mailers in many countries have made increasing use of special postage stamps vended by machines that also print values on the stamps at the time of purchase.

These stamps begin as blank or decorated labels that have no denomination. The value is printed when the stamp is dispensed.

Although this may sound similar to the postage labels and im-prints created by post-age meters, these machine-printed postage stamps are available to any postal customer who inserts payment into the appropriate vending machine.

Figure 288 shows an outdoor stamp-vending machine manufactured by Sielaff, operating in Germany after that country converted to euro currency in 2002. Also shown is a €0.56 postage stamp with Letterbox design dispensed by the machine. These stamps are not dated, as postage meter stamps are, so they may be used for postage at any time, the same as more traditional postage stamps.

These vending machine postage stamps come in many different styles and go by many different names. In the United States, they are referred to as computer-

Figure 288. Postal patrons in Germany can purchase variable-denomination postage stamps from this outdoor vending machine. The stamp shown was obtained in 2002 from the Sielaff machine in the photograph.

vended postage or variable-denomination stamps. In many other countries, they are known as ATM stamps, an abbreviation for the German term "Automatenmarken" (automatic stamps). Some collectors call them "Framas" after the name of one of the more prominent vending-machine manufacturers, Frama. Deutsche Post, the German postal service, specifically refers to the stamp pictured in Figure 288 as a "Sielaff-type" postage stamp.

As use of these stamps has increased, so has interest in collecting them.

A catalog that identifies the many variable-denomination stamps around the world is compiled by the German stamp catalog publishers Michel (most English-speakers pronounce the name as MISH-ul or MIK-ul).

The 2002 edition of the Michel *Automatenmarken-Spezial-Katalog*, shown in Figure 289, is written in German, but it includes a page of symbols and abbreviations that are used in the catalog, defined in both German and English. The catalog includes detailed listings and values for all known variable-denomination stamps. Mint stamps are usually valued in sets of stamps representing the more common postage rates.

For example, Hong Kong has issued variable-denomination stamps for several years. Each year a new design is created that corresponds to the Asian new year cycle represented by 12 different animals. In 1988 — the Year of the Snake — the stamps featured the image of a snake, as pictured in Figure 290. Each stamp also included the

Figure 289. The Michel *Automatic Stamp Specialized Catalog* provides information about variable-denomination stamps worldwide.

Figure 290. Hong Kong variable-denomination stamps from 1988 marked the year of the snake. The two stamps shown here have different machine numbers printed in the upper-right corners.

denomination, shown as "00.10" in the pictured examples.

The Michel ATM specialized catalog suggests that a mint set of Hong Kong's 1989 Year of the Snake variable-denomination stamps should include (in Hong Kong currency) values of 10¢, 60¢, $1.40 and $1.80.

The catalog also identifies several varieties of these stamps, including one difference that can be seen in the two stamps illustrated in Figure 290. Near the upper-right corner of each stamp is a two-digit number: "01" on the stamp at the top of the illustration and "02" on the stamp at bottom. The catalog notes that the number identifies whether the stamp came from the main Hong Kong post office (01) or the Tsim Sha Tsui annex office on Hong Kong's Kowloon Peninsula (02).

Other information provided includes stamp-paper color varieties (there are two), the existence of fluorescent tagging on the stamps, the type of machine that created the stamps (Frama FE 264), the name of the designer (Michael Tucker) and the printing method used for the stamps (offset lithography).

Similar details are provided for most of the stamps listed in the Michel ATM specialized catalog.

The catalog provides descriptions of 38 different manufacturers of variable-denomination stamps, including Frama of Switzerland, Klussendorf of Germany, and Electrocom (Eca-Gard) and Unisys of the United States.

The modern age of variable-denomination postage stamps goes back to 1976, when postal authorities in Switzerland installed machines that would print and dispense postage labels with values of the customer's choice, ranging from 0.05 francs to 99.95fr. Among the forerunners for this type of stamp are the 1936 Mailomat postage meter stamps from the United States that were sold publicly at coin-operated stations.

The Michel catalog lists more than 50 countries that have sold variable-denomination stamps. The listings for

Figure 291. In 1992 the United States began to sell variable-denomination coil stamps in selected post offices. Customers could create strips of stamps with different values, as shown here.

the United States begin with the Autopost labels issued in 1989, the Shield and Bunting Eca-Gard-printed perforated coil stamps from 1992, and the similar Unisys-printed coil stamps from 1994.

Figure 291 shows a strip of the U.S. Eca-Gard issue. The stamps inside the Eca-Gard vending machine were in large coils originally printed with the Shield and Bunting design by the Bureau of Engraving and Printing.

When the Eca-Gard machines were first installed in a limited number of post offices, mailers could purchase stamps in any denomination they desired. The stamps came out as a continuous strip until the purchaser detached them from the machine. As a result, it was possible to create and purchase strips of stamps with different denominations on each stamp. As an example, the Figure 291 strip begins with a 1¢ stamp followed by a 2¢, a 3¢, a 4¢ and so on up to 10¢.

The Postal Service eventually adjusted the machines so the minimum value that could be printed was 19¢ (the postcard rate at the time).

A second type of machine that vended similar coil stamps was manufactured by Unisys. The earlier Eca-Gard machines were finally removed from service in 1998.

Variable-denomination stamps from most countries are dispensed as single detached stamps and cannot be collected in long strips as the later U.S. coil stamps can. The Hong Kong stamps shown in Figure 290 are somewhat typical of the formats found in other countries.

Often these stamps come from machines with preset value choices. Instead of being able to select any specific value for the stamps, mailers have the choice of several common rates, such as postcard, first-class, airmail and so on.

Along with collecting these variable-denomination stamps in mint sets, some collectors save postally used stamps on cover.

Figure 292. A Danish variable-denomination stamp postally used on a cover mailed to Germany. The stamp's 3.50-krone value paid the economy postage rate in effect at the time.

Figure 292 shows a 3.50-krone stamp from Denmark on an envelope mailed to northern Germany in 1995. The 3.50kr value fulfilled Denmark's 20-gram economy letter rate to European countries that went into effect June 10, 1991. This nice example is tied to the cover by a dated postmark from Ostjyllands Postcenter.

The term "tied" means the postmark covers both the stamp and part of the envelope paper.

Many collectors choose to save postally used stamps on cover, rather than soaking them off the paper. In some cases, soaking damages variable-denomination stamps, destroying some or all of the stamp design.

Figure 293 shows two very similar stamps from Spain. The stamp at top was soaked in water, and much of the design has dissolved or flaked off the label. The stamp at bottom was not soaked: It is saved on envelope paper.

Collectors can create specialized collections of variable-denomination stamps from a single country and look for uses that fulfill various rates.

The Michel catalog also lists errors and varieties that collectors may watch for, including doubled printings of denominations, misaligned numerals, improper denomination printed, no denomination printed, partial printing, and so on.

Topical stamp collectors may be attracted to variable-denomination stamps because many of the postage labels contain background designs

Figure 293. Some variable-denomination stamps can suffer damage if immersed in water. Shown at top is a soaked stamp from Spain. Much of the printed design of the stamp dissolved or flaked off in water. At bottom is an unsoaked stamp.

that fit well into different topical collections.

Obviously the Hong Kong stamps picture a variety of New Year animals, including dragons, horses, monkeys, tigers and more. Several countries have featured birds on their stamps, including Japan and France. Greece, Portugal and Spain have shown ships, Australia has shown kangaroos and lizards, Finland has pictured Santa Claus, and Macau has shown a bridge.

Many countries have issued variable-denomination labels that have only very plain single-color imprints with no pictorial design. Others, such as Denmark, started out plain but evolved into interesting and colorful stamps with a variety of designs.

Along with the worldwide listings in the Michel specialized catalog, collectors can find listings for individual countries in specialized catalogs for that area.

Variable-denomination stamps of the United States are listed in the Scott *Specialized Catalogue of United States Stamps & Covers* under the heading "Computer Vended Postage." They're also in the Scott *Standard Postage Stamp Catalogue.*

There are stamps on postal stationery, too

You may be surprised to learn that the first four hologram issues from the United States Postal Service were placed on sale between 1989 and 1995. These holograms were the vignettes (pronounced vin-YETS) or central designs of the imprinted stamps on stamped envelopes.

Stamped envelopes, postal cards and aerograms (or air letters) are known collectively as postal stationery. The defining characteristic of most postal stationery is that the items are imprinted with stamp designs with full postage value.

The imprinted stamp on a stamped envelope, therefore, pays the amount that is shown by the denomination, so it is not necessary to buy a stamp if the envelope is current and is to be used for mailing.

Stamped envelopes and postal cards are sold at U.S. post offices for a slight premium over the postage value, to pay for the additional costs associated with manufacturing the envelope or card.

Postal stationery items share many characteristics with postage stamps, and they can be collected in much the same way.

Collectors can choose to save mint or postally used examples of postal stationery, or they can save postal stationery as first-day covers. Because the imprinted stamps often bear pictorial design elements, postal stationery items can be important additions to topical or thematic collections as well.

The first four hologram issues from the United States were created from two different designs. A space station scene appeared three times: on envelopes issued in 1989 (with a 25¢ value imprint), 1992 (29¢) and 1995 (32¢). The first

Figure 294. Three stamped envelopes issued by the United States during the 1990s. The 1989 25¢ Space Station envelope at top was the first U.S. issue to feature a holographic image.

U.S. hologram envelope is shown at the top of Figure 294. The hologram on the 25¢ stamped envelope issued in 1990 showed the Vince Lombardi trophy and football players in action.

The hologram on each of these four envelopes is visible through a die-cut rectangular window in the upper-right corner of the envelope paper. It is actually affixed to the inside of the envelope so that the design displays outwardly through the cut out. The same procedure was used in 1991 to create the 29¢ Protect the Environment envelope shown in the center of Figure 294, but the vignette is a multicolor lithographed print rather than a hologram.

More frequently, the stamp designs are simply printed on the surface of the envelope paper, though often part of the design is also embossed.

The envelope shown at the bottom of Figure 294 is the 32¢ Liberty Bell issue of 1995, with a typographed and embossed design.

The first federal stamped envelopes from the United States were issued in 1853. For the next 100 years, literally hundreds of stamped-envelope varieties were created, most featuring the embossed profile of a U.S. political dignitary within a printed oval frame.

Figure 295 shows the imprinted stamp of the 12¢ Henry Clay stamped envelope issued in 1870. The item as shown in the illustration is known as a "cut square." It was trimmed from the corner of an envelope specif-

Figure 295. A cut square from the 12¢ Henry Clay stamped envelope issued in 1870.

ically to save in a collection. Cut squares were created both from unused and postally used items. Most collectors today who come upon an entire stamped envelope save the "entire," as it is known, rather than cutting it down to save the cut square.

In the 2003 Scott *Specialized Catalogue of United States Stamps & Covers*, the unused 12¢ Henry Clay cut square in the illustration has a listed value of $100, but the value for an entire of the same issue is $240. Given a choice, it obviously would be wise to save the intact envelope for the additional value. The 12¢ Henry Clay cut square shown in Figure 295 is identified in the Scott U.S. specialized catalog as Scott U93.

U.S. postal stationery items are found in the Scott catalog following the listings for regular postage stamps and those stamps designated for special duty, such as airmails, Official stamps and parcel post issues. For that reason, postal stationery is often referred to as a back-of-the-book collecting area.

Modern U.S. stamped envelopes are created in a variety of sizes. The Figure 294 illustration shows, from top to bottom, a number 9 size envelope, a number 10 size envelope and a number 6¾ size envelope.

Additionally, envelopes are regularly issued in varieties with address windows, so that the delivery address on enclosed correspondence can be seen through a die-cut window. A windowed envelope is shown without its contents in Figure 296. The illustrated envelope is the 29¢ Great Seal stamped envelope of 1991, Scott UO85, an Official stamped envelope. Official postal stationery (and stamps) can be used only by authorized federal agencies.

Figure 296. Some modern postal stationery can be difficult to find postally used. The value of this 1991 29¢ Official Mail envelope is greater postally used than mint.

A number of modern postally used Official envelopes have relatively high catalog values because examples are infrequently found. Mint envelopes are much more common. The Figure 296 envelope, postally used, is valued at $20, though the value for a mint example of the same issue is merely 70¢.

The United States also has issued numerous stamped envelopes specially marked for airmail use.

"Postal cards," like stamped envelopes, are imprinted with postage before they are sold by the post office. That's what distinguishes them from "postcards," which require the addition of a postage stamp before mailing.

Figure 297 shows two U.S. postal cards issued more than 100 years apart: the 1¢ black Thomas Jefferson of 1897 (Scott UX14), and the 20¢ Washington and Lee University of 1999 (Scott UX302).

Whether collected mint or postally used, postal cards are saved only as entires, not as cut squares.

Between 1873 and 1993, the United States issued 245 different postal cards. The stamp designs show many different subjects, ranging from presidents to American scenic views to historic sites.

From 1994 through 2000, the United States issued a staggering 191 postal cards. The numbers are inflated by

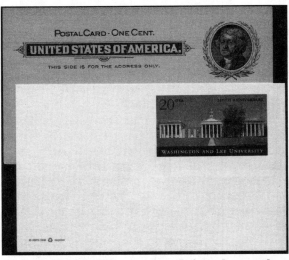

Figure 297. Two U.S. postal cards issued more than 100 years apart: the 1¢ black Thomas Jefferson issue of 1897, and the 20¢ Washington and Lee University issue of 1999.

Figure 298. U.S. picture postal cards are issued in sets and sell for more than the postage value. Shown is the 20¢ Francis Hopkinson Flag postal card of 2000.

the regular issuance of picture postal cards in large sets that correspond to multiple-design issues of commemorative postage stamps.

For example, a set of 20 33¢ Stars and Stripes postage stamps was issued June 14, 2000. At the same time, 20 20¢ Stars and Stripes picture postal cards were also issued. Picture postal cards bear an imprinted stamp, but they also feature a colorful picture, similar to a postcard. One of these cards, the 20¢ Francis Hopkinson Flag picture postal card, is shown in Figure 298. The front of the card has the imprinted stamp design in the upper-right corner, while the reverse of the card shows a larger image of the design used on the stamp.

The Postal Service sells picture postal cards in sets at a substantial premium over the postage value of the cards.

Postal cards have also been issued for airmail and Official mail. Paid-reply postal cards, which include an attached prepaid postal card to encourage a reply, have also been issued periodically.

Aerograms are postage-paid letter sheets intended for overseas mail. They are

Figure 299. The 60¢ Voyageurs National Park aerogram of 1999. Aerograms with imprinted stamps are another example of postal stationery.

cut into a special shape that can be folded and sealed to resemble an envelope. The imprinted stamp on the 1999 60¢ Voyageurs National Park aerogram in Figure 299 can be seen near the upper right. The back side of the aerogram, and the bottom portion of the front, are left blank for messages.

The United States has only issued about 30 aerograms since they first appeared in 1947. Collecting them postally used can be a wonderful challenge because most were sent overseas and can be difficult to find in the United States.

Postal stationery items can be stored in albums or stock books, or they can be preserved in cover sleeves and protected by a sturdy storage box. Stamp hobby supply dealers offer many different storage options.

As with stamps, the condition of postal stationery is very important. An unused stamped envelope with a dirt mark, bent corner or crease has substantially less value than a pristine example and is less appealing to the collector.

Chapter 9
Covers and Postal History

Denominations figure into postal history

The denomination of a stamp is the postage value, which is usually shown by numerals that are part of the stamp design.

Figure 300 shows stamps from three different countries. Each stamp was issued during spring 2000. The Library of Congress stamp at left was issued by the United States. The number "33" represents 33¢, the cost (in 2000) of sending a letter weighing 1 ounce or less from one U.S. address to another. In the center of Figure 300 is a 46¢ stamp from Canada honoring the Boys and Girls Clubs of Canada. At the time this stamp was issued, the domestic letter rate in Canada was 46¢ (in Canadian funds). At right in the same illustration is a 110-pfennig stamp from Germany commemorating 350 years of daily newspapers. In 2000, German postal customers paid 110pf to mail a letter from one location in Germany to another.

At the time these stamps were issued, Canada's letter rate was the equivalent of about 31¢ in U.S. currency. Germany's rate was higher, equaling about 53¢.

Each of the three stamps shown pays the respective country's domestic letter rates by themselves, but each also may be used in combination with other stamps to pay higher rates: for delivery to a foreign country or for delivery of a larger envelope or package, for instance.

The denomination of a stamp is important to many stamp collectors and to anyone studying postal history.

Many collectors prefer to collect postally used envelopes or cards bearing stamps, used postal cards or used parcel wrappers, which are known collectively as "covers." The appeal of a collectible cover often depends upon the stamp or stamps that were used to mail it.

Collectors of postal history look for covers that show how stamps are used dur-

Figure 300. The denomination of a stamp is indicated by a number that states its postage value. Shown are a 33¢ stamp from the United States, a 46¢ stamp from Canada, and a 110-pfennig stamp from Germany. Each represents the domestic letter rate for the respective country.

ing their normal sales period to properly pay a required postage rate.

Some collectors enjoy finding a cover that illustrates a complicated rate paid as simply as possible with contemporary postage stamps.

One example of such a use is shown in Figure 301. The 9-inch by 12-inch envelope was mailed June 24, 2000, from Pennsylvania to Ohio. Instead of bearing 33¢ in postage, however, the envelope bears two 22¢ stamps paying 44¢ in postage.

Was the postage simply overpaid by the collector?

Actually, the postage paid on the envelope is precisely correct. The envelope contained only one piece of paper and altogether weighed less than 1 ounce, but the oversize envelope exceeds the letter-mail dimensional standards followed by the U.S. Postal Service.

Because it weighed less than 1 ounce but was greater than 11½ inches tall and 6⅛ inches high, an 11¢ nonstandard surcharge was applied to the basic postage rate.

Most post offices would not have had 11¢ stamps on hand, and at the time, no U.S. 44¢ stamps were then on sale at post offices, but 22¢ stamps were readily available to pay additional per-ounce postage

Figure 301. The two 22¢ stamps on this envelope pay a 44¢ postage rate that includes an unusual nonstandard surcharge.

for a mailed letter weighing more than 1 ounce. To fulfill the unusual 44¢ rate, the mailer simply used two common 22¢ stamps. As a result, the cover nicely demonstrates how the nonstandard surcharge rate is properly paid.

To pay the 55¢ 2-ounce rate in 2000, a U.S. postal customer could have chosen to use the 55¢ Alice Hamilton stamp, Scott 2940, that was issued in 1995 and remained on sale in 2000. A 55¢ Victorian Love self-adhesive stamp issued in 1999, Scott 3275, was another option, as was the 55¢ Ohio Class Submarine stamp, Scott 3375, that was issued March 27, 2000, as part of the U.S. Navy Submarines prestige booklet containing 10 stamps with five different designs and denominations.

The five different Submarine stamps in the Submarines booklet are each denominated to pay a specific postal rate. They are a 22¢ S Class stamp (to pay the additional ounce rate), a 33¢ Los Angeles Class stamp (to pay the first-class letter rate), a 60¢ USS Holland stamp (for overseas letter mail), and a $3.20 Gato Class stamp (for Priority Mail parcels weighing two pounds or less), along with the 55¢ Ohio Class stamp.

The vast majority of U.S. mail sent with postage stamps is domestic letter-rate mail, so the Postal Service creates many different letter-rate stamps each year.

The residents of some foreign countries may make more frequent use of stamps paying a variety of rates, including international rates. As a result, postal

Figure 302. Nondenominated stamps are issued by countries throughout the world. The three examples shown here are (left to right) from the United States, Finland and Singapore.

authorities in those countries may regularly issue stamps in sets that provide several different denominations.

Great Britain, for example, often issues commemorative stamps in sets of four. The Millennium Projects issue of June 6, 2000, includes one 19-penny stamp for second-class mail service, one 26p stamp for first-class mail service, one 44p stamp for airmail service outside Europe and one 65p stamp for airmail items that weigh between 10 grams and 20 grams. The 19p and 26p stamps in this set do not show the denominations in the stamp designs. Instead, the stamps are inscribed "1st" and "2nd," respectively, indicating the class of mail the stamp fulfills, not the denomination.

Such stamps are called nondenominated stamps, because the price of the stamp does not appear on it. Figure 302 shows three other nondenominated stamps from the United States, Finland and Singapore. The lack of a denomination on each of these stamps can be confusing for stamp collectors, but fortunately, the face values of nondenominated stamps are usually described in stamp catalogs.

Nondenominated U.S. stamps are usually issued in conjunction with changing postal rates. The 1995 Love stamp (Scott 2948) at left in Figure 302, for example, was issued Feb. 1, 1995, just one month after U.S. domestic letter rates increased from 29¢ to 32¢. Because the amount of the rate increase was not known when the stamps were printed months in advance of their release, they were printed without a denomination and then sold for 32¢ each.

The Spring Anemone stamp from Finland in the center of Figure 302 was issued May 9, 2000, and sold in sheets of 10 for 35 markkaa. The stamp is marked "1 luokka klass" to indicate it is for first-class postage.

The 1995 Philatelic Museum stamp from Singapore (Scott 729) is designated "FOR LOCAL ADDRESSES ONLY" and sold for 20¢ in Singaporean currency.

U.S. nondenominated stamps generally keep the postage value assigned to the stamp at the time of issue. For example, the nondenominated A-rate Eagle stamp issued in 1978 with a value of 15¢ is still worth 15¢ in postage today.

Some countries allow mailers to use nondenominated first-class postage stamps to pay the current postage rate, regardless of the cost of the stamp when first issued.

If that were true in the United States, the A-rate stamp could have been used to pay 33¢ in postage in 2000.

The familiar values of many European stamps changed at the beginning of 2002 when 12 European nations converted from their traditional currencies to the euro (Figure 303), a new single currency of the European Monetary Union. Each nation continued to set its own postage rates, so the rates still varied from country to country after the change, though all were denominated in the same new euro currency. Collectors are certain to consider the changeover to the euro as a significant period in European postal history.

Reviewing the denominations of the stamps you collect and the purposes they serve can help you better understand how they fit into the world of postal history.

Figure 303. Luxembourg issued the first euro-only denominated stamps on Oct. 1, 2001. Several other countries had previously issued dual-denominated stamps with values in euro and in their traditional currencies.

Many elements make up a complete cover

Stamp collectors and cover collectors have many things in common, including a desire to collect objects that are in good shape. Stamp collectors don't much care for damaged stamps, and cover collectors aren't very fond of tattered covers.

The word "cover" refers to an envelope, postal card or other item that has been mailed or has received postal markings. Many collectors seek out covers that show how a stamp was properly used or how a specific postal rate was fulfilled. In many cases, a postage stamp has more value if it is kept on a cover than if it is soaked off and placed into an album.

Many cover collectors research postal history, learning about how specific stamps were used to mail letters at different rates and during different periods. Other cover collectors also look for social history, including advertising information that appears on covers or military usage during war or foreign occupation.

First-day covers (FDCs) bearing postmarks that indicate when (and often, where) a stamp is issued are also popular collectibles.

As with postage stamps, the condition of a cover plays an important role in the value of the collectible item. Though two similar covers may show the same rate fulfillment, postal marking or stamp usage, a difference in the condition of the covers can make one more desirable than the other.

Condition is just one factor that can affect the value or cost of a cover in a dealer's inventory. The relative scarcity of the cover is another important element. There are times when rarity makes a cover desirable despite serious faults.

When given a choice between similar covers, though, collectors should always take the time to examine the available items, to determine which would be the best example to add to a collection. Here are a few of the characteristics that collectors can examine when looking though covers. These characteristics are illustrated in Figure 304.

Paper. The condition of envelope paper varies from one extreme to another with covers, and the collector has a lot to look for when inspecting a cover. Paper from decades ago is prone to signs of aging that range from yellowing to actual

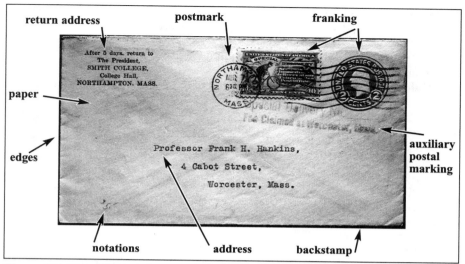

Figure 304. The different characteristics of a cover may vary in condition. Collectors generally seek out the best examples of each.

deterioration. Older covers that have been exposed to extremes of humidity, heat or light may have become the home for microorganisms that can cause spots and damage to the paper.

Any cover of any age can have detracting wrinkles or folds. Some folds may be a natural part of the cover, as with folded letters or parcel wrappers, but envelopes that have been inadvertently or intentionally creased are another matter.

Even modern first-day covers that are plentiful on the market may be damaged by improper storage or handling. Stains, including fingerprints, grease and food remnants, are another form of damage to the paper of a cover.

Overall, collectors should look for examples that have been handled carefully and do not have obvious areas of damage to the paper.

Edges. Postcards and envelopes both are vulnerable to damage along their edges. For postcards this often includes edges that are worn soft (instead of being crisp and sharp). Envelopes may have tears that come from mishandling or from deterioration of the paper.

Sealed envelopes that were opened come in all sorts of conditions. Some are opened so cleanly that it's hard to tell it was ever sealed, while others are carelessly torn by hand and show shredded envelope paper across the length of one side.

The corners of envelopes and postcards also can suffer blunt edges and creases from striking hard surfaces.

Notations. Some collectors and dealers have made pencil notations on covers, a practice that may cause damage to the collectible item. The notation might be a price for the cover or some identifying information.

In some cases pencil marks can be removed with a soft gum eraser, but the indentation of the writing often remains. Erasing can cause damage to the paper as well or leave an unnaturally lightened area on the paper of the cover.

Some specialist collectors consider any added notations to be a part of the cover's history. It is best to learn what the notations indicate, and whether or not they should be preserved, before any attempt is made to remove such markings.

Address. Many collectors of modern first-day covers prefer to find examples that are unaddressed, while earlier FDCs and most other mailed covers are naturally found with a mailing address. In most cases the address does not affect the desirability of the cover, though covers addressed to celebrities or well-known personalities may add interest.

Some collectors believe that covers addressed to stamp collectors are philatelically contrived, and often that is the case. For example, a cover bearing an unusual combination of stamps that is addressed to a collector may have been created specifically for collecting, rather than for the everyday carriage of mail.

It's up to the collector to decide if this type of philatelic cover is somehow less worthy than a more conventional cover that is not addressed to a stamp collector. There are collectors who seek out philatelic covers as examples of collector activity from years past.

One important aspect of the address is the location, for often the destination helps to determine the postage needed to mail the cover. An envelope mailed in the United States, for instance, would be charged a different rate for delivery within the United States than it would for delivery to a destination overseas.

Auxiliary postal markings. Postal authorities worldwide have applied many different auxiliary markings to mailed items. These markings can take the form of handstamps, labels or written notations.

Some indicate a problem with the mailed item, such as insufficient postage or address. Others help to clarify the class of mailing or properly direct the item.

Often these markings are applied to the cover in a hurry, so the best find is one that is clear and legible. There are some collectors who seek out varieties of auxiliary postal markings.

The type of marking used may help to make the cover even more desirable. Learning about such markings involves research and study. Because some markings are rare or hard to find, the study may pay off with some exciting discoveries.

Backstamp. Most backstamps are another form of auxiliary postal marking, often a receiving mark to indicate the date and location of delivery for a cover. Although this usually is applied when an item is mailed using a special service, a cover also can receive a backstamp if it is accidentally missent to a location other than its intended destination. It's a good idea to check every cover for markings on the reverse.

Franking. Franking is the postage that is applied to pay for delivery of the mail piece. This can take the form of postage stamps, postage meter stamps or even the word "free" written on some U.S. military mail.

Collectors who study postal rates try to find examples that are properly franked to meet a specific rate: that is, bearing the exact value in stamps or metered postage to fulfill the rate.

Overfranked and underfranked covers can be specialty collecting areas.

Stamps used on mail may suffer damage while in the mailstream, and a collector should watch out for scuffs, tears, folded stamps and other forms of damage. Sometimes stamps are damaged by the mailer or postal clerk before they are applied to the cover.

Postmark. The word "postmark" is a general term for any postal marking, but it is often used to describe the marking that cancels the stamp and gives information about the location and date of mailing. The term **cancellation** specifically refers to the marking that obliterates the stamp.

A clear strike of a postmark provides the greatest amount of information. Many times, information in a postmark cannot be read because it was applied very quickly and some element is illegible. Collectors seek out the clearest examples possible.

Information in the postmark can be used to research the cover. Given a specific date of mailing, the collector can then find out the prevailing rates for postage and special services. The location where the item was mailed may also play a part in the study of the cover.

Postmarks constitute another area of postal history study. Examples of some specific postmarks may be very difficult to find.

Return address. Usually found in the upper-left corner of the front of the envelope, the return address gives information about the mailer. Sometimes it can be used to guess at a point of mailing on an item with an illegible or mute postmark (one that intentionally has no location information), but generally this cannot be the only source for the information. A cover, after all, may have one city named in the return address but can be transported to another location for mailing.

A preprinted return address is called a "corner card." These may include advertising messages or other interesting details about the mailer.

Return addresses are sometimes found on the reverse of envelopes, on the back flap.

As with postage stamps, it is difficult to find a cover that has appealing characteristics in every area. Often the collector has to determine which features are most important for the type of collection that is being assembled, and use that information to decide which cover is the best choice.

Stampless mail: something old, something new

A large amount of modern mail is delivered without postage stamps affixed, a fact that aggravates more than a few stamp collectors.

Instead of finding a postage stamp in the upper-right corner of the envelope, postal customers frequently encounter postage paid permit imprints, the boxed-up messages shown in the four examples in Figure 305.

The fact is, a postage stamp is simply a receipt that indicates postage has been paid. That's why most stamps bear a denomination, just as any other receipt tells you how much you paid for a product or service.

For any company that has to send out a lot of mail, it is easier, cheaper and faster to have a "postage paid" message printed directly on the outgoing envelope and to use the post office's permit system than it is to purchase postage stamps and hire a person to make sure they all get affixed correctly.

Permit imprints are allowed when a company or organization sets up an advance deposit account with the United States Postal Service to prepay the mailer's postage fees. Similar systems exist in many other parts of the world as well.

In the United States, permit mail is set up in three main categories: first-class mail, bulk rate (also known as standard mail) and mail from nonprofit organizations.

Many different payment levels exist for these three categories, depending in part upon how thoroughly the mail has been prepared for handling before it is handed over to the Postal Service.

If the mailer reduces the Postal Service's workload by sorting the mail and adding automation barcodes, the mailer is rewarded with a reduction in the amount of postage that has to be paid.

There are a few stamp collectors who save examples of these privately imprinted envelope markings, usually watching for unusual designs or varieties. They recognize that a permit imprint is just as valid as a postage stamp when it comes to showing that postage has been paid.

However, most collectors, like the public in general, discard these imprinted envelopes without giving them a second thought.

The first postage stamp created by any country was the Penny Black from Great Britain, a 1-

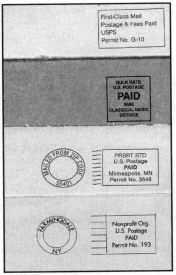

Figure 305. Paid postage permit imprints indicate that postage has been paid and tell what class of mail is being used.

penny stamp issued in 1840. The first U.S. issues came seven years later, when a 5¢ stamp picturing Benjamin Franklin and a 10¢ stamp honoring George Washington were released.

Postal systems were organized and mail deliveries were being made long before there were postage stamps, however, and the letters and envelopes sent during this prestamp period are now known as stampless mail.

Unlike today's stampless permit mail, though, stampless mail from before the postage stamp era is very collectible and treasured by many individuals who study postal history.

Figure 306 shows just one example of what classic stampless mail looks like. Instead of an envelope holding the correspondence, the sheets were simply folded and addressed on the blank side of the outer sheet.

This type of mail is referred to as a folded letter sheet. Postage rates in those days were based in part on the number of sheets mailed. An enve-

Figure 306. How did mail travel before there were stamps? In some cases, mailers paid a fee that was noted on the cover. This 1843 letter between two Ohio cities cost 20¢ to mail.

lope, if used, counted for extra postage.

Mailed in 1843, the letter was sent from Sidney, Ohio, to the town of Kalida, Ohio, about 45 miles due north.

Although stamps were not yet part of the mailing procedure, postmarks did exist, as evidenced by the Sidney circular marking in the upper-left corner.

Letters to be mailed were presented at the local post office, where payment was accepted and then marked with the amount and the word "paid" in the upper-right corner, or they could be sent unpaid.

The postage fee charged on the letter in Figure 306 was 20¢, and the cover is marked "Paid 20."

American Stampless Cover Catalog, edited and published by David G. Phillips, notes that in some instances the word "free" was applied to mail that was sent free of postage under existing regulations.

Another alternative was mail sent unpaid: The recipient would pay the postage fee when the mail was delivered. The catalog notes that the absence of the words "paid" or "free" indicated this method of payment was used.

Although U.S. stamps were made available in 1847, the prepayment of domestic letter mail postage was not compulsory until Jan. 1, 1856.

Figure 307. Free-franking privileges have been extended to active service personnel and certain U.S. government officials. Shown are a 1944 cover from a Coast Guard installation and a 1973 cover from then-Congressman Gerald R. Ford.

Figure 308. Are these stamps? Shown are a postage meter stamp (top), a post office postage value imprint label (center) and postage printed by the mailer using a computer (bottom).

The Postal Service has long allowed mail to be sent free of charge under a few very special circumstances. Collectors refer to this privilege as "free-franking."

Once again, though postage stamps are not used on these items, the complete covers (envelopes, postcards or outer wrapping) are saved by many collectors interested in postal history.

Letter mail sent by certain military personnel stationed in designated locations may be sent without charge. In the upper-right corner, the serviceman writes the word "FREE." The sender's name and military address must appear in the upper-left corner.

An example is shown at top in Figure 307: a World War II-era cover mailed from the United States Coast Guard Station in Tawas, Mich., to an address in Alcoa, Tenn. The word "FREE" is printed in the upper-right corner, and the envelope received a Feb. 21, 1944, postmark.

The president of the United States, the vice president and members of Congress have some free-franking privileges as well. When these officials exercise this privilege, the envelope must bear their signature or a facsimile of their signature in the upper-right corner.

Figure 307, bottom, shows an example of free-franking on an envelope mailed by Gerald R. Ford in 1973, when he was the minority leader of the U.S. House of Representatives. Ford became the 38th president of the United States the following year.

Postal regulations also allow free-franking for correspondence and the mailing of select items to or from persons who are blind.

Of course, other types of mail can be sent using prepaid postage other than conventional postage stamps.

Three examples are shown in Figure 308: the postage meter stamp (top), the postage value indicator label (center) created at U.S. post office counters, and a postage imprint generated by a home or business computer.

These may not be thought of as stamps by most collectors, but there are others who watch for varieties of all of these items and even create specialized collections showing how they are used.

After all, these labels and imprints are prepaying the postage rate that delivers the mail, the same function that is fulfilled by the conventional postage stamp.

U.S. handcancels prevented stamp reuse

From the earliest days of U.S. postage stamp production, one of the great concerns of the post office has been preventing the illegal reuse of stamps. This is generally accomplished by applying a postmark or other cancellation that invalidates the stamp.

The terms "postmark" and "cancellation" have specific meanings that are different from one another.

A postmark is usually considered to be a marking applied by the post office to a piece of mail as it travels to its destination, including markings identifying the town of origin, as well as transit markings such as "PAID" or "FORWARDED."

Some collectors prefer to think of a postmark as being only that portion of a marking that identifies the date and location where the item was mailed, but that definition is generally too narrow.

A postmark may be struck upon a postage stamp to invalidate it for future use. Other postmarks may provide additional information about the mail delivery.

Cancellation is a more specific term that refers only to the postal marking that obliterates a postage stamp to indicate it has been accepted for use and cannot be used again.

A cancellation, therefore, is always a postmark, but a postmark is not always a cancellation.

Postmarks were developed long before postage stamps, mostly to indicate the point of origin for a specific mail piece.

Postage on early mail usually was paid by the recipient rather than the mailer. The postmark allowed the post office to calculate the distance the letter traveled and thereby determine the amount of payment that was due.

The first U.S. postage stamps issued in 1847 brought with them the concern that instead of buying new stamps, recipients might reuse the stamps they received on mail. To prevent this, postmasters marked each stamp on each letter to indicate that it had been used and could not be used again.

Three postally used examples of the 5¢ Benjamin Franklin stamp of 1847, one of the first two U.S. postage stamps, are shown in Figure 309. Each is marked with a different type of cancellation.

The stamp at left is marked with a handwritten cancel (usually called a "manuscript cancel") in the shape of a simple "X." This method of cancellation was very common on early stamped mail. Manuscript pen or marker cancels are still seen from time to time on today's mail, when the automatic machinery designed to deface modern stamps has somehow failed in its mission.

Figure 309. Three very different postal markings, as found on the 5¢ U.S. Benjamin Franklin stamp of 1847.

At the center of Figure 309 is a stamp bearing a town postmark used as a cancel across the stamp's face.

The stamp at right in the illustration was canceled with a black rectangular grid of squares.

Siegel Auction Galleries of New York, which offered these three stamps in one of its sales, identified the grid-of-squares cancel as originating from Wilkes-Barre, Pa.

While the three cancels shown in Figure 309 are all quite different from one another, they all accomplish the intended goal of sufficiently marking the stamp to prevent reuse.

Linn's Postal History columnist Richard B. Graham wrote in his book *United States Postal History Sampler* that standardized postmarking handstamps were distributed by the Post Office Department in 1799.

Figure 310. The Bridgeport Fireman cancel on this 1866 letter was one of several well-known and highly collectible fancy cancels created by the postmaster of Waterbury, Conn.

When postage stamps came into use nearly half a century later, the town postmarks were often struck elsewhere on the envelope, and the stamp was canceled with a separate marking known as the "killer."

The grid-of-squares cancel shown at right in Figure 309 is one example of a killer marking.

However, as the stamp in the center of the same illustration shows, town marks were sometimes used to cancel the stamps.

After 1860, the use of town marks for cancellation purposes was prohibited by a Post Office Department edict. The new regulation was put into effect because the information in the town marking often could not be read when it was struck upon the stamp. Another factor that came into consideration was that the town markings often did not sufficiently obliterate the stamp to prevent its reuse.

Postmasters and postal clerks around the country used a number of different devices to cancel stamps, from simple segmented corks to elaborately carved images depicting everything from humans to insects and other animals.

One example is shown in Figure 310. Known as the

Figure 311. The duplex handstamp applied the town postmark and killer obliteration with just one strike.

Bridgeport Fireman, the image of the man's head canceling the 1861 3¢ stamp on the envelope in the illustration was used by the Waterbury, Conn., post office in 1866.

Herman Herst Jr. wrote in the January 1983 *Scott Stamp Monthly* that the marking was created by John W. Hill to commemorate a baseball rivalry between the fire departments of Waterbury and Bridgeport. Even more well-known is the famous Waterbury "Running Chicken," which some believe actually may have been a running turkey, since the cancel appeared close to Thanksgiving Day 1869.

Figure 312. The Chicago postmark on this stamp was applied by a duplex handcancel device similar to the device shown in Figure 3.

Other cancellation designs used by offices around the country included stars, geometric patterns and many more.

The government supplied many larger offices with postmarking devices, but smaller offices were forced to buy or create their own.

In 1859 Marcus P. Norton of Troy, N.Y, patented a duplex-style handstamp. This device imprinted the circular town stamp at left and the obliterating killer at right with a single motion. One example from the 1880s, illustrated in Graham's book, is shown in Figure 311.

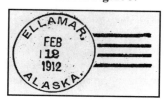

Figure 313. A four-bar-killer handstamp from Alaska in 1912. Similar handstamps are still used today in post offices across the country.

The device created adjoining marks that both identified the sending office and obliterated the stamp, as shown in Figure 312.

While this duplex cancel is no longer in use, another well-known handcancel is still found today in many U.S. post offices.

The four-bar killer cancel also combines the circular town marking with an obliterating cancel in a single device.

An example from Ellamar, Alaska, dated Feb. 12, 1912, is shown in Figure 313.

Today's handcancels are primarily made from hard rubber or similar synthetic, unlike the earlier steel or wood devices used decades ago.

There are still standardized cancels as well as individualized varieties that can be distinguished from town to town.

Metal cancels are primarily used in canceling machines, which debuted in 1876.

Different varieties of handcancels can substantially increase the value of an older stamp and cover.

Listings for early U.S. postage stamps in the Scott *Specialized Catalogue of United States Stamps & Covers* often give premium values for stamps marked by specific postmarks, including steamship and packet boat markings, markings such as "FREE," "PAID," "STEAM," "WAY" and others, various numeral cancels, and cancels in different ink colors.

The Scott U.S. specialized catalog provides six pages of information about postmarks and cancels in its introduction.

Modern U.S. postmarks are also collectible

Most of the postmarks seen on mail today are applied by machine through a high-speed automated process that effectively conveys millions of pieces of mail each day.

When U.S. postage stamps first appeared in 1847, each stamp was postmarked by hand, either with a hand-cancel device or with an ink line across the face of the stamp.

Postmarking machines were first used in the United States in 1876, but hand-cancels have remained in use, often employed when a mailed item cannot be processed by machine.

Today's letter mail is most often sorted and postmarked by a large and complex machine known as an automatic facer-canceler (AFC), part of which is shown in Figure 314. Letter mail is dumped into the AFC, which properly faces each envelope to automatically apply a postmark to the stamp.

The AFC is able to accomplish this because most U.S. stamps printed since 1963 are tagged with a small amount of phosphorescent material that glows when exposed to shortwave ultraviolet light. The machine detects the phosphor in the stamp and positions the envelope so the stamp will be struck by a metal postmarking cylinder as the envelope flies past it.

Figure 315 shows the stamp corners of three envelopes postmarked by the AFC.

The marking shown in the top illustration is an example of a common U.S. machine cancel. At left is a round portion known as the circular datestamp, or CDS. It includes the date and location where the postmark was applied.

This location may not be the same as the post office where the letter was deposited. The envelope in the illustration bears a Yellow Springs, Ohio, return address and was most likely mailed from that location, although it is postmarked Dayton, a larger city located about 15 miles to the west.

Smaller post offices may cancel some envelopes from time-to-time using a simple hand-fed machine, but more often the smaller office will simply ship the

Figure 314. Part of the complex automatic facer-canceler (AFC) machine, which correctly positions envelopes so the postmark will land directly on the postage stamp.

mail it receives to a nearby larger city where the AFC quickly sorts and postmarks each piece.

The local machine cancels usually can be distinguished from the AFC cancels because of format differences in the CDS and the killer lines. The right side of the AFC postmark is known as the "killer," because it marks (or kills) the postage stamp so it cannot be used again.

Most killers resemble the seven wavy lines shown at the top of Figure 315, but many post offices regularly use slogan cancels that promote the U.S. Postal Service, a social cause or some event of regional interest.

The postmark in the center of Figure 315 has a pictorial killer that includes the message "Fall in Love with stamp collecting."

The bottom postmark reads, "Heart disease— your #1 enemy— your #1 defense heart fund."

It so happens that these two markings both have a theme relevant to the design of the heart-shaped 33¢ Love stamp, Scott 3274, used for postage.

Such combinations of themes matching the stamp with the slo-

Figure 315. Three cancels from the AFC. The standard wavy-line cancel is shown at top. The two slogan cancels below it are by chance appropriate for the heart-shaped 33¢ Love stamp.

gan cancel occur by chance, but they make nice additions to a collection of either stamps or cancels.

Some slogan cancels have pictorial elements that make them suitable for a topical or thematic collection.

Obtaining a slogan cancel is often a matter of chance, though some collectors have had good luck submitting a stamped, addressed envelope to the postmaster in a city with a known slogan and politely requesting the envelope be serviced so that it receives the desired slogan.

It's a little easier to obtain one of the many pictorial commemorative postmarks offered each week by offices of the U.S. Postal Service.

Handstamped postmarks, often with pictorial elements, are used to commemorate everything from museum openings to civic anniversary celebrations to local festivals and much more.

These markings are listed each week in *Linn's Stamp News* and a few other stamp-hobby publications.

To obtain one of the postmarks described in the listing, a collector must mail a stamped, addressed envelope or card (also known as a "cover") to the address provided within 30 days of the announced postmark date. The postmarked cover is then returned through the mailstream.

Some collectors use peelable address labels that can be removed once the cover is returned, so that it may be saved unaddressed.

Figure 316 shows two different cancels on the 1998 32¢ Year of the Tiger stamp, Scott 3179. The marking at the bottom is a commemorative cancel that was applied for a limited time in Alhambra, Calif., to mark a local festival. The top marking is a first-day cancel that commemorates where and when the Year of the Tiger stamp was issued.

Almost every time the U.S. Postal Service issues a new stamp, it allows collectors to obtain a first-day cancel marking the event. The Year of the Tiger stamp was officially issued in Seattle Jan. 5, 1998, as the postmark shows.

The procedure for obtaining a first-

Figure 316. These two souvenir cancels were available by request for a limited time. At top is a first-day cancel; below it is a commemorative cancel marking a local festival.

day cancel is just about the same as the procedure given in previous paragraphs for obtaining a commemorative cancel.

The address for the first-day cancel is announced by the Postal Service before the new stamp is issued. Instructions for obtaining the first-day cancel are usually published in stamp-hobby periodicals.

Some first-day cancels are applied by hand while others are marked by a machine. Collectors sometimes find first-day cancels for the same stamp that differ slightly in style, because one is a handcancel and the other is from a machine.

Local post offices use a variety of handcancel devices every day. Markings from four of these devices are shown in Figure 317.

One of the more common markings is the cancel shown at upper left in Figure 317. This cancel, from a device known as a round-dater, is usually struck in red and is sometimes used on larger envelopes that cannot be sent

Figure 317. Various handcancels regularly used in post offices across the United States. All include the post office name or location, ZIP code, and the date the marking was struck.

through the AFC. The same postmark device is often used to mark receipts and other USPS paperwork.

The postmark directly below it is a variation of the round-dater, also seen most frequently in red.

At right are two markings in black, both known as "four-bar killers." Each includes a large round CDS at left and four straight-line killer bars to the right.

Collectors may request handcancels at local post offices, but not every office has every type of cancel available.

Some collectors like to obtain handcancels from specific locations on specific dates to complete a commemorative cover of their own design.

For example, the post office won't create a special commemorative cancel to mark a 50th wedding anniversary, but it may be possible to obtain a handcancel from the city where the couple was married, dated on the exact anniversary date.

All requests for cancels from the Postal Service must include a stamped envelope or postcard. The Postal Service only applies cancels to stamps, not blank paper. Unlike commemorative cancels, handcancels from a post office are applied only with the present day's date. Therefore, requests for a specific cancel must be timed carefully.

Often a mailed request to a postmaster asking for a marking on a particular future date is successful. A collector may wish to include an addressed return envelope bearing sufficient postage for return of the envelope or envelopes submitted. Otherwise, the canceled covers may pick up unwanted markings on their way back to the collector.

Most collectors prefer to save entire covers with the markings intact, though some cut their postmark collections into 4-inch by 2-inch shapes known as "two by fours."

Collectors should take particular care when cutting covers, to make sure they aren't destroying a significant postal history item.

Some collectors simply ignore the postmark as they look for stamps that interest them, but there are many ways that postmarks can be used to add variety to any collection.

First-day covers mark the stamp's issue date

For almost every new stamp that is issued in the United States, the United States Postal Service provides a special postmark that tells the date the stamp was issued and identifies the official first-day city. This postmark is called a first-day cancel, and the words "first day of issue" usually appear somewhere in the marking.

Many stamps are issued with a special ceremony, often open to the public, where the stamp is placed on sale for the first time. Postal Service dignitaries and special guests usually attend these ceremonies. Sometimes the stamp designer or some other celebrities attend the ceremony as well. Of course, the ceremony is called a "first-day ceremony."

As preparations are made to issue a postage stamp, the Postal Service schedules an issue date and selects a city or town to be the site of the first-day ceremony. If all goes well, the new stamp will be sold for the first time in that town on that date. The stamp is placed on sale nationwide on the next business day.

However, sometimes a window clerk at some other post office accidentally sells the stamp before the first day of issue. Some collectors like to look for covers (stamped, mailed envelopes) that show the stamp postally used before the designated issue date. The earliest documented use of such a stamp is called the "earliest known use" (EKU) or "earliest documented use" (EDU).

Once in awhile the Postal Service will issue a stamp nationwide on the first day. In such cases, one city is usually selected where the official first-day cancel can be obtained, but the stamp is placed on sale at post offices all over the country on the same first day.

When an envelope or postcard is prepared by a collector to receive the first-day cancel, that item is called a "first-day cover" or FDC.

There are many collectors who like to prepare first-day covers and obtain the first-day cancel themselves. There are two main ways of doing this: in person at the first-day ceremony or by mail.

First-day ceremonies are often held during stamp shows and exhibitions, but some take place at locations and on dates that are related to the subject of the stamp. For instance, the 32¢ stamp honoring playwright Thornton Wilder was issued April 17, 1997, the 100th anniversary of Wilder's birth. The ceremony took place in Hamden, Conn., where Wilder made his home.

On the other hand, the 50¢ Benjamin Franklin and 60¢ George Washington stamps

Figure 318. Collectors may use a cacheted envelope (top) or a plain envelope for a first-day cover. After the stamp is affixed, the Postal Service applies the first-day cancel, creating the finished first-day cover shown at bottom.

celebrating 150 years of U.S. postage stamps were issued in San Francisco, Calif., May 29 and May 30, 1997, respectively, during the Pacific 97 World Stamp Exhibition.

Hundreds of collectors at that international stamp show enjoyed creating their own FDCs and having them canceled as they waited. The four photographs in Figure 318 help show how this is done.

First, the collector selects an envelope to use for the cover. It may be plain and undecorated, or it may have a "cachet" (pronounced, "ka-SHAY"), which is a design related to the stamp issue.

At the top of Figure 318 is a cacheted envelope manufactured by ArtCraft that was sold at Pacific 97 by Washington Press. Without the stamp and first-day cancel, such an envelope might also be called "unserviced." Some collectors create their own cachet designs, though permission should be obtained to use or reproduce any copyrighted material.

Next, the collector affixes the postage stamp to the envelope. Sometimes larger envelopes are used to obtain the first-day cancel on a block of stamps or a full pane of stamps.

The Postal Service clerk inks the handcancel and positions it over the envelope and stamp. He carefully applies the cancel to the cover, and the end result is the finished FDC shown at the bottom of Figure 318. Because the cancel extends over both the stamp and the envelope, it is said that the stamp is "tied" to the cover, because the cancel shows that the stamp was affixed at the time the cancel was applied.

Collectors who attend first-day events can get cancels on almost any kind of souvenir, including photographs, artwork or posters, as long as the proper stamps are affixed to the item.

Some collectors also like to purchase the stamp at the first-day ceremony and get an "unofficial" first-day cancel at another location. For example, a collector could have taken a Benjamin Franklin cover from the Pacific 97 show, traveled to the downtown San Francisco post office, and asked at the post office window for a standard San Francisco handcancel on the stamp.

Because mailed-in first-day cancels can be obtained after the actual first day of issue, an unofficial first-day cancel from downtown San Francisco would prove that the stamp was actually obtained by the collector on the first day.

Even though a collector may not be able to attend the first-day ceremony or obtain the stamp until after the official first day, he may mail a stamped cover to the first-day city within a specified grace period (usually within 30 days from the issue date) to obtain the first-day cancel.

Here's how it's done.

Soon after the stamp is issued, the collector buys it at his local post office and affixes it to the cover he wants canceled. Because the cover will be returned in the mail, it must be addressed. Most collectors of modern covers prefer to save examples that are not addressed, however. To solve this problem, the collector prints or types his name and address on a plain removable (peelable) label and places that label where the mailing address normally goes on the envelope.

A thin piece of flat cardboard or a folded sheet of paper placed inside the envelope helps make a better impression for the cancel. Most collectors do not lick and seal the back flap of the envelope. Instead, they tuck the flap into the opening.

The prepared, unserviced stamped envelope is placed inside a larger stamped envelope and mailed to the designated first-day location for the stamp. The address to obtain a first-day cancel is provided by the Postal Service and published in *Linn's Stamp News* and the USPS *Postal Bulletin*.

The first-day cover is returned to the collector through the mail with the stamp canceled "FIRST DAY OF ISSUE." The collector can remove the peelable address label and add the cover to his collection.

Sometimes mistakes can make some interesting first-day collectibles. The 32¢ James Dean commemorative was issued June 24, 1996, in Burbank, Calif., but confusion over the first-day site resulted in some collectors sending their covers to Hollywood, Calif., instead. Though most collectors prefer only one cancel on the first-day cover, the Dean cover shown in Figure 319 is worth saving.

Figure 319. Though the 32¢ James Dean commemorative was issued June 24, 1996, in Burbank, Calif., this unofficial first-day cover was postmarked in Hollywood, Calif.

Two covers marked "FIRST DAY OF ISSUE" for the 1995 Women's Suffrage stamp are shown in Figure 320. It's not unusual for the collector to see different styles of first-day cancels used on the same stamp, depending on how or when the cancel is obtained. That's the case with the two covers in Figure 320, where the cancel on the cover at top is smaller and has a different type style than the cancel on the cover at bottom.

Another difference exists between the two, however: A mistake was made on the date on the cancel at top. The Women's Suffrage stamp was issued Aug. 26, 1995, but the top example is marked "first day of issue" exactly one month later. Such dating errors on first-day covers also are

Figure 320. These two Women's Suffrage first-day covers have different styles of cancels as well as different dates. The cancel on the cover shown at top is dated Sept. 26, 1995, instead of the correct date, Aug. 26, 1995.

great additions to a collection.

Along with standard first-day-of-issue cancels, the U.S. Postal Service sometimes creates special pictorial cancels to mark the first day a stamp is released. When the 37¢ Andy Warhol stamp was issued Aug. 9, 2002, the Postal Service used a first-day-of-issue cancel that included the pop artist's name and a caricature of him wearing dark glasses (Figure 321).

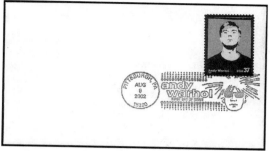

Figure 321. The first-day-of-issue cancel for the 37¢ Andy Warhol stamp is pictorial; it includes the artist's name and likeness.

First-day covers from the first stamp onward

What makes a cover a first-day cover? It's not the cachet, which is a decorative illustration that is often found on a first-day cover.

There are plenty of cacheted envelopes from recent years that are not first-day covers. They illustrate other things, like special local events or stamp shows and exhibitions. There are also plenty of first-day covers that do not have a cachet on them.

The identifying characteristic of a first-day cover (FDC) is that it bears a postage stamp that is postmarked on the date the stamp was issued.

Postal stationery, such as postal cards, stamped envelopes and aerograms, also can be found as first-day covers.

First-day covers have been around just as long as postage stamps, for the world's first stamp is known on a first-day cover. Shown in Figure 322 is a rare cover that was sent from London to Yorkshire in England on the first day that the Penny Black was issued, May 6, 1840. The cover has a dated handstamp on the back.

Covers of the Penny Black postmarked before the first day of issue are also known, but they are very rare.

There are no known FDCs for the first two U.S. stamps. Both were issued July 1, 1847.

The 5¢ stamp is listed in the

Figure 322. The world's first adhesive postage stamp, Great Britain's Penny Black, is shown on a cover postmarked on the stamp's first day of issue, May 6, 1840.

Scott *Specialized Catalogue of United States Stamps & Covers* on an earliest-documented-use cover of July 7. A July 2 cover is known bearing a pair of 10¢ stamps. The cover is shown in Figure 323.

The same listings also appear in the Scott *U.S. First Day Cover Catalogue & Checklist* by Michael A. Mellone. The Mellone catalog notes that although FDCs

Figure 323. The earliest-documented use of the 10¢ George Washington stamp of 1847 (U.S. Scott 2) on cover, marked July 2, 1847.

were known and collected for many years, the special first-day cancel from the Postal Service (then known as the U.S. Post Office Department) was not developed until 1937, when a "first day of issue" machine cancel was authorized for use on the Ordinance of 1787 commemorative (Scott 795) issued July 13, in Marietta, Ohio.

Before then, U.S. FDCs were postmarked with the standard machine cancels or handcancels that were used on normal mail. Most FDCs after that date have had the specially designated first-day cancel applied to them.

Before the first-day cancels were created, the covers sought and collected by specialists were simply uses of the stamp on the first day it was issued. Most of the examples were mail that was sent in the course of normal business or correspondence.

The Post Office Department began designating a first day of issue for its stamps during the 1920s, and most FDCs from that point on have been philatelic creations, rather than standard uses. The first cacheted FDC was created soon after by George W. Linn who in 1928 would start a publication he called *Linn's Weekly Stamp News*. Following the death of President Warren G. Harding on Aug. 2, 1923, the Post Office Department prepared a 2¢ memorial stamp that was issued less than one month later, on Sept. 1. The stamp was available on its first day of issue in Washington, D.C., and in Marion, Ohio, where the president was buried.

Linn, who lived and worked in Columbus, Ohio, about 40 miles south of Marion, made the trip to Marion that day to obtain the new stamps and create some souvenir covers. A printer by trade, Linn used black-bordered mourning envelopes for his FDCs and imprinted in the lower-left corner the message, "In Memorium/Warren G. Harding/Twenty-Ninth President/Born Nov. 2, 1865/Died Aug. 2, 1923."

It is estimated that Linn created at least a couple hundred covers, addressing each by hand to his address in Columbus. An example of one of these covers is shown in Figure 324. As one of the first cacheted FDCs ever created, this example was auctioned in 1996 by James T. McCusker for $1,100, plus a 10 percent buyer's premium. Linn sold his cacheted FDCs for 50¢ each in 1923.

A few first-days from earlier issues are known with cachets that were applied long after the stamp was canceled on cover.

For many years, FDCs addressed by hand (like Linn's) or typewritten were the standard. Most col-

Figure 324. The first cacheted first-day cover was created by George W. Linn, who founded *Linn's Weekly Stamp News*.

lectors of modern FDCs now prefer unaddressed cacheted first-day covers.

A collector should never attempt to alter or remove an address on a cover.

Soon after George Linn created his cacheted FDCs, collectors and cover-makers realized that a cachet on an FDC added an interesting new feature to the collectible. Printed messages like Linn's were followed by illustrations and designs related to the stamp being issued.

Cachets may be printed, rubber-stamped or handpainted designs, or affixed illustrations or labels.

For many collectors, cachet collecting has become a critical element in their FDC collections. Some collect only cachets by certain artists or manufacturers. Others seek out the most beautifully cacheted FDC to add to their collections.

Simple illustrations have given way to all sorts of innovations, including covers that are fully illustrated, presenting an allover design on the envelope.

Shown in Figure 325 is a foldout cover created for the 1996 Folk Heroes block of four stamps issued by the United States.

Figure 325. Cachetmakers have brought about numerous first-day cover innovations. This foldout cover for the 1996 Folk Heroes issue was created by Bennett Cachetoons.

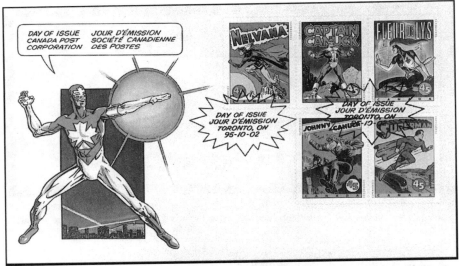

Figure 326. Foreign postal services often manufacture and sell first-day covers for their new stamp issues. This 1995 cover from Canada is for its Superheroes stamps.

Other covers use transparent windows in the front to show items displayed inside the cover.

FDCs without cachets are still prepared and saved by collectors, and the United States Postal Service also sells uncacheted FDCs for some of its new issues.

Postal services from many foreign countries manufacture and sell FDCs for their own stamp issues, usually using cacheted envelopes to create the cover. An example is the FDC from Canada shown in Figure 326. The phrase "Jour d'emission" in the cancel is French for "day of issue."

There are really no limits to the types and varieties of cachets used to illustrate modern FDCs.

Many cover manufacturers advertise subscription programs that send serviced cacheted FDCs to the collector soon after the new stamp is issued. Others offer their covers for sale individually through advertisements in popular philatelic publications like *Linn's Stamp News* and *First Days*, the journal of the American First Day Cover Society.

Chapter 10
Multiples and More

Sets and series are tailor-made for collecting

Stamps issued in sets and in series appeal to many collectors for a variety of different reasons.

Every dedicated stamp collector has some concept of order and organization that he methodically applies to his stamp collection. Even the worldwide collector, who welcomes into his collection almost any stamp ever printed, still arranges that collection by country or by year, or both. The topical collector also fits his stamps into a sequence that he finds pleasing or that succeeds in conveying an established theme.

We probably don't think of it consciously, but the desire to neatly organize our collections, and our ability to do so, are appealing elements of the stamp hobby. It is apparent that the stamp collector possesses some trait that makes accumulating and sorting attractive activities. That may also explain why the appeal of the stamp hobby is so strong for some people and so incomprehensible to others who by their nature are not collectors.

It may have happened by accident, but postal administrations around the world have tapped into the collector's instinct for organization by regularly issuing stamps that can be collected in sets and series.

Figure 327. A set of three stamps from Luxembourg issued Sept. 21, 1998, to mark the 1,300th anniversary of the Abbey of Echternach. Each stamp has a different design and value.

The terms "set" and "series" as they apply to postage stamps are sometimes confused by collectors, and they do have a tendency to overlap in meaning. Both terms refer to groups of stamps that share common characteristics of design or theme.

A series of stamps is issued over a period of time, often several years. A set of stamps may be issued all at once, or it can be issued over a period of time, but generally not an extended period.

The three Luxembourg stamps shown in Figure 327, Scott 996-98, constitute a complete set of stamps. The stamps commemorate 1,300 years of the Abbey of Echternach. All were issued on the same day: Sept. 21, 1998. Each stamp was issued in separate panes of 20 stamps, and each carries a different denomination to pay specific domestic or international mail rates.

These are all characteristics of this particular set from Luxembourg. Stamps from other sets may be issued on different days or may all have the same denomination.

For example, in 1973 the United States Postal Service issued a set of four 8¢ stamps individually honoring composer George Gershwin (Scott 1484), poet Robinson Jeffers (1485), painter Henry O. Tanner (1486), and novelist Willa Cather (1487). All four stamps share very similar designs created by Mark English, but they were issued on four different days, ranging from Feb. 28 for the Gershwin stamp to Sept. 20 for the Cather issue.

Stamps in a series may be issued on a regular schedule, or they may appear as a postal need for new denominations arises.

One series of commemorative stamps from the United States is the Black Heritage series. Beginning in 1978, one stamp in this series has been issued each year to honor one individual.

Commemorative stamps are usually printed in a predetermined quantity and are taken off sale after a year or two. Definitive stamps, on the other hand, may be printed over and over again as the need arises, and they are often available for many years.

A 33¢ Black Heritage series stamp honoring Patricia Roberts Harris, a Cabinet secretary during the administration of President Jimmy Carter, was issued Jan. 27, 2000. Some collectors simply save the Harris stamp as part of their general U.S. stamp collection. Others may maintain a specialized collection of the Black Heritage series or a topical collection of black Americans on stamps, and they will add the Harris stamp to it.

While the Black Heritage commemorative series continues beyond 2000, another popular U.S. stamp series ended a few years earlier.

The Transportation coil definitive stamp series began in 1981 with the issuance of an 18¢ single-color stamp depicting a surrey from the 1890s (Scott 1907). New stamps in the same series were issued from time to time, each showing a different form of transportation and most bearing different face values ranging from 1¢ to $1. More than 50 different designs were created over the course of 15 years.

Many collectors have been fascinated by the Transportation coil series and found different ways to build collections of the various stamps.

While 23 years or even 15 years may seem like a long time for a series to continue, the longest-running stamp series in the world has existed for more than 125 years.

Norway's Posthorn definitive stamp series began with a 3-skilling rose stamp issued in 1872 (Scott 18). The 2sk stamp of the same design (17), issued in 1874, is shown at upper left in Figure 328.

Over the course of more than a century, stamps have been issued in the Posthorn series to reflect changing postage rates and printing techniques. Five stamps from the series are shown in Figure 328. At lower left in the illustration is a 20-øre blue stamp (1142) issued in 1997.

There are more than 100 major varieties in Norway's Posthorn series, and countless minor varieties exist as well. Though there have been some small changes in the basic design, the stamps in the Posthorn series all closely resemble one another.

Design similarities can be a distinguishing characteristic among sets or series, but sometimes stamps in the same series may bear little resemblance to one another. Again, the Black Heritage series provides an example. The designs of the various stamps in the series include multicolor paintings and monochromatic photographs with a variety of type styles and arrangements. In this case, the series is defined by the subject matter, not the design. Sometimes the series subject is formally announced by the issuing postal authority. Sometimes it is defined by collectors.

There are many instances where stamps are issued in sets that become part of a larger series.

In 1993 the United States began its Legends of American Music series with a single 29¢ stamp issued Jan. 8 to honor Elvis Presley (Scott 2721). Later that same year, the Postal Service began issuing booklets and panes of stamps with similar designs honoring other musicians or musical productions. The series ended with the release of six 33¢ Broadway Songwriters stamps on Sept. 21, 1999.

Three panes in the Legends of American Music series are shown in Figure 329: the Country & Western issue of 1993 (2771-74), the Popular Singers issue of 1994 (2849-53), and the Jazz Musicians issue of 1995 (2983-92).

As the illustration shows, these issues contain more than one design on the pane. The Jazz Musicians pane

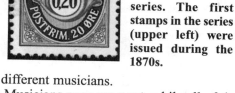

Figure 328. The longest-running stamp series in the world is Norway's Posthorn definitive series. The first stamps in the series (upper left) were issued during the 1870s.

of 20 stamps, for example, honors 10 different musicians.

The 10 different stamps on the Jazz Musicians pane are a set, while all of the different Legends of American Music stamps (a total of 93) make up the series.

Stamp collectors decide for themselves how they like to collect stamps that have been issued in sets or in series. Mint stamps can be collected singly, such as the three stamps from Luxembourg shown in Figure 327, or even in full panes, as shown in Figure 329.

Many collectors prefer to save postally used stamps, such as the five Posthorn issues shown in Figure 328. Another option for the collector of used stamps is to save the stamps intact on cover. Figure 330 shows one of the 33¢ Sonoran Desert stamps of 1999 (Scott 3293) on cover. The 10 stamps in the Sonoran Desert pane

Figure 329. The Legends of American Music series issued by the United States consisted of many different sets (such as the three panes shown here) as well as individual stamps. The series began in 1993 and ended in 1999.

all have different designs, but together they are considered a set.

Commemorative stamps frequently see less use as postage than definitives, so on-cover examples are sometimes hard to come by. Creating a collection of the 10 Sonoran Desert stamps on cover can be quite a challenge.

Covers bearing stamps from earlier definitive series are popular with many collectors. Examples showing

Figure 330. Individual stamps from a set or series may be collected on covers. Shown is one of the 10 stamps from the 33¢ Sonoran Desert set issued by the United States in 1999.

stamps paying special postage rates, such as certified or registered mail, are particularly interesting.

Different catalogs list sets and series of stamps in different ways. The Scott catalogs often group related stamps together, assigning them individual sequential catalog numbers. A handy Identifier section near the beginning of the Scott *Specialized Catalogue of United States Stamps & Covers* helps to locate and identify U.S. definitive stamp series.

Sometimes the standard catalog listing for a series is broken into different sections, and the catalog will lead you to later sections with a note at the end of the first section.

Fascinating collections have been created using stamp sets and series as a starting point.

On some occasions, postal authorities have created immensely popular sets and series, while other sets or series have turned out to be great flops. The success or failure of each set usually depends upon collectors and the general public. It is up to the individual collector to decide which stamps he enjoys and how he wants to add them to his own collection.

Se-tenant stamps are different designs united

A special term describes stamps that are attached to one another but bear different designs. The word "se-tenant" translates from French as meaning "holding together." The French pronunciation of the word is "say-tah-NON," but American collectors often pronounce it "say-TEN-ent."

One example of a se-tenant pair from the United States is shown in Figure 331. The 13¢ Capt. James Cook issue of 1978 consisted of two designs printed together on a single pane of 50 stamps: five rows down and 10 across. The stamps on the left half of the pane (five rows down and five stamps across) all show a portrait of Cook (Scott 1732). Each stamp on the right half shows the ships *Discovery* and *Resolution* (1733).

Up and down the center of each Capt. Cook pane were five se-tenant pairs of

259

stamps such as the example shown in Figure 331. Many collectors chose to save a pair. In the Scott catalog, the attached pair of Capt. Cook stamps is specifically identified as Scott 1733b.

Sometimes when two different designs appear on a single pane, the stamps are arranged like a checkerboard, with the different designs alternating in each row horizontally and vertically.

Some collectors question whether self-adhesive stamps, such as the ten 33¢ Sonoran Desert stamps issued by the United States in 1999, can be se-tenant. After all, the die cut that separates each self-adhesive stamp completely severs it from its neighbor, whereas stamps that are perforated

Figure 331. The 1978 13¢ Capt. James Cook issue can be collected as a se-tenant pair, where two different stamps are attached. Each Cook pane of 50 included five se-tenant pairs.

with rows of holes are still attached to one another by the small bit of stamp paper between each hole that is known as a "bridge."

Even though the self-adhesives are not really attached to one another, they are held together by their proximity and their placement on the backing paper. Two unused adjacent self-adhesives of different designs may be called se-tenant. If one stamp is removed from the backing paper, it is no longer se-tenant with its neighbors, just as when an attached pair of perforated stamps is separated, it is no longer se-tenant.

In the early years of stamp production, the stamps in a given printing were all the same design. For example, every stamp of the Penny Black issue of 1840 (Great Britain Scott 1) shows a portrait of Queen Victoria with the inscriptions "POSTAGE" and "ONE PENNY."

The Penny Black is acknowledged as the world's first adhesive postage stamp. Yet, in the left and right lower corners of each Penny Black stamp there appear two very small letters that identify the position where the stamp appeared on the sheet.

Therefore, any Penny Black stamp attached to another can be considered se-tenant because these plate-position letter combinations are different for each stamp on the sheet.

While the distinguishing differences on the Penny Blacks are intentional, other early se-tenant stamps were created unintentionally.

In 1851 Spain produced a sheet of 170 6-real blue stamps featuring a portrait of Queen Isabella II. As described in the *Linn's* book *Philatelic Gems*, a single 2r cliché (a metal unit with a single stamp design used to construct a form to make a plate) was accidentally inserted in the form for the 6r stamp. When the stamps were printed from the resulting plate, one stamp on each sheet was inscribed "DOS REALES" rather than the correct "SEIS REALES."

The 2r blue stamp is considered an error of color because the 2r stamp was normally printed in red. At least one example has survived that shows the 6r stamp se-tenant with the 2r error from the same sheet.

A few similar examples are known among U.S. stamps. Figure 332 shows a block of nine stamps from the 1916 George Washington issue. The stamps shown are all carmine red. If you look closely at the illustration, you'll see that all of the stamps have 2¢ denominations, with the exception of the center stamp, which is 5¢.

Once again, the 5¢ stamp is considered an error of color because the proper color for the 5¢ stamp of this issue was blue.

As one of the steel printing plates was being manufactured for the 2¢ issue, for some reason it became necessary to re-enter three subjects (individual stamp designs) on the plate. An impressing device called a transfer roll, which bore the design of the

Figure 332. The stamp in the center of this block is a 5¢ carmine error of color. It is se-tenant with the remaining 2¢ stamps.

5¢ stamp, was used to place the design on the plate, instead of the proper transfer roll with the 2¢ design.

Apparently no one noticed the difference because the stamp designs were very similar, so sheets of 400 stamps were printed with three stamps bearing the wrong denomination.

To illustrate the se-tenant nature of the issue, collectors save this interesting error with examples of the proper stamp attached. The 2¢ stamp is Scott 463, and the 5¢ carmine error of color is Scott 467.

In 1936 the United States issued an imperforate four-stamp souvenir sheet (778) commemorating the Third International Philatelic Exhibition. The sheet reproduced the designs of four different stamps that had been issued between April 1935 and March 1936. Similar imperforate souvenir sheets were issued in 1947 (948) and 1956 (1075).

Stamps with attached labels are also considered to be se-tenant with the label, and they are normally saved in that form by collectors whenever possible. Most of Belgium's stamps issued from 1893 through 1913 were printed with a detachable label at the bottom of the stamp. The label requested no delivery of the mail on Sunday. Other nations have included advertising labels se-tenant with booklet stamps. Examples include the booklet issues of Denmark from 1927 to 1934, with labels attached to common letter-rate stamps. The labels promote automobiles, magazines, soap and other items.

In 1962 the United States began to issue 5¢ George Washington booklet stamps with se-tenant slogan labels (1213a) promoting proper use of ZIP codes and offering other mailing suggestions.

Many countries have issued se-tenant stamps in various ways.

As early as 1905, Germany issued booklet panes with se-tenant Germania stamps of different denominations.

Beginning in 1926, the stamps of South Africa were printed alternately with English and Afrikaans inscriptions in the same sheet. Most collectors of South Africa's stamps from this period look for se-tenant pairs of stamps that show one of each type.

The United States issued four perforated se-tenant multicolor 5¢ Christmas stamps in 1964. Each stamp showed a different type of flora associated with the holiday: holly, mistletoe, poinsettia and conifer (1254-57).

Se-tenant stamps began as issues of separate designs that were simply attached to one another, but as the concept became more popular, postal administrations looked for ways to make the stamps part of a larger continuous design.

A se-tenant pair of 5¢ U.S. stamps shows a space-walking astronaut on one stamp (1331) and the Gemini 4 space capsule on the other (1332), but the pair together shows those elements as a single outer-space scene (1332b).

The 1972 Cape Hatteras National Park issue (1448-51) consists of four 2¢ stamps in a se-tenant block that together creates one seashore scene.

A single scene made up of four se-tenant stamps is called a quadripartition.

When three stamps make up the scene, the issue is called a triptych (pronounced "TRIP-tik"). The U.S. 13¢ Spirit of '76 stamps from 1976 recreated Archibald M. Willard's well-known portrait of a fife and drum trio as three se-tenant stamps (1629-31) to commemorate the U.S. bicentennial. This triptych is shown in Figure 333.

Figure 333. Three se-tenant postage stamps completing a single continuous design are referred to as a triptych.

The postal services of several countries have created single contin-uous scenes with as many as 10 or 20 se-tenant stamps. The U.S. Sonoran Desert issue is just one such example.

Many collectors enjoy looking for postally used examples of se-tenant issues. Since the stamps are frequently separated when used on mail, examples of se-tenant stamps still attached can be a little harder to find.

The cover shown in Figure 334 bears seven stamps from Denmark, on an enve-lope mailed from Copenhagen to the United States in 1978. The first five stamps from left to right are all attached; only the two 20-øre stamps in positions 3 and 4 are alike.

Together the five stamps form the first pane of Denmark's machine-vended se-tenant definitive booklet stamps, issued in 1977 (544a).

Like most booklet stamps with varying denominations, this example was cre-ated to offer a variety of stamps at a nice round rate that can be easily paid into a machine. In this case, the five stamps cost an even 2 kroner.

Se-tenant stamps have been issued in many forms by countries around the world. Every variety provides collectors with a great number of different ways to collect and enjoy their stamps.

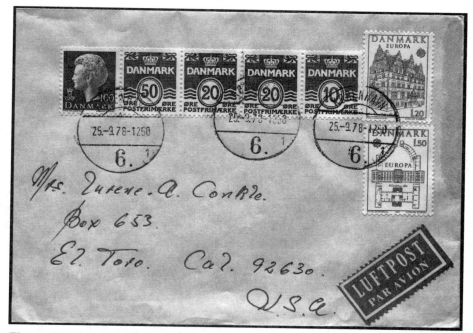

Figure 334. Se-tenant stamps are sometimes found used on cover. The envelope shown here was sent from Denmark to the United States in 1978. The five stamps at left are all se-tenant, from a booklet sold by machine beginning in November 1977.

U.S. plate blocks exist in numerous formats

There's something about a plate block that motivates many of us to keep collecting them.

It may be that for some collectors, looking at four or more stamps in a block is simply more interesting than examining a single stamp. Or maybe we appreciate the plate-block format because having a plate number attached to the stamps provides us with additional information about the item we've saved.

Whatever the reason, plate-block collecting has persisted for decades. It is likely to continue in some form as long as stamps are bought and sold.

Plate blocks, also known as plate number blocks, are groups of attached stamps in specific quantities taken from the corner or side of a pane, including the selvage (margin paper) bearing the numbers identifying the printing plate or cylinder used to print the entire stamp sheet.

A pane, as previously explained, is a quantity of stamps trimmed from a full press sheet and later delivered to the post office.

Some older press sheets, for example, had 400 stamps printed upon them, but before they left the printing plant, they were cut into four 100-stamp panes that were eventually sold through post office windows.

With the exception of some of the earliest issues, U.S. stamps have plate numbers printed in the selvage of each sheet. In most cases, the plate number appears at least once in the margin of the pane.

In his 1982 *Census of United States Classic Plate Blocks 1851-1882*, John C. Chapin wrote, "There were no plate numbers on the panes of the 5 cent and 10 cent 1847 issue and its 1875 reproductions (Scott Nos. 1-4) and types I, Ib, and Ia of the 1 cent blue of 1851 (Scott Nos. 5, 5A, and 6) cannot have them since their plate positions preclude it."

The blocks illustrated in Figures 335-336 are from the Eliot H. Weisman private collection that was offered for sale May 8, 1998, in New York City by Shreves Philatelic Galleries Inc.

In Figure 335 is shown a plate block of Scott 26, the 1857 3¢ dull red George Washington (type II). The plate number on this block is "No. 20 P.," which can be read in the margin paper attached to the block of eight stamps.

The listing for Scott 26 in the Scott *Specialized Catalog of United States Stamps & Covers* describes the plate block as "P# block of 8, Impt."

"Impt." is an abbreviation for "imprint." Many early plate blocks also included imprinted information that identifies the stamp printer. Along the margin paper of the block in Figure 335, for example, are the words, "Toppan, Carpenter & Co. BANK NOTE ENGRAVERS, Phila, New York, Boston & Cincinnati." The imprint is usually found centered in at least one margin on early U.S. stamp panes.

Figure 335. A plate block of U.S. Scott 26. It includes two vertical rows of stamps and attached margin paper bearing plate number and imprint information.

Why does this plate block require eight stamps when others need only six or four?

For stamps of a single design, such as Scott 26, a plate block consists of two rows of the minimum number of stamps attached to the margin that encompasses all of the plate number and imprint information.

In this case, saving fewer than eight stamps (in two rows) would mean removing part of the imprint information. Therefore, even though the plate number information might still be attached, anything less than eight stamps would not be considered a plate block.

The Scott U.S. specialized catalog, however, lists numerous early U.S. stamps with both "plate strip" and "plate block" values. An example is Scott 73, the 2¢ Black Jack of 1863, a black stamp featuring the portrait of Andrew Jackson.

Among the listings for the Black Jack in the Scott U.S. specialized catalog are both "P# strip of 4, Impt." and "P# block of 8, Impt." The "P# strip" for this issue is four stamps in a single-row horizontal strip with selvage attached bearing imprint and plate number information. The "P# block" for this issue is eight stamps (two horizontal rows of four) in a block with selvage attached bearing imprint and plate number information.

Of course, the larger block is the preferred multiple, and the catalog values reflect this: In 2003, for example, the value was $4,250 for the strip versus $14,000 for the block.

Though plate number strips are listed for a few of the earliest issues from the 20th century, plate number blocks became the more accepted format to collect, and most later sheet stamps are not listed with a plate number strip value.

On many U.S. issues, the location of the imprint and plate number information can help identify the section of the sheet from which the plate block came.

The 3¢ stamp in Figure 335 was printed in sheets of 200 (20 across and 10 down) that were divided by a vertical cut into two panes of 100 (10 across and 10 down). The pane on the left included plate information in the left margin. The pane on the right included plate information in the right margin. Therefore, by examining the plate block in Figure 335, it is possible to tell by the position of the plate information that the block came from a left-hand pane.

This method of locating the pane position could not be used for every early issue, however. When rotary-press stamp issues with corner plate blocks were introduced in the 1920s, a similar method developed that was much more consistent.

The companies that produced early U.S. postage stamps created plate number imprint blocks in many different styles. The Bureau of Engraving and Printing began manufacturing postage stamps in 1894 and used several similar imprints until discontinuing them in December 1911, according to the *Durland Standard Plate Number Catalog.*

One of the later plate number imprint blocks is shown at the left of Figure 336. The 50¢ violet Benjamin Franklin stamp of 1912 (Scott 422) includes the Bureau imprint, letter "A" and plate number 5749 in the margin.

Many issues of the time were printed in sheets of 400 (cut into four panes of 100), and the Bureau imprint appeared twice in the margins of each pane: once at top or bottom and once at left or right. The pane from the upper-left portion of the sheet, for example, would have numbers in the top and left margins.

Figure 336. Plate blocks of six stamps can be found with imprint information (Scott 422, left) or with plate number alone (Scott 479, right). Catalogs describe the format.

Scott 422 was printed in sheets of 200, however, and divided into panes of 100. Plate numbers were found in the top and bottom margins of each pane.

When the Bureau eliminated imprints, the plate number remained. Since the numbers still appeared roughly centered in the pane margin, plate blocks of six were the prevalent format, as illustrated by the block of Scott 479, the $2 James Madison issue of 1917 shown at the right of Figure 336.

Numerous other formats were also created. Higher value bicolor stamps are particularly interesting. Figure 337 shows a plate block of the $2 orange-red and black Benjamin Franklin issue of 1918, Scott 523. In the Scott U.S. specialized catalog this block is described as "P# block of 8, 2# & arrow."

The illustrated block shows two plate numbers (one for each color used in the printing process) and an orange-red arrow guideline (shaped like a "V") in the center of the margin.

The formats for the known plate blocks are described in both the Scott U.S. specialized catalog and the Durland catalog.

Figure 337. Plate blocks of some bicolor high-value stamps, including Scott 523 from 1918, consist of eight stamps, two different numbers and a V-shaped guideline arrow.

Plate blocks affected by printing changes

In the early years of U.S. postage stamp production, stamps often were printed using flat steel plates that produced one sheet at a time.

In 1914 the director of the Bureau of Engraving and Printing revealed that a new postage stamp printing press was in operation that used curved printing plates wrapped around a cylinder rather than the flat plates of the past. Called the rotary press, this new machinery allowed the Bureau to manufacture long, continuous rows of stamps that could be slit into coils easily, and the first rotary-press issues to appear were 1914 coil stamps.

When the rotary press was used in 1923 to create stamps that would be sold in panes, small changes were made in the full-sheet layouts that transformed the structure and appearance of the plate block. Plate numbers were printed only four times on each sheet, once at each corner. When the sheet was divided into four panes of 100 stamps, each pane included just one plate number.

The plate numbers on earlier stamps that were printed using flat plates often were centered in the margin at top, bottom and sides, so collectors saved plate blocks of six or more with the plate information centered along the edge of the block. With the new rotary sheet stamps, a corner block of four stamps became the established plate-block format. An early rotary-press plate block, the 3¢ perf 10 Abraham Lincoln issue of 1925 (Scott 584), is shown at upper left in Figure 338.

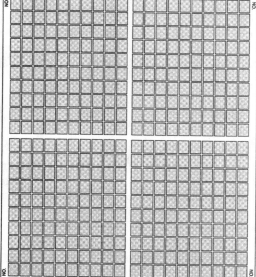

Figure 338. Plate blocks of the earliest rotary-press stamps, including the 3¢ Abraham Lincoln of 1925 (Scott 584), were corner blocks of four with plate information attached (upper left). The same format was still used years later for some issues, including the 1994 20¢ Virginia Apgar (Scott 2179, upper right). Both issues were printed in press sheet layouts resembling the diagram at left. The two plate blocks shown are from the upper-left corner.

Shown at upper right of Figure 338 is a plate block of the 20¢ Virginia Apgar stamp, Scott 2179, issued in 1994. Both the Lincoln stamp and the original printing of the Apgar stamp that was issued nearly 70 years later were printed in sheets of 400 stamps that roughly resemble the diagram shown in Figure 338. Those sheets were separated through the center both vertically and horizontally before they left the manufacturing plant. Post offices received panes of 100 stamps, with one plate number at one corner of each pane.

The location of the plate number on these two issues also tells collectors exactly where on the press sheets the blocks came from.

If you look at the upper-left corner of the sheet diagram in Figure 338, you can see how the location of the four stamps and plate number on the Lincoln and Apgar blocks correspond to that part of the sheet: They could not have come from any other area.

This method of determining the original location of the block was reliable for about 70 years, but it was negated not long after the Apgar stamp was issued.

267

Some plate-block collectors particularly enjoyed tracking plate-block positions and sought to collect blocks representing each of the four corners of the press sheet. The example in Figure 339 shows four plate blocks of the 4¢ Flag stamp from 1960, Scott 1153. Each block has the same plate number, 26639, in the selvage. This is called a matched set of plate blocks.

On many issues, more than one plate was used to print the stamps, and each plate had its own number. The 4¢ Flag, for instance, was printed using plate numbers 26639, 26640, 26647 and 26648. With four corner plate blocks for each plate, a collector could obtain all 16 possible plate blocks. This is called a complete matched set of plate blocks.

While 16 is a manageable number of plate blocks, 1,424 is not. That's how many different blocks a collector would need to put together a complete matched set of plate blocks for the 3¢ Thomas Jefferson issue of 1938, Scott 807. Over the many years this workhorse stamp was used for daily mail, 356 different plates were used to manufacture it.

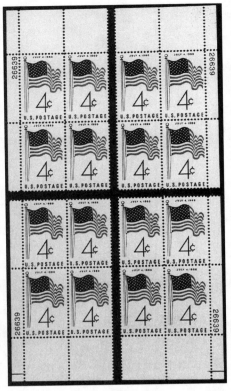

Figure 339. A matched set of plate blocks includes all four corner positions with the same numbers on each block.

The rise and limited fall of big plate blocks

The specialty of plate-block collecting was enjoyed for decades by many stamp collectors in the United States, but a combination of factors contributed to a decline in its popularity in the later decades of the 20th century.

Extra-large plate blocks of 10 or 12 stamps or more were created in the late 1960s by the new Huck multicolor printing press installed at the U.S. Bureau of Engraving and Printing. Within five years, collectors who were used to paying 24¢ for plate blocks of four 6¢ stamps were finding that in some instances they had to buy plate blocks of 12 8¢ stamps for 96¢, a four-fold increase in price.

When that cost increase was multiplied by the numerous issues that were placed on sale each year, many collectors decided they did not want to pay that much. Some simply abandoned their plate-block collections and went to collecting one each of U.S. issues. Others stopped collecting stamps entirely.

Another factor that contributed to a decline in plate-block collecting was the development of se-tenant U.S. postage stamp issues.

Though collectors today are quite accustomed to stamp issues that include more than one design, such a thing did not exist in the United States before the

1964 5¢ Christmas issue, Scott 1254-57. For the first time, four different U.S. postage stamp designs appeared together on one pane. While this particular se-tenant issue did not affect plate-block collectors since the plate block of four contained all four designs and the plate numbers, later se-tenant issues would grow considerably in size.

Issues with 10 different designs appeared in 1968 (6¢ Historic Flags, Scott 1345-54) and 1973 (8¢ Postal Service Employees, Scott 1489-98). Each of these issues required the plate-block collector to save 20 stamps to obtain every design in two rows with the necessary plate number information.

Two problems were quickly apparent. The big plate blocks once again cost much more than the smaller blocks of four, and they took up more than their

Figure 340. When every stamp on a pane is different, as with the 50 State Flags issue of 1976 (Scott 1633-82), the full pane must be saved for a plate-block collection.

share of room on an album page.

In 1976 the Postal Service issued the 13¢ 50 State Flags stamps (Scott 1633-82, shown in Figure 340), the first U.S. issue consisting of 50 different stamps. What does a collector save as a plate block for this issue? The answer is everything you see in Figure 340. To have at least one stamp of each design in the plate block, the collector needs to save the entire pane.

Multiple designs continue to be issued today by the Postal Service, and large plate blocks are still the requirement in such cases.

Even issues with fewer se-tenant designs, such as the five from the 1998 32¢ Alexander Calder issue (Scott 3198-3202), require a large plate block. A Calder plate block of 10 is shown in Figure 341.

The Postal Service made an attempt in 1980 to woo back plate-block collectors who had left the specialty by promising to eliminate the multidigit monster plate blocks. In a press release dated Dec. 10, 1980, the agency announced a new plate numbering system that, except in cases where more than four designs appear on a pane, would "establish a plate block as consisting of four stamps regardless of the number of inks used or the press used to print the stamps."

The agency's Stamps Division said its goal was "to make plate number collecting a less expensive pursuit based upon logic and consistency."

The memo, two-and-a-half pages long, was attached to a 12-page report describing, among other things, how a gravure-printed single-design issue that had been printed with six five-digit number combinations along the selvage (each combination in a different color) would be printed henceforth with a single six-digit number combination (with each digit in a different color).

The system of showing sequential plate numbers on the pane would end, replaced by a digit grouping that reflected the cylinder use for each specific issue. For example, the initial printing of a six-color issue would begin with the digits 111111. If one color printing cylinder was replaced, the corresponding color digit would change from 1 to 2.

While the new system decreased the size of most plate blocks for multicolor issues to four, it did not change another printing-press characteristic that affected a number of U.S. issues.

Figure 341. Issues with multiple designs often must be saved in plate blocks of more than four stamps. The plate block of the 1998 32¢ Alexander Calder consists of 10 stamps.

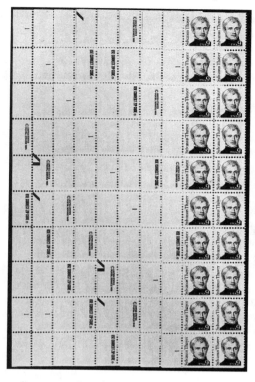

Figure 342. Various strips of 20 9¢ Sylvanus Thayer stamps are shown at left to illustrate the floating plate number. Above is the plate block of six recommended by catalogs.

Stamps printed on the Bureau's combination intaglio-gravure A-press, which was installed in 1973, featured plate numbers that would appear virtually anywhere in the stamp margin. Shown at left in Figure 342 are eight different strips of 20 9¢ Sylvanus Thayer stamps of 1985 (Scott 1852) placed one on top of another. A close inspection of the image shows the single digit "1" appearing in various positions in either one or two spots in the selvage of each strip.

These so-called floating plate numbers posed another problem for collectors who were used to saving corner blocks with selvage along two adjacent margins. The collector's initial instinct was to save all 20 stamps in the strip, but most catalogs today suggest that a plate block on these single-color floating-number issues can be considered two rows of three stamps with the number centered in the margin paper.

An example of a plate block of six Thayer stamps is shown at right in Figure 342. Some collectors will recognize that this plate-block format closely follows that of stamps printed by the flat-plate method in the earliest years of the 20th century.

The floating-plate-number system was directly caused by the size of the A-press printing cylinder. The layout of the printing sleeve created 920 of these small-sized stamps, a number that couldn't be divided evenly into panes of 100 without waste.

In *Linn's Plate Number Coil Handbook*, Ken Lawrence reported that not long after the Thayer stamp was produced, a change in perforating technology made it economical to reconfigure the A-press printing sleeves, and corner blocks of four stamps became the norm for these issues as well.

Plate-block collectors contend with changes

So far we have followed the evolution of U.S. plate blocks from the earliest examples of classic stamp issues printed by flat plates to the oversized blocks that appeared on rotary-press issues during the late 1960s and the 1970s.

As printing methods and machinery have changed, so has the appearance of the plate block.

In the 1990s, two new developments particularly affected collectors of plate blocks: the pane position diagram and the change to four plate blocks on each pane.

On July 24, 1992, the Postal Service issued a pane of 50 29¢ American Wildflowers stamps. Ashton-Potter America Inc. produced the stamps on two different offset presses. One printed sheets containing six panes (or 300 stamps total), and the other produced four-pane sheets of 200 stamps each. Both sheet sizes were trimmed into panes of 50 that were sold at post offices.

For the interest of collectors, though, each pane of 50 stamps included a diagram that showed which size press sheet the individual pane came from. The Figure 343 illustration shows the diagram that appears near the upper-left corner of a pane from the four-pane sheet. The upper-left box of the four boxes in the diagram is shaded to indicate that the pane this particular diagram appeared on came from the upper-left section of the full press sheet.

Similar diagrams continue to appear in a modified state on many of today's stamp issues. The diagram is labeled "PLATE POSITION" on many issues, but it is referred to as a pane position diagram by *Linn's Stamp News*, for it shows the position of the pane in relation to the full press sheet.

Figure 344 shows an uncut press sheet of the 32¢ Stephen Vincent Benét stamp issued July 22, 1998. While many recent stamps have been sold to the public in press-sheet form, the Benét stamp was not. The photograph of the sheet shown here was provided by the United States Postal Service.

As you can see, the Benét press sheet consists of nine panes of 20 stamps. Enlarged at top right in Figure 344 is one of the nine pane position diagrams that appears on the sheet. One diagram is found directly below each of the nine blocks of 20 stamps on the sheet.

Figure 343. The pane position diagram was introduced on the American Wildflowers issue of 1992. The four-square grid represents the sheet layout.

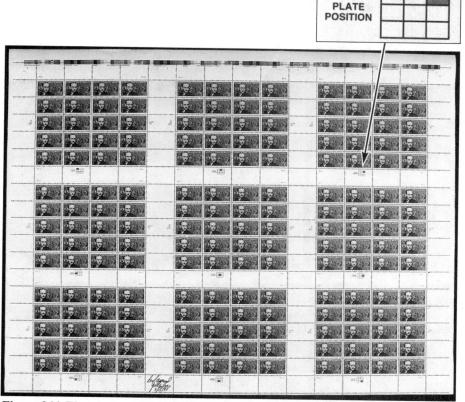

Figure 344. The nine panes of 20 stamps on this press sheet of the 1998 32¢ Stephen Vincent Benét stamp are each indicated by the nine rectangles in the position diagram.

For some issues the diagram can be collected as part of the plate block. This is true for the Benét stamp, as the diagram appears on each of the lower-left plate blocks from each pane.

Figure 345 shows a collection of nine plate blocks that represent the nine pane positions of the Benét press sheet. The diagram on each block indicates a different location on the press sheet. This type of collection is similar to the collections of matched plate blocks that were formed by enthusiastic collectors decades earlier.

The diagram is not an essential element of the plate block, however. Although the Scott U.S. specialized catalog notes for some issues that "some plate blocks contain plate position diagram," collectors interested in saving just one plate block for each issue are not required to seek out a block that includes the diagram.

On the other hand, in recent years the diagram has become the only indicator of the pane position that collectors can rely upon. As early as 1992, the Postal

Figure 345. Collectors may specifically seek out plate blocks that include a pane position diagram, such as these, but many plate blocks having no diagram are quite collectible.

Service began issuing first-class-rate stamps in panes of 20 with plate numbers appearing in all four corners of every pane from the press sheet.

As noted previously, the single plate number on most rotary-press issues had previously been a reliable indicator of the pane position. If a corner block of four stamps had margin selvage and a plate number adjacent to the upper-left stamp in the block, this showed that the plate block had come from a pane from the upper-left position of the press sheet.

With numbers at all four corners of every pane, that indicator was suddenly no longer valid. The introduction of the pane position diagram became a necessity for specialists who desired pane location information.

Figure 346 shows a pane of 20 32¢ Lila and DeWitt Wallace stamps, Scott 2936, issued July 16, 1998, as part of the Great Americans series. The plate number "P1" is visible in each corner of the pane. The plate block for this issue contains four stamps.

Collectors may choose to save any or all of the four plate blocks that appear on this pane. To include the pane position diagram, some may decide to save a block of six or 10 stamps from the bottom half of the pane. Such decisions are completely up to the collector.

While the new format is convenient for collectors who save plate blocks, it also reduces the scarcity of the blocks and diminishes their potential value.

Consider that in 1993 the 29¢ Thomas Jefferson stamp (Scott 2185) in the same Great Americans definitive series was issued in panes of 100 stamps with

Figure 346. Many recent issues have four plate blocks in the pane as well as a pane position diagram.

a single plate number in one corner. That single block made up just four percent of the full pane. On the Lila and DeWitt Wallace stamp, the four corner plate blocks make up 80 percent of every pane.

Collectors who have pursued plate-block collecting for years continue to enjoy their specialty, realizing that most modern plate blocks will never appreciate considerably in value. Value is not always the motivation for building such a collection, however. The reasons are based much more on the challenge of accumulating the blocks that one seeks and the satisfaction of building a collection that best suits the collector.

Save the whole sheet or collect the pieces

The United States Postal Service began selling a few of its new commemorative stamps as uncut press sheets in 1994. The program caught the interest of many U.S. collectors, but just as many have asked, "What am I supposed to do with these things?" Uncut press sheets, after all, are large and unwieldy.

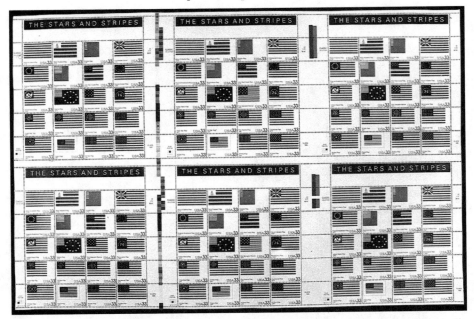

Figure 347. The 33¢ Stars and Stripes stamps issued June 14, 2000, were sold in individual panes of 20 at the post office, but uncut press sheets of six panes like this could be ordered by mail.

Stamps today are almost always printed as large press sheets in continuous rolls, but most of the time no one sees them that way except for the stamp printer. Before the sheets leave the printing plant, they are cut apart into the smaller formats that are sold at the post office. The press sheet may contain as many as nine of the 20-stamp panes that are sold over the post office counter, so some press sheets measure nearly two feet square.

When the Postal Service decides to make a stamp available for purchase as an uncut press sheet, the printing contractor usually trims away excess margin paper around the outside of the printed stamps but leaves the individual panes together, unsevered.

Figure 347 shows the uncut press sheet of the 33¢ Stars and Stripes stamps issued June 14, 2000. The local post office sold the Stars and Stripes issue only as panes of 20 stamps, but the press sheet, sold through the USPS mail-order division, contains six 20-stamp panes as one large unit.

The Postal Service often sends the press sheets through the mail rolled up in reinforced cardboard tubes, but that's not a good way to store stamps long-term. The uncut sheets are too big to fit into a conventional album, and until recently, there just wasn't an established way to store these large items safely and protect them from creases.

These days many collectors save the large sheets intact in specially designed press-sheet storage units developed by stamp hobby supply dealers. The sheets are saved flat in oversize stock pages created from chemically safe materials. A special press-sheet storage box is also available.

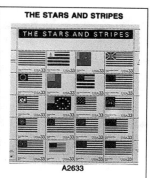

THE STARS AND STRIPES

A2633

Designed by Richard Sheaff. Printed by Banknote Corp. of America.

Designs: a, Sons of Liberty Flag, 1775. b, New England Flag, 1775. c, Forster Flag, 1775. d, Continental Colors, 1776. e, Francis Hopkinson Flag, 1777. f, Brandywine Flag, 1777. g, John Paul Jones Flag, 1779. h, Pierre L'Enfant Flag, 1783. i, Indian Peace Flag, 1803. j, Easton Flag, 1814. k, Star-Spangled Banner, 1814. l, Bennington Flag, c. 1820. m, Great Star Flag, 1837. n, 29-Star Flag, 1847. o, Fort Sumter Flag, 1861. p, Centennial Flag, 1876. q, 38-Star Flag, 1877. r, Peace Flag, 1891. s, 48-Star Flag, 1912. t, 50-Star Flag, 1960.

LITHOGRAPHED

Perf. 10½x11

2000, June 14		**Tagged**	
3403	A2633 Pane of 20	13.00	—
a.-t.	33c any single	.65	.30
	Sheet of 120 (6 panes)	80.00	
	Horiz. block of 8 with vert. gutter	10.00	—
	Vert. block of 10 with horiz. gutter	12.00	—
	Cross gutter block of 20	22.50	—
	Vert. pairs with horiz. gutter (each)	2.25	—
	Horiz. pairs with vert. gutter (each)	2.25	—

Inscriptions on the back of each stamp describe the flag.

Cross gutter block of 20 consists of six stamps from each of two panes and four stamps from each of two other panes with the cross gutter between.

Figure 348. When stamps are issued as press sheets, the catalog listing describes the various position pieces that collectors can create and save.

A number of collectors, however, prefer to save what are known as "position pieces": pairs and blocks of stamps that, because they contain gutters, clearly show they were removed from a press sheet. The gutter is the uncut margin paper between adjoining panes on the sheet.

Look again at the Figure 347 sheet. It contains two gutters that run from top to bottom. On this issue, some colored boxes are printed within each of these two gutters. The sheet also has one narrow gutter that runs through the middle of the sheet from side to side, just above the printed banner "THE STARS AND STRIPES" on the bottom three panes.

The Scott *Specialized Catalogue of United States Stamps & Covers* lists the different collectible configurations that can be extracted from the sheet. The Scott catalog listing for the Stars and Stripes press sheet is shown in Figure 348, as printed in the August 2000 issue of *Scott Stamp Monthly*.

The catalog listing identifies the standard pane of 20 as Scott 3403 and assigns minor letters to each of the 20 different flag stamps. It also lists a series of position pieces from the press sheet, beginning with the complete press sheet of 120 stamps.

Also listed are a horizontal block of eight with vertical gutter, a vertical block of 10 with horizontal gutter, a cross-gutter block of 20, vertical pairs with horizontal gutter, and horizontal pairs with vertical gutter. One example of each of these items is pictured in Figure 349. On the top left side of the illustration are the horizontal pair with vertical gutter (at left) and the vertical pair with horizontal gutter (at right). This sheet contains five different horizontal pairs and four different vertical pairs to collect. Only one of each is shown in the illustration.

At bottom left in Figure 349 is the horizontal block of eight with gutter. Notice that it contains the bottom row of stamps from one pane, the gutter, the printed banner "THE STARS AND STRIPES" from the top of the pane below it, and the top row of stamps from that lower pane.

The center of Figure 349 shows the vertical block of 10 with gutter. At the left side of the block is the vertical row of stamps from the right side of one pane. The gutter runs down the center of the block, and the right side of the block contains the vertical row of stamps from the left side of an adjoining pane.

At right in Figure 349 is the cross-gutter block of 20 stamps. Notice that this block contains parts of both the vertical and horizontal gutters, intersecting to make a cross, and 20 different stamps from four adjoining panes.

The catalog listing states, "Cross gutter block of 20 consists of six stamps from

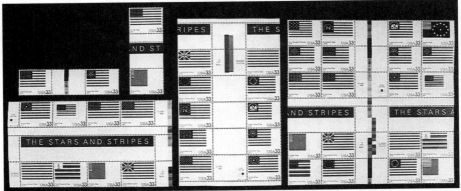

Figure 349. Position pieces from the press sheet. At left, horizontal and vertical pairs (top) and the horizontal block of eight with vertical gutter (bottom). In the center, the vertical block of 10 with horizontal gutter. At right, the cross-gutter block of 20 stamps.

each of two panes and four stamps from each of two other panes with the cross gutter between."

Extracting all of these pieces from the press sheet takes a little advance planning. In some cases, it also takes more than one press sheet. That's true with the Stars and Stripes issue: If you look at the Figure 347 photo and consider the various blocks in Figure 349, you'll see that to gather them all you need to take apart two press sheets, not just one.

A steel straight-edge ruler and a razor knife are handy to separate the pieces. Of course, you have to be very careful when using the razor knife and its extra-sharp blade, and children should not handle it at all.

As shown at left in Figure 350, the knife is used to cut through unperforated areas of the press sheet. On the cross-gutter block at right in Figure 349, for example, a razor knife was used to cut through the printed banner. Don't use the knife through perforations though.

Once you've cut through the unperforated areas, fold the sheet as shown at right in Figure 350. You may wish to wear light cotton or powder-free rubber

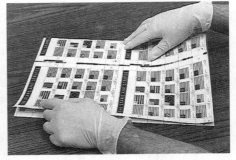

Figure 350. At left: a razor knife and straight-edge ruler can be used with care to cut through unperforated areas of the press sheet, but not through perforations. The press sheet should be folded back and forth through perforated areas to separate stamps, as shown at right.

gloves while handling the stamps to avoid getting fingerprints on the stamps or gum.

Once again, if you're going to divide up your press sheet, look at the catalog listings first and plan your strategy carefully. Press sheets are manufactured in several different formats, and sometimes only one sheet is needed to create the position pieces — if you're careful.

In the 2003 edition of the Scott specialized catalog, the horizontal block of eight and vertical block of 10 were removed from the listing for Scott 3403. However, these items are still interesting collectibles.

Keep in mind that another option is to save the entire sheet intact.

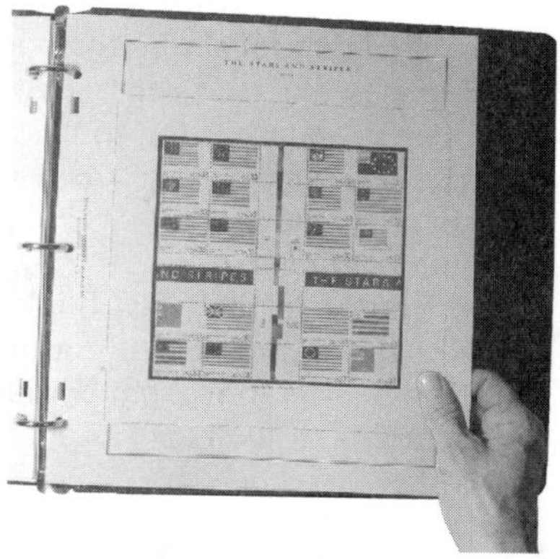

The position pieces are small enough to fit

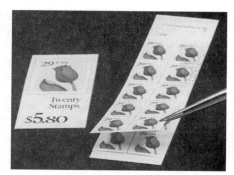

Figure 351. Position pieces can be stored in stock sheets or on preprinted album pages.

on standard album pages. Figure 351 shows a sample album page from Scott Publishing Co. for a cross-gutter block from the Stars and Stripes issue.

When you're done creating your position pieces, you'll find that from the remains of the press sheet you can make extra vertical or horizontal pairs with gutters between. These are often good items to trade with other collectors, or they can be used to create first-day covers with a little extra appeal. They also can be used for postage on mail to other collectors or to friends who will return the unusual covers to you for your collection.

There's no end to the varieties of booklets

According to the Scott *Specialized Catalogue of United States Stamps & Covers*, the first booklet of U.S. postage stamps was issued April 18, 1900. It contained the red type IV variety of the 2¢ George Washington stamp of 1899, Scott 279B.

The booklet format, with small panes of stamps between thin covers, makes it convenient for postal customers to carry and store unused postage stamps. They remain clean and undamaged, even when carried in a pocket or purse.

Figure 352 shows a booklet of 20 29¢ Tulip stamps from 1991, Scott 2527.

The complete booklet of two 10-stamp panes is identified as Scott BK185 in the Booklets: Panes & Covers section of the Scott U.S. specialized catalog.

The 25¢ booklet of 1900 contains two panes of six 2¢ stamps arranged two across and three down. A 49¢ booklet contains four such panes, and a 97¢ booklet holds eight panes.

Figure 352. From 1900 to 1996, the United States issued booklets of perforated stamps with individual stamp panes.

The extra charge of 1¢ per booklet was compensation for the extra cost of manufacturing and processing the booklets.

The panes are each separated by what writer John Luff described as "paraffined paper" interleaving to ensure that the adhesive stamps would not stick to one another. Interleaving was used in booklets until the 1970s, when the development of a synthetic dry or dull gum eliminated concerns about the stamp panes sticking together.

The stamps in that first booklet and in most U.S. booklets were perforated between the stamps but not around the outer edges of the booklet pane. As a result, every stamp in each booklet had at least one straight edge. Stamps in the outer corners of the panes (opposite the binding end) had two adjoining straight edges.

Figure 353. Two 20¢ Flag Over Supreme Court stamps from 1981. The straight edge on the right side of the stamp at right helps to identify it as the booklet variety.

Many collectors used this straight-edge characteristic to identify a U.S. booklet stamp.

Figure 353 shows two 20¢ Flag Over Supreme Court stamps of 1981. The stamp at left, perforated on all four sides, is from the pane of 100 (Scott 1894). The stamp at right, with a straight edge on its right side, is the booklet stamp of the same design, Scott 1896.

The booklet panes of 1900 were manufactured with a short paper tab or stub at the top. After the stamps were positioned between cardboard covers, the panes were stapled through this tab to hold the booklet together. The U.S. Bureau of Engraving and Printing used this binding process for many years.

Booklet stamps actually existed before the 1900 issue appeared in U.S. post offices.

Luxembourg began selling stamps in booklets in 1895, and U.S. telegraph companies had created booklets for their own stamps around 1870.

Most U.S. booklet stamps have been varieties of definitive issues that were sold in larger standard panes, usually of 100 stamps.

Stamp collectors generally take note of any variety that occurs on the issues they collect, so booklets and booklet stamps have long held collector interest.

The varieties grew even more pronounced when the 8¢ deep claret Eisenhower booklet stamp was issued in 1971. Although it resembled the blue-gray 6¢ Eisenhower stamp issued the year before in panes, booklets and coils, the 8¢ stamp in deep claret (a reddish violet color) was not available in larger non-booklet panes, though it was manufactured in coil form.

Before long, a number of different stamps appeared with designs that could only be found in booklet form, including the 13¢ Flag Over Capitol of 1977 (Scott 1623).

As early as 1912, the Post Office Department began selling combination booklets that contained more than one kind of pane.

A 73¢ booklet (BK34) issued that year contained four panes of six 1¢ George Washington stamps (Scott 405) and four panes of six 2¢ George Washington stamps (Scott 406).

Slogan labels appeared on U.S. booklet panes in 1962 when new booklets of 20 5¢ George Washington stamps (BK110) were issued in anticipation of a hike in letter rates effective Jan. 7, 1963.

Many collectors preferred saving only individual panes from booklets (for easy display on a stamp album page), and others saved what are known as exploded booklets. The booklets were dismantled and carefully fanned out on a page to show at least part of each cover, pane and interleaf in the booklet. Even the staples were saved by some collectors and displayed as well.

Exhibiting an exploded booklet was easy enough to do when the booklets were stapled, but by the mid-1970s U.S. booklets were being assembled with an adhesive holding the panes to the booklet covers, instead of staples.

Many collectors wanted to save individual booklet panes intact with the binding tab attached to the edge of the pane. This was difficult to do with glued-in panes, though collectors had some success removing panes from booklets using moistened cotton swabs to carefully dampen the tab so the adhesive would release.

For years booklet tabs had shown identifiable markings of various styles. These tabs became even more interesting in 1981 when plate numbers were printed in the tab attached to the 18¢ American Wildlife pane of 10 different designs (Scott 1880-89).

Collectors searched post offices and traded with each other to obtain booklets that contained the markings and plate numbers they didn't yet have in their collections. Plate numbers can be seen on the 29¢ Pledge of Allegiance booklet of 1993 with red denomination (Scott 2594) shown in Figure 354.

Many modern booklets contained larger panes that were folded between the booklet covers, and in 1988 the United States Postal Service began to offer never-folded booklet panes of the same issues that were sold folded between cardboard covers. These varieties were offered for several years until the U.S. perforated booklet stamp program was discontinued in 1996. The perforated issues were shouldered out of the way by mailer demand for self-adhesive booklets, according to the Postal Service.

Figure 354. Plate numbers are printed on the tabs of most perforated U.S. booklet panes issued since 1981.

A flat pane of 18 25¢ Eagle and Shield stamps issued in 1989 is considered to be the first booklet of self-adhesive stamps, though there was a do-it-yourself factor involved. Mailers had to peel off and discard two narrow strips of self-adhesive paper to fold the flat pane into thirds.

Such issues, including the 1999 Fruit Berries booklet shown at the top of Figure 355, came to be called convertible booklets by the Postal Service.

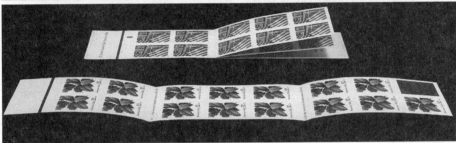

Figure 355. U.S. booklets of self-stick stamps in three formats: unfolded convertible booklet (top), where peel-off strips removed by the mailer allow the booklet to be folded as shown; folded booklet with panes on liner (center); and folded booklet with cover acting as liner (bottom).

Prefolded booklets of self-adhesive stamps were also offered within a few years. The bottom of Figure 355 shows two popular varieties: with individual panes on liner paper, and with the inside of the booklet cover serving as the liner paper.

Most of these self-adhesive issues have also included plate numbers to add to the varieties collectors seek. Some booklet stamps have plate numbers printed directly on them (Figure 356, left), while plate numbers are printed on the peel-off strip on many modern booklets of self-adhesive stamps (Figure 356, right).

Although the United States Postal Service quit producing standard booklets of perforated

Figure 356. Some self-adhesive booklet stamps have had plate numbers printed directly on one stamp in the booklet (left). Most issues show the plate number on a peel-off strip (right).

stamps after releasing the 32¢ Winter Flowers issue of 1996, in 2000 it released an oversized booklet of perforated stamps with water-activated adhesive. The U.S. Navy Submarines booklet shown in Figure 357 contains five different stamps along with pages of descriptive text and photographs. This type of deluxe

stamp booklet with additional features is known as a prestige booklet.

The concept of the prestige booklet was pioneered by Great Britain in 1969 and has since been used by other countries. The U.S. version is a combination of something old (the perforated, gummed stamp) with something new (the prestige booklet format) to further interest booklet stamp collectors.

Figure 357. The United States followed the lead of Great Britain and other countries when it issued its first prestige booklet in 2000.

Stamps in booklet form have created uncountable varieties for collectors in the United States and many other countries as well.

There's little doubt that as stamp technology continues to advance, collectors will continue to see new and exciting items appear.

Coil development led to collecting specialty

Coil stamps serve a number of specific duties for postal customers, but they are also of special interest to many stamp collectors around the world. Coil stamps are processed and issued as long single rows of stamps, usually 100 or more, that are wound into a roll.

Figure 358 shows four U.S. issues in four different coil roll sizes, stacked one upon another in full rolls. The top roll contains 100 of the self-adhesive 20¢ Pheasant coil stamp of 1998, Scott 3055. Below it is the 20¢ Cog Railway coil originally issued in 1995, Scott 2463, in a roll of 500. The next roll down contains 3,000 1¢ American Kestrel coils from 1996, Scott 3044. Finally, the bottom roll contains 10,000

Figure 358. Coil stamps are sold in rolls of different sizes. The four rolls shown here in a stack contain (from top to bottom) 100 stamps, 500 stamps, 3,000 stamps and 10,000 stamps.

nondenominated (10¢) Eagle and Shield coil stamps, Scott 3270, from 1998.

Individuals may go to the post office and buy full rolls of coil stamps in selected denominations, such as postcard or letter-rate values, but other coil stamps or roll sizes may be available only by special order.

One of the more common uses for coil stamps is for dispensing from vending machines in post office lobbies and elsewhere, as shown in Figure 359.

Businesses that send mail in great quantities sometimes use coil stamps in special affixing machines that apply coil stamps to envelopes automatically.

The need for stamps that would fulfill these vending and affixing requirements led to the development of coil stamps at the beginning of the 20th century.

When the first postage stamps were issued in the 1840s, they were printed in large sheets that usually were divided into smaller panes for sale at post office windows. The first U.S. postage stamps, issued in 1847, for instance, were printed in sheets of 200 that then were cut into panes of 100.

Worldwide industrial development in the latter half of the 19th century included the development of numerous mechanical devices designed to accomplish tasks previously performed by hand.

Figure 359. Coil stamps are often used to stock post office vending machinery.

In 1905, New Zealand began trials of stamp vending machines known as "Penny-in-the-slot" machines (or slot machines) at the post office in Wellington. In the 1965 *Catalogue of New Zealand Stamps*, Campbell Paterson wrote, "The [slot machine] issues have a proud place in New Zealand philately, being evidence of the invention by New Zealanders of a device now in use in all parts of the world." The stamps initially used in these devices were the 1-penny carmine Commerce issue of 1901.

However, Hans Jaffe and R.E. Kuntz, in *Coils A Worldwide Catalog,* reported the existence of coil stamps as early as 1903 for the Netherlands, which Burton E. Bauder affirms in his *Poko Issue of The Netherlands.*

"Printing stamps in coils was proposed by the Englishman Mr. Benjamin Cleverton as early as 1839," Bauder writes, "but the first trials in Holland date from 1903. In that year a vending machine for both 2½ and 5 cents stamps was installed in the main PO in the Hague. Rolls made from the normal sheets were too weak and a special printing of the 2½ cent stamps on the paper for the recess printing stamps was made." All attempts failed, Bauder reports, though more successful trials began anew in 1908.

In the United States, the manufacturers of stamp-affixing machinery were encountering difficulties similar to the Dutch innovators. Richard McP. Cabeen writes in his *Standard Handbook of Stamp Collecting* that soon after 1900, U.S. vending-machine manufacturers created coils by pasting together strips of perforated sheet stamps, but "they were so weak at the perforations that they tore apart and clogged the machines. In 1906 the U.S. government responded to requests from these manufacturers by providing imperforate sheets of 400 stamps that the manufacturers then could perforate in whatever manner would best work in their specific vending machinery."

Several different vendors are identified with their own characteristic privately applied coil stamp perforations in the Scott *Specialized Catalogue of United States Stamps & Covers*, in a special section titled Vending & Affixing Machine Perforations. Some of these privately perforated coil stamps are fairly common, while others are remarkably scarce.

Figure 360. Early U.S. coil stamps were created from imperforate stamps supplied to mailers by the United States Post Office Department. Shown is a horizontal pair of the imperforate 4¢ brown Grant issue, Scott 314A, with holes added privately by the Schermack Mailing Machine Co. of Detroit.

One of the earliest and most valuable of these is the 4¢ brown Grant issue, Scott 314A, issued imperforate in 1908, although all stamps were perforated with oblong holes by the Schermack Mailing Machine Co. in Detroit. The unused pair shown in Figure 360 was sold for $105,000 plus a 10-percent buyer's premium by Robert A. Siegel Auction Galleries during the October 1998 sale of the Zoellner collection.

Recognizing the general need for coil stamps, the U.S. Post Office Department began creating its own perforated coil stamps not long after the private companies began pasting together coil strips cut from imperforate sheets.

The government created its first coils by pasting together strips cut from sheets of 400 perforated horizontally only, Max G. Johl said in *The United States Postage Stamps of the 20th Century*. The sheets were divided into vertical strips of 20 and pasted together to form rolls of 500 and 1,000 stamps.

The first attempt at U.S. government coil production was experimental and short-lived, Johl writes. Few coils were made, and collectors either didn't know about them or paid them little attention. As a result, these first federal coil issues of the United States — the 1908 1¢, 2¢ and 5¢ coils (Scott 316, 321 and 317, respectively) — are now extremely scarce.

The 1¢ coil pair shown in Figure 361 is another gem from the 1998 Zoellner sale, hammered down at $80,000.

Because of the tremendous value of the early coils, there have been many attempts made to create fakes by trimming perforations or creating counter-

Figure 361. The first U.S. government-issued coils were assembled by hand from sheets of stamps. Shown is a pair of 1¢ green Franklin stamps from 1908, Scott 316, sold at auction in 1998 by Siegel Auction Galleries.

feit private perforations.

Note that most of the illustrations with this article show pairs of coil stamps. Because of the way the stamps are created and sold, collectors have become fond of saving coil stamps in pairs or longer strips to indicate the way the stamps are adjacent to one another.

The Scott catalog listings for these early coil stamps include a premium variety identified as a "guideline pair." Consider that the flat sheets of 400 stamps (20 stamps by 20 stamps) that were used to create these coils were printed one at a time on a flatbed press, with the intention of dividing them into panes of 100 stamps each that would be sold at post office windows. Each sheet of 400 was printed with two thin inked lines: one splitting the large sheet from top to bottom, and another splitting the left and right halves horizontally. These guidelines simply showed where the large sheet was to be cut apart before it was sent to the post office for sale. When the uncut sheets were used to create coil stamps, each strip of 20 stamps would include a bit of the guideline that fell along the perforations directly between the 10th and 11th stamps.

Because only one guideline appeared in each strip of 20, collectors recognize that they are more scarce than coil pairs without the guidelines; therefore, they normally sell for a little more as well.

At left in Figure 362 is a guideline pair of the flat-plate printed 5¢ blue Washington coil stamp of 1914, Scott 447, which has a catalog value of $170 for a never-hinged pair and $375 for a never-hinged guideline pair.

As the demand for coil stamps increased, the Bureau of Engraving and Printing looked for ways to automate its production. By 1914 the Stickney rotary press was put into production, and the BEP began printing coil stamps in continuous strips on a long roll of paper called a web.

The rotary press used two curved printing plates affixed to the exterior of a rotating cylinder so that the edges of each plate adjoined its partner. That meeting spot between the two plates created a natural gap where printing ink would be trapped and then would be printed at regular intervals as a line between stamp images across the web of stamp paper. The result was a marking on the rotary-printed issues that was virtually identical to the guidelines that appeared on coil stamps from the flatbed press.

Figure 362. Many specialty collectors of coil stamps place a premium on coil pairs that have guidelines (left, on Scott 447, the 5¢ blue Washington of 1914) or joint lines (right, on Scott 1614, the 7.7¢ Saxhorns issue of 1976) printed between the two stamps. Although they look very similar, guidelines and joint lines are created by two very different circumstances.

And once again collectors sought these infrequent joint-line pairs just as they did the earlier guideline pairs.

At right in Figure 362 is a joint-line pair of the 7.7¢ Saxhorns coil issue of 1976, printed on the Cottrell rotary press that replaced the Stickney rotary press in the 1950s.

There's always something new in coil stamps

Coil stamps are created and issued by postal authorities around the world for use in vending machines and automatic stamp-affixing equipment, as well as for the personal use of mailers who prefer their stamps in convenient rolls. Most coil stamps worldwide are definitive stamps that return to press again and again as postal needs require.

In the United States nearly all coil stamps have straight edges at top and bottom and perforations or wavy-line die cuts on the left and right. The straight edges are at left and right on coils with horizontal perforations or die cuts.

Coil stamps from many other countries, however, are perforated on all four sides.

Over the years, collectors in the United States developed a preference for collecting coils in pairs, a format that remains popular today. Figure 363 shows three pairs of the 33¢ Flag Over City coil stamps introduced by the United States Postal Service in 1999. At top is the perforated lick-and-stick variety, Scott 3280; in the middle is the self-adhesive stamp from coils of 100, Scott 3281; at bottom is a different self-adhesive, from coils of 10,000, Scott 3282.

Long before self-adhesive stamps became popular, many collectors were saving pairs of coil stamps with their general collections, while some also were saving pairs that showed guidelines (from flat-plate printed coils) or joint lines (from rotary-press printed coils) along the perforations between the two stamps.

In 1980 the United States Postal Service began printing tiny plate numbers at the bottom of coil stamps at spaced intervals that usually were determined by the type of printing press used to create the stamps. The first U.S. coil stamp produced under this new system with plate numbers printed on periodic stamps was the 18¢ Flag of 1981, Scott

Figure 363. The 33¢ Flag Over City stamp has been issued in three coil varieties: perforated with water-activated adhesive (Scott 3280, top), and self-adhesives in coils of 100 (Scott 3281, center), and in coils of 3,000 and 10,000 (Scott 3282, bottom).

1891. The plate number appears on every 52nd stamp in the roll.

Just a few weeks after the 18¢ Flag coil was issued, a second 18¢ coil was released, marking the debut of an attractive new definitive series that would catch the imaginations of stamp collectors across the country.

This launch of the Transportation series of coil stamps with the issuance of the 18¢ Surrey coil (Scott 1907) led to a growth in collector interest in coil stamps and in the new coil plate numbers.

The collecting specialty soon came to be known as "PNC" for "plate number coils," and new terminology grew out of the collectors' acquisitions, such as "PNC5," which refers to a strip of five coil stamps with the center stamp bearing the tiny plate number. The PNC5 format eventually became the most widely accepted among coil enthusiasts.

Figure 364 shows the $1 Seaplane coil stamp (2468) from the Transportation series as a plate number single on cover and as a PNC5. The single stamp on the cover precisely pays the $1 one-ounce airmail rate to Germany in 1996. Both examples show plate number "1."

While a few coil stamps are known with only one or two different plate numbers, more have been printed with several different numbers. Multidigit plate numbers with each digit in a different color soon appeared

Figure 364. Two ways plate number coils can be collected: postally used on cover (top) and mint strips of five (bottom).

on multicolored coil stamps.

Many coil collectors try to locate examples of every known plate number or number combination to add to their collections.

Collectors who were looking more closely at their coil stamps began noticing varieties in paper, gum, separations, phosphor tagging and other features that made coil collecting all the more intriguing. The Plate Number Coil Collectors Club, a popular

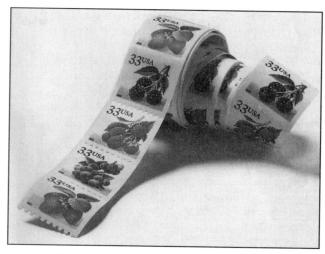

Figure 365. Two linerless self-adhesive coil stamps were issued by the United States in 1997. The third linerless example is the 33¢ Fruit Berries coils issued June 16, 2000.

collecting group, developed as a result of this interest.

In 1989 the 25¢ self-adhesive Eagle and Shield stamp (Scott 2431) was made available in strips of 18 that have been described as the first U.S. self-adhesive coil stamps. The coil stamps were sold only through the USPS mail-order division, then known as the Philatelic Fulfillment Service Center (later, Stamp Fulfillment Services).

Early U.S. self-adhesive coil stamps were spaced apart on liner paper, similar to the 33¢ coil stamps shown at the bottom of Figure 363. Later advances brought about coils in full rolls with stamps that were adjacent to one another, separated only by wavy-line die cuts that resembled perforations. The 33¢ coil pair in the center of Figure 363 is an example of this production change.

All self-adhesive coil stamps were produced with a coated backing liner paper until 1997, when two different linerless self-adhesive coil stamps were issued. These stamps were rolled up like adhesive tape and could be separated one at a time for use on mail or were kept in longer strips for collectors to save on liner cards supplied by the Postal Service.

Figure 366. British coil stamps issued in 1971. The coil strip shows five different stamps with three denominations, sold together for 5 pence. Note that these British coil stamps are perforated on all sides.

The first linerless coils issued were the 32¢ Flag Over Porch (Scott 3133) and the nondenominated (25¢) Juke Box coil (Scott 3132). Figure 365 illustrates the third U.S. linerless coil issue, the 33¢ Fruit Berries stamps issued June 16, 2000.

The Berries coil issue is additionally unusual because it has more than a single design. This is rare among U.S. coils, but it's not necessarily so among coils from some other countries.

Great Britain, for example, occasionally has produced definitive coil stamps sharing the same basic design but with different colors and denominations in a single roll. Figure 366 shows a strip of five British Queen Elizabeth II coil stamps, Scott MH25a, with three different denominations. The five coil stamps add up to 5 pence and sold for that amount when they were issued in 1971.

The five 100-pfennig German coil stamps shown in Figure 367 demonstrate another interesting characteristic: a printed number on the back of one stamp to assist postal clerks when they inventory their stamps. These back numbers are printed on every fifth German coil stamp and first appeared in the 1950s. Many specialty collectors of German coils save mint strips of stamps with the back number at one end (as shown in the illustration).

Counting numbers began appearing on the backs of some U.S. coil stamps with the issuance of the nondenominated (32¢) G-rate coil in 1994. Some U.S. self-adhesive coil stamps have back numbers as well; however, they appear on the back of the liner paper, not on the back of the stamp.

Figure 367. Germany is just one country that has issued coil stamps with printed back numbers. Clerks use the numbers to determine how many stamps remain in the roll.

Both the German and U.S. back numbers usually wash away when soaked in water.

Coil stamps have a long history and offer the collector a chance to study many aspects of postage stamp production. Collectors can choose to save mint or postally used examples, and many collectors have found specialty areas within the coil collecting field that suit their individual interests.

Joint issues show international postal accord

Joint issues are created when two or more countries agree to issue stamps celebrating the same topic at about the same time. Often the issues are released on exactly the same date, but sometimes several days or even weeks may separate the joint issues.

A joint issue is a coordinated effort between the countries, and it reflects cooperation between the national postal services.

Sometimes the designs of the stamps issued are nearly identical, as shown by the two Cinco de Mayo stamps illustrated in Figure 368. The United States and Mexico each issued stamps April 16, 1998, to mark this Mexican holiday. The 32¢ U.S. stamp was designed by Robert Rodriguez of Pasadena, Calif. The same design was used for the slightly larger 3.50-peso issue from Mexico.

Figure 368. Similar designs were used on a 1998 Cinco de Mayo joint issue from the United States (left) and Mexico.

Stamps that have similar designs are not necessarily joint issues, however. The main requisite for a joint issue is the agreement between the issuing nations.

As an example, the nation of The Gambia scheduled the release of a Year of the Rabbit stamp for late December 1998. The design includes a paper-cut image of a rabbit and what appears to be Kanji script lettering along the left edge of the stamp. In many ways it is similar to the 33¢ Year of the Hare stamp issued Jan. 5, 1998, by the United States. However, there was no official agreement between the United States and The Gambia to issue these similar stamps, so they are not considered joint issues.

Some collectors find such stamps of similar design interesting, though, and obtain them to create collections of what may be called "stamp twins."

Stamps that are official joint issues also may have designs that are considerably different from one another.

A U.S.-Mexico issue from 1996 featured animals that are endangered because of their limited numbers. The U.S. Endangered Species issue consists of 15 stamps with individual designs, each featuring a photograph of the endangered animal and its name. The Mexican counterpart consists of 24 stamps that together make a large painting that shows dozens of animals. Each stamp shows several creatures and includes their names in small type.

As of the end of 2002, the United States had participated in 38 joint issues with other countries. A listing is shown on the following page.

Official joint issues between countries can be identified by notes that appear in the Scott *Standard Postage Stamp Catalogue* and the Scott *Specialized Catalogue of United States Stamps & Covers*. If a stamp is a joint issue, there will be a reference in the Scott listing that directs you to the corresponding stamp from the other country. For example, the listing for the U.S. Endangered Species issue, Scott 3105, notes, "See Mexico No. 1995," which is the corresponding 24-stamp Endangered Species issue from Mexico.

Sometimes the effort to create a joint issue goes one step further.

The countries of San Marino and Italy produced a small pane in 1994 that contained one stamp from each country to mark the 900th anniversary of the Basilica of St. Mark. That joint issue is shown front and back in Figure 369. Each

United States joint issues

Issue date	Subject	U.S. Scott No.	Country	Scott No.	Designs
6/26/1959	4¢ St. Lawrence Seaway	1131	Canada	387	similar
9/16/1960	4¢ Mexican Independence	1157	——	——	
9/15/1960	[same]	——	Mexico	910	similar
8/28/1965	5¢ Florida Settlement	1271	Spain	1312	similar
7/15/1975	10¢ Apollo-Soyuz	1569-70 (2)	Russia	4339-40	similar
6/1/1976	13¢ U.S. Independence	1690	Canada	691	similar
8/4/1977	13¢ Peace Bridge	1721	Canada	737	different
10/13/1980	40¢ Philip Mazzei	C98	——	——	
10/18/1980	[same]	——	Italy	1439	different
10/13/1981	18¢, 20¢ James Hoban	1935-36 (2)	——	——	
9/29/1981	[same]	——	Ireland	504	similar
4/20/1982	20¢ Diplomatic Recognition	2003	Netherlands	640-41	similar
3/24/1983	20¢ Amity and Commerce	2036	Sweden	1453	similar
4/29/1983	20¢ German Immigration	2040	——	——	
5/5/1983	[same]	——	Germany	1397	similar
9/2/1983	20¢ Treaty of Paris	2052	France	1899	different
6/6/1984	20¢ John McCormack	2090	Ireland	594	similar
6/26/1984	20¢ St. Lawrence Seaway	2091	Canada	1015	similar
1/23/1986	22¢ Stamp Collecting	2198-201 (4)	Sweden	1585-88	similar
5/24/1986	14¢ Francis Vigo	UX111	Italy	——	similar
7/4/1986	22¢ Statue of Liberty	2224	France	2014	similar
7/17/1987	22¢ Friendship/Morocco	2349	——	——	
7/22/1987	[same]	——	Morocco	642	similar
1/26/1988	22¢ Australian Bicentennial	2370	Australia	1052	similar
3/29/1988	44¢ New Sweden	C117	Sweden	1672	similar
[same]	[same]	——	Finland	768	similar
7/14/1989	45¢ French Revolution	C120	France	2145a	different
1989	[same]	——	France	2143-45	different
11/24/89	45¢ Futuristic Mail	C126 (4)	Russia	5837	similar
9/28/1990	25¢ Micronesia	2506	Micronesia	124-26	similar
9/28/1990	25¢ Marshall Islands	2507	Marshall Is.	381	similar
10/3/1990	25¢ Sea Creatures	2508-11 (4)	Russia	5933-36	similar
2/22/1991	50¢ Switzerland Anniversary	2532	Switzerland	888	similar
5/22/1991	29¢ William Saroyan	2538	Russia	6002	similar
4/24/1992	29¢ Voyages of Columbus	2620-23 (4)	Italy	1877-80	similar
5/22/1992	(various) Columbian reprints	2624-29 (16)	Italy	1883-88	similar
[same]	[same]	——	Portugal	1918-23	similar
[same]	[same]	——	Spain	2677-82	similar
5/29/1992	29¢ Space Accomplishments	2631-34 (4)	Russia	6080-83	similar
3/24/1993	29¢ Grace Kelly	2749	Monaco	1851	similar
10/9/1994	29¢ Cranes	2867-68 (2)	China	2528-29	similar
9/29/1995	32¢ Republic of Palau	2999	——	——	
10/1/1995	[same]	——	Palau	377-78	similar
10/2/1996	32¢ Endangered Species	3105 (15)	Mexico	1995	different
10/22/1996	32¢ Hanukkah	3118	Israel	1289	similar
4/16/1998	32¢ Cinco de Mayo	3203	Mexico	2066	similar
2/26/1999	33¢ Irish Immigration	3286	Ireland	1168	similar
3/22/2001	34¢ Nobel Prize Centenary	3504	Sweden	2415	similar

Joint issues of the United States and other countries that did not take place on the same day are listed with the foreign issue information on the line immediately following the U.S. issue information. The 1986 Francis Vigo issue is a postal card for both the United States and Italy. All other listings are regular issue or airmail postage stamps.

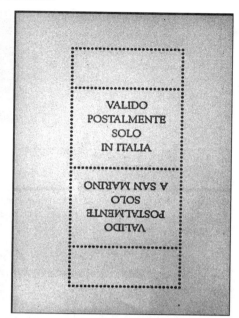

Figure 369. San Marino and Italy created a joint issue in 1994 that included one stamp from each country on a souvenir sheet. Each stamp was valid only in the country named.

stamp was valid for postage only in the country named on the stamp. This fact was emphasized with printing on the back of each stamp explaining "postally valid only in San Marino" or "postally valid only in Italy."

Finally, there are even examples where two countries jointly issued one stamp with both country names upon it. Figure 370 shows a single 1995 stamp issued by both Switzerland and Liechtenstein to celebrate the 75th anniversary of a postal treaty between the two nations. The denomination "60" on the stamp refers to 60 centimes in Switzerland and 60 rappen in Liechtenstein. The stamp was valid for postage in either country.

Figure 370. A 1995 joint issue from Switzerland and Liechtenstein consisted of a single stamp accepted for postage in either country.

Omnibus issues link colonies, economic allies

A joint issue occurs when two or more nations agree to issue stamps at the same time to recognize a single subject.

The first official U.S. joint issue occurred in 1959, when the United States and Canada both issued stamps to celebrate the opening of the St. Lawrence Seaway. United States Scott 1131 was a 4¢ stamp and Canada Scott 387 was a 5¢ stamp, but the two had very similar designs.

The idea of similar stamps from different stamp-issuing entities goes back to the early days of the postage stamp, when Queen Victoria ruled Great Britain and its many colonies around the world. In the 1880s, for example, Great Britain issued numerous stamps depicting the queen on behalf of its overseas colonies.

Two examples, Cyprus Scott 25 and Montserrat Scott 3, are shown together in Figure 371. Obviously the stamps in the illustration are nearly identical. They are printed in different colors and have different colony names and denominations printed upon them, but they share the same design.

Figure 371. Two key types from Cyprus (Scott 25, left) and Montserrat (Scott 3, right) share a common design featuring Queen Victoria. Both stamps were issued in the 1880s.

This type of standardized design is known as a key type. The vignette (central design), borders and ornaments are printed by a single printing plate known as a key plate. The area for the colony name and denomination are blank. A second plate known as the duty plate adds the name and value information in the blank spaces.

Many definitive stamps from British colonies have been printed as key types. Some depict more recent British monarchs, including Queen Elizabeth II. Other countries made use of key types of various designs for their colonial holdings, including Germany, France and Portugal.

In 1898 Portugal and its colonies took this common design theme one step further by issuing what is considered by many to be the world's first omnibus stamp issue. Eight stamps with different designs commemorated the fourth centenary of Vasco da Gama's discovery of the route to India. Identical stamps were issued for Portugal and six colonies: Azores, Macau, Madeira, Portuguese Africa, Portuguese India and Timor. Each stamp was inscribed with the name of the issuing colony. Figure 372 shows the 75-reis value from the set as issued by Portugal (left, Scott 152) and Madeira (right, Scott 42).

The omnibus idea didn't really catch on until many years later, when France and Great Britain released commemorative issues during the 1930s on behalf of their many colonies. The French colonial exposition issue of 1931 is a set of four stamps with common designs that was issued by 26 colonies. The complete omnibus set of

Figure 372. Portugal and its colonies issued identical eight-stamp commemorative sets in 1898 to mark the 400th anniversary of Vasco da Gama's successful voyage to India. The two stamps here show the same design: Portugal Scott 152 (left) and Madeira Scott 42 (right).

Figure 373. A 1996 omnibus from 10 members of the British Commonwealth cele-brated Queen Elizabeth II's 70th birthday. In all, 46 stamps were issued in the set.

this issue, therefore, consists of 104 different stamps. The King George V Silver Jubilee issue of 1935 from Great Britain and its colonies consists of 249 stamps from 59 entities, according to the Scott *Standard Postage Stamp Catalogue*.

The Scott catalog lists numerous stamps with common designs near the beginning of each volume, under the heading "Common Design Types." A single illustration provided for each omnibus issue in the common-design listings helps reduce the bulk of the catalog.

Members of the British Commonwealth of Nations continue to issue omnibus sets on a fairly regular basis. In 1996 a group of 10 nations united to issue similar stamps marking the 70th birthday of Britain's Queen Elizabeth II. Figure 373 shows one stamp from each of those countries: Ascension, British Antarctic Territory, British Indian Ocean Territory, Falkland Islands, Pitcairn Islands, St. Helena, Samoa, Tokelau, Tristan da Cunha and Virgin Islands. Each participating country actually issued either four or five stamps for the event, for a total of 46 stamps in the omnibus set.

The first common-design listings a collector encounters in the Scott catalog usually are for Europa issues.

In 1951, six nations known collectively as the European Coal and Steel Community agreed to a free market concept known as the Schuman plan. This economic alliance between Belgium, France, Germany, Italy, Luxembourg and the Netherlands led to the formal establishment of the European Economic Community in 1957. The six nations released the first Europa stamps in 1956 to symbolize their cooperation. The designs of the stamps were all similar to the 10¢ issue from the Netherlands, Scott 368, shown in Figure 374.

In 1960 the Europa stamp issues celebrated the establishment of the European Council of Postal and Telecommunications Administrations, abbreviated CEPT

for its French name, "Conference Europeenne des Administrations des Postes et des Telecommunications." Eighteen
nations participated in the 1960 release.

For many years the Europa stamps all shared common
designs. In 1974 the various nations participating began to
issue Europa stamps with different designs on the same
theme. That tradition continues, as evidenced by the three
stamps shown in Figure 375. From left to right are the
1998 Europa issues of Germany, Faeroe Islands and San
Marino. Each stamp has a very different design, but they
all celebrate the 1998 Europa theme of national holidays
and festivals. The German stamp celebrates the day of German unification. The Faeroese stamp shows the Faeroe
national festival of music. The San Marinese issue commemorates the feast day of the nation's patron saint. Notice
that each stamp includes the word "Europa" in stylized lettering somewhere in the design.

Figure 374. The first Europa stamps in 1956 were similar in design to this issue from the Netherlands, Scott 368.

Europa and other omnibus issues can serve as ready-made specialties for any
collector with an interest in worldwide issues.

**Figure 375. Numerous European nations still create Europa stamps each year, as
shown by these issues from Germany, Faeroe Islands and San Marino. More recent
stamps share a common theme, rather than a common design.**

Stamp anniversaries celebrated with stamps

If you've been collecting stamps for a while, you probably already know that
most stamps are categorized as either commemoratives or definitives. These are
just two types of stamps used for mailing; there are many others.

Commemorative stamps were originally designed to remember, or commemorate, a special event or person. What many collectors consider the first U.S. commemorative stamp set, issued in 1893, marked the 400th anniversary of Christopher Columbus' expedition to North America.

Definitive stamps also mark such anniversaries from time to time, usually the birth

Figure 376. The first two U.S. stamps, issued in 1847, are shown at left. In 1997 two similar stamps, shown at right, were issued to celebrate 150 years of U.S. stamps.

of a prominent individual. The 29¢ Thomas Jefferson definitive in the Great Americas series, Scott 2185, was issued April 13, 1993, on the 250th anniversary of Jefferson's birth.

Commemorative stamps are usually large and colorful, while definitive stamps are usually smaller and often printed in a single color.

There are certainly many exceptions to these general observations.

The U.S. commemorative stamp program for 1997 included news of two stamps that marked an important anniversary for U.S. stamp collectors.

On July 1, 1847, the first stamps of the United States were placed on sale. The 5¢ stamp pictured Benjamin Franklin, the first U.S. postmaster general, and the 10¢ stamp showed George Washington, the first U.S. president. These two stamps are shown at left in Figure 376.

The designs of these two definitive issues were reproduced in special commemorative panes that were issued May 29 and May 30, 1997, in conjunction with Pacific 97, the world stamp exhibition that took place in San Francisco, Calif., May 29-June 9, 1997. The new stamp issue marked the 150th anniversary of those very first U.S. stamps.

There are some very evident differences between the original stamps and the 1997 reproductions (which are shown at right in Figure 376). While much of the stamp design is the same on the 1997 stamps as it was on the 1847 originals, the denomination at the very bottom of the stamp was changed.

The 5¢ Franklin became a 50¢ stamp (to fulfill the then-current international postcard rate) and the 10¢ Washington became a 60¢ stamp (meeting the international letter rate). To change the denomination, a horizontal box with the new value in the center and a pair of horizontal lines on either side of the number appears at the bottom of the each stamp. There is no cent sign.

Each of the two stamps is designed to make the box appear as though it was placed over the old denomination: The edges of the "5" and "X" (for 10) from the original designs peek around the sides of the boxes.

The colors of the stamps were changed on the 1997 issues. The original red-brown Franklin stamp was printed in blue, and the black Washington stamp was bright red-orange in 1997.

Also, the first stamps were imperforate — they had no perforations, so postal clerks and mailers cut the stamps apart with scissors. The 1997 stamps are perforated all around, in panes of 12 stamps each.

The full panes of the 1997 stamps are shown in Figure 377. An enlarged reproduction of the corresponding original die proof for the 1847 designs appears in the selvage of each pane.

This isn't the first time that the designs of the first U.S. stamps have been reproduced. Many collectors will recognize the souvenir sheet shown in Figure 378, which was issued May 19, 1947, during the Centenary International Philatelic Exhibition (Cipex) held in New York, N.Y. The Cipex sheet, Scott 948, pictured the first two stamps in colors nearly identical to the stamps that were issued in 1997: 5¢ blue and 10¢ brown-orange.

Of course, the 1947 date marked the 100th anniversary of U.S. postage stamps, and that fact was clearly marked across the lower portion of the sheet.

A single 3¢ commemorative stamp issued three days earlier, Scott 947, showed the portraits of Franklin and Washington from the first stamps on a scene depicting early and modern mail-carrying vehicles. At the bottom of this commemorative was the message, "U.S. Postage Stamp Centenary."

These centenary tributes were printed in plentiful quantities and are still easily available today. Even though the stamps are nearly 50 years old, collectors can usually obtain one each of Scott 947 and 948 for less than $1.

Figure 377. The 1997 anniversary stamps were issued in panes of 12 with a decorative border selvage.

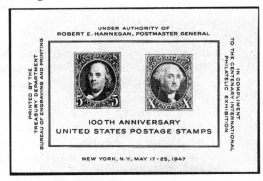

Figure 378. The Cipex souvenir sheet was issued May 19, 1947, to mark the centennial of the first U.S. stamps.

Most collectors know that the first postage stamps in the world were issued seven years before the first U.S. stamps appeared.

Great Britain's Penny Black, a definitive stamp depicting Queen Victoria, was placed on sale May 6, 1840.

When the 150th anniversary of the Penny Black was celebrated in 1990, Great Britain issued a set of five definitive stamps that showed the reigning monarch,

Queen Elizabeth II, side by side with a portrait of Queen Victoria from that very first issue. The five stamps are shown on a special anniversary cover at the top of Figure 379. The cover celebrates the anniversary of the Penny Black with a special cachet (the design at the left of the cover) and a postmark with the words "150 years Penny Black."

A special souvenir sheet also was issued to celebrate the stamp anniversary. Scott MH193f, shown at the bottom of Figure 378, includes one 20-penny stamp showing the two queens and a reproduction of the Penny Black. The dates "1840-1990" appear at the bottom of the sheet to mark the anniversary, and the portrait, *Britannia Rules the Waves*, is featured in the surrounding margin paper. The souvenir sheet sold for £1.

Throughout 1990 a number of

Figure 379. The special cover at top is franked with the five definitive stamps issued by Great Britain in 1990 to mark the 150th anniversary of the world's first postage stamp. A souvenir sheet, shown at bottom, was also issued.

countries, particularly from the British Commonwealth, paid philatelic tribute to the Penny Black. Among these were Ascension, Bangladesh, The Gambia, Ghana, India, South Africa and Zambia.

The British 1990 definitive anniversary issues bear some similarity to the stamps Britain created for the centennial celebration of the Penny Black of 1940. Commemorative stamps with six denominations ranging from ½ penny to 3p were issued showing the reigning monarch, King George VI (father of Elizabeth II), and Queen Victoria, again from the 1840 portrait that appeared on the Penny Black. The set is

Figure 380. A 1940 British stamp from a set of six noting the 100th anniversary of the Penny Black.

cataloged as 252-57. The ½d value from that set is shown in Figure 380.

Many other countries have celebrated their first stamp issues with centennial remembrances. An example is a set of three 1943 stamps from Brazil, Scott 609-11, reproducing the designs from the first three Brazilian stamps issued in 1843.

Look through the Scott catalog at the first issue of a country, and then check the listings for stamps issued by that country 100 years later. Often you'll find that if you couldn't possibly afford the first issue, you can probably add an appropriate reproduction to your collection.

Change is nothing new to stamp collecting

Stamp collecting is both a hobby of stability and a hobby of change.

From the classic stamps of the 19th century to the colorful commemoratives issued today, most stamps have been released, collected and have remained relatively unchanged over the course of time.

But a closer look at stamps throughout history reveals that change always has been an element of the stamp hobby.

The first U.S. stamps in 1847 showed statesmen of the past, such as George Washington and Benjamin Franklin, followed in later years by Thomas Jefferson, Andrew Jackson and, one year after his death, Abraham Lincoln (Figure 381).

Figure 381. Early U.S. stamps, including the 1866 15¢ Lincoln, Scott 77, showed presidents and other famous statesmen.

After 22 years, the U.S. Post Office Department issued its first pictorial issues showing locomotives, eagles with shields, and the arrival of Columbus on America's shores.

Think of it. The first U.S. stamp showed only the face of Ben Franklin surrounded by ornamental scrollwork. The scrollwork remained, though it became even more ornate, but the 24¢ stamp issued in 1869, Scott 120, included in its design the images of more than 40 men participating in the signing of the Declaration of Independence (Figure 382), all reproduced on a paper canvas the size of, well, a postage stamp.

In *United States Postage Stamps of 1869,* a *Linn's* handbook authored by Jon Rose, it is noted that there was criticism when the stamp was issued that it failed to identify the scene depicted.

"For a foreigner, the only clue as to what the design signified was the tiny date, '1776,' placed just below the central picture," Rose wrote.

Figure 382. One early change in U.S. stamps involved the introduction of the pictorial issues of 1869. A familiar scene showing the signing of the Declaration of Independence is shown on the 24¢ value, Scott 120.

"This may well be a valid criticism considering that the 24¢ value was created largely for foreign-mail use. However, since many uses of the stamp would involve British mails, the ambiguity might have been intentional."

Is it possible that in 1869 the design of a U.S. stamp was modified to circumvent problems with a foreign government?

Many of today's stamp collectors will recall how one design from the 1995 World War II commemorative issue was changed prior to its release because protests from Japan convinced the U.S. president and the postmaster general that the intended design of one stamp depicting an atomic bomb explosion was insensitive to the agony that had been suffered by thousands of Japanese citizens.

There are great differences between the 24¢ stamp of 1869 and the Atomic

Bomb nonstamp of 1995, but it appears there are some similarities as well. Perhaps the familiar phrase "history repeats itself" also can apply to stamp collecting.

Two dozen years passed between the issuance of the 1869 pictorials and the release of what some collectors think of as the first U.S. commemorative stamp set, in 1893.

Placed on sale just prior to the World's Columbian Exposition in Chicago, Ill., the Columbian commemoratives were a history-making departure from previous U.S. stamps. Yes, the Columbian issue had pictorial elements like the 1869 stamps, but the 1893 set was issued specifically to mark the 400th anniversary of the landing of Columbus and the great exposition about to take place. The 10¢ Columbian issue in Figure 383 shows some strong similarities to the 24¢ 1869 issue, with intricately engraved human figures in the vignette (the pictorial section of the design), though only half as many figures as in the Declaration of Independence stamp.

Figure 383. In 1893, commemorative stamps marked the landing of Columbus and promoted the Columbian World Exposition planned for later that year.

But there are changes evident as well. The engraved frame of the stamp consists almost entirely of straight lines with very little ornamentation, a design development that evolved during the 1870s, but indications of which can be seen even in the 6¢ value from the 1869 set. And, an explanation of the depicted scene is clearly lettered under the vignette of the 10¢ Columbian, as it is under all the stamps of that set. The 10¢ features the phrase, "Columbus presenting natives."

Engraved scrollwork with elaborate ornamentation reappeared on many later stamps, including, quite notably, the definitive series of 1902-03, but consider how commemoratives changed from those first issues.

Jump forward about a half-century, to a simple commemorative from 1944 marking the 150th anniversary of the first steamship to cross the Atlantic Ocean (Figure 384, top). This representative stamp has no ornamentation and only a line frame. Yet it is engraved like its ancestors and includes a description of the depicted scene.

Some things have changed, and some have remained the same.

Figure 384. Issued nearly 50 years apart, these two stamps show similarities and striking differences. Scott 923 (top) was issued in 1944. Scott 2805 was issued in 1993.

During the 1970s, the engraved stamp began to give ground to stamps created by lithography and photogravure, and by the late 1980s, engraved stamps were almost entirely limited to definitive issues. Commemoratives evolved into more colorful designs that some collectors enjoyed and others loathed.

The year 1993 is another half-century jump from 1944, and the landing of Columbus is again celebrated, this time on a photogravure stamp shown at the bottom of Figure 384. The black-and-white illustrations in Figure 384 point out the similarities that prevailed: a set of anniversary dates, a denomination and a simple design.

But the stamps have great differences, including the prominent multicolor artwork of the 1993 issue and the overall difference in appearance that is the result of two different printing methods: intaglio (for the engraved 1944 issue) and photogravure (for the 1993 stamp).

As with almost everything else in this world, evolution and change have proceeded more quickly in stamp collecting over the past decade than at any other time in the history of the hobby. And it's not likely that the changes in the hobby are going to slow down very soon. In recent years the United States Postal Service has expanded its line of self-adhesive stamps, introduced linerless coils and developed a revolutionary new postage meter technology.

Not all changes are good, but many are inevitable. Changes in printing technology have brought about varieties in mind-boggling quantities, including sheet stamps, coils, booklets, self-adhesive panes and coils, many with multiple die-cut and design varieties. Examples include the G-rate and Flag Over Porch stamps of 1994-97.

But anyone who thinks such an extraordinary variety of stamps is unprecedented needs to take a look in the Scott *Specialized Catalogue of United States Stamps & Covers* at the long list of stamps that are assigned Scott design type number A140, the George Washington definitives that were first issued in 1908 (Figure 385). The many varieties of the 1994-95 G-rate stamps will never hold a candle to those of the Washington head definitives issued more than 80 years earlier.

Figure 385. U.S. Scott 406 is only one of the numerous major varieties of George Washington definitives that have kept specialists occupied for years.

Stamp collectors can have an influence on the changes that occur in U.S. postage stamps, though doing so requires strong and active voices that will keep the hobby involved in whatever the Postal Service plans.

Collectors who want to speak out about the changes in U.S. stamps can express their opinions by contacting the United States Postal Service. The USPS office of stamp management in Washington, D.C., works with the Citizens' Stamp Advisory Committee in selecting stamp designs.

Though the element of change has a powerful effect on the stamp hobby, collectors should remember that it's not a new thing. Much of what we experience today is not that different from what occurred decades before.

That doesn't mean that if you don't like it you have to accept it, but it does mean that the stamp hobby has weathered changes in the past, and it survived because enough collectors cared about the hobby to see it through.

Chapter 11
Stamp History

Postal reforms brought about the first stamps

Every country that has ever issued postage stamps can point to a single stamp or set as the first to come from that country. There are some wonderful stories associated with many of these first issues, and together they contribute to the history and lore of postage stamps worldwide.

Great Britain was the first country in the world to issue an adhesive postage stamp. The year was 1840, and the introduction of stamps to verify the prepayment of postage was just part of a much larger revision in Britain's national mail service.

Prior to that year, British postage rates were determined in part by the distance that the letter had to travel, and the responsibility for paying that rate usually fell to the recipient of the letter rather than to the sender. The rates were complex and costly, and there was a call throughout the country to straighten out the mail mess and provide a way for people to send letters at a reasonable price.

Rowland Hill is credited with bringing about the British postal reforms that included the introduction of the adhesive postage stamp.

A delightful story has been told how Hill was on his way to work one morning when he saw a teary-eyed young lass dejectedly declining the delivery of a letter, apparently because she did not have the money to pay for its delivery. Hill sensed that the girl was being deprived of a message from a distant loved one, and he approached the scene, paid the postman his due and handed the letter to the girl.

To his surprise, she informed him she didn't want the letter, prompting Hill to question her about the exchange.

It turns out that because of the costly postage rates, her sweetheart included a coded message as he addressed the letter, and the girl discerned the message with a glance before handing the mail back to the waiting postman.

The story goes that this incident provided Hill with the inspiration to suggest that postage should be paid in advance.

Hill was a businessman and educator who had previously demonstrated an interest in postal affairs. In 1837 he published a pamphlet titled *Post Office Reform: Its Importance and Practicability.*

Hill submitted his plan to the British government, and the concept of uniform postage, set at a uniform rate of 1 penny for a prepaid half-ounce letter, went into effect Jan. 10, 1840. As these changes were taking place, Hill also had a hand in the development of the postage stamp.

Previously, the rate of postage was simply marked by hand or handstamp upon the outside of the letter, and payment usually was rendered when the letter was delivered.

In 1837 a Scottish printer named James Chalmers suggested that the prepayment of postage could be verified with "Stamped Slips" bearing a design on the front and "rubbed over on the back with a strong solution of gum, or other adhesive substance." Hill incorporated this idea in a later printing of his pamphlet.

Once the British government approved the plan, the British Treasury sponsored a competition to create a design for the first adhesive postage stamps. None of the submitted designs was accepted. Instead, it was decided to use a portrait of Queen Victoria by William Wyon that had appeared on a medal issued in 1837, when Victoria was but 18 years old.

The assignment for engraving the design was awarded to printer Charles Heath, but most likely it was executed by his son Frederick.

Figure 386. The world's first adhesive postage stamp is the Penny Black from Great Britain, issued in 1840 following the implementation of massive reforms to the British postal system.

As shown in Figure 386, the 1-penny stamp known as the Penny Black features a line-engraved portrait of Queen Victoria that stands against a black background of delicate engraved lathe-work. The background design was created by Jacob Perkins, an American inventor living in Great Britain who developed the engine-turning lathe and whose London firm — Perkins, Bacon & Petch — actually printed the first stamps.

Each stamp also includes two letters, one in each lower corner, known as check letters. These letters can be used to determine the original placement of each stamp in a sheet of 240.

Each of the 20 horizontal rows in the sheet contained 12 stamps. All of the stamps in the first row had the letter A in the lower-left corner. The letter in the lower-right corner progressed across the sheet from left to right, beginning with A on the first stamp and ending with L. In the next horizontal row, all of the stamps contained the letter B in the lower-left corner and progressed similarly.

The stamps themselves went on sale May 1, 1840, but they were not accepted for use until May 6.

However, a folded letter sheet, now known as the "May 1st cover," exists with the Penny Black affixed and bearing a May 1 postmark. Because the stamp was used before it was authorized, the cover is marked with a large "2" indicating that the recipient was to pay 2 pence postage due, twice the prepaid rate.

In February 1999 this cover was sold in Switzerland for the equivalent of $404,800 at an auction by David Feldman.

The Penny Black is listed in the Scott *Standard Postage Stamp Catalogue* as Great Britain Scott 1. It was not the world's only postage stamp for long. On May 7, Britain placed on sale a second stamp, the Two-Penny Blue.

Collectors who are not aware of the second country to issue postage stamps are sometimes surprised by the answer.

Less than two years after Britain instituted its sweeping postal reforms, a similar package of changes was approved by the congress of Brazil. Like Britain,

Brazil in the 1830s had a maze of rates that made sending mail long distances a very costly venture.

In the July 1943 issue of the *American Philatelist*, Lester G. Brookman described the changes in the Brazilian postal system.

"Under the new rate a letter weighing not more than 4 octaves (15 grammes) was carried anywhere in the country by land for 60 reis, or, if carried by sea, for 120 reis. Letters weighing more than 4 octaves but not more than 6 octaves required 90 reis. 30 reis was required to pay carriage on printed matter and on letters, circulars and other papers of the judiciary."

Like Britain, Brazil decided to issue postage stamps that would prove the delivery fee had been paid in advance.

It has been said that Brazil in the 1830s did not have the ability to create a postage stamp that would adequately foil potential stamp forgers, but in 1841 Brazilian customs authorities confiscated an engraving machine that would solve part of the problem. The later purchase of an engraving transfer machine gave the Brazilian mint the accessories necessary to produce its engraved issues in 1843.

The 30r, 60r and 90r stamps were all released Aug. 1, 1843 — in fact, they were all printed on the same sheet. The earliest printing of the stamps included 18 each of the three denominations on one 54-stamp sheet. Separate 60-stamp sheets of the 30r and 60r values were printed at a later date.

Figure 387. The second country to issue postage stamps was Brazil. The 30-reis Bull's Eye from 1843 is one of three stamps Brazil initially issued.

The 30r stamp, Brazil Scott 1, is shown in Figure 387. The design of the stamp simply shows the numeral of value in a rounded vignette with engraved background. The shape of the design caused the stamps to be called "Bull's Eyes."

Of the few stamps that were printed, many were intentionally destroyed in 1846 because a new stamp issue had been created. Examples of Brazil's Bull's Eyes therefore are relatively scarce.

The concept of postal reform initiated by Great Britain swept across the globe during the 1840s, and the next nation to follow suit was the United States. Once again, it was a tangle of complicated and costly postage rates that made mailing letters in the United States an expensive and problematic endeavor.

Facing demands in their own country for postal reforms, U.S. postal officials looked at the changes taking place in the British postal system and considered whether such changes would work in America.

One concern was that the reformed British system appeared to lose money in its earliest years, and government officials in the United States were uneasy about the prospect of financial losses.

Private postal companies began operating in the United States during the first half of the 1840s, and several even created their own postage stamps.

Following the initial establishment of reformed postal rates in 1845, the postmaster in New York became the first to offer provisional postage stamps in the United States.

It soon became apparent to federal officials that the postage stamp was clearly the mailing instrument of the future.

In 1847 the U.S. government authorized the use of postage stamps, and the first federally issued stamps were placed on sale July 1, 1847. Once again, the stamps were printed using engraved designs. Two denominations were issued: a 5¢ red-brown stamp picturing Benjamin Franklin and a 10¢ black stamp picturing George Washington. The two stamps are shown together in Figure 388. The 5¢ Franklin is U.S. Scott 1; the 10¢ Washington is Scott 2.

In *The United States Postage Stamps of the 19th Century, Vol. 1,* Lester G. Brookman noted, "There has been some discussion about the correctness of placing the portrait of Franklin on the first stamp value and that of Washington being relegated to the second value but the reason this was done was no doubt due to the fact that Franklin was the 'father' of the American Postal Service."

Figure 388. The first stamps issued by the United States were both placed on sale July 1, 1847. The 5¢ Franklin (left) is United States Scott 1; the 10¢ Washington (right) is Scott 2.

Linn's U.S. Stamp Facts 19th Century lists the designers of the two stamps as "not known; attributed to James P. Major." Similarly, the book conditionally lists the engraver as Asher B. Durand.

The earliest-known use of any U.S. postage stamp is a cover mailed July 2, 1847, using two 10¢ Washingtons. No first-day use for either denomination has been discovered.

Just months after the United States issued its first stamps, the island of Mauritius in the Indian Ocean, then a British colony, became the fourth stamp-issuing entity. It was followed by the German state of Bavaria and the country of Belgium, both in 1849, and another 10 countries in 1850.

Though the first stamp of any country is traditionally listed first in most stamp catalogs, this rule is not steadfast. Denmark issued its first postage stamp April 1, 1851, a brown square adhesive denominated 4 rigsbank-skilling. The stamp identified as Denmark Scott 1, however, is a 2rbs stamp issued exactly one month later on May 1. The 4rbs brown is listed as Scott 2. The two stamps are shown together in Figure 389.

Figure 389. Catalogs don't always list the first stamps first. Denmark Scott 1, the 2-rigsbank-skilling stamp at right, was issued one month after Scott 2, the 4rbs stamp at left.

The stamps are listed in the same reverse order in the well-known Facit catalog published in Sweden. The Danish AFA *Danmark Frimaerkekatalog*, however, lists the two stamps following the actual order of their appearance.

These stamps are the legends of the hobby

The real celebrities of the stamp hobby always have been the postage stamps themselves, from the very first issue of 1840 to the greatest rarities of all time.

While some stamps are so common they seem to turn up in every collection and mixture, others are much harder to find. The rarities described here have achieved a reputation that places them foremost among the true gems of philately.

Some of the shining stars of the stamp world are incredibly rare, and there are instances where only one known example of a given stamp has ever been verified. Other famous stamps are a little more plentiful but still draw the attention of collectors because of their place in the history of the stamp hobby.

Following are the biographies of six well-known stamps from five different countries. The stamps described here have all been known for many years by special nicknames that many collectors recognize immediately.

Let's begin with the first adhesive postage stamp issued by any country in the world, honoring a young queen shortly after she ascended her country's throne at the tender age of 18.

Penny Black (Great Britain Scott 1: 1840 1-penny definitive)

The Penny Black is known primarily for being the first adhesive stamp created and sold by any national government for the prepayment of postage. It was issued by Great Britain May 1, 1840, following a campaign by Rowland Hill to make mail services available to all by simplifying Britain's complicated system of charging for the delivery of mail.

The design of the stamp reproduces a portrait of Britain's Queen Victoria, who was ruler of England when the new postal reforms were put into effect. A delicate engraved pattern makes up the background of the design, and a small alphabet letter appears in each of the two lower corners. As noted previously, these letters tell the position of the stamp in the full sheet of 240 stamps (20 horizontal rows of 12 stamps each).

The letter in the left corner indicates the horizontal row, and the letter in the right corner gives the exact position in that row, with A indicating the first row or position, B the second and so on. For example, a stamp with the letters B and C in the left and right lower corners, respectively, show that the stamp comes from the second horizontal row (B) and was the third stamp in the row (C).

The Penny Black shown at left in Figure 390 is marked with the letters Q and G, so it came from the 17th horizontal row (Q), seventh position (G).

Figure 390. A pair of the 1840 Penny Black from Great Britain.

The word POSTAGE is inscribed across the top of the stamp, while ONE PENNY is lettered along the bottom.

The name of Great Britain does not appear on the Penny Black, and as a tradition the stamps of Great Britain do not show the country's name to this day. Instead, the image or cypher of the ruling monarch is printed somewhere in the design.

Like many early stamps, the Penny Blacks were not perforated. Postal clerks and customers used scissors to cut the stamps apart.

The Penny Black is not a rare stamp, but it is rather expensive. An unused stamp is valued in the 2003 Scott *Standard Postage Stamp Catalogue* at $3,000, and a used one is valued at $180.

Post Office Mauritius (Mauritius Scott 1-2: 1847 1-penny orange and 2d blue definitives)

While the Penny Black is a costly stamp, it pales in comparison to the values for the first two issues of Mauritius.

A 1993 auction by David Feldman of the Hiroyuki Kanai collection of Mauritius resulted in numerous record-setting prices, including the sale of one unused example of each of the first two Mauritius issues. The 1d orange stamp sold for $1,072,260, and the 2d blue sold for $1,148,850. Both amounts include the 15 percent buyer's premium.

Only one example of the 1d stamp is known in unused condition; three unused 2d stamps are known.

Mauritius is a small island in the Indian Ocean encompassing about 720 square miles. It is more than 500 miles east of a much larger island, Madagascar, which is located off the southeast coast of the African continent.

The first two Mauritius stamps, shown in Figure 391, were also the first stamps authorized by any British colonial government. A local engraver named Joseph O. Barnard prepared the two designs, which, like the Penny Black, show the image of Queen Victoria.

One peculiarity of the two stamps is that they are inscribed with the words "POST OFFICE" along the left edge of the design. Later issues of nearly identical

Figure 391. Unused copies of the rare 1-penny orange and 2d blue Mauritius Post Office definitive stamps issued in 1847.

design were marked "POST PAID" instead. These 1848 Post Paid issues (Scott 3-6) are also somewhat rare, but not nearly to the extent that the Post Office issues are. Only 500 each of the Mauritius Post Office stamps were printed, and most have been lost forever.

A few rare covers bearing one or both of the stamps also survive, and they command enormous sums when they are sold. The only known cover bearing one each of the two Mauritius Post Office stamps sold at the 1993 Feldman auction for $3,829,500, setting a new record for the highest price ever paid for a single philatelic item.

Three-Skilling Yellow (Sweden Scott 1a: 1855 3-skilling-banco definitive orange-yellow error of color)

Some stamps are cherished because they are rare. Others are distinguished by the fact that they are errors that show some major mistake in production. Sweden's Three-Skilling Yellow, shown in Figure 392, fits both of these descriptions.

The Three-Skilling Yellow is an error of Sweden's very first stamp issue from 1855. The normal stamp, which in itself is rather scarce, has a blue-green color.

However, as the name of the stamp implies, the Three-Skilling Yellow is a shade of yellow that is close to orange.

And there is only one example known.

It is thought by some that the Three-Skilling Yellow error may have been created when a cliché (the printing element showing a single stamp subject) of the 3sk value was inadvertently used during the printing of the yellow-orange 8sk stamp of the same issue.

The unique Three-Skilling Yellow error was discovered in 1885 in Stockholm by a youngster named Georg Backman, who sold it for 7 krone a few months later. In the intervening years, many wealthy collectors have owned the Three-Skilling Yellow. During the 1990s, the

Figure 392. The Three Skilling Yellow, a rare color error of the first stamp from Sweden.

stamp was auctioned twice by the Feldman auction firm, but according to reports, the winning bidders in both sales did not pay in full for the stamp, and in 1998 it reportedly was finally sold privately to an anonymous collector.

The stamp is listed in the 2003 Scott catalog for $3 million. It is certainly one of the most valuable stamps of all time.

Penny Magenta (British Guiana Scott 13: 1856 1¢ black on magenta)

East of Venezuela, on the northern coast of South America, is a small country that is now called Guyana. In 1856 it was British Guiana, a colony well known to stamp collectors because of its notorious Penny Magenta stamp. Printed by typeset in black ink on magenta (red) paper, the example shown in Figure 393 is believed to be the only one in existence.

Figure 393. The 1856 Penny Magenta of British Guiana.

Despite its rarity, the stamp is not much to look at. It is cut into an octagonal shape and is marked with a very heavy cancel.

The story of the Penny Magenta is in itself remarkable. A 12-year-old boy named Vernon Vaughan found the Penny Magenta in Demerara, the capital of British Guiana, in 1873. He sold it to stamp collector N.R. McKinnon for six shillings, or about $1.50.

Over the years the stamp has been owned by some of philately's greatest collectors, including Count Philippe Ferrari and Arthur Hind.

In 1980 the stamp was consigned to the Robert A. Siegel firm of New York, which auctioned it for $935,000 to chemical-fortune heir John E. duPont. In 1997 duPont was convicted of murdering a wrestler he was sponsoring, and the only known British Guiana Penny Magenta has since remained in a bank vault in Philadelphia, Pa.

Inverted Jenny (United States Scott C3a: 1918 24¢ airmail invert error)

The Inverted Jenny is not the scarcest U.S. stamp, and it's also not the most valuable, but more people can tell you about the stamp with "the upside-down airplane" than about any other U.S. stamp rarity.

On May 14, 1918, a 29-year-old stamp collector named William T. Robey went to a Washington, D.C., post office to buy some of the new 24¢ airmail stamps that had just been placed on sale. The stamps were the first airmail issue of the United States, and Robey purchased a full pane of 100, a pretty expensive purchase at $24.

When he looked at his stamps, however, Robey realized his money was very well spent, for all 100 stamps were printed with the blue airplane in the center flying upside down within the carmine red frame. The printing mistake is called an invert. The red and blue parts of the design were printed in separate passes through the press, and when the sheet containing Robey's stamps was inserted to receive the image of the airplane, it is thought that the blue printing plate was unintentionally inserted upside down, resulting in the error.

Robey hurriedly left the post office with his prize. Word of the discovery circulated quickly, but no other Jenny inverts were ever found.

The stamps were sold within a week to an eccentric millionaire, Col. E.H.R. Green, for $20,000. Robey received $15,000 from the dealer who brokered the sale.

Col. Green eventually broke the pane into single stamps and blocks, retaining some of the stamps but selling many to interested collectors.

Singles and blocks of the inverted Jenny have been bought and sold with some regularity over the years, and the values have increased substantially since the days when Col. Green was selling individual stamps for $250.

Figure 394. The Inverted Jenny.

Because of its condition and centering, the stamp illustrated here in Figure 394 is among the finest examples of the inverted Jenny known. Siegel Auction Galleries of New York sold the stamp May 13, 2000, for $155,000.

Many other stamps are incredible rarities, including some with values far greater than those of the inverted Jenny or the Penny Black.

The six stamps described here, however, are almost certainly the most famous issues cherished by stamp collectors. Some of these legendary stamps can be viewed from time to time at major stamp shows and exhibitions around the world.

Chapter 12
Stamp Designs

Many creative people develop stamp designs

Long before U.S. postage stamps start rolling off printing presses, a small army of people work together and independently to create the designs that will appear by the millions in post offices all across the country. Some of those people get very little public credit for their work.

Although it seems like there are a hundred different hands involved in designing the items we collectors save, the process all appears orderly and organized when each area of responsibility is considered.

CSAC: The idea for a postage stamp may come from almost anywhere. The Citizens' Stamp Advisory Committee (CSAC) is responsible for sorting through all the suggestions and pleas to determine what will become a stamp and what will not. Because the committee receives up to 40,000 letters a year from individuals suggesting topics for postage stamps, the 100 or so annual winners in this contest are greatly outnumbered by the also-rans.

The 15 members of CSAC are appointed by the postmaster general, who also may decide that a specific subject will appear on a stamp or who may decide to reject a stamp subject recommended by the committee.

The committee meets four times a year in Washington, D.C. Along with approving stamp subjects, the committee makes recommendations on stamp designs in progress. Many members of the committee have had backgrounds in the arts, and some serve on the CSAC design subcommittee.

Project manager: A project manager is assigned for each subject that becomes a U.S. postage stamp. The selection of the project manager is made by the Postal Service's manager of stamp development, and the lead designer and project manager for stamp design, a part of the Postal Service's stamp development division.

Terrence McCaffrey has served as project manager for numerous U.S. issues, and he described some of the responsibilities of the position.

"The project manager oversees the whole project," McCaffrey said. "He works directly with the art director and sometimes with the artist or designer or illustrator or photographer who is actually doing the stamp.

"The project manager does a lot of the behind-the-scenes work. He writes up the contract and oversees things to make sure that things are on target and meeting deadlines, and he also interfaces directly with our research group that does the visual research and fact verification."

In the past, the United States Postal Service has had a small group of project managers that served regularly on stamp projects.

McCaffrey added that the project manager is also responsible for running "political traps, to make sure that we're not offending anyone," with the subject or portrayal of a specific stamp design.

Art director: The responsibility of the art director is to act as a go-between for many of the people involved in the design process, to select the artist for the stamp illustration and to produce a top-notch finished product. The art directors who work regularly with the Postal Service all have many years experience dealing in the arts, which they use to select an artist whose strengths are best suited for the subject of the stamp.

Carl Herrman has worked as art director for many U.S. stamps, including those honoring Marilyn Monroe, James Dean, James K. Polk, Recreational Sports and Comic Strip Classics. Herrman notes that the direction provided by the art director may vary, depending on the artist and the subject matter.

"In some cases the art director is very dominating," Herrman said, "and in some cases the art director gently guides the illustrator."

As an example, he described the choice of artist Michael Deas to prepare the 32¢ Marilyn Monroe stamp issued in 1995. As art director for that stamp, Herrman was responsible for picking the right artist and seeing to it that the artist had available any necessary reference materials. The art director keeps the project on track, Herrman noted. In the case of the Monroe stamp, it was important to keep the subject dignified by presenting a sophisticated image of Monroe, rather than an image that would portray her as a sexy bombshell.

McCaffrey added that the selection of the artist is approved by the project manager, who writes up the contracts.

Stamp designer and illustrator: The concept of stamp designer changed during the 1990s. Where previously one individual was usually credited as the stamp designer, the responsibilities of designing and illustrating the stamp were often undertaken by two different individuals.

McCaffrey pointed out that many elements of the stamp are actually designed by the art director. For many years, the individual named as designer was the artist who created the illustration, though the design of the stamp may have originated elsewhere.

Artist Dean Ellis, who has designed and illustrated U.S. postage stamps for more than 30 years, explained that when he receives a call from an art director for a new U.S. postage stamp, he may be given a specific assignment, or the art director may be looking for concepts and visual ideas.

Figure 395. Artist Dean Ellis stands next to an enlargement of the 32¢ Sylvan Dell postage stamp. Ellis designed the five Riverboats stamps issued Aug. 22, 1996, in Orlando, Fla.

For the 32¢ U.S. Naval Academy stamp issued in 1995, Ellis said, "I did eight or 10 rough sketches." The final design of midshipmen on a racing sloop was based on a photograph by Diane Olmstead.

Ellis creates his finished artwork most frequently as a gouache, a painting of opaque watercolors, though he has used oil or acrylic paint in some cases.

The Postal Service puts specific limits on the size of the artwork the designer may submit, though the artist can request permission to submit a larger piece. Ellis was granted such permission for his paintings that appeared on the five 32¢ Riverboats stamps issued Aug. 22, 1996. Still, the wonderfully detailed original paintings that appear on those stamps were only nine inches across.

Ellis is shown in Figure 395, standing next to an enlargement of one of his designs during the issuing ceremony in Orlando, Fla. Ellis' first U.S. stamp design was the Arkansas River Navigation commemorative issued in 1968 (Scott 1358).

Other U.S. stamps have shown artwork created by engraving, photography, scratchboard and many other methods. Some stamps have been designed on computer using previously archived images. In 1999 artist Steve Buchanan created 20 incredibly detailed illustrations for the 33¢ Insects and Spiders issue entirely by computer, from blank screen to finished image.

As the artist works on a stamp design, it requires the approval of the CSAC design subcommittee and eventually the entire CSAC membership. Usually the final design is approved by the CSAC members, though a change may be requested.

McCaffrey recalled that when Thomas Blackshear's design for the 1993 29¢ Joe Louis stamp was presented before the CSAC members, actor Karl Malden, who serves on the committee, noticed that the gloves worn by Louis in Blackshear's proposed design were training gloves with stitching between the fingers, instead of the boxing gloves Louis wore in the ring.

That original design and the finished stamp are shown in Figure 396.

Figure 396. The training gloves worn by Joe Louis in the illustration at left were changed to ring gloves, at the suggestion of Citizens' Stamp Advisory Committee member Karl Malden. The finished stamp is shown at right.

Typographer: The typographer is responsible for any letters or numbers (called the "inscription") that appear on the stamp, including the denomination, the letters "USA" or the words "United States," and any additional wording that appears as part of the stamp design. The job includes selecting the style of type for the inscription and its position on the design. In many cases the typography will be done by either the art director or the stamp designer.

Artist Mark Stutzman painted the illustration for the 1993 Elvis Presley stamp (shown at left in Figure 397). The art director for the stamp, Howard Paine, worked with graphic designer Tom Mann to complete the typography. The finished stamp is shown at right in Figure 397.

As with many aspects of today's stamp designs, the typography for the Elvis stamp was completed using a computer. Art directors also use computers to scan in the final designs and create an image that has perforations and all lettering on it, for proofs to be approved by the CSAC design subcommittee.

Figure 397. The illustration for the Elvis stamp (left) was created by artist Mark Stutzman. The typography used on the finished stamp (right) was determined by art director Howard Paine, working with graphic designer Tom Mann.

Modeler: Clarence Holbert is a banknote designer with the U.S. Bureau of Engraving and Printing. He has a number of different responsibilities, including his work as a modeler on many U.S. postage stamp issues. "When artwork comes in, it might be out of scale," Holbert said, "so we bring it into proportion, bring it down to size."

Holbert and other modelers make changes on computer, scanning the artwork in, checking the accuracy of the color, arranging the typography if necessary, and adjusting any other elements until it compares as close as possible to the original artwork, matching the specifications put forth by the Postal Service. "We're doing whatever it takes to make a good-looking piece of artwork," Holbert said.

When the modeler is done preparing the finished product, it goes to the Postal Service for final approval before production of the actual stamps begins.

It takes the combined effort of all these individuals to create the design of one stamp. A new army takes over to actually print and process millions of stamps for every single issue.

Some designs may be hugely popular while others do their service with little notice, but each design requires a great deal of hard work, patience and cooperation among many people to become the miniature work of art that is a U.S. postage stamp.

The engraver's skill creates lines of beauty

So, who's prettier? Grace Kelly or Marilyn Monroe?

The purpose of my question is not to examine the beauty of these two famous actresses, but to point out the difference in the two U.S. stamps that portray them. You can see both stamps in Figure 398. You may already know what difference I'm talking about.

Figure 398. The engraved image of Grace Kelly is shown at left on a 29¢ U.S. stamp. The image of Marilyn Monroe on the 32¢ stamp at right was printed by gravure.

The 29¢ stamp at left featuring Grace Kelly was issued March 24, 1993. The 32¢ Marilyn Monroe stamp at right was issued June 1, 1995. Both stamps feature attractive portraits of the actresses.

The image of Grace Kelly was engraved and then printed by the intaglio process. The image of Marilyn Monroe was painted and then printed by gravure. Which stamp do you like better?

Although I think both stamps are nicely designed, I'll admit that I prefer stamps with line-engraved images, so the Grace Kelly stamp gets my vote in this little beauty contest.

Line engraving is part of a process that has been used to produce postage stamps ever since the first stamp, the Penny Black, was issued by Great Britain in 1840. The printing process that uses an engraved design is called "intaglio," (pronounced "in-TAHL-yo"). An engraver uses a sharp, finely pointed tool called a burin (pronounced "BYUR-en") to cut into a special piece of steel plate called a die.

There are two very remarkable features of engraved postage stamp art. One is that the engraver must create the image in precisely the same miniature size that it will appear on the postage stamp. And secondly, all elements of the design — portraits, lettering and frames — must be engraved as reversed or mirror images of how they will appear on the stamp.

Through a series of production processes, the engraved steel die is used to create a printing plate with recessed lines that are filled with ink and pressed onto stamp paper with great pressure. The resulting design shows depth and dimension that other printing processes lack.

Intaglio printing has long been the preferred printing process for security items such as postage stamps and currency, because the printing method creates a raised surface where the ink is printed on the paper. That raised surface can be felt with the fingertips, even on postage stamps, and that quality is very difficult to duplicate or counterfeit.

Each engraver works a little bit differently. Some use microscopes while working, to more clearly see the detail of the engraving in process. Others prefer to use a hand-held magnifier to inspect their work. Some engravers also use a process called "etching," where lines deliberately scratched on a plate are deepened with a special bath of etching acid. Other engravers do not etch but rather create designs only with the point of the burin.

The engraver who created the image of Grace Kelly shown in Figure 398 is Czeslaw Slania (pronounced "CHESS-wav SWAN-ya"). He is shown in Figure 399, at work creating an

Figure 399. Renowned engraver Czeslaw Slania at work on a stamp design. The 44¢ United Nations stamp of 1986 (Scott 474), engraved by Slania, shows an engraver at work.

engraved image. Also shown in Figure 399 is a 1986 United Nations postage stamp that uses an engraved design created by Slania. The design shows an engraver (who looks a lot like Slania) with his burin, magnifier and steel die.

Slania, who was born in Poland, has created more engraved designs for postage stamps than anyone else in history. His 1,000th stamp engraving was created for his adopted country, Sweden, where he has lived and worked since 1956. The huge, intricately detailed 50-kroner stamp, Scott 2374, was issued March 17, 2000.

Slania has engraved stamps for more than 25 nations, including Denmark, Iceland, Monaco, Sweden, Poland, Great Britain and the United States. He has also engraved designs for currency for a number of different countries.

Slania is the most famous stamp engraver in the world, but he is one of many who have practiced this extraordinary art form.

André Lavergne has engraved many stamps for France and its related territories, and several other countries, including Monaco and Andorra. He works in a studio near his home in Paris, engraving stamp images and other artwork, for which he has won several prizes, including a gold medal at a 1992 Paris art show.

When I met Lavergne in Toronto, Canada, in 1996, he told me that he has engraved designs for nearly 100 stamps. He contracts for each project. The length of time he spends on each stamp design depends on the size and difficulty of the design.

Lavergne's engraving of the research ship *Marion Dufresne* is the design of the 1993 stamp from French Southern and Antarctic Territories shown in Figure 400.

The enlarged details of the stamp image at left show how the engraver uses lines of varying depth, thickness and length to reproduce different textures and shapes. To create darker parts of the designs, like the bow of the ship, the engraver cuts lines that are closer together.

In the United States, the premier stamp engraver is Thomas Hipschen of the U.S. Bureau of Engraving and Printing. Hipschen told me during a telephone interview that his first U.S. stamp engraving was the 7¢ Benjamin Franklin definitive stamp, Scott 1393D, issued

Figure 400. The engraver uses short and long lines to create depth, form and texture in the design. Cross-hatched lines and lines engraved closely together create darker shading.

Oct. 20, 1972. Hipschen was an apprentice engraver at the time, undergoing a 10-year process of work and study that led to becoming a master engraver.

It's important to remember that the engraver is not the designer of the stamp. Instead, the engraver must faithfully reproduce a design created by someone else.

Figure 401. Thomas Hipschen is a greatly admired veteran engraver with the U.S. Bureau of Engraving and Printing. Among the many stamp engravings to his credit is the 32¢ Bessie Coleman commemorative issued April 27, 1995.

There are exceptions, however, where the engraver both designs and engraves a stamp. Slania designed the Grace Kelly stamp in Figure 398, for instance.

Hipschen shares credit for one U.S. stamp design, the 22¢ Knute Rockne commemorative issued in 1988, with Peter Cocci.

The work of the engraver varies, Hipschen told me. He worked on the 1995 32¢ Bessie Coleman stamp for "three or four weeks," working on four or five versions and even coping with a denomination change during the process. The finished stamp is shown at right in Figure 401.

So how long does a stamp engraving take to complete? "I think I did one in six hours one time," Hipschen said, following that with a description of the five-month effort he put into the 1988 25¢ Carousel Animals set of four stamps. "I had to do a separate engraving for each color," Hipschen said, adding that some of those engravings were photographed for offset printing plates.

Hipschen uses hand-held magnifying glasses while engraving. "I get a bigger variety of line widths and depths that way," he said.

Hipschen engraves not only stamp designs, but portraits printed by the BEP as well. At left in Figure 401, he's shown engraving a portrait of John Philip Sousa. His most well-known works are the portraits used on the redesigned U.S. currency, starting with the $100 bill first released in 1996. Once again, Hipschen's subject was Benjamin Franklin.

Armandina Lozano is a U.S. engraver who does contract work for printing companies that create U.S. stamps. She told me that she is the only female portrait and figure engraver in the United States. Her best known stamp engravings, shown in Figure 402, are the two triangular 32¢ Pacific 97 stamps issued March 13, 1997. Her other U.S. stamp-engraving credits are the 1991 $2.90 and $9.95 Eagle designs, the four 29¢ National Postal Museum stamps issued in 1993, and the 32¢ Olympic Discus Thrower stamp issued in 1996.

Lozano has also engraved stock certificates for Banknote Corporation of

Figure 402. The designs of the 32¢ Pacific 97 triangular stamps were both engraved by Armandina Lozano.

America and Northern Bank Note, and has engraved the designs on many U.S. commemorative panels.

The Eagle and National Postal Museum stamps were printed using a combination process, where engraved details are added to stamps that are printed primarily by lithography. The Discus Thrower and Pacific 97 stamps are entirely intaglio-printed.

Lozano does not use etching as part of her work; everything she does is by line engraving. "I like the burin," she told me.

When a stamp-engraving project begins for her, she receives from the stamp printer a large image of the design that she is to reproduce by engraving. She does a cellophane tracing of the design, which is reduced photographically and is used to transfer the design to the steel die, which is covered with a thin layer of wax.

Some engravers frequently make proofs while they work, a print of the design made by filling the recessed lines of the engraving with ink and pressing it under pressure onto special proof paper. Lozano often makes only one proof, checks for areas that need special attention, and then submits her finished die to the stamp printer.

"It's very sad that they don't do more engraved portraits," Lozano said, referring to the designs on U.S. stamps. "I know it's also a disappointment for the collectors. I used to go to shows — all the people that I met, they told me they wanted more engraved stamps."

The number of engraved designs on U.S. postage stamps declined dramatically near the end of the 20th century. By 2000, no commemorative stamps were produced by the intaglio printing process, though a few new engraved designs have appeared sporadically since then.

Some countries, including Sweden and Austria, have continued to issue numerous stamps with line-engraved designs.

Lozano appreciates the affection collectors have for the engraved image. She told me about a collector and his wife who visited with her at a stamp show. The wife told her how the husband would get up in the middle of the night to inspect the engraved images on stamps. "They spend the same time looking at the engraved stamps that I spend doing the engraving," Lozano said.

As she related the story, her voice conveyed the same kind of admiration for the collectors and their appreciation of the difficult art of engraving that collectors so often bestow upon the engravers themselves.

The processes used to print postage stamps

In the middle of March 1895, the Rev. Ernest Millar of the Church Missionary Society sat at his typewriter in Mengo, Uganda, and created the first postage stamps for that East African nation. One example of those early Ugandan stamps is shown in Figure 403.

More than half a century before the Ugandan typewritten stamps were issued, Great Britain created the world's first postage stamps: intricately line-engraved portraits of Queen Victoria reproduced using the intaglio printing method on watermarked white paper.

Though primitive stamps like the Ugandan issues exist, the very first postage stamps — and most postage stamps since then — were printed using more sophisticated methods.

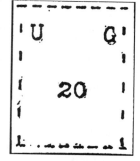

Figure 403. One of Uganda's 1895 typewritten stamps.

Four printing processes have been used to create most stamps since the first appeared in 1840: intaglio, gravure, lithography and letterpress (also known as typography). The first three, commonly used today, will be discussed. Stamps printed using combinations of these processes, such as intaglio and lithography together on one stamp, are common.

Intaglio: The printing process called intaglio (pronounced, "in- TAHL-yo") usually begins with the work of the engraver, a skilled craftsman creating an image referred to as a "line engraving." Using a small, sharp tool called a burin (pronounced "BYUR-en"), the engraver cuts into a soft steel plate to create a die.

The engraver actually creates the image that will be printed on the stamp as a mirror image, the reverse of how it eventually will appear.

The finished steel die has recessed areas where the engraver cut into the plate with the burin and removed bits of steel in lines of various lengths and thicknesses. Crosshatching and lines placed close together create darker areas of the design.

The engraver may fill those recessed areas with ink, press a special paper against the die, and create a printed image called a "proof" that is similar to the stamp image.

But how is this one engraved die used to create millions of postage stamps?

What normally happens next is that the engraved die is hardened and then used to reproduce the image in reverse onto another soft steel surface called a transfer roll. This is done by pressing the transfer roll onto the engraved die with great pressure. The steel of the roll is forced into the recessed areas of the die, creating an image that is right-reading and in relief of the engraved image. That is, where the engraved image was dug into the surface of the die, it is reproduced as a raised image on the transfer roll.

The process is still not finished, though. The transfer roll is hardened and then used to reproduce the image again, this time on a soft steel printing plate.

The reproduction in this part of the process is repeated over and over to create however many images should appear on the plate. For instance, if a stamp is printed in press sheets of 200 images, then the transfer roll is pressed into the printing plate 200 times. The finished plate has 200 images that reproduce that single engraved die created by the engraver: a recessed image that will be filled with ink and printed on paper under great pressure.

The special ink used for intaglio printing, combined with the pressure of the printing process, creates a raised image on the surface of the paper that can be felt by lightly running the fingers over the printed image.

The 32¢ Stagecoach and Clipper Ship triangular stamps issued March 13, 1997, by the United States (shown in Figure 402) are examples of intaglio-printed stamps. Even without magnification, the engraved lines can be seen clearly.

Another example of an intaglio-printed stamp is shown at left in Figure 404. This 1976 12-kopeck issue from Russia (Scott 4523) shows a space exploration medal with a portrait of cosmonaut Yury Gagarin. Enlarged above the stamp is the detail from the center of the design, to the left of Gagarin's face, showing the lines created by the engraver's burin.

The line-engraved image of this stamp can be compared to a nearly identical lithographed stamp issued by Russia the following year. At right in Figure 404 is Russia Scott 4602, using the same design as Scott 4523, but printed by

Figure 404. A 1976 intaglio-printed Russian stamp (left) and a nearly identical lithographed stamp issued the following year. Details of the two stamps are shown enlarged at top.

lithography. The differences are obvious under magnification. The sharp engraved lines of the earlier issue are replaced by small dots, blotches of ink and less clearly defined lines in the later stamp.

Almost all U.S. stamps issued before the 1960s were printed by the intaglio method.

By the end of the 20th century, intaglio printing was evolving as many printing companies still using the process looked for more efficient and less costly ways to achieve the security features that intaglio printing offered. Although recessed plates were still used to print the stamps, new mechanical, film or digital transfer processes often led to a final product that blunted much of the depth that the initial line engraving achieved and resulted in a less faithful finished image.

Gravure: Like intaglio printing, gravure is a recess printing process. Ink is filled in recessed areas of the printing plate (or printing cylinder), and then applied to paper.

Gravure printing does not involve line engraving, however. Usually the image of the design is photographed and then chemically etched onto the surface of the printing plate in the form of "cells," tiny circular indentations that hold the ink. The cells are created after the photographic image is screened, breaking it up into a pattern of extremely small dots. Darker tones are reproduced by cells etched more deeply that hold more ink.

Nearly solid colors can be created this way, making it difficult to see the screen effect. A characteristic of gravure printing is that under great magnification the edges of these colors are not sharp but instead appear rough-edged or bubbled, like on the 1993 AIDS Awareness stamp shown in Figure 405. The letter "A" from "Awareness" is shown magnified above the stamp.

The image on multicolor gravure-printed stamps is usually created by separating the photographed image into four screened colors: magenta (red), cyan (blue), yellow and black. A separate printing cylinder is created for each color, and the cylinders are used in combination to create a variety of hues and tones.

Because of the involvement of photographic processes, the term "photogravure" is sometimes used to describe this printing method.

Figure 405. Screened lettering on the 1993 AIDS Awareness stamp appears rough-edged under magnification, a common characteristic on gravure-printed stamps.

In Figure 406 are two stamps from the United States issued during September 1994. The Bing Crosby stamp at left, from the Popular Singers set, was printed by photogravure. The Muddy Waters stamp at right, from the Jazz and Blues Singers set, was printed by offset lithography.

The two stamps appear very similar, even viewed side-by-side, but differences become apparent under magnification. The letters "SI" from the word "SINGER" along the left margin of each stamp are shown under magnification at the top of Figure 406. The letters from the gravure-printed Crosby stamp have rough edges, and the vertical edge of the illustration has a rounded or scalloped effect.

The letters on the lithographed Waters stamp have much sharper edges, and the edge of the illustration, though not perfectly straight, is more linear than the edge of the Crosby stamp design. The letters on the Waters stamp are not screened, which is why they appear so sharp. This selective screening is possible on lithographed stamps, but not on gravure stamps, where the entire stamp image is created by etched cells.

Lithography: The differences between stamps printed by gravure and by lithography can be very difficult to discern. Both methods use screened dots to produce multicolor images, but the dots of lithographed stamps are larger and the uniformity of the dot pattern can be seen more easily. Viewed together, stamps from both processes often appear nearly identical.

Lithographed stamps are printed by a completely different process, however, based on the fact that oil and water do not mix. The printing sur-

Figure 406. Differences between the gravure-printed Bing Crosby stamp and the lithographed Muddy Waters stamp can be seen in the outlines of the printed letters and the structure of the vertical edge of the central design.

face in lithography is coated with a greasy ink, which is kept from spreading beyond its designated area by the use of water.

Postage stamps are printed by a process called offset lithography, where the inked design is transferred from the printing plate to a cylindrical rubber blanket, and then onto the paper.

The artwork and images on stamps printed using this method are usually reproduced as screened halftone dots of varying sizes, so even under magnification there are similarities to stamps printed by the gravure process.

However, a couple of clues help distinguish the two.

As noted earlier, the gravure dots usually produce rougher edges, even on the straightest printed lines. The definition between unprinted areas and printed areas on lithographed stamps is much cleaner and sharper.

Lithographed stamps can and often do have unscreened areas, particularly on sections of solid color, numerals and inscriptions. The difference between the Bing Crosby and Muddy Waters stamps in Figure 406 provides a good example of this.

Another similar pair of U.S. stamps to compare is the 32¢ Tennessee Williams commemorative of 1995 (lithographed) and the 23¢ F. Scott Fitzgerald of 1996 (gravure).

On single-color stamps, distinguishing between gravure and lithographed examples can be maddening, but often the border where the design meets the margin is the best indicator, as the gravure stamps under magnification have a characteristic bumpiness, even on straight lines.

Distinguishing the printing methods used for different types of postage stamps becomes more difficult as these methods continue to evolve. Computers are frequently used in the creation of stamps, including computer-generated and controlled engraving of photogravure printing cylinders.

Collectors can train themselves to understand differences between similar processes by studying and comparing similar stamps that are identified in stamp catalogs as being printed by different methods. A 30-power magnification helps to provide a very detailed look at the printed characteristics of designs.

Proofs are part of the stamp creation process

Collectors who purchased the Pacific 97 souvenir sheets (U.S. Scott 3139-40) noticed that the margin of each small sheet included a decorative enlargement of what appeared to be one of the original 1847 stamps. The designs of those first U.S. stamps were used as a basis for the designs of the 1997 stamps. After all, the souvenir sheet was marking the 150th anniversary of the two originals, a 5¢ Benjamin Franklin stamp and a 10¢ George Washington stamp, the first ever issued in the United States.

The oversized version in the margin of the souvenir sheet (one of which is shown at the top of Figure 407) was not a stamp reproduction, however. It was actually a reproduction of a proof.

The word "proof" is used in many different fields, often with similar meanings. In photography, a proof is a test print of a negative. In the minting of coins, a proof is a special edition coin that is struck from a highly polished die.

A stamp proof is another item that is the result of a creative production process. Though it looks like a postage stamp, a proof is actually a test printing of the stamp design on special paper or card.

At the bottom of Figure 407 is a proof of the 5¢ Benjamin Franklin design, hinged in the center of a card with handwritten notations. This proof was used as a reference by engravers

Figure 407. The enlarged design on the right side of the souvenir sheet at top is a reproduction of a proof. The card at bottom has the actual proof hinged in the center.

of the 1947 Cipex souvenir sheet, Scott 948. The same proof design was reproduced in the margin of the Pacific 97 souvenir sheet featuring the Benjamin Franklin design, Scott 3139.

The printed designs of all proofs are the same size as the printed designs of the corresponding postage stamps as issued.

During the manufacturing of an original stamp design, those involved in the production create proofs to examine the design for any flaws that need repair or any changes that need to be applied to the design before the stamps are printed.

The person creating the proof may be the design engraver. The design engraver creates the stamp design by cutting into a small plate of soft steel called a die, using a sharp tool called a burin.

Because of the way engraved images are produced, the engraver creates the design as a mirror image of how it will finally appear.

When a test impression of the engraving is printed, it is referred to as "pulling a proof." The engraver may pull a proof during the course of creating the engraving as a way to see how the work is progressing and if any changes need to be made.

This engraver's progress proof is created by filling the recessed areas of the steel die engraving with special ink. Proof paper is applied under pressure to the surface of the die, creating an inked impression of the design on the paper.

When the engraver's work is completed, the steel die is checked by the printer as an early part of the production process. To do this, die proofs are created by the printer in different formats.

One way that different die proofs are distinguished is by the size of the paper upon which the design is printed.

Generally, a proof on a larger piece of paper, allowing margins around the stamp of 5 millimeters or greater, is called a large die proof. A proof on a smaller piece of paper is called a small die proof.

Some large die proofs have had much of the margin paper trimmed off at some point, leaving them at a size that qualifies them as small die proofs. If it can be determined for certain that a small die proof was created from a large die proof that was trimmed, it may be referred to as a "cut-down" or "trimmed large die proof."

One large die proof of the 5¢ Franklin is shown at left in Figure 408. It is printed in the red-brown color used for the actual 1847 stamp.

Notice that the design is surrounded by crosshatched lines. This is a little unusual for a stamp proof, though it is more common for the 1847 issues.

There are a couple of theories why these cross-hatched lines were used. One is that they would prevent slippage during printing. In *The Congress Book 1997*, George W. Brett disagrees, stating that "the cross-hatching was for decorative purposes only."

By the way, the engraved crosshatching was added to the die in 1858, so the large die proof at left in Figure 408 actually was created years after the original stamps were printed.

Why create a proof after the stamps are printed? There are various reasons. The printer may want a record of the condition of the die after it is used to prepare the printing plates. The die also may have been used to create proofs for special exhibits or even as gifts to officials. Such items are referred to as post-issue proofs. Proofs created prior to the manufacturing of the stamp printing plates are referred to as pre-issue proofs.

Another reason for the creation of proofs is to determine which color should be used to print the stamp. The resulting impressions are called trial color proofs.

Figure 408. At left is a large die proof printed in the red-brown color used on the 1847 stamp issue. The trial color proof at right is printed in yellow green. The designs on each are the same size, though they appear different in these photos.

The engraved design may be printed in many different colors before one color is selected for actual stamp production.

Nineteen colors are cataloged for trial color proofs of the 5¢ Franklin design. They are listed in the trial color proofs section of the Scott *Specialized Catalogue of United States Stamps & Covers.*

Shown at right in Figure 408 is a trial color proof of the 5¢ Franklin issue that is printed in yellow-green ink. Remember, the actual stamp was printed in red-brown ink. An assembled collection of trial color proofs can make a dazzling display.

Most of the proofs already described here are created by the steel die with the engraved image of the design. To create a printing plate for stamps, the steel die is hardened and the engraved image is impressed upon a soft steel transfer roller. The transfer roller is then hardened and repeatedly impressed onto the printing plate. For the 5¢ Franklin stamp, 200 images of the design were made on a single printing plate that was used to print postage stamps.

It is also possible to create proofs from the finished printing plate, rather than from the single die. Such items are called plate proofs. Plate proofs of the 1847 5¢ Franklin in red-brown ink were printed on a thin, soft opaque paper called India paper.

Other plate proofs of the same image were printed on India paper in black or orange. These items are known as trial color plate proofs.

Plate proofs of other stamp designs may be printed on cards rather than paper.

Proofs of early U.S. stamps often are sold at auction and by stamp dealers. Both die and plate proofs, as well as color trial proofs, are listed in the Scott U.S. specialized catalog.

Collectors who are unfamiliar with proofs could be fooled by proofs that are sold improperly as stamps. The small die proof at left in Figure 409, for instance, bears a very strong resemblance to an actual unused 5¢ Franklin stamp, shown at right in Figure 409. The proof, however, sold at auction in 1989 for $350. The unused 5¢ Franklin (Scott 1) has a catalog value of $6,250.

It is therefore wise to obtain authentication for

Figure 409. Can you tell the difference? The small die proof is shown at left; the issued stamp appears at right.

any valuable stamp that also can be purchased as a proof. Though proofs are usually printed on different paper than stamps, a collector who is unfamiliar with the differences could be deceived.

Proofs for hundreds of U.S. postage stamps, Official stamps, revenue stamps and more are cataloged and occasionally offered for sale. Often, the proof impressions are actually much more valuable than the stamps. Such values vary from issue to issue.

Chapter 13
Selling Your Collection

Selling your stamps? Consider all the options

Being a stamp collector will not make you rich.

It will make you smarter, it may help you relax and it will doubtless provide you with countless hours of enjoyment, but don't count on it making you rich.

Yes, sometimes you hear that a stamp collector scored a tidy profit when he sold his collection, but those stories are outnumbered by tales of stamp collectors who thought the sales of their collections would bring in much more money than they did.

For those who decide at some point to sell some or all of a stamp collection, the experience can be difficult in more ways than one. Not only are they letting go of a lifetime pursuit, but they may have trouble finding someone who is interested in buying what they have to sell.

And when it comes time to sell, many collectors learn that the monetary value they place on their pastime is quite unrealistic.

Did you pay full catalog value for every stamp in your collection? Probably not. And whoever buys those stamps from you won't want to pay full catalog value for them either. If your buyer is a stamp dealer, he probably won't be able to sell most of those stamps at full catalog value. He'll have to sell them at a discount.

And he has to buy them from someone at an even deeper discount, so he can make enough profit to pay his staff, his travel expenses, his store rent, insurance, utility bills and all other overhead, property taxes, income taxes, and maybe even put a little food on the table.

But don't be naive and sell your stamps for next to nothing if they actually have some value to collectors.

A smart collector has to look at the many selling options that exist, compare the offers that he hears for the stamps he wants to sell, and decide how much time and effort he wants to invest in selling his collection.

There are many ways to go about selling your stamps. The easiest methods will generally net you the least amount of money, because you're passing the work on to the buyer.

Selling strategies that may bring in more money for your items will probably take up a lot more of your time.

The interest potential buyers may have in your collection will depend on many different factors. Is there an active market for the stamps you want to sell? Are your stamps in excellent condition?

The values you find published in catalogs are for undamaged stamps, usually in very fine condition. Condition and grading problems will affect that value in a big way.

When it comes time to sell some of your stamps, your main options are to sell to a dealer or to sell to collectors.

Here are some of the most popular selling options for you to consider.

Selling directly to a dealer

There are many ads in *Linn's Stamp News* from dealers who are buying stamp collections. Sometimes they will sell the collections they buy intact to another collector or dealer. Often they have to spend hours taking the collection apart to stock their inventory of single stamps, or approvals books, and so on.

Ads from dealers interested in buying stamps are found throughout *Linn's* and under the "Wanted to Buy" headings among the classified ads. Look through these ads to find dealers who may be interested in the kinds of stamps you hope to sell.

When you speak with any stamp dealer on the phone, be prepared with your facts and be completely honest. The stamp dealer will need an accurate description of the stamps you have, including an approximate catalog value, and he'll likely ask you many questions about your collection. He may want to see it.

Figure 410. Stamp collectors at dealers' booths during a stamp show. A collector with stamps to sell can visit with different dealers to get a sense of the market for his collection.

Your patience will make the whole process easier for you and for the dealer.

If you have purchased your stamps from a few specific stamp dealers over the years, they may be the dealers you need to consult when you are interested in selling.

If there isn't a stamp dealer near you, try to attend a stamp show in your area.

Figure 410 shows collectors visiting dealers' booths during a large stamp show in Canada. At the stamp show, you will find a number of dealers who can tell you if they are interested in looking over your collection or individual stamps. Some may be willing to give you an offer.

Don't be insulted if the offer you hear is far less than you expected. The dealer is factoring in what he has to do to resell your collection, and he may have to discount your stamps considerably.

Be polite if you decide to reject a dealer's offer. There's no point in creating ill will just because you think you should get more money than you're being offered.

What's the best thing about completing an outright sale to a dealer? You give the stamps to the dealer, the dealer gives you payment, and the deal is done. There's no waiting to see if the sale is successful.

Selling at auction

Auction houses that specialize in stamps handle everything from single stamps to the largest collections.

Every auction transaction is different. Some collections are auctioned intact, while others are broken into individual lots.

Figure 411 shows the 1¢ Franklin stamp of 1869, which catalogs unused at $800. This type of excellent stamp is likely to appeal to auction buyers as an individual lot.

You can learn much more about consigning your stamps at auction by calling one of the many firms advertising in *Linn's* and consulting with an auction house representative.

Consignment means the auction house will try to sell the stamps on your behalf at a scheduled sale. If they do not find a buyer, the stamps go back to the original owner.

If the stamps sell, the auction house will take a portion of the sale price to cover its expenses in handling the sale. Ask the auction house representative to describe the charges you can expect to incur.

Figure 411. Individual higher-value stamps of superior quality may sell well as individual auction lots. Shown is a wonderfully well-centered unused copy of the 1¢ Franklin stamp of 1869, U.S. Scott 112.

Many auction houses accept only larger lots, but if you have some individual high-value, high-quality stamps to offer, the auction house may be interested. Auction house representatives are often present at larger national stamp shows.

Selling at club auction

If you want to sell smaller groups of less valuable stamps, you can consider participating in a stamp club auction, as shown in Figure 412.

If there is interest in your items, club members will bid to purchase them. Most clubs also take a percentage of the sale price to support the club.

Club members are probably looking for a bargain, so your stamps may sell for far less than catalog value, but the club auction can be a good way to dispose of duplicates and unwanted stamps that others may appreciate.

Figure 412. The stamp club auction is one way to dispose of individual items and sets from a collection. Stamp collectors are always looking for a bargain, so items at smaller club auctions are likely to sell at levels far below catalog values.

Selling through club circuits

Circuit books are offered by the American Philatelic Society and some other clubs as a means for members to sell individual stamps and covers. An example of an APS circuit is shown in Figure 413.

The seller has to identify and price each individual item, mount each in the circuit book, and return the books to the sponsoring organization. The books are then sent around to other interested collectors who review the offerings and make purchases, if they wish.

You may sell some or even most of the stamps that you place in the circuit, but you also may sell very few. And it often takes many months before the final tally comes in from the organization, because the stamps have to go from collector to collector to generate sales.

In the end, you may find that your good stamps have all sold and you have a number of stamps remaining that no one is interested in.

You can always consider donating these stamps to the youth collecting programs of the American Philatelic Society or the Junior Philatelists of America, or to one of the schools or organizations requesting stamp donations in the pages of *Linn's*.

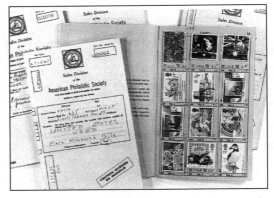

Figure 413. One way to sell individual stamps is through club circuit books. Although this selling method is popular, it can be quite time-consuming and does not guarantee sales.

Online sales

Since the late 1990s, the Internet's World Wide Web has opened up a number of selling opportunities for collectors who want to sell their stamps themselves. They're not always successful, and there can be some hazards.

Again, collectors must properly identify and price each item or group of items they want to sell.

Internet stamp sales options include selling at set prices or at online auction. Fixed-price sales can be conducted through other online retail databases. Collectors can set the price for their stamps, and for a fee the sponsoring organization handles most of the actual sales transaction.

The seller also must pay a fee to sell his items through online auctions, and he must properly describe what he is selling. Here the seller handles the transaction. The auction site simply supplies the venue and charges a fee.

Remember, if you are selling the stamps yourself, you may have to contend with a buyer who is not satisfied with your stamps once you complete the transaction. That means you may have to conduct a refund and resell the item again.

Selling stamps is rarely easy; that's probably why the professional stamp dealer calls it work.

Every online sales venue is different. Check with the sponsoring organizations for specific details.

Every stamp collector who is selling his stamps would like to find a simple and very profitable way to do so. Sometimes a transaction with a stamp dealer will bring about this happy conclusion, but it's not always that easy.

Consider the many options that are available when it comes time to sell your stamps, and proceed cautiously to ensure that you find the deal that is right for you.

Chapter 14
Conclusion

Stamp hobby appeal depends on collector

Those who are familiar with stamp collecting and those who have taken the time to learn about the stamp hobby know that it has earned its title as "the king of hobbies and the hobby of kings."

Great Britain's King George V, the grandfather of Queen Elizabeth II, was an avid stamp collector, taking a great personal interest in the development of the Royal Philatelic Collection. In 1906, before he ascended the throne, he entered his Mauritius and Hong Kong collections in competition at the International Philatelic Exhibition and won two silver medals.

Figure 414. The hobby of kings was also the hobby of presidents when Franklin D. Roosevelt was in office.

King Carol II of Romania at one time was the owner of Sweden's 1855 3-skilling-banco orange-yellow error of color, which in 1996 claimed the title as the world's most valuable stamp when it sold for more than 2.5 million Swiss francs (about U.S. $2.27 million). Considering the size of that single postage stamp, it certainly must be, ounce for ounce, the most valuable object in the world.

One of the world's most prominent stamp collectors was Franklin D. Roosevelt, president of the United States from 1933 until his death in 1945. The fact that he was a stamp collector was so well known that a label promoting his involvement in the hobby was once used to advocate his election (Figure 414).

Along with these eminent representatives, this "hobby of kings" also is enjoyed by millions of people around the world, from children to retirees, from all possible walks of life.

A fortune can be spent creating a majestic prize-winning collection, yet someone less wealthy can enjoy the hobby at virtually no cost by saving stamps that were used to pay postage and which arrived affixed to the collector's daily mail. This universal appeal has sustained the stamp hobby since its beginnings in the mid-19th century. Each week it brings together business leaders and laborers, young and old, at stamp clubs, shows and exhibitions in cities and communities all over the world.

What is it about the stamp hobby that appeals to so many different people?

Though stamp collecting has many different features, it seems specifically to attract individuals with inquisitive minds, those who have a desire to learn more about the world. Collectors feed that desire through their stamps, learning about history, geography, social culture and more.

Some collectors cherish the solitude that stamp collecting offers. It is an opportunity to be alone with a collection that is distinctly personal, to create something that no one else has a hand in. Others enjoy the camaraderie of stamp clubs or correspondence with other collectors. Here is a chance to meet, talk and exchange ideas with people who have similar interests and who enjoy this very distinctive pastime.

One important aspect of the hobby is the continuous search for stamps still needed to complete a collection. Putting together a stamp collection is, for many, like piecing together a fantastic jigsaw puzzle. However, not only must the puzzler figure out where all the pieces go, he must also go out in the world and find all the pieces.

Some of the best collectors discover pieces that no one ever knew existed.

These features endear stamp collecting to those who already enjoy the hobby. What is it that makes stamp collectors begin their accumulating ways?

Figure 415. *Mona Lisa* for $1? It's easy if you're a stamp collector. This 5-pfennig German stamp was issued in 1952.

No matter at what age the collector starts out in the hobby, the design of the stamp is often the first appealing feature. Someone who has always admired Leonardo da Vinci's *Mona Lisa*, for example, may be enchanted to learn that it has been reproduced on a postage stamp (Figure 415) and can be owned and enjoyed by anyone who desires it.

This combined appreciation of art and history can take another form. Those who collect covers (the entire envelopes that are used to send mail) may follow this interest because they are drawn to owning something that is historic in nature and composed with the elegance of a time that has long since passed.

As the example in Figure 416 shows, the flourish of a handwritten address, combined with the beauty of an engraved stamp design and the simple strike of a classic postmark, creates a collectible object that after more than a century is still a pleasure to look at, to study and to learn from.

Often the attraction of collecting stamps is a link to family history or national pride. A youngster whose parents moved to the United States from another country may find pleasure in collecting the stamps that arrive on letters from relatives and friends still living overseas. The father or mother may enjoy collecting the stamps that show images reflecting the history and culture of the new country that they now call home.

Other reasons for beginning a collection may be less easy to define.

Stamps have always conveyed a sense of value, a simple enough connection considering that the value of the stamp is normally printed on the face of it for all the world to see. This idea of value is reinforced from time to time by newspapers and television when reports of a remarkable stamp sale tell the story of a single stamp worth millions. It may be easy to imagine that

Figure 416. An illustrated stagecoach cover bearing the 1857 10¢ green, type V — a classic stamp on a classic cover.

the stamp on a cover from Grandma mailed from overseas 30 years ago could also be worth a bundle.

It is easy to imagine, and on very rare occasions it actually happens. The 3-skilling-banco orange-yellow error was discovered by a schoolboy stamp collector only 30 years after it was issued.

The fact that stamps, for the most part, are issued by government agencies adds to the assurance that the stamp has an intrinsic value, like coins, currency and government savings bonds. This is in contrast to some other collectibles that are manufactured by companies with no responsibility beyond the creation and sale of the product.

Figure 417. Stamps have been used to promote many philosophies. Peace is advocated in seven languages on a 1986 stamp from the United Nations.

The postage stamp has a purpose, and a rather noble one at that: to act as a carrier for the mail. Throughout its existence, the stamp has conveyed news of joy and discovery, sorrow and loss, and reports of historic magnitude.

As a device of communication, the stamp again represents history. History pops up everywhere in stamp collecting, from the world leaders and historical events portrayed on stamps from every country to the documents of the past that have been carried from one distant land to another.

As we've learned, one specialty of the stamp hobby, the study of postal rates, classifications and usages, has even earned the name "postal history."

Stamps are a link through history to our past, much as the aging photographs in a family album provide a link to relatives from a time long ago. Even the newest stamp issued today will be one more link in that historical chain.

Stamps have provided the world with mystery, fantasy, hidden marks and secret codes. They have rallied the home front as war waged overseas, they have raised money for the needy with voluntary surtaxes, and they have suggested a better world with messages of peace and friendship (Figure 417).

For all these reasons and many, many more, stamp collecting has repeatedly proven itself to be a hobby quite worthy of pursuit.

And the one truth that should be remembered by all who begin a stamp collection is that it is indeed a hobby. It is a leisure activity, a diversion, a chance to have fun, to challenge oneself and to relax. The pursuit of that last remaining stamp and the desire for a complete collection can always be maintained. But the collector should never forget that he is engaged in a hobby, quite possibly the world's finest.

Figure 418. Though the stamp hobby has many remarkable qualities, the young collector on this 1968 stamp from Poland reminds us that we're here to have some fun.

Like the cheerful young collector shown in Figure 418 on Poland's 1968 Philately issue, let's put on our stamp-collecting hats and have a little fun.

GLOSSARY

Philatelic terms and abbreviations
This glossary defines terms frequently
encountered in the stamp hobby. Precise definitions for many philatelic
terms do not exist. One collector, dealer or society may define a term one
way, while others may use the term in
a slightly different way. Specialist
groups may be able to provide additional information for specific terms.
This glossary defines more than 330
terms.

A

Accessories: Various products and
tools commonly used by the stamp collector, including hinges, mounts,
stamp tongs, perforation gauges, stock
books and magnifiers. Stamp albums,
catalogs and philatelic literature can
also be regarded as accessories.

Adhesive: 1) The gum on the back
of a stamp or label. Some stamps have
been issued with no adhesive. Stamp
adhesive may be water-activated or
pressure-sensitive (self-adhesive). 2) A
word generally referring to a stamp
that may be affixed to an article to prepay postal fees, in contrast to a design
printed directly on an article, as with
postal stationery. An adhesive can also
refer to a registration label or other
label added to a cover.

Admirals: A nickname for three
British Commonwealth definitive
series, those of Canada, 1912-25
(Scott 104-34); New Zealand, 1926
(182-84); and Rhodesia, 1913-19
(119-38). These stamps depict King
George V of Great Britain in naval uniform.

Aerogram: A postage-paid air letter
sheet with gummed flaps that is written on and then folded to form an
envelope. Aerograms are normally carried at less than the airmail letter rate.
No enclosures are permitted.

Aerophilately: A specialized area of
collecting concentrating on stamps or
covers transported by air.

Agency: 1) An extraterritorial post
office maintained at various times by a
government within the territory of
another government. Examples are the
post offices maintained by many European powers in the Turkish Empire
until 1923. 2) An organization authorized to publicize or sell new issues of
stamps on behalf of a stamp-issuing
entity.

Air labels: Adhesives issued by private organizations for specific, unofficial flights.
See also Etiquettes.

Airmail: The carriage of mail by air.
Also, stamps specifically issued to
prepay postage for mail transported by
aircraft. The first regular airmail service began in 1870, when mail was carried from Paris, then besieged by German forces, over enemy lines by balloon. Many countries have issued
postage stamps, stamped envelopes,
postal cards and aerograms specially
designated for airmail use. The first
airmail stamp was issued by Italy in
1917 (Italy Scott C1).

Albino: An uninked impression
made by a printing plate. Such errors
are scarce on stamps. They are found
more frequently on postal stationery.

Album: A binder and pages
designed for the mounting and display
of stamps or covers. Many early
albums were permanently bound
books. Albums come in many sizes,
styles and themes.

Album weed: In general, a forged
stamp. It also refers to unusual items
that resemble postage stamps but were

not intended to pay postage, like publicity labels and bogus issues. *Album Weeds* is the title of a reference book series on forged stamps, written by the Rev. R. Brisco Earée.

Aniline: Ink with a coal-tar base. Aniline inks are very sensitive and may dissolve in water or other liquids or chemicals. To prevent the erasure of cancellations and reuse of stamps, aniline inks were used to print some stamps.

Approvals: Priced selections of stamps or covers sent to collectors by mail. The collector purchases the items he chooses, returning the rest to the approval dealer with payment for the purchased items.

APO (Army Post Office): An official United States post office established for use by U.S. military units abroad. An army post office or military post office is set up to distribute mail to and from military personnel. The APO is indicated by numbers during wartime to prevent revealing personnel locations. The locations become generally known after the conflict ends.

Arrow: On many sheets of stamps, V-shaped arrowlike markings appear in the selvage, generally serving as guides for cutting the sheets into predetermined units. Some collectors save stamps or blocks displaying these marks.

arrow

As is: A term written in auction descriptions, or spoken or written during a retail transaction. It indicates that an item or lot is sold without guarantee or return privilege. Stamps are usually sold "as is" when they are damaged or are possibly not genuine.

ATM: 1) In the United States, panes of self-adhesive stamps on a liner the approximate size and shape of U.S. currency, designed for dispensing from automated teller machines. 2) "Automatenmarken," automatic stamps produced individually by a machine. *See also* Computer-vended postage, Frama.

Auction: A sale of stamps, covers and other philatelic items where prospective purchasers place bids in an attempt to obtain the desired items. The highest bidder for each lot (described item or items) makes the purchase. Auctions are generally divided into mail sales, where bids are accepted by mail, and public sales, where mail bids are combined with live bidding from individuals present at the auction or participating by telephone.

Authentication mark: A marking, such as initials, placed on the reverse of a stamp examined and certified to be genuine by an expert. Such markings do not detract from the value of the stamps when they represent the endorsement of recognized authorities.

B

Backprint: Printing on the reverse of a stamp. Some stamps have numbers, symbols, advertising or information about the stamp subject printed on the reverse of the stamp.

Backstamp: A postmark applied to mail by the receiving post office or by a post office handling the piece while it is in transit. Backstamps are usually on the back of a cover, but they can be on the front.

Bank mixture: A high-quality mixture of stamps. It generally represents clippings from the mail of banks or other businesses with extensive overseas correspondence, and thus includes a relatively high proportion of foreign stamps of high face value. *See also* Mission mixture.

Bantams: The nickname of the South African definitive series of 1942-43 (Scott 90-97). Wartime economy measures prompted the manufacture of stamps of small size to conserve paper.

Batonne: A wove or laid paper with watermarklike lines deliberately added in the papermaking process and intended as a guide for handwriting.

Bicolor: Printed in two colors.

Bilingual: Inscribed in two languages. Most Canadian stamps include both English and French text. South African stamps from 1926-49 were printed alternately with English and Afrikaans inscriptions in the same sheet.

Bisect: A stamp cut or perforated into two parts, each half representing half the face value of the original stamp. Officially authorized bisects have often been used during temporary shortages of commonly used denominations. Unauthorized bisects appear on mail from some countries in some periods. Bisects are usually collected on full cover with the stamp tied by a cancel. At times, some countries have permitted trisects or quadrisects.

Bishop mark: The earliest postmark, introduced by Henry Bishop in England circa 1661. A Bishop mark was used to indicate the month and day that a letter was received by a post office. It encouraged prompt delivery by letter carriers.

Black Jack: The nickname of the United States 2¢ black Andrew Jackson stamp issued between 1863 and 1875.

Blind perforation: Intended perforations that are only lightly impressed by the perforating pins, leaving the paper intact, but cut or with a faint impression. Some stamps that appear to be imperforate really are not if they have blind perfs. Stamps with blind perfs are minor varieties carrying little, if any, price premium over normally perforated copies.

Block: A unit of four or more unsevered stamps, including at least two stamps both vertically and horizontally. Most commonly the term refers to a block of four (a block of stamps two high and two wide), though blocks often contain more stamps and may be irregularly configured (such as, a block of seven consisting of one row of three stamps and one row of four stamps).

Bluenose: The nickname for Canada Scott 158, the 50¢ issue of 1929, picturing the schooner *Bluenose*.

Bluenose

Body bag: An informal term for the plastic bag used by U.S. postal authorities to protect and preserve mailed items such as envelopes that have been damaged during handling or processing. The bag usually bears a preprinted message apologizing to the recipient

bisect

337

for the damage caused to the article.

Bogus: A fictitious stamplike label created for sale to collectors. Bogus issues include labels for nonexistent countries and nonexistent values appended to regularly issued sets and issues for nations or similar entities without postal systems.

Booklet: A unit of one or more small panes or blocks (known as booklet panes) glued, stitched or stapled together between thin card covers to form a convenient unit for mailers to purchase and carry. The first officially issued booklet was produced by Luxembourg in 1895. For some modern booklets of self-adhesive stamps the liner (backing paper) serves as the booklet cover.

booklet

Bourse: A meeting of stamp collectors and/or dealers, where stamps and covers are sold or exchanged. A bourse usually has no competitive exhibits of stamps or covers. Almost all public stamp exhibitions include a dealer bourse, though many bourses are held without a corresponding exhibition.

Bull's-Eyes: 1) The nickname for the 1843 first issue of Brazil, Scott 1-3. The similar but smaller issues are called goat's eyes. 2) A bull's-eye cancel refers to a "socked-on-the-nose" postmark with the impression centered directly on the stamp so that the loca-

tion and date of mailing are shown on the stamp.

bull's-eyes

Burelage: A design of fine, intricate lines printed on the face of security paper, either to discourage counterfeiting or to prevent the cleaning and reuse of a stamp. The burelage on some stamps is part of the stamp design.

Burele: Adjective form for burelage, meaning having a fine network of lines. Some stamps of Queensland have a burele band on the back. Also called moiré.

burelage

C

Cachet: In French, cachet means a stamp or a seal. On a cover, the cachet is an added design or text, often corresponding to the design of the postage stamp, the mailed journey of the cover, or some type of special event. Cachets appear on modern first-day covers, first-flight covers and special-event covers.

Canceled-to-order (CTO): Stamps are "canceled to order," usually in full sheets, by many governments. The cancels may be printed on the stamps at the same time that the stamp design is printed. A stamp with a cancel and with full gum is likely a CTO stamp, as CTOs do not see actual postal use. CTO stamps are sold to stamp dealers at large discounts from face value. Some stamp catalogs identify if CTO stamps or genuinely used stamps are priced from known CTO-issuing countries.

Cancel, cancellation: A marking intended to show that a stamp has been used and is no longer valid as postage. Modern cancels usually include the name of the original mailing location or a nearby sorting facility and the date of mailing. Most cancellations also include a section of lines, bars, text or a design that prints upon the postage stamp to invalidate it. This part of a cancel is called the killer.

Cantonal stamps: Issues of Switzerland's cantons (states) used before the release of national stamps. The cantonal issues of Basel (1845), Geneva (1843-50) and Zurich (1843-50) are among the classics of philately.

Carriers' stamps: Certain stamps of the United States issued from the 1840s to the 1860s, plus special government reprints of official issues in 1875. The stamps prepaid the fee for home delivery of letters by appointed carriers. When carrier fees were discontinued in 1863, mail carriers became salaried government employees.

Cape Triangles: Common name for the triangular Cape of Good Hope stamps of 1853-64, the first stamps printed in triangular format. The distinctive shape helped illiterate postal clerks distinguish letters originating in the colony from those from other colonies.

Catalog: A comprehensive book or similar compilation with descriptive information to help identify stamps. Many catalogs include values for the listed items. An auction catalog is published by the auction firm in advance of a planned sale to notify potential customers of the specific items that will be offered.

Catalog value: The value of a stamp as listed in a given catalog for the most common condition in which the stamp is collected. Some catalogs list stamps at a retail value, though actual dealer prices may vary substantially for reasons of condition, demand or other market factors. Most catalogs have a set minimum value for the most common stamps.

Censored mail: A cover bearing a handstamp or label indicating that the envelope has been opened and the contents inspected by a censor.

Centering: The relative position of the design of a stamp in relation to its margins. Assuming that a stamp is undamaged, centering is generally a very important factor in determining grade and value.

Certified mail: A service of most postal administrations that provides proof of mailing and delivery without indemnity for loss or damage.

Chalky paper: A chalk-surfaced paper for printing stamps. Any attempt to remove the cancel on a used chalky-paper stamp will also remove the design. Immersion of such stamps in water will cause the design to lift off. Touching chalky paper with silver will leave a discernible, pencillike mark and is a means of distinguishing chalky paper.

Changeling: A stamp whose color has been changed: intentionally or unintentionally: by contact with a chemical or exposure to light.

Charity seals: Stamplike labels that are distributed by a charity. They have no postal validity, although they are often affixed to envelopes. United

States Christmas seals are one example.

Charity stamp: *See* Semipostal.

Cinderella: A stamplike label that is not a postage stamp. Cinderellas include seals and bogus issues, as well as revenue stamps, local post issues and other similar items.

cinderella

Classic: An early issue, often with a connotation of rarity, although classic stamps are not necessarily rare. A particularly scarce recent item may be referred to as a modern classic.

Cleaning (stamps): Soiled or stained stamps are sometimes cleaned with chemicals or by erasing. The cleaning is usually done to improve the appearance of a stamp. A cleaned stamp can also mean one from which a cancellation has been removed, making a used stamp appear unused.

Cliché: The individual unit consisting of the design of a single stamp, combined with others to make up the complete printing plate. Individual designs on modern one-piece printing plates are referred to as subjects.

Coil: Stamps processed in a long single row and prepared for sale in rolls, often for dispensing from stamp-vending and affixing machines. Some coils, including most U.S. coils, have a straight edge on two parallel sides and perforations on the remaining two parallel sides. Some coils are backprinted with sequence or counting numbers.

coil

Collateral material: Any supportive or explanatory material relating to a given stamp or philatelic topic. The material may be either directly postal in nature (post office news releases, rate schedules, souvenir cards, promotional items) or nonpostal (maps, photos of scenes appearing on stamps).

Combination cover: Cover bearing the stamps of more than one country when separate postal charges are paid for the transport of a cover by each country. Also stamps of the same country canceled at two different times on the same cover as a souvenir; for example, first-day combination covers, created when a new stamp is applied to an earlier thematically related FDC and submitted for a new first-day cancel.

Commatology: Specialized collecting of postmarks. This term was invented before World War II to describe postmark collecting. It is rarely used. Usually, collectors refer to postmark collecting or marcophily.

Commemorative: A stamp printed in a limited quantity and available for purchase for a limited time. The design may note an anniversary associated with an individual, an historic event or a national landmark, or the subject may be primarily decorative. *See also* Definitive.

Compound perforations: Different gauge perforations on different sides of a single stamp. The sides with the different gauge measurements are usually perpendicular.

Computer-vended postage: Postage stamps and undated postage labels with denominations of the customer's choosing (variable denomination), printed on demand and sold from self-service machines. This term is typically used in reference to U.S. stamps. *See also* ATM, Frama.

Condition: The overall appearance

and soundness of a stamp or cover. Positive condition factors include fresh full color, full original gum on unused stamps, and so on. Damage such as creases, tears, thinned paper, short perforation teeth, toning and so on negatively affect condition.

Controlled mail: A system in which the mailer selects philatelically desirable issues for outgoing mail, arranges for a specific manner of cancellation and secures the stamps' return by the addressee. In some cases such controlled mail operations may provide rare examples of specific rate fulfillment or other similar postal use.

Copyright block: Block of four or more United States stamps with the copyright notice marginal marking of the United States Postal Service. The copyright marking was introduced in 1978 and replaced the Mail Early marking.

Corner card: An imprinted return address, generally in the upper-left corner of an envelope, from a commercial, institutional or private source, similar to business card or letterhead imprints.

Counterfeit: Any stamp, cancellation or cover created for deception or imitation, intended to be accepted by others as genuine. A counterfeit stamp is designed to deceive postal authorities.

Cover: An envelope or piece of postal stationery, usually one that has been mailed. Folded letters that were addressed and mailed without an envelope and the wrappers from mailed parcels are also covers.

Crash cover: A cover that has been salvaged from the crash of an airplane, train, ship or other vehicle. Such covers often carry a postal marking explaining damage or delay in delivery.

Crease: A noticeable weakening of the paper of a stamp or cover, caused by its being folded or bent at some point. Creases substantially lower a stamp's value. Creases particularly affect cover values when they extend through the attached stamp or a postal marking. Stamp creases are visible in watermark fluid.

Cut cancellation: A cancellation that intentionally slices into the stamp paper. Often a wedge-shaped section is cut away. On many issues, such cancellations indicate use of postage stamps as fiscals (revenues) or telegraph stamps rather than as postage. Cut cancellations were used experimentally on early United States postage stamps to prevent reuse.

Cut square: A neatly trimmed rectangular or square section from a stamped envelope that includes the imprinted postage stamp with ample margin. Collectors generally prefer to collect stationery as entire pieces rather than as cut squares. Some older stationery is available only in cut squares.

cut square

Cut-to-shape: A nonrectangular stamp or postal stationery imprint cut to the shape of the design, rather than cut square. Cut-to-shape stamps and stationery generally have lower value than those cut square. One of the world's most valuable stamps, the unique 1856 British Guiana "Penny Magenta" (Scott 13), is a cut-to-shape stamp.

Cylinder: A curved printing plate used on a modern rotary press. The plate has no seams. For United States stamps, cylinders are used to print gravure stamps. *See also* Sleeve.

D

Dead country: A former stamp-issuing entity that has ceased issuing its own stamps. Also, the old name of an active stamp-issuing entity that has changed its name so that the old name will no longer be used on stamps.

Definitive: Stamp issued in a large indefinite quantity and for an indefinite period, usually several years or more. The United States Presidential issue of 1938 and the 1995 32¢ Flag Over Porch stamps are examples. Definitive stamp designs usually do not honor a specific time-dated event.

Deltiology: Picture postcard collecting.

Denomination: The face value of a stamp, usually indicated by numerals printed as part of the design. Some modern U.S. stamps produced for rate changes are denominated with a letter. A numerical value is assigned when the letter stamps are issued. An example of this is the H-rate Hat stamp of 1998, which represented the first-class rate of 33¢.

Die: The original engraving of a stamp design, usually recess-engraved in reverse on a small flat piece of soft steel. In traditional intaglio printing, a transfer roll is made from a die and printing plates are made from impressions of the transfer roll. When more than one die is used in the production of an issue, distinctive varieties are often identifiable.

Die cut: A form of separation usually employed on self-adhesive stamps. During processing, an edged tool (die) completely penetrates the stamp paper on all sides of the printed stamp, making the removal of the individual

stamps from the liner possible. Die cuts may be straight, shaped in wavy lines to simulate perforation teeth, or take other forms.

Directory markings: Postal indication of failed delivery attempt, stating the reason for failure. Examples are "No Such Number," "Address Unknown" and "Moved."

Duck stamp: Popular name for the United States Migratory Bird Hunting and Conservation stamp, issued and sold for use on hunting licenses. Each annual stamp depicts waterfowl. Also used to describe similar issues from the various states for use by hunters or for sale to collectors.

duck stamp

Dummy stamp: Officially produced imitation stamp used to train employees or to test machinery, such as automatic stamp-dispensing machines. Dummy stamps are usually blank or carry special inscriptions, blocks or other distinguishing ornamentation. They are not valid for postage, and most are not intended to reach the hands of stamp collectors. Some do reach collectors by favor of postal employees.

Duplex cancel: A two-part postal marking consisting of a canceler and a postmark. The canceler voids the stamp so it cannot be reused. The postmark notes the date and place of mailing.

Duplicate: An additional copy of a

stamp that one already has in a collection. Beginners often consider stamps to be duplicates that really are not, because they sometimes overlook perforation, watermark or color varieties.

E

EDU (earliest documented use): The verified date of the first-known use of a stamp in the mail. The EDU for a classic issue may be after the official issue date. New discoveries can change an established EDU. By requiring documentation, this term has replaced the similar EKU (earliest known use).

EKU (earliest known use): *See* EDU (earliest documented use).

Embossing: The process of giving relief to paper by pressing it with a die. Embossed designs are often found on the printed stamps of postal stationery (usually envelopes and wrappers). Selected stamps of certain countries have been embossed, such as Germany-Berlin Scott 9N472, a 1982 issue commemorating the Berlin Philharmonic.

Encased postage stamp: A stamp inserted into a small coin-size case with a transparent front or back. Such stamps were circulated as legal coins during periods when coins were scarce.

Entire: An intact piece of postal stationery, in contrast to a cutout of the imprinted stamp. This term is sometimes used in reference to an intact cover or folded letter.

Error: A major mistake in the production of a stamp or postal stationery item. Production errors include imperforate or imperforate-between varieties, missing or incorrect colors, and inversion or doubling of part of the design or overprint. Major errors are usually far scarcer than normal vari-

eties of the same stamp and are highly valued by collectors.

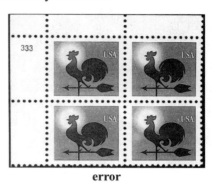

error

Essay: The artwork of a proposed design for a stamp. Some essays are rendered photographically. Others are drawn in pencil or ink or are painted. Most essays are rejected. One becomes the essay for the accepted design.

essay

Etiquette: A gummed label manufactured for application to an envelope to designate a specific mail service. Airmail etiquettes, or air labels, are most common and are used by Universal Postal Union member nations to denote airmail carriage. They are inscribed "Par Avion" (French for "By Airmail"). The text usually includes the same message in the language of the country of origin.

etiquette

Europa: The "United Europe" theme celebrated annually on stamps of western European nations since 1956. The original Europa stamps were issued by the nations in the European Coal and Steel Community. Today, European nations that are members of the postal and telecommunications association (PostEurop, formerly CEPT) issue Europa stamps.

Europa

Expertization: The examination of a stamp or cover by an acknowledged expert to determine if it is genuine. As standard procedure, an expert or expertizing body issues a signed certificate, often with an attached photograph, attesting to the item's status.

Exploded: A stamp booklet that has been separated into its various components, usually for purposes of display. Panes are removed intact; individual stamps are not separated from the pane.

Express mail: Next-day mail delivery service in the United States, inaugurated in 1977.

F

Face: The front of a stamp; the side bearing the design.

Face value: The value of a stamp as inscribed on its face. For letter-denominated or nondenominated stamps, the understood postal value of the stamp.

Facsimile: A reproduction of a genuine stamp or cover. Such items are usually made with no intent to deceive collectors or postal officials. Catalog illustrations may also be considered facsimiles.

Fake: A stamp, cover or cancel that has been altered or concocted to appeal to a collector. In a broad sense, fakes include repairs, reperforations and regummed stamps, as well as painted-in cancels, bogus cancels or counterfeit markings. Sometimes entire covers are faked.

Fancy cancel: A general term to describe any pictorial or otherwise unusual obliterating postmark. More specifically, the term is used to describe elaborate handmade pictorial cancels of the 19th century, such as the Waterbury "Running Chicken" of 1869 or the many intricate geometric shapes used during that period in post offices around the country.

fancy cancel

Farley's Follies: During 1933-34, U.S. Postmaster General James A. Farley supplied a few imperforate sheets of current commemorative issues to President Franklin D. Roosevelt and other government officials. The resulting uproar from U.S. collectors forced the government to release for public sale 20 issues in generally imperforate and ungummed sheets. They are United States Scott 752-71. Numbers 752-53 are perforated.

Fast colors: Inks resistant to fading.

Field Post Office (FPO): A military postal service operating in the field, either on land or at sea. *See also* FPO (Fleet Post Office).

Find: A new discovery, usually of something that was not known to exist. It can be a single item or a hoard of stamps or covers.

First-day cover (FDC): A cover bearing a stamp tied by a cancellation showing the date of the official first day of issue of that stamp.

first-day cover

Fiscal: A revenue stamp or similar label denoting the payment of tax. Fiscals are ordinarily affixed to documents and canceled by pen, canceler or mutilation. Because of their similarity to postage stamps, fiscals occasionally have been used either legally or illegally to prepay postage. *See also* Postal fiscal, Revenues.

Flat plate: A flat metal plate used in a printing press, as opposed to a curved or cylindrical plate.

Flaw: A defect in a plate that reproduces as an identifiable variety in the stamp design.

FPO (Fleet Post Office): An official United States post office for use by U.S. military naval units abroad. *See also* Field Post Office.

Forerunner: A stamp or postal stationery item used in a given location prior to the issuing of regular stamps for that location. Turkish stamps before 1918 canceled in Palestine are forerunners of Israeli issues. So are the various European nations' issues for

use in Palestine and the subsequent issues of the Palestine Mandate. The term "forerunner" is also used to describe a stamp issued before another stamp or set, if the earlier issue may have influenced the design or purpose of the later issue.

Forgery: A completely fraudulent reproduction of a postage stamp. There are two general types of forgeries: those intended to defraud the postal authorities (*see also* Counterfeit), and those intended to defraud the collectors (*see also* Bogus).

Frama: A general name used for a vended postage stamp printed on demand with a denomination selected by a customer, derived from the name of the Swiss firm, Frama AG, an early producer of such issues. There normally is no date on the stamp, as there is on a meter stamp. Also called ATM from the German word Automatenmarken. *See also* ATM, Computervended postage.

Frama

Frame: The outer portion of a stamp design, often consisting of a line or a group of panels.

Frank, franking: An indication on a cover that postage is prepaid, partially prepaid or that the letter is to be carried free of postage. Franks may be written, handstamped, imprinted or affixed. Free franking is usually limited to soldiers' mail or selected government correspondence. Postage stamps and postage meter stamps are modern methods of franking a letter.

Freak: An abnormal, usually nonrepetitive occurrence in the production of stamps that results in a variation from the normal stamp, but falls short of producing an error. Most paper folds, overinking and perforation shifts are freaks. Those abnormalities occurring repetitively are called varieties and may result in major errors.

freak

Front: The front of a cover with most or all of the back and side panels torn away or removed. Fronts, while desirable if they bear unusual or uncommon postal markings, are less desirable than an intact cover.

Fugitive inks: Printing inks used in stamp production that easily fade or break up in water or chemicals. To counter attempts at forgery or the removal of cancellations, many governments have used fugitive inks to print stamps.

G

Gauge: A measurement indicating the number of perforation holes or teeth within the space of 2 centimeters on perforated stamps, or the number of peaks or valleys within the space of 2cm on die-cut stamps. When the gauge for all sides is the same, one number is indicated, for example, "perf 11½." In the case of compound perforations (where the horizontal and vertical gauge differ), the horizontal gauge is given first, followed by the vertical gauge ("perf 11½ x 10"). *See also* Perforation gauge.

Ghost tagging: The appearance of a faint image impression in addition to the normal inked impression. This is caused by misregistration of the phosphor tagging in relation to the ink. Sometimes, a plate-number impression will have an entirely different number from the ink plate, giving the impression of an error: one dark (normal) number and one light (ghost) number.

Glassine: A thin, semitransparent paper that is moderately resistant to the passage of air and moisture. Envelopes made of glassine are commonly used for temporary stamp storage.

Glassine is also used in the manufacture of stamp hinges.

Goldbeater's skin: A thin, tough, translucent paper. The 1886 issue of Prussia was printed in reverse on goldbeater's skin, with the gum applied over the printing. These stamps are brittle and virtually impossible to remove from the paper to which they are affixed.

Granite paper: A paper with small colored fibers added when the paper is made. This paper is used as a deterrent against forgery.

Gravure: A printing process using a recessed intaglio printing plate or cylinder created by photographic and chemical means rather than by hand engraving. *See also* Intaglio, Photogravure.

Grill: A pattern of parallel lines (or dots at the points where lines would cross) forming a grid. A grill is usually: 1) the impressed breaks added to stamps as a security measure (United States issues of 1867-71 and Peru issues of 1874-79); or 2) a grill-like canceling device used on various 19th-century issues.

grill

Gum: The mucilage applied to the backs of adhesive postage stamps, revenue stamps or envelope flaps. Gum is an area of concern for stamp collectors. It may crack and harm the paper of the stamp itself. It may stain or adhere to other stamps or album pages under certain climatic conditions. Many collectors are willing to pay extra for 19th- and some 20th-century stamps with intact, undisturbed original gum.

Gutter: The selvage separating panes on a sheet of stamps. The gutter is usually discarded or divided during processing. The gutter may be unprinted, or bear plate numbers, accounting or control numbers, advertising or other words or markings. Gutter pairs and gutter blocks are unsevered groups of stamps separated by an intact gutter or gutters between them.

gutter

Gutter snipe: One or more stamps to which is attached the full gutter from between panes, plus any amount

of an adjoining stamp or stamps. This term is typically used in reference to U.S. stamps. Gutter snipes are freaks caused by misregistration of the cutting device or paper foldover.

H

Handstamp: Cancellation or overprint applied by hand to a cover or to a stamp.

Highway Post Office (HPO): Portable mail-handling equipment for sorting mail in transit on highways (normally by truck). The last official U.S. HPO ran June 30, 1974.

Hinge: Stamp hinges are small, rectangular-shaped pieces of glassine paper, usually gummed on one side. Folded with the gummed side out, the hinge is used to mount stamps. Most modern hinges are advertised as peelable. Once dry, they may be easily removed from the stamp, leaving little trace of having been applied.

Hologram: An image usually reproduced on silver foil that appears to reflect light with three-dimensional qualities and prismatic effects. The first postage stamp with a hologram as part of its design was issued by Austria in 1988 (Scott 1441). Because the hologram is affixed to the stamp paper, the hologram portion of the stamp may separate when soaked in water.

I

Imperforate: Refers to stamps without perforations, rouletting, die cuts or other separations between the individual stamps in a pane. The earliest

imperforate

stamps were imperforate by design, but after about 1860, most stamps were perforated. Modern imperforates are usually errors or are produced specifically for sale to stamp collectors.

Imperforate between: A pair of stamps that is fully perforated at the top, side and bottom but has no perforations between the stamps.

Impression: Any stamped or embossed printing.

Imprimatur: Latin for "let it be printed." The first sheets of stamps from an approved plate, normally checked and retained in a file prior to a final directive to begin stamp production from a plate.

India paper: A thin, tough opaque printing paper of high quality used primarily for striking die proofs.

Indicium: The stamp impression of a postage meter or the imprint on postal stationery (as opposed to an adhesive stamp), indicating prepayment and postal validity. Plural: indicia.

Inscription: The letters, words and numbers that are part of a postage stamp design.

Intaglio: Italian for "in recess." A form of printing in which the inked image is produced by that portion of the plate sunk below the surface. Line engraving and gravure are forms of intaglio printing.

International Reply Coupon (IRC): A redeemable certificate issued by member nations of the Universal Postal Union and sold through their post offices to provide for return postage from recipients in other countries. IRCs may be redeemed for postage at a post office.

Invert: An error where one portion of the design is inverted (upside down)

international reply coupon

in relation to the other portion(s). An overprint applied upside down is also an invert.

invert

J

Joint issue: An officially sanctioned stamp or postal stationery issue by two or more countries to commemorate the same subject. Joint issues are often stamps bearing similar designs issued on the same day by both countries.

Joint line: A printed line of ink found at regular intervals on the perforations separating two coil stamps. The line marks the meeting point of two adjoining curved printing plates on the press.

K

Keytype: A basic stamp design utilized for the issues of two or more postal entities, usually differing in the

keytype

country name and inscription of value. Many of the earlier colonial issues of Britain, France, Spain, Germany and Portugal are keytypes.

Kiloware: A stamp mixture consisting of miscellaneous postally used stamps on envelope corner paper from various sources. Kiloware is sometimes sold by the kilogram (about 2.2 pounds).

L

Label: Any stamplike adhesive that is not a postage stamp or revenue stamp.

Laid paper: One of the two basic types of paper used in stamp printing. Laid paper is distinguished from wove paper by the presence of thin, parallel lines visible when the paper is held to light. The lines are usually a few millimeters apart. *See also* Batonne.

Letterpress: Printing done directly from the inked raised surface of the printing plate.

Line engraving: Printing done from an intaglio plate produced from a hand-engraved die and transfer roll rather than by photographic or chemical means. *See also* Gravure.

Line pair: A pair of coil stamps with a printed line between them. Older stamps produced on a flatbed press have a line from the guideline between panes. Stamps produced on a rotary press have a joint line from the space where ink collects between the sections of curved rotary plates.

line pair

Liner: Coated paper used as a back-

ing for mint self-adhesive stamps. The liner allows the release of the stamp, which may then be applied with pressure to envelope paper.

Linerless: An experimental form of self-adhesive coil stamp that requires no liner. The mint stamps are rolled upon each other in a manner similar to adhesive tape. See United States Scott 3132, 3133; also 3404-07 and 3680-83.

Lithography: Printing from a flat surface with a design area that is ink-receptive. The area that is not to print is ink-repellant. The process is based on the principle that an oil-based design surface will attract oily ink.

Locals: Stamps valid within a limited area or within a limited postal system. Local post mail requires the addition of nationally or internationally valid stamps for further service. Locals have been produced both privately and officially.

M

Machin: The name given to a well-known series of British definitive stamps first issued in 1967. The design of the stamp depicts a plaster portrait of Queen Elizabeth II created by artist Arnold Machin.

Machin

Mail Early Block (ME block): U.S. marginal marking block with the selvage bearing the inscription "Mail Early (in the Day)." This first appeared on U.S. marginal selvage in 1968. It was replaced subsequently by the copyright notice. ME blocks typically consist of four or six stamps.

Makeshift booklets: U.S. stamp

booklets manufactured using stamps normally issued in individual panes that have been packaged in generic blue cardboard covers and dispensed by vending machines.

Marcophily: Postmark collecting.

Margin: 1) The selvage surrounding the stamps in a sheet, often carrying inscriptions. 2) The unprinted border area around the stamp design. The collectible grades of stamps are determined by the position of the design in relation to the edge of the stamp as perforated or, in the case of imperforate stamps, as cut from the sheet.

Mat: A hard rubber plate used to apply overprints on postage stamps.

Maximaphily: Maximum card collecting.

Maximum card: A picture postcard, a cancel and a stamp effectively combined to create a thematic collectible. The stamp is usually affixed to the picture side of the card and is tied by the cancel. Collectors of maximum cards seek to find or create cards with stamp, cancel and picture in maximum agreement, or concordance. The statutes of the International Federation of Philately (FIP) for exhibiting give specific explanatory notes for the postage stamp, the picture postcard, the cancel, concordance of subject, concordance of place and concordance of time.

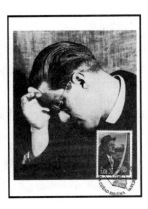

maximum card

Meter (postage meter): The mechanical or digital device that creates a valid denominated postage imprint known as a meter stamp. Postage is prepaid to the regulating postal authority. Meters were authorized by the UPU in 1920. They are used today by volume mailers to cut the cost of franking mail.

Microprinting: Extremely small letters or numbers added to the designs of selected stamps of the United States and other countries as a security feature. In most cases, 8-power magnification or greater is needed to read microprinting.

Miniature sheet: A smaller-than-normal pane of stamps issued only in that form or in addition to full panes. A miniature sheet is usually without marginal markings or text saying that the sheet was issued in conjunction with or to commemorate some event. *See also* Souvenir sheet.

Mint: A stamp in the same state as issued by a post office: unused, undamaged and with full original gum (if issued with gum). Over time, handling, light and atmospheric conditions may affect the mint state of stamps.

Mirror image: An offset negative or reverse impression.

Mission mixture: The lowest grade of stamp mixture, containing unsorted but primarily common stamps on paper, as purchased from missions or other institutions. *See also* Bank mixture.

Missionaries: The first stamps of Hawaii, issued 1851-52, considered among the great classics of philately.

Mixed perforation: *See* Compound perforation.

Mixed postage: The franking on a cover bearing the stamps of two or more stamp-issuing entities, properly used. *See also* Combination cover.

Mixture: A large group of stamps, understood to contain duplication. A mixture is said to be unpicked or picked. A picked mixture may have had stamps, probably of better quality, removed by a collector or dealer.

Mobile Post Office (MPO): Portable mail-handling equipment and personnel, generally in railroad cars, streetcars, trucks or buses.

Money, Stamps as: During periods of coin shortage, stamps have circulated officially as small change. Often, stamps used in this way are printed on thin card stock, enclosed in cases of various kinds or affixed to cards. *See also* Encased postage stamp.

Mount (stamp mount): Acetate holders, clear on the front and with some sort of adhesive on the back. Collectors use mounts to affix stamps or covers to album or exhibit pages.

Multicolor: More than two colors.

Multiple: An unseparated unit of stamps including at least two stamps, but fewer than the number included in a full pane.

N

Native paper: Crude, handmade paper produced locally, as opposed to finer, machine-made paper.

Never hinged (NH): A stamp without hinge marks. A never-hinged stamp usually has undisturbed original gum, but this is not always the case.

New-issue service: A dealer service that automatically supplies subscribers with new issues of a given country, area or topic. The issues provided are determined by a prearranged standing order that defines the quantity and types of issues.

Newspaper stamps: Stamps issued specifically for the prepayment of mailing rates for newspapers, periodi-

cals and printed matter.

Nondenominated: A stamp with no numerical inscription designating the face value. The value of some nondenominated stamps are marked by a designated letter. Others may have a service inscription that indicates the rate the stamp fulfills.

nondenominated

NVI: No value indicator. Primarily British term for nondenominated stamps, where the postage value of the stamp is indicated by inscribed rate abbreviations: "1st" for first-class mail use, "2nd" for second-class mail use, "E" for mail to Europe, and so on. NVI stamps remain valid for the inscribed rate class, even if the rate increases after the stamp is sold.

O

Obliteration: 1) A cancellation intended solely to deface a stamp: also called a killer. 2) An overprint intended to deface a portion of the design of a stamp, such as the face of a deposed ruler.

Obsolete: A stamp no longer available from post offices, although possibly still postally valid.

Occupation issue: An issue released for use in territory occupied by a foreign power.

Off-center: A stamp design that is not centered in relation to the edges of the stamp. Generally, off-center stamps are less desirable than stamps more nearly centered in relation to the edges. Stamps that are extremely off-center may be added to collections as production freaks.

Offices abroad: At various times, many nations have maintained post offices in other countries, usually because of the unreliability of the local postal system. In China and the Turkish Empire, especially, many foreign nations maintained their own postal systems as part of their extraterritorial powers. Usually, special stationery and stamps were used by these offices. Most consisted of overprints on the regular issues of the nations maintaining the offices.

Official: Stamp or stationery issued solely for the use of government departments and officials. In many countries such items may be available to collectors in unused condition from the postal authority.

Official

Offset: 1) A printing process that transfers an inked image from a plate to a roller. The roller then applies the ink to paper. 2) The transfer of part of a stamp design or an overprint from one sheet to the back of another, before the ink has dried (also called set off). Such impressions are in reverse (*see* Mirror image). They are different from stamps printed on both sides.

OHMS: Abbreviation for On His (or Her) Majesty's Service. Used in perfins, overprints or franks to indicate official use in the British Commonwealth.

Omnibus issue: An issue released by several postal entities to celebrate a common theme. Omnibus issues may or may not share a keytype design.

On paper: Stamps (usually postally used) that are affixed to portions of an original envelope or wrapper. Often used to describe stamps prior to soaking.

On piece: A stamp on a portion of the original envelope or wrapper showing all or most of the cancel. Stamps on piece are usually saved that way.

on piece

Original gum (OG): The adhesive coating on a mint or unused stamp or envelope flap applied by a postal authority or security printer, usually before the item was issued. Upon request of stamp collectors, postal authorities have at times offered to add gum to items first issued ungummed. *See also* Regummed.

Overprint: Any printing over the original completed design of a stamp. An overprint that changes the value of a stamp is also called a surcharge. *See also* Surcharge.

overprint

Oxidation: Darkening of the ink on certain stamps caused by contact with air or light. Some inks used to print stamps, especially oranges, may in time turn brown or black.

P

Packet: 1) A presorted selection of all-different stamps, a common and economical way to begin a general collection; 2) a ship operating on a regular schedule and contracted by a government or post office to carry mail.

Packet letter: A letter carried by a ship operating on a regular schedule and carrying mail by contract with a government or a post office.

Pair: Two unseparated stamps.

Pane: The unit into which a full press sheet is divided before sale at post offices. What a post office customer may refer to as a "sheet of stamps" is more properly called a pane. Most United States full sheets are divided into four or more regular panes or many more booklet panes before they are packaged and shipped to post offices.

Paquebot: Cancellation indicating an item was mailed aboard a ship.

Par Avion: A French phrase meaning "By Air," it appears on airmail etiquettes of most countries, along with a similar phrase in the predominant language of the country of origin.

Parcel post stamps: Special stamps created for payment of parcel post fees.

Part-perforate: A stamp with all perforations missing on one or more sides, but with at least one side perforated. *See also* Imperforate, Imperforate between.

Paste-up: The ends of rolls of coiled stamps joined together with glue or tape.

Peaks and Valleys: On the outer edge of self-adhesive stamps with simulated die-cut perforations, the high (peak) and low (valley) points of the wavy line die cuts. Collectors can identify varieties by comparing peaks and valleys on similar stamps.

Pelure paper: A strong, thin paper occasionally used in stamp printing. Pelure paper is translucent and resembles a slightly dark, thin onion-skin paper.

Pen canceled: Stamps canceled with an ink pen or marker pen rather than a handstamp or machine cancel. Many early stamps were routinely canceled by pen. A pen cancel may also indicate that a stamp was used as a fiscal. Modern stamps may be pen canceled if a sorting clerk or delivery carrier notices that a stamp has been missed by a canceling machine.

Penny Black: The black 1-penny British stamp issued May 6, 1840, bearing the portrait of Queen Victoria. It is the world's first adhesive stamp issued for the prepayment of postage.

Penny Black

Perfins: Stamps perforated through the face with identifying initials, designs or holes in coded positions. Perfins are normally used by a business or government office to discourage pilferage or misuse of stamps by employees. Perfins may be either privately or officially produced.

perfin

Perforation: The punching out of holes between stamps to make separation easy. 1) Comb perforation: Three sides of a stamp are perforated at once, with the process repeated in rows. 2) Harrow perforation: The entire sheet or unit of stamps is perforated in one operation. 3) Line perforation: Holes are punched one row at a time. Line perforations are distinguished by the uneven crossing of perforation lines and irregular corners. Comb and harrow perforations usually show alignment of holes at the corners. Some forms of perforation may be difficult to distinguish.

Perforation gauge: A scale printed or designed on metal, transparent or opaque plastic, cardboard or other material to measure the number of perforation holes or teeth (or die-cut peaks or valleys) within the space of 2 centimeters.

perforation gauge

Permit: Franking by the imprint of a number and additional information that identifies a mailer's prepaid postage account, thereby eliminating the need to affix and cancel stamps on large mailings. The mailer must obtain a document (permit) that authorizes his use of this procedure.

Phantom philately: The collection of bogus stamps. The name is derived from Frederick Melville's book *Phantom Philately*, one of the pioneer works on bogus issues.

Philatelic cover: An envelope, postal card or other item franked and mailed by a stamp collector to create a collectible object. It may or may not have carried a personal or business message. A nonphilatelic cover is usually one that has carried business or personal correspondence and has had its stamps applied by a noncollector. Some stamps are known only on collector-created covers. It is impossible to say whether some covers are philatelically inspired or not. *See also* Used, Postally used.

Philately: The collection and study of postage stamps, postal stationery and postal history.

Phosphor: A chemical substance used in the production of selected stamps to activate machines that automatically cancel mail. The machines react to the phosphor under ultraviolet light. In 1959, Great Britain began to print phosphor lines on some of its stamps. *See also* Tagging.

Photogravure: A modern stamp-printing process that is a form of intaglio printing. Plates are made photographically and chemically, rather than by hand-engraving a die and transferring it to a plate. The ink in this process rests in the design depressions. The surface of the printing plate is wiped clean. The paper is forced into the depressions and picks up the ink, in a manner much like the line-engraved printing process. *See also* Gravure.

Pictorial: Stamp bearing a picture of some sort, other than a portrait or coat of arms.

Plate: The basic printing unit on a press used to produce stamps. Early stamps were printed from flat plates. Curved or cylindrical plates are used for most modern stamps. *See also* Cylinder, Sleeve.

Plate block, Plate number block: A

block of stamps from the corner or side of a pane including the selvage bearing the number(s) of the plate(s) used to print the sheet from which the pane was separated. Some stamp production methods, such as early booklet and coil production, normally cut off plate numbers. In the United States, plate number blocks are collected normally as blocks of four to 20 stamps, depending on the press used to print the stamps. When each stamp in a pane is a different design, the entire pane is collected as the plate block.

plate number block

Plate number: Numerals or an alphanumeric combination that identifies the printing plate used to print postage stamp images. In the United States, plate numbers on sheet stamps often appear in corner margin paper or side margin paper. Plate numbers on coil stamps were commonly trimmed off until about 1980. Since then the number appears on stamps at specific intervals. Booklet plate numbers are often found on selvage attached to the pane; on some self-adhesive issues the number is printed on one stamp from the booklet. *See also* PNC definition 1.

Plating: The reconstruction of a stamp pane by collecting blocks and individual stamps representing various positions. This is possible for many older issues, but most modern issues are too uniform to make the identification of individual positions possible.

Plebiscite issue: A stamp issue promoting a popular vote. After World War I, a number of disputed areas were placed under temporary League of Nations administration until plebiscites could determine which nation the populace wished to join. Special issues note the upcoming vote in several of these areas, including Allenstein, Carinthia, Eastern Silesia, Marienwerder, Schleswig and Upper Silesia.

plebiscite

PNC: 1) A plate number coil stamp; that is, a stamp from a coil that is inscribed with a plate number. The abbreviations PNC3 and PNC5 identify strips of three or five coil stamps with the PNC located in the center position of the strip. 2) A philatelic-numismatic combination: a cover bearing a stamp and containing a coin, medal or token. The coin and stamp are usually related in such cases; often the cover is canceled on the first day of use of the coin.

Pneumatic post: Letter distribution through pressurized air tubes. Pneumatic posts existed in many large cities in Europe, and special stamps and stationery were often produced for this service.

Postage due: Stamps or markings indicating that insufficient postage has been affixed to the mailing piece. Postage dues are usually affixed at the office of delivery. The additional postage is collected from the addressee.

postage due

Postage meter: *See* Meter

Postal card: A government-produced postcard bearing a stamp imprint in the upper-right corner representing prepayment of postage. *See also* Postcard.

Postal fiscal: A postally used revenue or fiscal stamp.

Postal history: The study of postal markings, rates and routes, or anything to do with the history of the posts.

Postal stationery: Stationery bearing imprinted stamps, as opposed to adhesive stamps. Postal stationery includes postal cards, lettercards, stamped envelopes, wrappers, aerograms, telegraph cards, postal savings forms and similar government-produced items. The cost to the mailer is often the price of postage plus an additional charge for the stationery item.

Postally used: A stamp or cover that has seen legitimate postal use, as opposed to one that has been canceled-to-order or favor-canceled. The term "postally used" suggests that an item exists because it was used to carry a personal or business communication, without the sender thinking of creating an item to be collected.

Postcard: A small card, usually with a picture on one side and a space for a written message and address on the other. Postcards have no imprinted stamp, so the mailer must also purchase postage to mail the postcard. *See also* Postal card.

Postmark: Any official postal marking. The term is usually used specifically in reference to cancellations bearing the name of a post office of origin and a mailing date.

Precancel: Stamp with a special overprint cancellation allowing it to bypass normal canceling. In some cases the precancel also designates a specific mail-handling service, such as "Presorted First-Class." Other precancels may include the city and state of the issuing post office. Precanceled stamps are used by volume mailers who hold a permit to use them. U.S. precancels fall into two categories: 1) Locals have the mark or text applied by a town or city post office; 2) Bureaus have the mark or text applied by the U.S. Bureau of Engraving and Printing. *See also* Service inscribed.

Prestamp covers: Folded letters or their outer enclosures used before the introduction of adhesive postage stamps or postal stationery.

Prestige booklet: A stamp booklet with oversized panes, descriptive information and stamp issues commemorating a special topic. Prestige booklets often include panes with no stamps that instead bear labels or additional information, along with panes bearing stamps.

Prexies: The nickname for the U.S. 1938-54 Presidential definitive series, Scott 803-34, 839-51.

Printer's waste: Misprinted, misperforated or misgummed stamps often created during the normal process of stamp production. Printer's waste is supposed to be destroyed, but such material sometimes enters the philatelic market through carelessness and theft.

Printing: The process of imprinting designs on paper from an inked surface.

Processing: Steps that finish a printed stamp sheet. Processing includes perforation, trimming, dividing the sheet into individual panes or coils, and packaging for distribution.

Pro Juventute: Latin, meaning for the benefit of youth. Switzerland has issued Pro Juventute semipostal stamps nearly every year since 1913.

Proofs: Trial impressions from a die or printing plate before actual stamp production. Proofs are made to examine a die or plate for defects or to compare the results of using different inks.

proof

Provisional: A postage stamp issued for temporary use to meet postal demands until new or regular stocks of stamps can be obtained.

PVI: Postage validation imprint. A dated, denominated postage label computer-printed at U.S. post office counters, frequently used to frank parcels but also found on first-class mail.

Q

Quadripartition: A block or strip of four stamps that together complete a single entire design. See United States Scott 1448-51, the 1972 Cape Hatteras National Seashore issue.

R

Railway Post Office (RPO): Portable mail-handling equipment for sorting mail in transit on trains. The last official U.S. RPO ran June 30, 1977. RPOs were used in many countries. *See also* Mobile Post Office.

Receiving mark: A postmark or other postal marking applied by the receiving, rather than the originating, post office. *See also* Backstamp.

Redrawn: A stamp design that has been slightly altered yet maintains the basic design as originally issued.

Re-engraved: A stamp with an altered design as the result of a change made to a transfer roll or printing plate prior to a later printing, thereby distinguishing it from the original die.

Regional: Stamp sold or valid in a specific area of a stamp-issuing entity. Great Britain has issued stamps for the regions of Guernsey, Jersey, Isle of Man, Northern Ireland, Scotland and Wales. Regionals are usually sold only in a given region but are often valid for postage throughout a country.

Registered mail: First-class mail with a numbered receipt, including a valuation of the registered item, for full or limited compensation if the mail is lost. Some countries have issued registered mail stamps. Registered mail is signed for by each postal employee who handles it.

Registration labels: Adhesive labels indicating the registry number and, often, the city of origin for registered articles sent through the mail.

Regummed: A stamp bearing adhesive from an unauthorized source.

Reissue: An official reprinting of a stamp from an obsolete or discontinued issue. Reissues are valid for postage. *See also* Reprint.

Remainders: Stocks of stamps remaining unsold at the time that an issue is declared obsolete by a post office. Some countries have sold remainders to the stamp trade at substantial discounts from face value. The countries normally mark the stamps with a distinctive cancel. Uncanceled remainders usually cannot be distinguished from stamps sold over the counter before the issue was invalidated.

Repaired stamp: A damaged stamp that has been repaired in some way to reinforce it or to make it resemble an undamaged stamp.

Replica: A reproduction of a stamp or cover. In the 19th century, replica stamps were sold as stamp album space-fillers. Replica stamps are often printed in one color in a sheet containing a number of different designs. Replicas can sometimes deceive either a postal clerk or collectors.

Reprint: A stamp printed from the original plate after the issue has ceased to be postally valid. Official reprints are sometimes made for presentation purposes or official collections. They are often distinguishable in some way from the originals: different colors, perforations, paper or gum. Private reprints, on the other hand, are usually produced strictly for sale to collectors and often closely resemble the original stamps. Private reprints normally sell for less than original copies. Reprints are not valid for postage. *See also* Reissue.

Retouch: The repairing of a damaged plate or die, often producing a minor, but detectable, difference in the design of the printed stamps.

Revenues: Stamps representing the prepayment or payment of various taxes. Revenues are affixed to official documents and to merchandise. Some stamps, including many issues of the British Commonwealth, are inscribed

revenue

"Postage and Revenue" and were available for either use. Such issues are usually worth less fiscally canceled than postally used. In some cases, revenues have been used provisionally as postage stamps. *See also* Fiscal.

Rocket mail: Mail flown in a rocket, even if only a short distance. Many rocket mail experiments have been conducted since 1931. Special labels, cachets or cancels usually note that mail was carried on a rocket.

Rotary plate: A curved or cylindrical printing plate used on a press that rotates the plate to make continuous impressions. Flat plates make single impressions.

Rouletting: The piercing of the paper between stamps to make their separation more convenient. No paper is actually removed from the sheet, as it is in perforating. Rouletting has been made by dash, sawtooth or wavy line.

Rural Free Delivery (RFD): System for free home delivery of mail in rural areas of the United States, begun as an experimental service in 1896.

Rust: A brown mold resembling the rust in iron. Rust affects stamp paper and gum in tropical regions.

S

SASE: A self-addressed, stamped envelope. An unused envelope bearing the address of the sender and sufficient return postage. Enclosed with correspondence to make answering easy.

Secret mark: A minute alteration to a stamp design added to distinguish later printings from earlier printings by a different firm. Secret marks may positively distinguish genuine stamps from counterfeits.

Seebeck: The nickname for various Latin American issues produced 1890-99 in contract with Nicholas Frederick Seebeck, the agent for the Hamilton

Bank Note Co. of New York. Seebeck agreed to provide new issues of stamps and stationery each year at no charge, in return for the right to sell remainders and reprints to collectors. The resulting furor destroyed Seebeck and blackened the philatelic reputations of the countries involved.

Self-adhesive: Stamp gum that adheres to envelope paper by the application of pressure alone, or a stamp with self-adhesive gum. Most self-adhesive stamps are sold on a coated paper release liner. *See also* Liner, Linerless, Water-activated.

Selvage: The marginal paper on a sheet or pane of stamps. Selvage may be unprinted or may contain printer's markings or other information.

Semipostal (charity stamp): A stamp sold at a price greater than postal value, with the additional charge dedicated for a special purpose. Usually recognized by the presence of two (often different) values, separated by a "+" sign, on a single stamp.

semipostal

Series: A group of stamps with a similar design or theme issued over a period of time. A series may be planned or may evolve.

Service inscribed: A stamp with wording as part of the initial printed design that identifies the mail-han-

service inscribed

dling service for which the stamp is intended, such as "Presorted First-Class." *See also* Precancel.

Set: Stamps sharing common design elements, often issued at one time and usually collected as a group.

Se-tenant: French for "joined together." Two or more unseparated stamps of different designs, colors, denominations or types.

se-tenant

Shade: The minor variation commonly found in any basic color. Shades may be accorded catalog status when they are very distinctive.

Sheet (press sheet): A complete unit of stamps as printed. Stamps are usually printed in large sheets and are separated into two or more panes before shipment to post offices.

Ship letter: Mail carried by private ship.

Short set: An incomplete set of stamps, usually lacking either the high value or one or more key values.

Sleeper: Stamp or other collectible item that seems to be underpriced and may have good investment potential.

Sleeve: 1) A seamless cylindrical printing plate used in rotary intaglio printing. 2) A flat transparent holder, often specifically for protecting and storing a cover.

Soaking: The removal of stamps from envelope paper by immersion in water. Most stamps may be safely soaked in water. Fugitive inks, however, will run in water, and chalky-surfaced papers will lose their designs entirely, so some knowledge of stamps is a necessity. Colored envelope paper should be soaked separately.

Souvenir card: A philatelic card, not valid for postage, issued in conjunction with some special event. The souvenir card often illustrates the design of a postage stamp.

souvenir card

Souvenir page: An announcement of a new United States stamp issue created by the U.S. Postal Service, bearing a copy of the new stamp tied by a first-day-of-issue cancellation.

Souvenir sheet: A small sheet of stamps, including one value or a set of stamps. A souvenir sheet usually has a wide margin and an inscription describing an event being commemorated. Stamps on a souvenir sheet may be perforated or imperforate.

Space-filler: A stamp in poor condition used to fill the designated space in a stamp album until a better copy can be found.

Special delivery: A service providing expedited delivery of mail. Called Express by some nations.

Special handling: A U.S. service providing expeditious handling for fourth-class material.

Special printing: Reissue of a stamp of current or recent design, often with distinctive color, paper or perforations.

Specialist: A stamp collector who intensively studies and collects the stamps and postal history of a given country, area, or time period, or who has otherwise limited his collecting field.

Special stamps: Regular postage stamp issues that fall outside the traditional definitions of commemorative and definitive stamps. In the United States, holiday issues such as Contemporary Christmas, Traditional Christmas, Hanukkah and the like are considered special stamps. They are printed in substantially greater quantities than commemorative stamps and sometimes return to press for additional printings. Love stamps are also considered special stamps.

Specimen: Stamp or stationery items distributed to Universal Postal Union members for identification purposes and to the philatelic press and trade for publicity purposes. Specimens are overprinted or punched with the word "SPECIMEN" or its equivalent, or are overprinted or punched in a way to make them different from the issued stamps. Specimens of scarce stamps tend to be less valuable than the actual stamps. Specimens of relatively common stamps are often more valuable.

Speculative issue: A stamp or issue released primarily for sale to collectors, rather than to meet any legitimate postal need.

Splice: The repair of a break in a roll of stamp paper, or the joining of two rolls of paper for continuous printing. Stamps printed over a splice are usually removed and destroyed before the normal stamps are issued.

Stamp: An officially issued postage label, often adhesive, attesting that payment has been rendered for mail delivery. Initially used as a verb, meaning to imprint or impress; for example, to stamp a design.

Stampless cover: A folded sheet or envelope carried as mail without a postage stamp. This term usually refers to covers predating the requirement that stamps be affixed to all letters (in the United States, 1856).

Stock book: A specially manufactured blank book containing rows of pockets on each page to hold stamps.

Straight edge: Flat-plate or rotary-plate stamps from the margins of panes where the sheets were cut apart. Straight-edge stamps have no perforations on one or two adjacent sides. Sometimes straight-edge stamps show a guideline.

Strip: Three or more unseparated stamps in a row, vertically or horizontally.

Surcharge: An overprint that changes or restates the denomination of a stamp or postal stationery item.

surcharge

Surface-colored paper: Paper colored on the surface only, with a white or uncolored back.

Surtax: The portion of a semipostal stamp purchase price exceeding the postage value. The surtax is designated for donation to a charity or some other purpose.

Sweatbox: A closed box containing dampened spongelike material, over which stuck-together unused stamps are placed on a grill. Humidity softens the gum, allowing separation of stamps. In some cases, the sweatbox may be used to help remove a postally used stamp from envelope paper.

T

T: Abbreviation for the French "Taxe." Handstamped on a stamp, the T indicates the stamp's use as a postage due. Handstamped on a cover, it indicates that postage due has been charged. Several countries have used regular stamps with a perforated initial T as postage dues.

Tagging: Phosphor material on stamps used to activate automatic mail-handling equipment. This may take the shape of lines, bars, letters, part of the design area or the entire stamp surface. The tagging may also permeate the stamp paper. Some stamps are issued both with and without tagging. Catalogs describe them as tagged or untagged.

Teeth (perforation teeth): The protruding points along the outer edge of a perforated postage stamp when it has been removed from the pane.

Telegraph stamp: Label used for the prepayment of telegraph fees. Telegraph stamps often resemble postage stamps.

Test stamps: Officially created labels intended to test stamp manufacturing and processing machinery; also used to describe stamplike labels specifically used to train postal employees. *See also* Dummy stamps.

Tête-bêche: French for "head to tail." Two or more unsevered stamps, one of which is inverted in relation to the other.

tête-bêche

Thematic: A collection of stamps or covers relating to a specific topic. The topic is expanded by careful inquiry and is presented as a logical story. *See also* Topical.

Tied: A stamp on a cover or piece, struck by a cancel that also extends over the envelope paper to which the stamp is affixed. Stamps also can be tied by the aging of the mucilage or glue that holds them to the paper.

Tongs: Tweezerlike tool with rounded, polished tips, used to handle stamps. Tongs prevent stamps from being soiled by dirt, oil or perspiration.

Topical: 1) A stamp or cover showing a given subject. Examples are flowers, art, birds, elephants, the Statue of Liberty. 2) The collection of stamps by the topic depicted on them, rather than by country of origin. *See also* Thematic.

Transit mark: A postal marking applied by a post office between the originating and receiving post offices. It can be on the front or back of a cover, card or wrapper.

Triptych: A se-tenant strip of three related stamps forming one overall design. One example is United States Scott 1629-31, the 1976 Spirit of 76 issue.

Type: A basic design of a stamp or a set. Catalogs use type numbers or letters to save space. Catalogs show a typical design of one type rather than every stamp with that design or a similar design.

U

Underprint: A fine printing underlying the design of a stamp, most often used to deter counterfeiting.

Ungummed: A stamp without gum. Ungummed stamps are either stamps issued without gum or an uncanceled gummed stamp that has had its gum soaked off. Many countries in tropical climates have issued stamps without gum.

Unhinged: A stamp without hinge marks but not necessarily with original gum.

Universal Postal Union (UPU): An international organization formed in Bern, Switzerland, in 1874, to regulate and standardize postal usage and to facilitate the movement of mail between member nations. Today, most nations belong to the UPU.

Unused: An uncanceled stamp that has not been used but has a hinge mark or some other characteristic or defect that keeps it from being considered a mint stamp. Uncanceled stamps without gum may have been used and missed being canceled, or they may have lost their gum by accident.

Used: A stamp or stationery item that has been canceled by a postal authority to prevent its reuse on mail. In general, a used stamp is any stamp with a cancel or a precanceled stamp without gum. *See also* Postally used, Philatelic cover.

V

Valleys: *See* Peaks and Valleys

Variable-denomination: *See* Computer-vended postage.

Variety: A variation from the standard form of a stamp. Varieties include different watermarks, inverts, imperforates, missing colors, wrong colors and major color shifts. *See also* Freak, Error.

Vignette: The central part of a stamp design, usually surrounded by a border. In some cases the vignette shades off gradually into the surrounding area.

W

Want list: A list of stamps or covers that a collector needs, identified by catalog number or some other description. The list is submitted to a dealer, often with requirements on condition and price.

Water-activated adhesive: Stamp gum designed to adhere to envelope paper only if the gum is moistened. All gummed stamps before 1963 used water-activated adhesive.

Watermark: A deliberate thinning of paper during its manufacture to produce a semitranslucent pattern. Watermarks appear frequently in paper used in stamp printing or envelope manufacturing. *See also* Batonne.

watermark

Web: A continuous roll of paper used in stamp printing.

Wing margin: Early British stamps from the side of a pane with selvage attached. British sheets printed before 1880 were perforated down the center of the gutter, producing oversized margins on one side of stamps adjacent to the gutter. Such copies are distinctive and scarcer than normal copies.

Wove paper: A paper showing few differences in texture and thickness when held to light. In the production of wove paper, the pulp is pressed against a very fine netting, producing a virtually uniform texture. Wove paper is the most commonly used paper in stamp production.

Wrapper: A flat sheet or strip open at both ends that can be folded and sealed around a newspaper or periodical. Wrappers can have an imprinted stamp or have a stamp attached.

Z

Zemstvo: A local stamp issued by Russian municipal governments or zemstvos, in accordance with an imperial edict of 1870.

Zeppelins: The stamps issued for, or in honor of, zeppelin flights. Examples include the three United States airmail issues of April 19, 1930, Scott C13-C15. Cacheted covers carried on such flights are Zeppelin covers.

ZIP block: U.S. marginal marking block with the selvage bearing the image of the "Mr. ZIP" cartoon character and/or an inscription urging the use of a ZIP code. This first appeared on U.S. marginal selvage in 1964. Typically a ZIP block consists of four stamps.

ZIP code: The U.S. numerical postcode used to speed and mechanize mail handling and delivery. The letters stand for Zoning Improvement Plan.

This glossary was originally created by Linn's Stamp News *staff members and contributors for the 1977 first edition of* Linn's World Stamp Almanac. *It was revised by Michael Baadke in 1999 for* Linn's World Stamp Almanac, *6th edition, and updated again for this book in 2004.*

Subject Index

Four indexes are provided: The Subject Index presents all topics discussed in this book. The United States Stamps Index lists all U.S. stamps discussed in this book. The Foreign Stamps Index lists all non-U.S. stamps mentioned in this book. The Scott Number Index lists all stamps — both U.S. and non-U.S. — that are mentioned by Scott number.

All page numbers appearing in bold type refer to locations where a term is defined. All page numbers appearing in italic type refer to pages where the subject is illustrated but not mentioned in the text on that page.

United States Stamps Index

All page numbers appearing in italic type refer to pages where the subject is illustrated but not mentioned in the text on that page.

Foreign Stamps Index

All page numbers appearing in italic type refer to pages where the subject is illustrated but not mentioned in the text on that page.

Scott Number Index

This index lists all stamps — both U.S. and non-U.S. — that are mentioned by Scott number as assigned in the Scott *Standard Postage Stamp Catalogue* or Scott *Specialized Catalogue of United States Stamps and Covers*.

All page numbers appearing in italic type refer to pages where the subject is illustrated but not mentioned in the text on that page.

About the Author

photo by Patricia Baadke

Michael Baadke began his journalism career in 1975 as a music reporter and book critic for *The Michigan Daily* in Ann Arbor. He studied writing and literature at the University of Michigan, earning a bachelor's degree in English in 1978 and a master's degree in English in 1984.

He joined *Linn's Stamp News* as a staff writer in February 1993 and was named senior editor at *Linn's* in April 1996. Since March 2001, he has been the editor of *Scott Stamp Monthly*.

Baadke's parents introduced him to the stamp hobby at age 10, and his collecting interests include the United States, Denmark, Germany, the 1920 Schleswig plebiscite issues, and the topic of beer and brewing.

His interests outside the stamp hobby include music, literature, Michigan football and Arizona Diamondbacks baseball.

Baadke and his wife Patti were married in 1982. They have one daughter, Katie, and a cat named Perfin.